DETROIT

LAKE ERIE

french creek

Ft. Franklin
(Venango)

CLEVELAND

PENNA.

Ft. McIntosh

1st
Ft. Steuben

Ft. Pitt

Seven
Ranges
1785

Wheeling

OHIO

Ohio
Company
1787

Ft. Harmar   Marietta

VIRGINIA

MARCH TO MASSACRE

A History of the First Seven Years of the United States Army

1784–1791

Arms of the United States engraved for the
Columbian Magazine of September, 1786, by
James Trenchard. One of the earliest published
portrayals of this device.
Guthman Collection

MARCH TO MASSACRE

A History of the First Seven Years of the United States Army

1784–1791

by
WILLIAM H. GUTHMAN

McGraw-Hill Book Company

New York   St. Louis   San Francisco
Düsseldorf   London   Mexico   Sydney   Toronto

ALSO BY WILLIAM H. GUTHMAN

New England Militia Uniforms and Accoutrements
(with John Obed Curtis)

Book design by Robert L. Mitchell

23456789 HDBP 798765

Library of Congress Cataloging in Publication Data

Guthman, William H
  March to massacre.

  Bibliography: p.
  1. United States. Army—History. 2. United States
—History—1783–1865. 3. United States—History,
Military. I. Title.
UA25.G93   973.3   73–22322
ISBN 0–07–025297–1

Material from the Harmar Papers at the William L. Clements Library of the University of Michigan, and from the Knox Papers
owned by the New England Genealogical Society and deposited in the Massachusetts Historical Society, has been drawn
upon extensively throughout this book.

For Pam and Scotty

Preface

There is a vast expanse of land that lies east of the Mississippi River, north of the Ohio River, west of Pennsylvania, and south and west of the Great Lakes. Today it comprises five states: Ohio, Indiana, Illinois, Michigan, and Wisconsin. But in 1755, when John Mitchell drafted his map of British possessions in North America, this unknown wilderness area was incorrectly charted. Therefore, in 1783, when Mitchell's map was used in the formal negotiations for the peace treaty which officially ended the American Revolution, Great Britain ceded to the United States a territory far greater than she realized. According to the terms of the treaty, this land—officially called by the Continental Congress "the Territory Northwest of the Ohio River," but more commonly referrred to as the Northwest Territory—was to become part of the United States.

In reality, Great Britain was relinquishing an area over four times as large as both England and Wales together. It consisted of roughly a quarter of a million square miles of unexplored land that contained millions of dollars worth of furs, timber, and farmland, along with unknown inland waterways, all of which was controlled by hostile Indian tribes and the wild beasts that roamed the forests and prairies. Congress saw a way to relieve the financial worries caused by the late war through the sale of this newly acquired land. Riches from the fur trade and the attraction of rich, virgin farmlands was an overwhelming inducement to many would-be purchasers, but the threat of hostilities from both Indians and renegade Whites posed a serious problem and caused many sales to fall through.

People would not move to the new land until they were assured of adequate protection by the government. Also, they could not purchase land until it had been surveyed and divided into lots, and the surveyors had to be protected by the government. And so, on June 3, 1784, Congress authorized the establishment of the Federal army, primarily for the protection of this frontier. This army, whose job it was to protect an area of over 248,000 square miles of land, plus the area of the Great Lakes, was to consist of only 700 noncommissioned officers and privates.

For seven and a half years the underfed force barely survived. The Indians were constantly on the warpath, and the army was ill equipped. Finally on November 4, 1791, near present-day Fort Recovery, Ohio, a final confrontation took place between the Indian tribes and the United States Army. Five days later, on November 9, the commander of the army wrote a summary of the events that had occurred during the battle.

Addressing his report to Secretary of War Henry Knox in Philadelphia, the commandant, General Arthur St. Clair, stoically penned the following lines from Fort Washington (the site of present-day Cincinnati): "Sir: —Yesterday afternoon the remains of the army under my command got back to this place, and I have now the painful task to give you an account of as warm and as unfortunate an action as almost any that has been fought, in which every corps was engaged and worsted...." General St. Clair went on to describe this tragedy—the worst defeat ever suffered in the history of the United States Army. The steps that led to the defeat actually began at the end of the struggle between Great Britain and the United States.

Acknowledgments

The suggestion that the Jonathan Heart letters would form the foundation for a book came from Thompson R. Harlow, Director of the Connecticut Historical Society, who also read the manuscript and gave many helpful suggestions. Much of the research for the book was accomplished at the William L. Clements Library where Howard H. Peckham, Director, and William S. Ewing, former Curator of Manuscripts, were extremely helpful and generous of their time. The information obtained at the United States Military Academy Library was of extreme importance to this manuscript, and a deep debt of gratitude is owed to Egon Weiss, Librarian, and Assistant Librarian J. Thomas Russell, who, as Manuscript Librarian, gave freely not only of his time and knowledge, but allowed free access to the manuscript material needed for this book. Both Caroline Dunn, Librarian, and Leona T. Alig, Manuscript Librarian, at the William Henry Smith Memorial Library of the Indiana Historical Society, were understanding correspondents and supplied a great deal of material through photocopy and microfilm. Many out-of-print books were made available to me through Maude D. Cole, First Assistant, Rare Book Division, New York Public Library. The stacks of the Pequot Library were always available to me through the courteousness of Stanley Crane, Librarian.

Master photographer Harold Guthman, A.R.P.S., was an invaluable source of information for photographing many of the illustrations. Don A. Troiani's talented art work is not only a valuable asset to this book but was an inspiration during the actual work on the book.

The title, *March to Massacre,* was the generous creative gift of C. Gordon Carroll, whose initial guidance helped construction of the outline for the manuscript.

E. Norman Flayderman and Edward L. Wheat were kind enough to read and give their opinions about the weapons chapter of the book.

The late Joe Kindig, Jr. was an interested and patient sounding board for many of the ideas contained in the book.

The late Stephen G. C. Ensko, who was always generous with his great knowledge, was an inspiration for me.

Craddock R. Goins was helpful, not only with illustrations from the archives of the Smithsonian Institution, of which he is Associate Curator of Military History, but with his encouragement and interest.

For many of the illustrated examples I am deeply indebted to Rockwell Gardiner and Christopher Snow.

The preparation of this book required the help of many other generous people who contributed their time and knowledge and photographs from their collections:

Robert Abels, Ray A. Barrett, George R. Beyer, M. Patricia Black, Edward Charol, Laura Chase, George M. Chinn, Dr. Fred. J. Dockstader, Phillip H. Dunbar, Samuel E. Dyke, Martha G. Fales, Charles E. Hanson, Jr., Ann K. Harlow, Ruth Russell Harlow, Josephine L. Harper, Colonel Georgia D. Hill, William A. Hunter, John W. Huston, First Lieutenant Robert W. Janek, Albert T. Klyberg, Lee Jordan, Elizabeth B. Knox, Thomas Krasean, John R. Lawrence, J. Robert Maguire, Horace Mann, Elizabeth R. Martin, Dr. Robert Moore, Irving Moskowitz, Charles E. Parrish, Claire Pyle, Paul Rabut, Jim Sames, James Schleyer, Sam Shelnitz, Charles E. Smart, Dwight L. Smith, Bruce W. Stewart, William F. Stiles, Charles M. Stotz, the late Gerald C. Stowe, Nathan L. Swayze, George Terasaki, Timothy Trace, Prudence B. Trimble, B. Elizabeth Ulrich, Colonel Arthur P. Wade, General Charles West, Wester A. White, Norman B. Wilkinson, Mary E. Williams, William H. Work.

To my wife, Patricia, who typed, proofread, and tolerated, I am deeply grateful.

Contents

Preface   vii

Chapter 1   **Establishing the First American Regiment**   1
              Notes to Chapter 1   6
Chapter 2   **Discipline and Training**   9
              Notes to Chapter 2   14
Chapter 3   **Recruiting and Clothing the Army**   21
Chapter 4
   Part I: **Fortifications**   35
   Part II: **Living in the Forts**   55
   Part III: **Provisions**   63
              Notes to Part I   69
Chapter 5
   Part I: **Duties and Deployment of the 1st Regiment**   71
   Part II: **Exploring, Charting, Mapping, Spying**   81
   Part III: **Other Duties of the Regiment**   84
Chapter 6
   Part I: **Small Arms**   91
   Part II: **Edged Weapons**   99
   Part III: **Accouterments and Ammunition**   102
              Notes to Part I   106
Chapter 7
   Part I: **The Indian—A Skillful Soldier and Underrated Enemy**   115
   Part II: **Southern Indian Tribes**   130
              Notes to Part I   136
Chapter 8
   Part I: **Prelude to the Indian Campaigns of 1790 and 1791**   141

Part II: **The Events Leading Up to the Hostilities**   148

Part III: **Militia**   150

Part IV: **Treaties with the Northwest Tribes**   152

Notes to Part II   165

Notes to Part III   166

Chapter 9   **The First Campaign**   173

Chapter 10

Part I: **The Peace Mission and Militia Campaigns of 1791**   199

Part II: **The Plans Prepared in Philadelphia for St. Clair's Ill-Fated Expedition**   205

Part III: **Preparations and Delays**   211

Part IV: **March to Massacre**   220

Bibliography   249

Index   261

When the American Revolution ended the United States found itself land rich and specie poor. The only means to pay its debts was the sale of newly acquired land in the northwest. An army was needed to protect the settlers in that territory, but the fear of standing armies and strong central governments caused the Confederation to establish a force so small that it was unequal to face the task that lay ahead.

Chapter 1

Establishing the First American Regiment

Although for all practical and historic purposes the American War for Independence ended when the British surrendered at Yorktown on October 19, 1781, Congress did not officially proclaim the cessation of hostilities until April 11, 1783. Only then did the red-coated English soldiers begin to evacuate New York City, the great Tory stronghold. However, before the last troop ship set sail for England on November 25 of that year, a new threat to the future of the thirteen United States arose.

Seven years of warfare had delivered the infant nation into a depression that the postwar economy had been unable to overcome, chiefly because the weak, decentralized government could not solve its economic problems. Each state jealously guarded its privilege to tax the inhabitants within its own borders; together the thirteen states fearfully prevented the Confederation from obtaining the power to raise money through direct taxation. Indebted both internally and abroad for the cost of the war, and glutted with worthless paper currency from every State in the Union, the United States was not even able to pay for the past services of its returning veterans.

Hopefully, Congress turned to the sale of the approximately one quarter million square miles in the Northwest, acquired from Great Britain under the terms of the Treaty of Paris, signed September 3, 1783. Large land companies purchased tremendous tracts from the government and in turn advertised this land for public sale. Easterners were encouraged to migrate west to a new and promising life. Land speculation became a popular form of investment, and most men of means began to buy and sell thousands of acres in this new frontier. Suddenly the Northwest Territory appeared to be the solution to many economic problems and the salvation of thousands. The government even set aside certain portions of land as bounty for soliders whose services it could not pay for during the last war.

However, while government and private promoters were painting a promising and peaceful picture of this new frontier, many Eastern newspapers carried accounts from families that had already moved west, telling about flaming arrows, flashing tomahawks, and bloody scalping knives. Quickly it became clear to the Federal government and the land speculators that something had to be done to secure this wilderness and thus provide revenue for the struggling nation. The logical solution was a military force to police the northwestern frontier and guard the inhabitants of territory belonging to the United States.

The new Federal army was the result of a compromise with necessity. Born of unwilling parents and practically left to its own resources during 1784–1791, its very existence, ironically, was the outgrowth of the government's need to raise money to pay debts incurred by supporting the previous army during the late war.

Congress established a small, ineffective regiment to do a job that actually called for several well-trained and -equipped regiments. However, it did not want to incur the expense of a large army nor did it want to jeopardize the freedom of the thirteen states by imposing a force similar to King George's troops.

THE RESOLUTION OF JUNE 3, 1784

The steps involved in establishing the army were not simple. In spring 1783 Congress appointed a committee to study the feasibility of a permanent military establishment. General Washington told the committee that a small regular army was indispensable to "awe" the Indians but that a large standing army could be dangerous to the country during peace time. Besides, the country could not afford to maintain a large army. Congress debated the issue for over a year. Elbridge Gerry, Massachusetts representative to Congress, echoed the feeling of most New Englanders in June 1784 when he told his fellow representatives that if Congress were given the prerogative of requisitioning troops from the states during time of peace, this would eventually lead to that legislative body claiming the right to extend the term of enlistment and the number of troops beyond the original limit of its authority. Gerry felt that Congress thereby infringed on the rights of the individual states. While he agreed that standing armies in time of peace were dangerous to the liberties of free people, he felt that the United States should provide a small number of troops to garrison the posts and that a general state of defense would be provided by a well-regulated and disciplined militia provided by each state, as stated in the Articles of Confederation.

Finally, on June 3, 1784, Congress passed a resolution establishing a regiment of 700 men to be furnished by four states: Pennsylvania, New Jersey, New York, and Connecticut. Only the realization of the immediate need for sending troops to the northwestern frontier finally forced the states into agreement. However, they limited possible expenditures when they cautiously recommended that the four states "most practically situated" furnish the 700 men.

On June 2, 1784, Congress had passed a resolution disbanding the last remnants of the old Continental army, except for a company of artillery at West Point and a detachment at Fort Pitt—a total of eighty men, most of whom were from Massachusetts. These men, and their officers, none of whom ranked higher than captain, comprised the single transitional unit that spanned the Revolution and the Federal army, forming the nucleus of the two companies of artillery that were a part of the newly established regiment. (It still exists today as 1st Battalion, 5th Field Artillery,[1] and is thus the oldest unit of the U.S. Army.)

The humble wording of the resolution—"Recommended to the States" rather than "Requisitioned from the States," for their quota of men plus the tying in of the discharging of the old Continental army the day before—finally enabled Congress to pass the resolution.

On the surface there was nothing to associate this new Federal army with the old Continental army, except the eighty artillerymen who had been retained. However, there actually was little difference in the two organizations. The basic structure of this new organization was the same as that of the old Continental army, prescribed in the Articles of Confederation adopted November 15, 1777.

THE ARTICLES OF CONFEDERATION

The Articles had been written by a people fighting for their freedom, a people who anticipated they would always have to protect that freedom. The Articles were rules tailored for thirteen

---

[1] Department of the Army, Office of the Chief of Military History, Washington, D.C.

quasi-autonomous states, each jealously guarding its own boundary and protecting its own territory. This weak confederation, loosely tied together by geographic and linguistic bonds, was completely outmoded by 1784.

Although the Confederation was only a league, created for the common defense of the States, binding them to assist each other in their common defense, it did attempt to regulate the peacetime force to be maintained by each state.[2]

Each state had the prerogative to appoint its own officers in the Federal corps. This had a demoralizing effect upon the officers, who knew that their advancement depended solely upon their influence within their respective states and their military careers could be furthered only through political patronage, rather than by capabilities as a soldier. This, in effect, rendered the state more significant to an ambitious young officer than either his commander, his fellow officers, or his Federal government.[3]

Because of the influence of four different states over the selection and promotion of the officers, during the first five years of the regiment's existence the Federal corps never commanded the kind of respect from its country (or its enemies) that is acquired after team pride has created an esprit de corps. Unfortunately, the only esprit de corps that existed was based upon the belief of the superiority of the American over the savage.

Indian cunning and military acuity had never been properly appraised, and the white man was mistakenly as positive of his own superiority as he was overconfident of the Indians' inferiority. Even the lack of trained men, the hasty reinforcements of undisciplined militia, and inadequate supplies could not alter this fatal attitude. The inadequately endowed army had struggled through its first five years much like an infant whose parents had abandoned it in the wilderness. The corps had to scratch and claw its way to maturity by instinct and the drive to survive. Article VIII provided that every expense incurred for common defense by the thirteen states be defrayed in proportion to the value of all the land within each state.[4]

Even though Congress was able to support the army under the Constitutional government through the power of direct taxation, the pitiful and penniless five-year beginning was too great to be overcome when St. Clair was preparing for his expedition in spring 1791. Too many bad habits had been acquired by the army's suppliers, and by responsible legislators. The army's plight—starvation survival—had become an accepted part of the American way of life.

More often than not the paymaster, the commandant or the Secretary at War, had to plead with the various state officials in order to receive the appropriations that had been levied on the States by Congress. This antiquated system of finance, which should have ended with the termination of the Revolutionary War, prevented the army, prior to 1791, from ever developing beyond a small, weak force. Congress, in 1784, intended it to be just that, and no more.

COMMAND STRUCTURE OF THE NEW ARMY

Not until the Constitutional government of 1789 was there centralized direction of the army. Prior to this the representatives of the thirteen States in Congress directed the activities of the federal

---

[2] "Every state," it stipulated, "shall always keep a well-regulated and disciplined militia, sufficiently armed and accoutred, and shall provide and have constantly ready for use in public stores, a due number of field-pieces and tents, and proper quality of arms, ammunition and camp equipage" (*Journals of Congress,* Vol. 7, p. 39).
[3] A most detrimental rule for the newly created United States Army was Article VII, which read, "When land forces are raised by any State for the common defense, all officers of or under the rank of colonel shall be *appointed by the legislature of each State respectively,* by whom such forces shall be raised, or in such a manner as such State shall direct; and all *vacancies shall be filled by the State* which first made the appointment" (*ibid.*).
[4] "The taxes for paying that proportion shall be laid and levied by the authority and direction of the legislature of the several States within the time agreed upon by the United States in Congress assembled" (*ibid.,* p. 40).

regiment and the Secretary at War carried out their instructions. The Confederation reserved the right of Congress to appoint all officers of the army (and all naval officers) *above* the regimental status. Congress also retained the right to make all the rules and regulations for the land and naval forces, and to direct their operations.[5]

The assent of nine members of Congress was required before troops could be raised, their number determined, war declared, warships built or purchased, and a commander-in-chief appointed. Considering the lack of unity that existed in the country from 1784 to 1789, it is not difficult to understand how immediate needs were often snarled in a web of interstate disagreement.

Actually, it was not until the constitutional government was established that the army had any kind of executive direction other than by the members of Congress. Benjamin Lincoln had resigned as Secretary at War on November 12, 1783. Joseph Carleton assumed the duties of Secretary in the War Office (rather than Secretary at War) on November 4, 1783, functioning in fact as a secretary for Congress in matters concerning the army.

Washington resigned as commander-in-chief of the army December 23, 1783, and Henry Knox became commanding officer (not commander-in-chief) of the army and remained in that office until June 20, 1784. There was no Secretary at War, no commander-in-chief, only a legislative body, Congress, acting through their appointed secretary in the War Office, directing the operations of the army.

Henry Knox was appointed Secretary *at* War by Congress March 8, 1785, and when George Washington became President in 1789 he appointed General Knox as Secretary *of* War. Washington then became the commander-in-chief and Knox was responsible directly to the President. In short, the system was finally centralized and a chain of command established—headed by the commander-in-chief, who was a military genius—but the damage created by the old decentralized system was not easily rectified.

The patronage system was finally eliminated. Josiah Harmar, who had been bitterly opposed to the system, had received directions from Secretary at War Henry Knox in October 1789 to settle the matter of seniority of the officers of the Corps of Infantry and the Corps of Artillery. Knox, in turn, had received his instructions from President Washington.[6] This change came, however, too late to eliminate the effects of the "old army way" of doing things that had existed since the establishment in 1784. The corps had grown up with that system and it required more than a directive to correct its effect.

LIMITING THE SIZE OF THE ARMY

The resolution establishing the First American Regiment called for eight companies of infantry and two of artillery (totaling 700 men) to be enlisted for one year. Congress said in the resolution that "troops were immediately and indispensably necessary for taking possession of the western posts, as soon as evacuated by the troops of his Britannic majesty, for the protection of the Northwestern frontiers, and for guarding the public stores."[7] However, because Congress limited the size of the new army, the British government, realizing that the United States was going to establish merely a token corps, gave in to the constant pressure from Canadian fur traders and merchants unhappy with

---

[5] *Journals of Congress,* Vol. 3, November 22, 1777.

[6] *Harmar Papers,* Vol. II, Knox to Harmar, October 29, 1789, William L. Clements Library, University of Michigan.

[7] The Division of Archives and History of the University of the State of New York, in its booklet, "The Sullivan–Clinton Campaign in 1779," published in 1929, suggests that the seed for the protection of the Northwestern Frontiers was sown by Washington and his staff when they planned the Sullivan–Clinton campaign in 1779. Conquest of that territory, the booklet suggests, would give the United States possession at the end of the Revolution, and would not leave the new nation with "a mere fringe of land along the seacoast."

the terms of the peace treaty. The British commander in Canada was subsequently given secret orders not to evacuate the key posts in the Great Lakes region, Britain's prime fur trade area, as dictated in the terms of the Treaty of Paris.

When meek communications from the United States requesting the evacuation of the various forts was received by the British commander in Canada, he firmly replied that no orders had been given by his superiors. The British maintained that until the United States had paid British loyalists their war debt, as stipulated in the same treaty, the posts would remain in British hands.

The British utilized these strategic outposts to supply the Indians who had been British allies during the Revolution and to encourage them to continue to raid the American settlements. British agents told the chiefs that the Americans had no right to Indian lands ceded by the English to the United States under the terms of the same treaty. The Indians, ignorant of peace terms and discontented over their loss of hunting grounds, listened to the British emissaries and gratefully accepted guns and powder from them as tokens of friendship.

American officers on the frontier felt that as soon as the United States occupied Fort Detroit, the major British depot to supply the Indians, Indian trouble would cease. It soon became apparent to most of the officers, however, that no attempt was being made to occupy that post. Forts Niagara, Oswego, Michilimackinac, and Detroit were not evacuated until many months after General Wayne's victory at Fallen Timbers in 1794. Thus the English were able to hold onto their lucrative fur trade for more than eleven years after the Treaty of Paris, and the Indians frustrated America's attempt to settle the northwest frontier during that time.

PAY, SUBSISTENCE, AND RATIONS

The resolve of 1784[8] specified that the pay, subsistence, and rations of the regiment were to be exactly the same as that adopted for the old Continental army on July 29, 1775. A lieutenant-colonel received $40 a month, plus subsistence and rations; a major, $33.33; a captain, $22; a lieutenant, $13.33; ensign, $10; sergeant, $8; corporal, drummer, and fifer, $7.33; and a private, $6.67. The subsistence and rations were scaled down according to rank, the enlisted men receiving no subsistence or forage.[9]

A total of thirty-seven officers were called for in the 1784 resolve: one lieutenant-colonel–commandant (from Pennsylvania), one major (from Connecticut), one major (from New York), eight captains, ten lieutenants, one surgeon, and four mates. The army was "liable to call the rules and regulations formed for the government of the late army of the United States,"[10] plus any additional rules that the present Congress thought necessary to establish.

The regiment was established on a miniature scale patterned almost identically after the old Continental army. Officers' Commission read "according to the Rules and Regulations formed for the government of the late army of the United States."[11] Recruiting began almost immediately and troops began to assemble near the Schuylkill River outside Philadelphia.

Pennsylvania supplied the largest quota of men to the regiment and was therefore allowed to choose the commanding officer, Josiah Harmar. Harmar was commissioned lieutenant-colonel–

[8] On April 12, 1785, Congress would pass another resolution raising troops for three years, the first enlistments having expired. Then the lieutenant-colonel's pay was raised to $50 per month plus forage and subsistence and the private's pay decreased to $4 a month.
[9] See Notes to Chapter 1.
[10] *Journals of Congress*, Vol. 9.
[11] Josiah Harmar's Pennsylvania Commission, August 12, 1784 (dated), Clements Library.

commandant by the state of Pennsylvania. His pay was $10 less than the $50 a month he received as a colonel in the Continental army. In reality he was an officer of the Pennsylvania state militia on detached duty to the Federal government. He sent weekly returns of the Pennsylvania troops "in the service of the United States" to John Dickinson, president of the supreme executive council of Pennsylvania, as well as returns of the Federal regiment to the secretary in the War Office. Dickinson was kept completely informed about the affairs of the regiment by Harmar.

Harmar brought to the new regiment pride and color. He accepted his commission with enthusiasm, hoping to make the regiment of raw recruits into a military unit comparable to the finest in the late army. The ultimate failure was the fault of the times, not of the commander. He brought with him every military concept he had learned as an officer serving under men like Washington, Steuben, and Wayne. He was aware of the challenge before him and knew he would be working with rank-and-file who had reached the bottom rung of the ladder in postwar America. Realizing that his task was to create an esprit de corps among a group that had given up all semblance of pride in themselves and in their government, Harmar began immediately to try to inject discipline and regulation into their slovenly and disordered lives.

NOTES:
Chapter 1

Pay of the army was fixed by acts of Congress of April 12, 1785, and reconfirmed by acts of Congress of October 20, 1786, and October 3, 1787. The rate of pay was:

Lieutenant-colonel–commandant	$50 per month	Surgeon Mate	$30 per month
Major	45 ' '	Sergeants	6 ' '
Captain	35 ' '	Corporals	5 ' '
Lieutenant	26 ' '	Musicians	5 ' '
Ensign	20 ' '	Private	4 ' '
Surgeon	45 ' '		

Clothing allowance was fixed at:
For each noncommissioned officer and private soldier annually:

1 coat	1 stock	4 shirts
2 pairs of woolen overalls	1 pair of shoe buckles	4 pairs of socks
1 hat	1 vest	1 stock clasp
4 pairs of shoes	2 pairs linen overalls	1 blanket

Rations of noncommissioned officers and privates consisted of:

1 pound of bread or flour	1 quart of salt	
1 pound of beef or 3/4 pound of pork	2 quarts of vinegar	
1 gill of common rum	2 pounds of soap	for every 100 rations
	1 pound candles	

Forage and subsistence for the officers consisted of:
Subsistence in lieu of rations, the same as during the Revolution.

Forage		*Subsistence*	
Majors	$12 per month	Lieutenant-colonel–	
Surgeon	6 per month	Commandant and Major	$20 per month
Regimental		Captain	12 per month
Staff—each	6 per month	Lieutenant	8 per month
		Ensign	8 per month
		Surgeon	16 per month
		Surgeon Mate	8 per month

By the act of July 31, Harmar was promoted to brigadier-general, by brevet, and to receive the emoluments of that rank, but the pay of lieutenant-colonel–commandant. The emoluments were: Subsistence—$64 per month Forage—18 per month[12]

[12] *American State Papers*, Vol. 1, Military Affairs, Gales & Seaten, Washington, 1832.

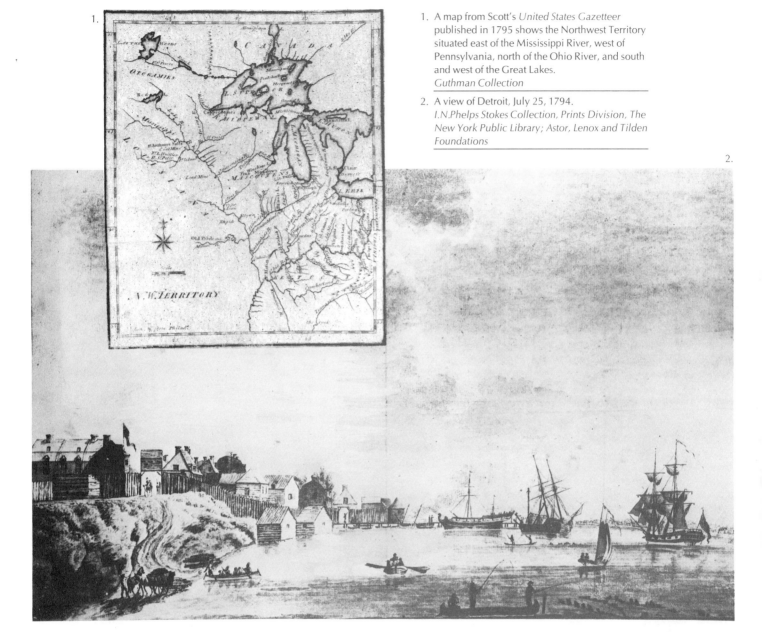

1. A map from Scott's *United States Gazetteer* published in 1795 shows the Northwest Territory situated east of the Mississippi River, west of Pennsylvania, north of the Ohio River, and south and west of the Great Lakes.
   Guthman Collection

2. A view of Detroit, July 25, 1794.
   I.N.Phelps Stokes Collection, Prints Division, The New York Public Library; Astor, Lenox and Tilden Foundations

3. West Point as viewed from the north, after a painting by Henry Livingston. This view, engraved for the March, 1791, *New York Magazine* by Cornelius Tiebout, shows:

   A—Constitution Island; B—Chain across the Hudson River; C—Fort Clinton; D—Fort Putnam.
   Guthman Collection

West Point viewed from the North as it appeared at the Close of the War.

4.

No. 305

Treasury-Office, Aug 10th 1789.

I CERTIFY That *Ebenezer Frothingham*
has lodged in this Office the following Notes, *viz.*
Army Notes due June 1, 1785, amounting to
Ditto   — —   1786,
Ditto   — —   1787,
Ditto   — —   1788,
Ditto   — —   1789,
Notes issued February   1781, ——— 12 2 7
Ditto per Act of May   1781,
Ditto per Ditto, payable to the Bearer,
Ditto per Act of May 1783, &c.
         Amounting to £. 12 2 7
For which I have issued / Notes for — 11 10
    Leaving the Sum of   ——— 12 7
             £ 12 2 7

For which he is entitled to receive Certificates in pur-
fuance of an Act of the General Affembly paffed in May
1789.

            J Huntington   Treafurer.

4. Connecticut Treasury Office note indicating past due Revolutionary War army pay owed to Ebenezer Frothingham, a lieutenant in the 3rd Connecticut Regiment. Frothingham served as a lieutenant in the 1st American Regiment. Killed in the Harmar campaign October 22, 1790, he was one of the first officers in the Federal Corps to die in battle.

5. One of a pair of shoe buckles worn during the period of Washington's inauguration. Silver backed with brass, they are decorated with finely sculptured medallions of the first president. *Guthman Collection*

6. Papier-mâché tobacco box lid circa 1789. Transfer of respect from "God Save The King" to "God Save The President Washington" is indicated by the decoration.

The patriotic design was one of many used during the period of the adoption of the Constitution and Washington's presidency. *Guthman Collection*

5.

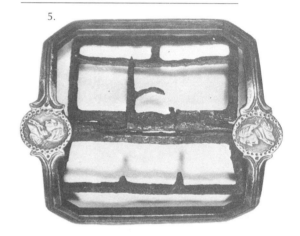

6.

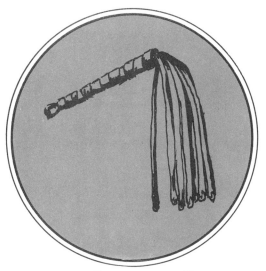

When Josiah Harmar was appointed commander, the experience he had acquired as an officer during the Revolution was handed down to his officers and men in the new regiment. Drill, discipline, and court-martials, as taught by Steuben's manual, were the new diet for those recruits who could find no other means of survival than to join the army for shelter, food, and clothing.

Chapter 2
Discipline and Training

Josiah Harmar was a lieutenant-colonel attached to the 6th Pennsylvania Regiment when General Washington issued the following order from his headquarters at Middlebrook, New Jersey, May 12, 1779:

> The Honorable the Congress Having been pleased by a Resolve of the 29th of March last, to establish a system of Regulations for the order and Discipline of the troops of the United States (written by Major General Baron de Steuben).
>
> The Commander in Chief Flatters himself that all officers Impress'd with the Importance of a regular system of Manoeuvres and Discipline, will Zealously Employ themselves with their Regulations, and with all possible puntulity and Despatch, to put them in practice within the limits of their Respective Commands. To forward this desirable purpose the Inspector General will Immediately enter upon the Exercise of this office, as Established by Congress . . .[1]

During the six post–Revolutionary War years when he was in command of the United States troops, Harmar continued to refer to the Baron's instructions in his regimental orders, and there is no question that this manual was the standard guide to the formation and discipline of the Federal army, as it had been to the Continental army and as it continued to be for another thirty years. Harmar carried his own manuscript copy of Steuben's instructions with him during his Federal campaigns.

Harmar's first orders, issued August 7, 1784, at Philadelphia, outlined the training and discipline of his small force.

> Rolls are to be called at Troop, At Noon and Retreat and all absentees reported.... The Troop is to be beat at 8 in the morning, the Retreat at sunset.... Any soldier who presumes to be absent himself shall be punished with severity.... The Adjutant will

---

[1] Orderly Book of Captain Seth Drew, 2nd Massachusetts Regiment, USMA Library, West Point.
Note: In most instances, in quoting from early sources the misspelling and other stylistic peculiarities of the originals have been preserved.

cause the men to be drilled morning and evening.... The Commanding Officer is confident that the officers will use the utmost diligence in recruiting their companies, and be careful to enlist none but good men...by a strict observance of all orders and constant attention to parade, the Regiment must soon cut a Military Figure ...[1]

ROUTINE ORDERS TO HIS MEN

The hours for Troop and Retreat varied according to the season—and also according to the danger that prevailed at the time. These two assemblies were essential to the routine of the regiment and served as the commandant's most direct means of communication to his men. Musters were taken, courts-martial, court-martial boards, and court-martial verdicts read aloud, punishment carried out (in front of the men), and the regimental and/or garrison orders spelled out to the troops, oftentimes followed by the reading of the Articles of War. Harmar's orders of September 11, 1784 stated, "All orders relative to the men are to be distinctly read to them on parade."[2]

Those same orders stated that "the preservation of the clothing is an object of greatest importance." Emphasizing the need to insure the longest possible wear for the short supply of uniforms, they further stated, "no soldier is to presume to wear his uniform coat on fatigue, on pain of being severely punished."[3] Commanding officers were to inspect the clothing, arms, and ammunition of their respective companies every Monday and submit a written report (return) to the commander that same day, specifying the condition of every article.

Until that department was abolished July 25, 1785, Harmar instructed the quartermaster to pay strict attention to the cleanliness of the encampment and to see that "tents are pitched in regular order, agreeably to the Baron's Instructions."[4] The quartermaster was ordered to supply company books and orderly books to each company commander who, in turn, was required to keep them "in the same form and with the same precision and accuracy that they were kept during the late war."[5] The food and clothing contractors assumed the provision distribution responsibilities of the quartermaster when the department was abolished, and the inspection of the camps was assumed by other officers in the regiment.

THE REGIMENTAL RECORD BOOKS

The adjutant of each company maintained the record book in which the orders issued by the commanding officer of the army and those issued by the commander at the respective garrisons were entered. The adjutant, a subaltern, daily recorded the instructions issued from headquarters and those issued by the major or captain who commanded his company into this orderly book. These orders, as well as Congressional directives pertaining to the army, were read aloud to the men at parade.

The logistical accounts (number of men on duty, sick, on leave, deserters, detached, or captured) were kept in a company book, usually by the commanding officer of the company. This accounting was taken every week, and returns submitted to the commanding officer at headquarters, where a compilation of all the companies was entered into a regimental book. Similar records were maintained for provisions, clothing, and weapons. Headquarters, in turn, forwarded compilation returns for the entire army to the Secretary at War, usually on a monthly basis. The adjutant of the regiment was responsible for the regimental orderly book maintained at headquarters, while a higher-ranking officer was responsible for the regimental book which contained the logistics. Thus the commanding officer could know at any given moment the exact status of his command.

[1] *Harmar Papers,* Vol. 32, Order Books 1784–88.
[2] *Ibid.*
[3] *Ibid.*
[4] *Ibid.,* August 7, 1784.
[5] *Ibid.,* September 10, 1784.

Preparations were made for a review of the regiment on Tuesday, September 28, 1784, at 3:00 P.M. On the preceding Sunday, Harmar's orders read, "the attitude of the soldier will be paid great attention to, that they stand perfectly silent under arms, heads up, looking to the right, it is probably they will be viewed by several judge of the military."[6]

This was the first review by the critical eyes of officials and, obviously pleased, Harmar commented in his orders of September 29, 1784, "The commanding officer is happy to see that his troops begin to have a just idea of the noble profession of arms. The martial appearance they cut yesterday in their parade through the city entitled them to applause...."[7] Six weeks of training under guidance of the Baron's instruction book had changed an unruly group of vagabonds into a fairly presentable unit of military men.

VON STEUBEN'S REGULATIONS OF 1784

Washington's hungry and frozen army, struggling to stay alive at Valley Forge, desperately needed the military discipline that Steuben offered. In addition to basic training, the rigid exercise prescribed in the manual diverted the men's minds from their immediate deprivations and gave them something new and challenging to think about in the midst of their misery.

Josiah Harmar had seen the miracle that Steuben had worked upon the Continental army and, six years later, when he was appointed commandant of the Federal regiment, he depended almost completely upon the instructions of his former teacher to mold the raw Federal recruits into a disciplined regiment. Steuben's manual was aimed at combatting British and Hessian forces—not the backwoods guerrilla fighting of the highly skilled American Indian warriors the regiment would eventually face. Shortsightedness on the part of the military was the reason that no preparatory training in Indian guerilla warfare was ever imposed on the army. Steuben's manual, perfectly sound in normal European military tactics in the period, was used to train American troops throughout the first quarter of the nineteenth century. But no Federal unit under Harmar or St. Clair was ever instructed in the frontiersmen's method of warfare.

Harmar never missed an opportunity to direct his officers' attention to some part—or all— of the instruction book. The Regulations pointed out the exact function of every man in the regiment, from the commandant down to the private soldier. With Steuben's exercises in hand, any officer could prescribe basic instructions to his recruits, and in a short time boast of a well-disciplined and highly coordinated corps.

The Baron maintained that officers with experience were best qualified to train raw recruits. Only officers with commendable Revolutionary war records were appointed to the new corps. Practically taking an officer by the hand, the manual began by defining a suitable place for drill. It outlined how recruits should be taught to put on and wear their accouterments. It explained how to form a company, how to divide the company into platoons, how to form the men into ranks according to size, where the officers and noncommissioned officers were to stand on parade, and then prescribed the formation of a regiment, positions of every man, and maneuvers of the regiment on parade, emphasizing the commands and various marching maneuvers which the new recruits were required to learn.

Fifteen printed pages were devoted to the mass loading, priming, and firing of muskets, as well as the use of the bayonet. Unfortunately, there was never enough ammunition on hand to practice this exercise adequately, if at all. There was no instruction at all for the random firing needed in guerrilla warfare, nor any suggestions for the use of rifles, a necessity on the frontier. Steuben pointed out the

---

[6] *Ibid.,* September 26, 1784.
[7] *Ibid.,* September 29, 1784.

precise method for setting up a camp, detailing every position, from horses and wagons to camp kitchens and baggage. He described the proper method of entering camp, establishing the camp guard, and the regulations that were necessary for keeping the camp clean and preserving the health of the inhabitants.

Once beyond the primary commands that were basic to every recruit's training, the manual specified military maneuvers, formations for attack and retreat, the order of march and encampment, and the disposition of field pieces for the artillery.

THE SOLDIER LEARNS TO OBEY COMMANDS

The ability of a soldier to recognize and obey the different drum signals and commands was essential, for that was the major method of communication employed in camp, on parade, during the march and under combat conditions. The soldier was taught instant recognition and immediate obedience to the various drumbeats that dictated his routine and which might save his life.

"HANDS AND FACES WASHED CLEAN"

The Baron insisted upon cleanliness. "The oftener the soldiers are under the inspection of their officers the better," he says, "for which reason every morning at troop beating they must inspect into the dress of their men; see that their clothes are whole and put on properly; their hands and faces washed clean; their hair combed; their accoutrements properly fixed, and every article about them in the greatest order." He added: "Every day the commanding officers of companies must examine their men's arms and ammunition, and see that they are clean and in good order."

Baths were a necessary luxury, and Steuben pointed out that "when any river is high, and the season favourable, the men shall bathe themselves as frequently as possible, the commanding officers of each battalion sending them by small detachments successively, under the care of a non-commissioned officer; but on no account must the men be permitted to bathe when just come off a march, at least till they have reposed long enough to get cool."

Sickness was the deadly enemy of every army. Precautions were taken to preserve the health of the men and as much treatment as possible was afforded to them when they were sick. Steuben told the officers, "There is nothing which gains an officer the love of his soldiers more than his care of them under the distress of sickness." His instructions stated that each regiment should set aside two or three tents for those who were too sick to be moved to a general hospital, or who did not require it, and that every company should be furnished with two straw-filled sacks to serve as sick beds.

Whenever a soldier died, or was dismissed from the hospital, the straw upon which he lay was to be burned and the bedding washed and aired before reusing. Returns of the sick were given every morning at roll call, after which the patients were visited by the surgeon, who delivered a report on the sick once a week to the commanding officer, stating their disorders and deciding when a patient was able to return to active duty. The manual specified that a surgeon was to remain with the troops on a march as well as in camp in case of emergencies where his services would be required. (The Congressional Resolution of June 3, 1784, called for one surgeon and four mates to take care of the Federal regiment.)

In conclusion, the manual gave instructions for each rank in the army. It spelled out the duties of everyone from the commandant down to the private soldier. A regiment could be properly administered only if its officers were able to keep careful books which would be regularly reviewed. Steuben said discipline and accurate accounting were the key to his program. Private soldiers were so busy learning their drill and applying their newly acquired military knowledge on the parade ground, over and over again, that there was little time to get into trouble. The officers were also kept busy, training their charges and keeping strict records of their physical whereabouts, so they too found it difficult to stray from the prescribed course.

COURTS-MARTIAL AND PUNISHMENTS

However, the regimental history is, except for periods of marching and fighting, a succession of courts-martial and punishment. Harmar's order book is more than half filled with the trials of his men and whippings were apparently a routine part of military life. What appears to be brutal and inhuman today was accepted as normal procedure in the eighteenth century, and the men were obviously well aware of the penalty they would have to pay for their crimes if apprehended. Either sheer boredom or ignorance or both caused by large numbers to continually commit seemingly minor crimes, for which they paid, in terms of twentieth-century justice, heavily.

Drunkenness, petty thievery, swearing at officers, forging officers' names on permits for additional whiskey rations, as well as more serious offenses of falling asleep on guard duty (usually due to intoxication) and neglect of duty were the most usual crimes, punished by whippings which consisted of from twenty five to 100 lashes on the bare back, in front of the troops at roll call.

Desertion, stealing government property, murder, aiding a prisoner to escape, major thefts, and assaulting Indians or civilians were punishable by execution (although the death sentence was seldom ordered), running the gauntlet[8] and being drummed out of the service, or by major whippings carried out over a period of days. Major punishment, however, was restrained because of the necessity to retain the offender for military service, and severe sentences were not ordered unless the situation absolutely required it.

Minor crimes were often dealt with as severely as major ones. Physical punishment was the principal method of maintaining discipline and it is not overstating the fact to say that the army was literally "whipped into shape."

Those Rules and Articles governing the army of the United States, which had been in use throughout the Revolutionary War, remained unchanged until 1786, when the situation along the northwestern frontier demanded their revision. Officers in command of small detachments along the Ohio River did not have the authority to hold courts-martial and dispense punishment to offenders. Harmar and his officers complained of the handicap of having to govern an army under regulations that had been written for regimental judication and not for application by small forces removed from headquarters by many days of travel.

General Knox, to whom the complaints had been directed, urged Congress to change the method of administering justice in the army, and on May 31, 1786, Congress passed a resolution enabling commanding officers of frontier outposts to maintain better discipline within their forts.

This directive provided that courts-martial, with as few as three commissioned officers, could be ordered by commanders of any of the garrisons for other than capital crimes and for privates and noncommissioned officer offenders only. Trials involving capital crimes or officer offenders were to be tried by a general court-martial. Garrison trials could not impose sentences of imprisonment over one month or fines of over one month's pay.

The verdict of every trial was submitted to Harmar, who either approved or disapproved the sentence, in some cases altering the punishment. Verdicts of general courts-martial involving capital punishment, or involving officers, were submitted to Secretary at War Knox for his approval, and he in turn forwarded the proceedings and findings to Congress for their final approval.

A forthcoming court-martial was announced at roll call during the reading of garrison, regimental, or general orders. The announcement was made several days prior to the trial and,

---

[8] See Notes to Chapter 2.

although the number of officers and noncommissioned officers comprising the court was announced, their names (and the defendant's name) were withheld until the day of the trial. When the trial day arrived, the court was announced at roll call again, and the name of the officers, the accused, and the violation were read aloud to the troops.

The presiding officer of the court (called president) was usually a captain or higher-ranking officer, and the trial was held in his tent. He was assisted by two, three, four, or more subaltern officers and an orderly sergeant. After hearing the complaints, and listening to the defendant, the court deliberated and submitted its finding to a) the commanding officer of the army if it was a garrison trial; or, b) the commanding officer of the army, who in turn submitted his findings to the Secretary at War in instances of capital crimes or officers on trial.

Often the sentence of the court was changed by the commander of the army or by the Secretary at War or Congress. A soldier's past record sometimes influenced the sentence, while at other times circumstances dictated the final decision. Harmar always injected his personal opinion after reviewing a sentence, many times reducing punishment to a verbal reprimand. There was no fixed punishment for each type of crime, and often different treatment was given various offenders guilty of the same crime.[9]

DRUMMED OUT OF THE SERVICE

NOTES,
Chapter 2

When the regiment was being formed in September 1784, punishment was severe. On September 10, 1784, a private convicted of theft and bad conduct was sentenced to run the gauntlet at evening roll call and was drummed out of the service with a halter around his neck. A private, Thomas McElvey, convicted of being absent all night and losing his uniform coat, was sentenced September 29 to run the gauntlet through two companies at evening roll call and be drummed out with a halter around his neck.

Harmar wrote from Fort Pitt to secretary in the War Office Carleton December 5, 1784, suggesting that "Inclosed you will likewise to receive a list of deserters from the Pennsylvania Troops; perhaps it might be advisable to advertise and pardon them (as their number is considerable) if they deliver themselves up in a limited time." He went on to explain, "I wish the Corps complete, and if they give themselves up, or can be apprehended you will please to judge the propriety of forwarding them to the Corps as speedily as possible."

Prior to 1786, the conduct of army courts-martial was handicapped by the inadequacy of the Articles of War adopted ten years earlier and in use throughout the Revolutionary war. In 1784, Harmar said, "From the situation of the Corps, a General Court Martial cannot be convened for the trial of a deserter—be pleased to inform me how they are to be punished, when apprehended."[10]

Harmar was in an unenviable position at Fort Pitt in 1784—afraid to punish deserters because he needed their numbers to complete his rosters, and unable to punish deserters, if he chose to do so, because he could not fulfill requirements of the Articles of War required to convene a court-martial.

In 1784 no specific punishments were prescribed for a military court to follow when sentencing a soldier; circumstances usually dictated the punishment. For instance, when the regiment was marching to Fort McIntosh it convened a court near Fort Pitt on December 29, 1784. As fresh meat on the frontier was scarce and highly valued in winter, a Private Thomson was sentenced to receive 100 lashes on his bare back for stealing fresh pork. A Private Burke was sentenced to receive fifty lashes on his back, by the same court, for stealing musket balls from the laboratory and for disobedience of orders, neglect of duty, and insolent language to a sergeant. A third private received fifty lashes on his bare back for disobeying a sergeant and threatening to beat him.[11] The sentence was carried out at the evening roll call, and it is obvious that the most serious offense was the theft of fresh food during winter when the rivers were frozen and supplies could not be transported to the frontier. And discipline was a necessity in the newly recruited corps, and threats to a noncommissioned officer (or commissioned) were as serious as stealing public property or actually insulting a superior.

[9] See Notes to Chapter 2.
[10] *Harmar Papers*, Vol. 28, Letter Book A, Clements Library.
[11] *Ibid.*, Vol. 32, Order Books 1784–88, Clements Library.

As the winter grew more severe, so did the court sentences. Two privates were ordered to walk the gauntlet[12] twelve times through the detachment at Fort McIntosh on January 31, 1785. They were caught stealing blankets—a commodity that could mean the difference between survival or perishing on the frontier—from the contractor. The punishment was ordered to take place at the morning roll call, and the surgeon was requested to attend, after which the two men were ordered to rejoin their companies.[13]

Courts could also be lenient, and in many cases the past record of the soldier and, of course, circumstances produced rather surprising results. An artillery matross (gunner's assistant) was found guilty of being drunk while on guard duty. A Fort McIntosh court sentenced him to be reduced to bombardier and ordered to stand on the picket (camp security guard) for ten minutes. This sentence was ordered February 3, 1785,[14] several days after an Indian peace treaty had been concluded at the fort. Harmar felt the treaty was highly favorable[15] and therefore the danger of attack by Indians was not thought to be a reality during the soldier's trial.

When danger from Indian attack became a greater menace, the punishment for sleeping on guard duty logically became more severe. The punishment ranged from fifty to 100 lashes on the bare back, and on August 12, 1788, Harmar issued the following order:

> The shameful neglect of some of the Centinels within these nights past is a disgrace to the Corps—no militia could act worse. A centinel sleeping upon his post is a crime of the highest nature, no less to suffer death, by the Articles of War—Between every relief the Sentries must be visited by the Corporal of the Guard and if anyone should be found setting or even standing upon his post, he is to be confined and shall suffer exemplary punishment—the sentries are continually to walk upon their posts except in case of rainy weather, when they are permitted to enter the sentry boxes.[16]

Many times a soldier was convicted of a crime because an event occurred at his post which might have been prevented had he been more alert. A sentinel at Fort McIntosh,[17] at whose post a theft occurred, was sentenced to 100 lashes—and so was the thief. Two canoes drifted away while a sentinel was assigned to guard them, and he received 100 lashes on February 18, 1787. Firing upon Indians without proper authority was penalized by reduction to private sentinel, and the sergeant who had ordered the sentries under his command to shoot was "stripp'd of his epaulets."[18]

Weapons were not to be fired in the camp except at designated places during specified periods. Private Peter Garner was brought before a court-martial August 7, 1787, at Post Vincennes, for discharging his piece in camp. The court found him guilty, but since the act appeared unintentional they acquitted him.[19] A sergeant was sentenced to receive fifty lashes and a reduction in rank for speaking disrespectfully about a captain during the officer's absence. Other officers interceded, however, and the punishment was reduced to forfeiture of his sergeant's epaulets at parade, and a warning that future disrespect would not be tolerated.[20]

Harmar called desertion "the greatest crime" and wrote Knox that he "would impress the soldiers with the fact that if they deserted they are violating an oath they had taken and would face the loss of their ears" in addition to running the gauntlet being drummed out of the regiment and forfeiting their pay.[21]

Knox answered on January 22, 1787, saying that he agreed "except for the cropping" of the ears. On March 5, 1787, Knox commuted a sentence of death for desertion that Harmar had approved in July 1786 at Fort McIntosh.[22]

Desertions had become a major problem, and continued to be so throughout the period 1784–1791. Harmar's concern was not exaggerated. The suggestion to crop ears was not typical of him, as he had a great deal of compassion for his men. His orders from Fort Harmar April 14, 1787, reveal this: After approving severe whippings that the court had passed upon guilty offenders he rescinded his endorsement, saying: "The Commandant approves the above sentence of the Court—It gives him pain to see a soldier disgrace himself so

[12] Note: In running the gauntlet (or "gauntloss" or "gauntlope"), the regiment (or detachment) lined up in two ranks, facing each other. Each soldier had a switch in his hand. The prisoner, stripped from the waist up, ran through the column, and as he passed each soldier lashed the prisoner with his switch or beat him with his fist. While he ran, the drum beat at each end of the ranks. The number of times a prisoner must run through depended upon the nature of his crime. An officer on horseback supervised the punishment and saw to it that each soldier did his duty.

[13] *Harmar Papers, ibid.*

[14] *Ibid.*

[15] *Ibid.,* Vol. 28, Letter Book A, Clements Library, Harmar to his brother, Ft. M'Intosh, January 29, 1785.

[16] *Ibid.,* Vol. 32, Order Books 1784–88, Clements Library.

[17] *Ibid.,* March 30, 1785.

[18] *Ibid.,* Rapids of the Ohio, June 23, 1787.

[19] *Ibid.*

[20] *Ibid.,* Fort Harmar, September 21, 1788.

[21] *Ibid.,* Vol. 28, Letter Book A, Clements Library, Harmar to Knox, Fort Harmar, September 17, 1786.

[22] *Ibid.*

much as to be brought to Corporal punishment—As he [Harmar] sets out tomorrow morning for the Rapids of the Ohio he is induced to pardon all the Prisoners, they are therefore to be immediately released and join their respective companies...."[23]

On occasion, though, he could be relentless with malefactors. A month later, May 4, at Fort Harmar, he ordered a fifer to run the gauntlet ten times that evening at roll call and then be drummed out of the garrison with a halter around his neck.[24] The fifer had run away that morning and was apprehended four miles from camp. Obviously enraged about the number of desertions, Harmar took action immediately, without calling a court. He had the entry dated, and the time noted, in the order book, which was quite unusual. Harmar, in acting outside military law, probably was trying to set an example for the entire garrison. His noting the time of order in the book must have been his way of impressing upon his men the speed with which he could—and would—deal with deserters.

[23] *Ibid.*
[24] *Ibid.*

7.

7. The drum was an instrument of command during the eighteenth century. Armies attacked or retreated, awoke or went to sleep upon hearing the proper drumbeat. The eighteenth-century American military drum pictured has blue hoops, blue shell, and white stars. The color and thirteen stars indicate Federal period infantry.
Guthman Collection

Pl.20.

XI. *Fix your Bayonet, 3. Motion ended.*

8. An eighteenth-century English engraving illustrating a soldier performing one of the positions of the manual exercise. The musket and uniform are British, but similar to the weapons carried and attire worn during the Federal period in America. The print is from the Norfolk Militia Manual printed in 1768. *Guthman Collection*

Inspection Return of Capt. Jon.ᵗ Heart's Comp.ᵞ Infantry 1.ˢᵗ U.S. Reg.ᵗ Commanded by Josiah Harmar Esq.ʳ L.ᵗ Col.ᵒ Comman.ᵗ

On French Creek 27.ᵗʰ May 1787

Jon.ᵃ Heart Capt.

N.B. Coats, Vests & Hatts are very bad, so long a March through the Woods has made them almost irreparable; & for want of Lin. Overalls the Woolen Overalls are much wore. — Tents very bad. — Knapsacks & Haversacks nearly worn out. — Arms & Accoutrements in good Order.

9.

9. Inspection return of Captain Jonathan Heart's company, 1st U.S. Regiment, dated French Creek, May 27, 1787. Fit for duty were forty-six privates, nine noncommissioned officers, and three officers. There were two deserters.
William L. Clements Library, Harmar Collection, University of Michigan; University of Michigan photo

10. The first commandant of the Federal Corps, Josiah Harmar, from a nineteenth-century engraving, after a portrait by Raphael Peale.
Guthman Collection

10.

11. Commission issued by Congress under the Confederation appointing Josiah Harmar Lieutenant-Colonel Commandant of the 1st Regiment, dated June 10, 1786.

The format of commissions remained the same, from 1777 until 1789, when the Constitution was adopted.
William L. Clements Library, Harmar Collection, University of Michigan; University of Michigan photo

12. Commission issued by the Supreme Executive Council of Pennsylvania appointing Josiah Harmar lieutenant-colonel commandant "of the troops to be raised in pursuance of the Resolution of Congress—."

Dated August 12, 1784, this commission expresses as much authority over Harmar and demands as much allegiance to the state of Pennsylvania, as does the Federal commission command for the United States.
William L. Clements Library, Harmar Collection, University of Michigan; University of Michigan photo

George Washington,

Prefident of the UNITED STATES of America.

To all who fhall fee thefe Prefents, Greeting;

KNOW Ye, That repofing fpecial Truft and Confidence in the Patriotifm, Valour, Fidelity and Abilities of *Jofiah Harmar Efquire* I have nominated, and by and with the Advice and Confent of the Senate, do appoint him a *Brigadier General by Brevet, of the Troops* ———. —— in the Service of the UNITED STATES:---He is therefore carefully and diligently to difcharge the Duty of *Brigadier General by brevet.* by doing and performing all Manner of Things thereunto belonging. And I do ftrictly charge and require all Officers and Soldiers under his Command, to be obedient to his Orders as *Brigadier General by brevet.* And he is to obferve and follow fuch Orders and Directions, from Time to Time, as he fhall receive from Me, or the future PRESIDENT of the UNITED STATES of AMERICA, or the General or other fuperior Officers fet over him, according to the Rules and Difcipline of War. This Commiffion to continue in Force during the Pleafure of the Prefident of the United States for the Time being.

GIVEN under my Hand, at *the City of New York* this *Twenty Ninth* —— Day of *September* in the Year of our Lord One Thoufand Seven Hundred and *Eighty Nine* and in the *Fourteenth* Year of the Independence of the United States.

By Command of the Prefident
of the United States of America.

Knox

Secretary for the department of War.

G. Washington

13. Commission issued by the President of the United States, as commander-in-chief of the army, appointing Josiah Harmar brigadier-general by brevet.

Signed by George Washington, this probably was the first commission issued by the Constitutional government.
William L. Clements Library, Harmar Collection, University of Michigan; University of Michigan photo

13A. Company punishment at a frontier fort: running the gauntlet.
Drawing by Don Troiani

The newly established regiment was to consist of 700 men; this quota, however, was never fulfilled. Recruiting was the most difficult task that faced the new corps. An army career was considered the lowest rung on the professional ladder of the poverty-stricken infant nation. An inadequate government, whose bankrupt treasury could not meet the obligations contracted by the suppliers of food and clothing for the army, resulted in the weakest foundation for the beginning of the United States Army.

Chapter 3

Recruiting and Clothing the Army

Filling its quota of 700 enlisted men is an achievement that the 1st American Regiment never attained. All the fears over too large an army that had been expressed on the floor of Congress during the many hours of debate over the proposed size of the Federal army proved groundless after the results of the recruiting officers had been tabulated. Even if Congress had approved a large enough force to combat the Ohio Indians adequately, it is doubtful that enough men could have been recruited under the four-state quota system. The glamour and color of colonial militia days had vanished from the American military scene long before the Revolution ended; and, by the time the Treaty of Paris had been signed, the inhabitants of the thirteen colonies abhorred war and everything associated with it.

Young men did not want a military career. The memory of discharged soldiers of the Continental army who returned home with only partial pay, or none at all, to discover their old jobs or businesses had vanished along with all hopes for "Peace and Plenty" was still vivid in the minds of most men suitable for military duty. They remembered how veterans were greeted—not with a hero's welcome but with scorn and disapproval by many whose liberty they had so bitterly fought for and attained. Neighbors suffering from the economic strain of war wanted to detach themselves from the trouble of those who had served that cause which had brought on the existing depression.

The ideal that had inspired the fighting men in Washington's army had been their vision of liberty and opportunity that victory could bring. Instead, their triumph at Yorktown brought them only broken dreams and thwarted ambitions. Hundreds—many with more bandages showing than clothing, others whose bloodstains were brighter than their faded uniforms—sought refuge in the impersonal atmosphere of the busy cities along the Eastern seaboard. There they found understanding only among themselves, a pathetic fraternity of forgotten men. Unrewarded by a government that couldn't pay them for their war service, and ignored by their friends who chose to forget their military exploits, these bitter men soon fell into lives of drinking and drifting. Swallowed up by the masses of population, they quickly found security in anonymity.

The task of trying to enlist recruits for the newly created Federal regiment had proved an almost impossible chore. Failing to enlist the most desirable young men, the recruiting parties in New York,

Connecticut, Pennsylvania, and New Jersey[1] turned in desperation and with simple logic toward the masses of drifters loitering on the city streets in their respective states. Having nothing better to do than to listen, or being too intoxicated to move away, many of the hopeless wretches succumbed to the pleas of the army. Some felt that by joining the Federal corps they had everything to gain and nothing at all to lose.

Even though a military career was the least desirable occupation in the not-too-promising future of the United States, the pledge of food, clothing, liquor ration, and (for some) the vision of the new land in the Northwest, resulted in the formation of an army of enlisted men who were, for the most part, pathetic rejects. The recruiting parties were only partially successful. Verbal approaches were made wherever possible, but the state quotas were not sufficiently completed. Advertisements were placed in local newspapers similar to the one that appeared in *The American Daily Advertiser* in Philadelphia. Adjacent to a woodcut of a plow advertising Benjamin Mason's seeds, and another showing the schooner *Hannah,* under rull rigging, "For Sale or Charter," the name "CAPTAIN ARMSTRONG" stood out in bold capital letters in the lower right-hand corner of page one:

> CAPTAIN ARMSTRONG informs his fellow soldiers and others, who may wish to enlist, that he has commenced recruiting in the city of Philadelphia, where a generous Bounty and other Encouragement will be given. Young Men who wish to become Adventurers in the New Country, by joining this command, may acquire a Knowledge of the Western World, subject to no expense; and after serving a short period, set down in their own farms, and enjoy all the blessing of Peace and Plenty. John Armstrong, Captain, 1st Regt United States.[2]

The romantic wording in this, and other such ads, did not attract restless young city dwellers who had idyllic dreams of a free, untrammeled life in the wilderness with nothing to do but work a trap line from which they could collect thick, glossy furs worth a king's ransom. Nor did settled family men respond to the lure of a lonely log cabin with a tamped earthen floor in some wilderness where farmlands could be cleared only by backbreaking labor. Besides, the government had broken too many promises during the last war, and its disappointed soldiers did not forget their bitter experiences. None, that is, except the most destitute of the army of unemployed—the hungry and the shabbily clothed. The promise of basic necessities—clothing and satisfied stomachs—induced many to enlist. A Congressional study made four years later revealed that good clothing was the greatest inducement of all to enlist.[3]

Connecticut and New York recruits were issued clothing and accouterments at West Point, while those recruited in New Jersey or near Philadelphia were outfitted at the Philadelphia repository. Those troops enlisted westward of Philadelphia received their issue at Fort Pitt, the final rendezvous for all of the troops in 1784.

The clothing issued at those points consisted of salvaged Revolutionary war stores. An indiscriminate combination of artillery coats and infantry hats, or vice versa, was handed out to the recruits regardless of whether they were artillerymen or infantrymen but rather depending upon the available suply of clothing. The important point was whether or not they received a full suit of clothing. According to the department quartermaster at West Point, there was not enough to go around, and some of the men had to march all the way to Fort Pitt without shoes or without a

---

[1] Recruiting was carried out only in those states that supplied troops to fill the quota of the Federal corps.
[2] Issue of March 22, 1791.
[3] *Journals of Congress,* Vol. 13, October 2, 1788.

complete uniform. All of the clothing was ill-fitting. Similar incidents occurred at Philadephia, and all of the recruits who lacked portions of their uniforms were told they would be completely outfitted at Fort Pitt.

Vainly, each company commander tried to enlist his full quota, but none succeeded. Realizing that every company would fall short of its personnel quota, and that time was growing short, the recruiting parties were ordered to march to Fort Pitt as soon as the officers felt their respective companies were as near full strength as possible. The march was tiring and the men, inadequately attired, and unused to strenuous military travel, found sanctuary in the various towns at night with a crock of whiskey or flask of rum.

The officers could not control the drinking problem and many of the new enlistees, satisfied that they had received all the clothing they were going to be issued, deserted in large numbers. Officers assumed a role similar to sheepherders rounding up strays rather than that of military leaders. Stragglers, either too intoxicated to keep up with the group, or overcome with nausea from too much alcohol the night before, became a daily source of annoyance to the officers, who also had to retrieve the scores of deserters. It was unusual for an officer to arrive at Pittsburgh with the same number of men with which he started the march.

A steady stream of new recruits arrived at Fort Pitt, tired and sore from their long march, wearing ill-fitting clothing that varied from man to man, rendering the appearance of the new regiment as unmilitary as the aborigines lurking beyond the gates of the fort.

1784 ENLISTMENTS EXPIRE

When, by April 12, 1785, the army's term of enlistment was about to expire, Congress authorized another term of enlistment for the same number of men for three years. Many of the first-year men did not want to re-enlist, and even promises of better clothing and prompter pay could not induce them to remain in the corps.

Only partially successful, recruiting parties were hurriedly sent back east to their home states, but efforts to fill the quotas were no different than the previous year. With time running out and still under strength, the small army proceeded with its schedule.

In 1786 the threat of Shay's Rebellion prompted Congress to authorize an additional 1,340 men for the army. The resolve of October 20 called for 260 recruits from New Hampshire, 660 from Massachusetts, 120 from Rhode Island, and 180 from Connecticut, all of whom were to be part of the infantry and artillery. Maryland and Virginia were to contribute sixty cavalrymen each, and the total of 1,340 new men, together with the original corps, were to be formed into a legionary corps consisting of 2,040 noncommissioned officers and privates.

By April of the following year the rebellion had been crushed, and Congress cut the size of the army back to its original strength but retained the two additional batteries of artillery that had been raised in Massachusetts under the resolve of October 20, 1786.[4]

1785 ENLISTMENTS EXPIRE

The army had begun construction of the sixth fort in the Ohio River valley when the three-year enlistments were about to expire. On October 3, 1787, Congress passed another resolution, calling again for the same number of men to continue in service for another three years. Harmar told

---

[4] The army consisted of one regiment of infantry composed of eight companies. Each company consisted of four sergeants, four corporals, two musicians, and sixty privates, plus one battalion of artillery consisting of four batteries (each battery was composed of four sergeants, four corporals, two musicians, and sixty privates). Although this was the strength as specified by Congress, the ranks were never entirely filled.

Secretary at War Knox that he intended to "maneuvre with the older soldiers—in order to re-enlist them—one of them is worth half a dozen recruits—as they have a knowledge of the country and acquired the habits of a soldier,"[5] and he recounted his experience of 1785.

Although the government, as usual, was behind in its pay and clothing allowance, Harmar promised the men prompt settlement of their pay and assured them that the clothing allowance would be filled if only they would remain with the regiment. He even went so far as to assure them that they would receive the extra month's pay Congress promised to new troops. But, in spite of his efforts, only a small percentage of the men remained. Recruiting new troops now became a major project, and the General again made plans to send officers, with enlisted men, to their respective states for that purpose. The importance of filling their state's quota was stressed and officers were aware that, if quotas were not filled, commissions might be revoked.

Those chosen to recruit left Fort Harmar March 9, 1788, carrying ten days' provisions and double allowance of whiskey. They boarded a contractor's[6] boat and traveled down the Ohio River to Fort Pitt.[7] Lieutenant John Pratt's destination was his native Connecticut. Accompanied by a "trusty non-commissioned officer and 3 handsome privates,"[8] he carried written instructions from General Knox. The Secretary at War instructed Lieutenant Pratt to:

> Be careful to recruit men of the best character, for honesty and sobriety as far as you shall judge. Every recruit must be well formed in his body and limbs—perfectly sound in his organs and health and sufficiently robust to bear the fatigues of the military life—No recruit to be under five feet six inches high or under eighteen or more than forty-five years of age. Neither Negroes; Mullatoes, or Indians are to be received.[9]

Lieutenant Pratt, and the other recruiting officers, were not in a position to follow General Knox's instructions to the letter. They tried, but his specifications were too exacting and the selection of men quite limited. Only the homeless and hungry, dejected and rejected, listened to the roll of the drum as the recruiting party moved from one street to another in the large cities and small towns. The army still had a negative appeal as a career to most of the men eligible to enlist. So, whenever regulations became impractical, the bottom of the barrel was scraped.

Department Quartermaster William Price, issuing clothing to the new recruits at West Point, complained to General Knox: "One of the recruiting serjeants in Connecticut has sent one man and he is unfit for a Soldier by reason of a Continual running Sores upon his Breast so that he cannot wear his accoutrements, etc."[10] Price denied the man clothing but told the Secretary at War that the man had served, under the same physical handicap, during the "late war," and suggested that if General Knox wanted to accept him in the army the quartermaster would issue the clothing.

Beginning its life with the hand-me-down clothing of the disbanded Continental army, the Federal corps appeared more like a stepchild than the pride and joy of the new nation. On paper, however, Congress did grant its new infantry recruits ample clothing. The annual allowance was:[11]

[5] *Harmar Papers,* Vol. 32, Order Books, 1784–88, Harmar to Knox, January 10, 1788.
[6] Contractors supplied the army with provisions. Since the forts were spaced along the Ohio River, the contractor moved his suplies from Pittsburgh by boat.
[7] *Harmar Papers, ibid.*
[8] *Ibid.*
[9] Knox to Lieutenant Pratt, War Office, April 16, 1788, Guthman Collection.
[10] West Point Letter Book #1, USMA Library, William Price to Knox, West Point.
[11] *Harmar Papers,* Vol. 32, Order Books, 1784–88, Garrison Orders, Fort McIntosh, June 16, 1785.

1 regimental coat	2 pairs of woolen socks
1 woolen vest	4 pairs of shoes
1 pair of woolen breeches	1 blanket
2 pairs of linen overalls	1 stock clasp
4 shirts	1 pair of buckles } every two years
2 pairs of stockings	1 hat
1 pair of mitts	1 hunting frock

The artillery was issued the same amount of clothing as the infantry, except that the pair of mitts and the hunting frock were omitted from their allowance.[12]

The allowance was idealistically ample, but realistically it was impossible for the young nation to furnish all of the specified items to its soldiers—just as impossible was the attempt to attire the army with impressive styling and color. An advertisement that appeared in the *Connecticut Courant* when that state was trying to complete its quota of 180 men for the Legionary Corps described the uniform:[13]

> The uniform of the Regiment will be, blue ground, red facings and cuffs—white vests and overalls.
>
> The Non-Commissioned officers will be distinguished by shoulder-knots; and the clothing of the Sergeants will be better quality than that of the privates.
>
> Permission will be given to such Non-Commissioned Officers and Soldiers of the former Continental Army, as appear by their discharges to have been entitled to honorable distinctions for three or six years faithful services, to resume the same badges of merit they formerly wore. Every occasion will be taken to notice and reward extraordinary merit.[14]
>
> Regimental colours and uniform Drums are expected before the regiment takes the field.
>
> Uniformity of appearance will be studiously attended to, in the minutest articles, from the first formation of this corps. The men are to wear their hair plaited and fastened up behind their hats.

Secretary of War Knox issued uniform regulations January 30, 1787,[15] specifying that the artillery was to dress accordingly:

> Hats cocked—yellow trimmings—coats blue, scarlet lappells, cuffs and standing cape—length of the coat to reach the knee, Scarlet linings and yellow buttons—vests white with short flaps, three buttons on each pocket—overalls—cockades of black leather round with points four inches diameter—shoulder straps—blue, edged with red on both shoulders—feathers—black and red, tops to rise six inches above the brim of the hat—epaulettes—the Officers, gold—the Majors 2, a single row of bullion—captains 1 epaulette on the right shoulder, 2 rows of bullion—the lieuts. 1 epaulette on the left shoulder, 1 row of bullion—Sergt. 2 epaulettes, yellow

---

[12] *Order Book,* 2nd Regiment Artillery, USMA Library, War Office, December 12, 1786.

[13] Issue of January 15, 1787.

[14] The headquarters order book at the "Rapids of the Ohio" contained the following order June 12, 1787: "Old soldiers who have served during the late war are to have badges of distinction on their left arm, one badge for every 3 years service" (*Harmar Papers*).

[15] *U.S. Artillery Order Book,* 2nd Regiment, 1787–1800, *ibid.,* USMA Library, West Point.

worsted—Corporals 1 epaulette right shoulder—Swords—saber form, yellow mounted, the Majors 3 feet & Capts. and Subs. [subalterns] 2½ feet— the uniform of the Music to be red, faced with blue.

Knox's specifications continued, covering the entire regiment:[16]

The infantry white vests had white buttons and the artillery white vests had yellow buttons; all vests to be the same [both infantry and artillery]. . . .

All troops were ordered to wear black stocks or cravats; the entire army was to have "lapells of the whole & standing cape, 2 inches wide; cuffs, 3 inches;—" The infantry cockades were the same as those of the artillery, as were their shoulder straps; epaulettes of the infantry were to be silver, and the colonel–commandant was to have a double row of silver bullion on each epaulette. "Sergts. Major, Quarter Masters Sgt., drum & fife Major, two, silks and silver; Sergeants, two, worsted—cpls., one, right shoulder—Artillery, yellow, infantry, white."[17]

In 1786, Colonel Henry Jackson, who was directing the recruiting in Massachusetts for the Legionary corps, suggested to General Knox that the uniform button should display an eagle on the center with the regimental number.[18] Because the Legionary corps never materialized, Jackson, a former general of the Continental army, lost his would-be command when the Massachusetts troops were ordered disbanded by Congress, along with the other troops ordered raised in 1786. The eagle button, however, remained with the army to become standard decoration, in various forms, through the twentieth century. Jackson was quite possibly the first to suggest the eagle to decorate American military insignia.

Whether the eagle button was adopted as early as 1787 is not certain, but the attempts to instill a military appearance were apparent, even though the efforts were ineffective by the time results reached the men in the field. Invoices dated 1787 did, however, list artillery coats, infantry coats, short fatigue coats, and drummer coats,[19] indicating there was more than an attempt on paper to create a military appearance.

The standardization of dress among the officers was much more consistent and easier to carry out during the same period, simply because they ordered and paid for their own uniforms. Headquarters regulated the prices of officers' clothing at the various army posts where the clothes were made. The price schedule included uniform coats, uniform vests, breeches, great coats, overalls, boots, shoes and ruffled and plain shirts,[20] and each officer could supervise the tailoring of his own clothes and make certain they were delivered on time.

Josiah Harmar's attempt to standardize the uniform of the corps as specified in the official orders is a story of an energetic man struggling against overwhelming difficulties, attempting to achieve a national identity for his small army. The commander knew that the first step toward creating a spirit of unity within the Corps was to first achieve uniformity of clothing. One of his first orders issued instructed his captains, in September 1784, to furnish the men in their command with black leather stocks, the cost of which was to be deducted from the men's pay.[21] Several months later he ordered

[16] *Ibid.*
[17] *Ibid.*
[18] *Knox Papers,* Jackson to Knox, February 25, 1787, Roll 19, Massachusetts Historical Society.
[19] *Harmar Papers,* Vol. 6.
[20] *Harmar Papers,* Vol. 32, Order Books 1784–88.
[21] *Ibid.,* Camp near Schuylkill River, September 15, 1784.

Artillery Captain Derick Lane, who was recruiting for the New York quota in Albany, to create a more uniform appearance among the troops he was enlisting.

"I am sorry to observe," Harmar wrote, "that some of your men's coats are faced with white and some with red—I wish you to endeavor to procure a sufficiency of Scarlet, and alter the white in order that the Regiment may be uniform."[22] Captain Lane accomplished the procurement of the red facings by stoppage of his men's rum ration, he reported to Harmar, who replied: " . . . if we do join at a future day, we shall have the satisfaction of being uniform."[23]

On July 1, 1785, Harmar wrote to General Knox and explained that the cockade worn by the regiment was the "union," which was black and white. He suggested that perhaps the general would send directions about the colors for securing "a national one."[24] Knox replied three weeks later, instructing that the cockades should be black for both soldiers and officers in the regiment.[25] He observed that light-colored cockades were impractical and that those of black leather presented "a respectable appearance when they were well polished."

Despite the attempts of Harmar and Knox, the army wore a mixture of artillery and infantry uniforms and an odd assortment of colors. Economic circumstances made the various attempts to solidify the color scheme impractical. New Jersey Infantry recruits were issued yellow-bound artillery hats from Department Quartermaster William Price at West Point in 1786.[26] He also issued the infantrymen twenty artillery and fourteen infantry coats from the "old army."[27]

Secretary at War Knox apologized for the blue overalls that had been delivered instead of white, in 1787, and said it was because the white cloth could not be obtained.[28] Harmar replied, expressing his feeling that white was more military and regretting having received the blue. The Commandant added that future uniforms would look much smarter if they consisted of cocked hats, one side higher than the other, and long blue coats with red facings and white underdress.[29] General Knox's answer reveals insight into the thinking of the eighteenth century concerning the practical aspects of the uniform versus their eye appeal and into the desire for national identity:

> I readily concur with you in the white overalls and I stated to you the reason they were not forwarded because the materials could not be procured—The blue overalls will answer well for winter, and the white linen for summer, but in the future the woolen shall be white if to be obtained—but with respect to cocked hats and long coats I have to observe—that long coats appear to me not to be proper for the service of the frontiers as short ones—Overalls are conceived to be greatly preferable to breeches—but overalls and long coats and cocked hats are in my opinion an unseemly association—the few men who are in this town belonging to Captain Bradford's company are judged to be most properly clothed for real service.
>
> It has been my desire that the American troops should have a characteristically national uniform, blending utility and appearance together without implicitly following the customs of the Europeans—I have had the hope that something might be adopted in this respect, might evince a judgement of our own, although I confess that

22 *Harmar Papers*, Vol. 28, Letter Book A, Harmar to Lane, January 19, 1785.
23 *Ibid.*, May 3, 1785.
24 *Ibid.*, Harmar to Knox, Fort McIntosh, July 1, 1785.
25 *Ibid.*, Knox to Harmar, July 22, 1785.
26 West Point Letter Book I, 1784–86, Price to Knox., USMA Library, West Point.
27 *Ibid.*
28 *Harmar Papers*, Vol. 6, November 14, 1787, Knox to Harmar.
29 *Ibid.*, Letter Book C, Harmar to Knox, March 9, 1788.

the present uniform is very different from my wishes and judgement, yet long coats and cocked hats would not be parts of the uniform—I hope the time will arrive when a system of this kind may be adopted agreeable to troops and honorable to the nation.[30]

General Harmar issued orders dated September 22, 1788, directing that the white bindings be removed immediately from all hats, and replaced with bearskin and scarlet bucktail. By the fourth year, 1788, the army had moved from an assortment of uniforms and colors closer to a national unity and identity.[31]

Consistent with his desire for an "American uniform," Harmar requested General Knox to approve a national marching song, one that would not copy the British or the French.[32] Evidently Knox approved of the idea and told Harmar that "as soon as one can be formed that shall be peculiarly characteristic, I will order it to be practised."[33]

Whatever clothing was not stored in Revolutionary war suplus had to be manufactured. The Board of Treasury placed ads in newspapers inviting bids from those who wished to receive contracts to supply the clothing needed:

> The United States in Congress, having their act of the 20th October last, directed the Board of Treasury to contract for cloathing and rations necessary for the troops to be raised in pursuance to the act above mentioned; and having further by their act of the 21st of said month, made a Special Requisition on the several states for the sume of 500,000 dollars, to be expressly applied for the pay and support of the troops on the present establishment.
>
> THE COMMISSIONERS of the BOARD of TREASURY hereby give notice that proposals will be received at their office till the 20th of December next inclusive, etc., etc.[34]

The ad went on to say that the bidders must specify all information about the types of materials to be used and their prices, the longest credit, and terms of payment. Competitive bids were submitted and the lowest bidder chosen. Specifications for the clothing, and the amount of clothing needed, had been submitted to the Board of Treasury by the Secretary at War.

Because of the inadequate system of raising funds the government was often helpless, and the army found that clothing was only delivered by the contractor when money was available. Therefore, deliveries to the men were piecemeal, and this explains why they were not issued all of their clothing at the same time. Congress reported that the troops that had enlisted for 3 years in 1785 had received only two of the three suits of clothing they were promised—and that "Provision was made for the third year's clothing but the Secretary at War has been constrained to apply it for the [newly enlisted] recruits, otherwise they could not have been enlisted."[35] The army often found itself in this position, and not much could be done to resolve the situation. Often the states were far behind in their required portion of payment to the Board of Treasury for support of the army. When the money was finally

[30] *Ibid.,* Vol. 7, Knox to Harmar, April 21, 1788.
[31] *Ibid.,* Vol. 32, Order Book, 1784–88.
[32] Harmar's letter to Knox, July 1, 1785, *op. cit.*
[33] Knox's letter to Harmar, July 22, 1785, *op. cit.*
[34] Issue of *Connecticut Courant* of December 4, 1786.
[35] *Journals of Congress,* Vol. 13, October 2, 1788.

forwarded it frequently was refused because it was in the paper currency of a state unacceptable to the contractor. Although Congress had resolved that all payments must be made in specie, it could not control the attempts of the states to pay in their own paper money, often worthless outside of the state in question.

The thankless task of collecting the funds from the states, paying the contractor, and delivering the clothing oftentimes fell upon the much overburdened regimental paymaster, Erskurius Beatty. Journeying between the wilderness outposts to the War Office in New York, then to the Board of Treasury, pleading for the men's pay and for payment to the contractors, then on to the various states diplomatically seeking their quota of funds to support the army, and back to the wilderness, his time was consumed in the hardships of travel and in diplomatic pressure.

A typical mission of Beatty's took place in January 1785 when he delivered long-overdue shoes to the men at Fort McIntosh and was immediately told "to be in readiness to proceed from hence on Sunday next for New York, in order to have the new clothing for the troops forwarded on as soon as possible."[36] During the winter months, in the Ohio River valley, no one traveled—except the paymaster. Sometimes he was successful and secured the clothing from the contractor; but the quality was usually inferior.

Josiah Harmar complained bitterly to the Secretary at War about the quality of the clothing in 1786:

> The shirts are in general of a sleezy linen, very scanty made— not more I believe than 2 & 3/4ths yds 7/8ths linen in them—they will not last a soldier a week—One of the russia sheeting pattern shirts is substantial and worth twenty of them—
>
> The shoes which Hodgdon[37] shewed me are too small, fit only for boys of twelve or fourteen years of age, and of a bad quality—
>
> The hats are likewise too small and badly worked—the person whom the clothiers contracted with for them, in the presence of Mr. Hodgdon and myself declared that some of them were English hats and never were made under our contract—
>
> The coats are also of the worst quality being made of a kind of stroud or duffil which would wear out before the troops arrive at Fort Pitt, were it not for the benefit of having fatigue coats.[38]

The summer before, Harmar complained about the late deliveries of clothing to Fort McIntosh. He told Secretary at War Knox that each man in the corps was lacking one shirt, one pair of linen overalls, one pair of woolen socks, and one pair of mitts, to complete his annual allowance.[39] That same year the paymaster was told by Harmar to "use every exertion to obtain and bring on a further supply of cash"[40] in order to pay the troops. The frustrated commandant told his men that "Prospects of receiving money very flattering."[41] The hardships of winter on the frontier were ordeal enough, without requiring his men to go without pay, Harmar thought.

The army grew used to waiting. Clothing continued to arrive piecemeal, and the order books are filled with entries noting staggered deliveries. "The troops are to receive another shirt per man. The

[36] *Harmar Papers*, Fort McIntosh, January 7, 1785, Vol. 32, Order Books, 1785–88.
[37] Samuel Hodgdon, Commissary of Military Stores.
[38] *Ibid.*, Harmar to Knox, Vol. 28, Order Book A, April 26, 1786.
[39] *Harmar Papers*, Harmar to Knox, January 7, 1785, Vol. 28, Letter Book A.
[40] *Ibid.*, Garrison Orders, September 12, 1786, Fort Harmar.
[41] *Ibid.*

Artillery Company and Capt. Finney's Company are to receive one pair of linen overalls and one pair of socks per man."[42]

Incident upon incident recounting deliveries that were late is recorded in the regiment's record books. On January 13, 1787, Commandant Harmar announced that the second-year men would receive their allotment of woolen overalls, two shirts, two pairs of shoes and socks, stocks, clasps, and shoe buckles, long overdue. "They had set off from Philadelphia the *30th* last *November,* and may be hourly expected,"[43] Harmar said. The supplies did not arrive until February 21, 1787.[44] To climax the frustration, after the clothing had been distributed to the troops a great outcry arose because the overalls varied greatly in quality—some men receiving good overalls, others very poor.

Nothing that the army undertook was easy. Secretary at War Knox tried to solve the contracting problem by ordering uniforms in England. Ironic as it seems (since England was still an enemy thwarting the westward expansion of the United States), Knox wrote to P. Brett in London on February 6, 1788, asking prices for "Blue cloth coat with red facing without lace; waistcoat, white cloth with half thick backs; shirt; black leather stock; stock clasp; pair yarn stockings; shoes; hat."[45]

In spite of difficulties, obstacles were overcome, substitutions made, and the regiment began to assume a uniform military appearance.

---

[42] *Ibid.,* Vol. 32, Order Books 1784–88, Fort McIntosh, May 9, 1789.
[43] *Ibid.*
[44] *Ibid.*
[45] *Knox Papers,* Knox to P. Brett, February 6, 1788, Roll 21.

14. Recruiting advertisement that appeared in *The American Daily Advertiser,* a Philadelphia newspaper, March 22, 1791. The ad was placed by Captain John Armstrong, whose name appears in bold type.

In order to retain their commissions, officers of the 1st Regiment were responsible for filling the quotas of their respective companies.
Guthman Collection

14.

15.

16. United States Army insignia of the 1790 period. Defined as a cross belt plate, this handsome accouterment was worn on a sword belt or cartridge box belt. It is finely modeled silver backed with brass.
Guthman Collection

17. Josiah Harmar's cockade. A delicately made officer's insignia, as opposed to the plainer leather cockades that were prescribed in the regulations. The cockade is made up of individual silk loops arranged in circular rows. The center is white, the middle light blue, and the outer circle is dark blue.
William L. Clements Library, Harmar Collection, University of Michigan

17.

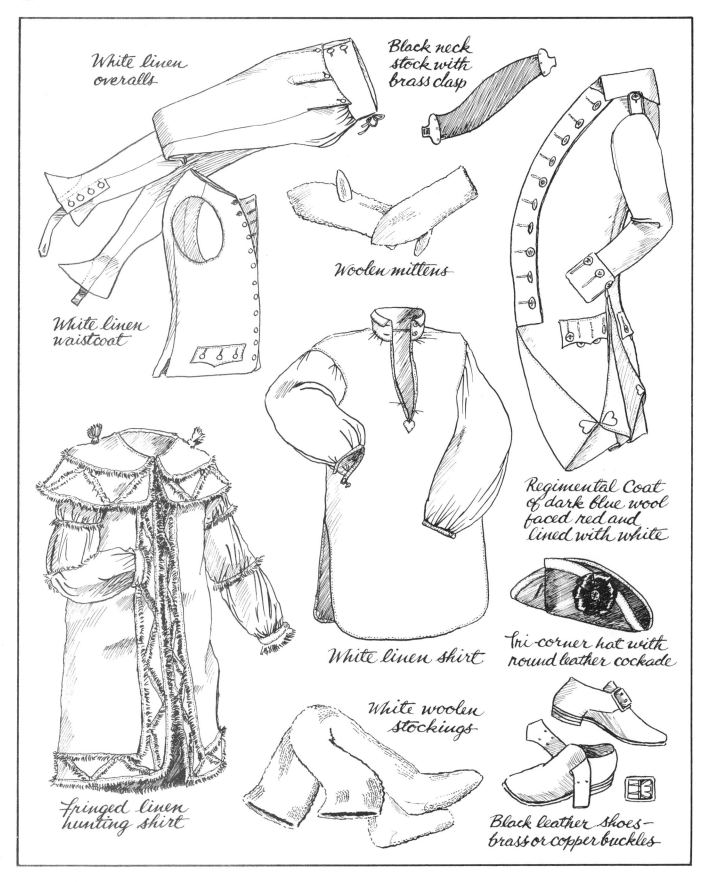

White linen overalls

Black neck stock with brass clasp

Woolen mittens

White linen waistcoat

Regimental Coat of dark blue wool faced red and lined with white

White linen shirt

Tri-corner hat with round leather cockade

Fringed linen hunting shirt

White woolen stockings

Black leather shoes— brass or copper buckles

19. An infantryman and musician of the 1st American Regiment drawn for *March to Massacre* by Don Troiani.

19.

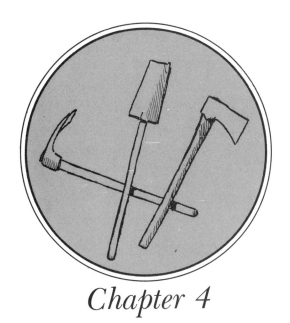

Chapter 4

A series of forts was constructed along the northwestern frontier. Fighting men were transformed into carpenters, and their needs—among Indians and the cruel winters of the wilderness—changed their life of misery and deprivation into an army of self-sufficient Americans.

Part I: Fortifications

The standard system of European fortification was not practical in the North American wilderness. Indians had no cannon; therefore the army was able to eliminate the expense of an elaborate defense against heavy weapons. But, since the forts were usually remote from large settlements, adequate storage space for provisions and supplies was required. On the other hand, as detachments were frequently dispatched from the forts on various assignments, it was necessary to provide for adequate defense of the fort with only half their complete garrison available.[1]

The basic design remained fairly constant: a walled square or pentagon with a two-story blockhouse located at every angle. A ditch seven to eight feet deep encircled the wall and loopholes in the cellar walls of the blockhouses, six feet above the ground, allowed firearms to be aimed directly into or over the ditch. Traders were permitted to build houses and stores along the inside of the wall, and a large area was left vacant to permit the planting of gardens, and the digging of wells and other out-of-doors facilities. Vegetables were also grown in the ditch surrounding the walls. The powder magazine containing most of the ammunition was placed in the center of the fort. Policy usually forbade more than a small quantity of cartridges to be kept in each blockhouse for emergency.[2] "The Garrisons of such Forts would be free from surprises, even if they had no Centries, for nothing can get at them, while the doors are bolted and barred."[3]

THE STRING OF FORTS

The Federal army devoted as much time learning the art of fort construction as they did learning the art of war. Throughout the first seven years of the corps, its men were constantly called upon to perform in the capacity of carpenters as well as soldiers, continuing to erect fortifications until October 1791, when they completed Fort Jefferson (Ohio), the final link in the supply chain for the extended troops.

[1]*Northwest Territory Collection,* Arthur St. Clair Papers, William Henry Smith Memorial Library, Indiana Historical Society. (An almost identical description of frontier fortifications is given in *An Historical Account of the Expedition Against the Ohio Indians in the Year 1764. Under The Command of Henry Bouquet, Esq.,* by William Smith.)
[2] *Ibid.*
[3] *Ibid.*

In order to execute its primary function of establishing military control of the recently acquired Northwest Territory and protecting the inhabitants from the depredations of the Indians and lawless whites, the regiment was called upon to construct a string of forts along the frontier border which extended from the Great Lakes to the St. Mary's River along the east bank of the Mississippi River. However, since the regiment consisted of only 700 men, the number at each fort was minimized. The forts were concentrated along the Ohio River, extending from a short distance north of Pittsburgh, southwest to Louisville, and then northwest to Vincennes on the Wabash River. As has already been pointed out, the American forces were to have taken possession of the already existing British forts at Detroit, Mackinac, and Niagara. This would have enabled the United States to dominate the new western territory. This, however, did not occur until 1796, and the failure to possess these three key strongholds created a weakness in the defense chain instead of adding the strength hoped for in the plan.

Those first troops enlisted in August 1784 marched from Philadelphia to camp on the Schuykill River, and then on to Fort Pitt, arriving at the fort November 14, 1784, where they remained for several weeks. Leaving a handful of men at the fort to maintain the post as a supply depot,[4] the small regiment departed by boat, traveling thirty miles down river to Beaver Creek and arrived December 18, 1784, at the old abandoned Revolutionary war fort, McIntosh, which they immediately began to rebuild. A Congressional resolution of June 3, 1784, required the newly enlisted troops, in addition to their other duties, to protect the commissioners who were to hold peace treaties with the Indians the following spring at McIntosh.[5]

The fort had fallen victim to vandalism and deterioration, and the corps was called upon to restore it so that the commissioners would be as comfortable as possible; and it was hoped that an imposing fortress would impress the Indians with America's strength in the wilderness. The transition to a construction crew took place at McIntosh. Josiah Harmar wrote to his friend, John Dickinson. "The whole Corps," he said, "has been on constant fatigue, since their arrival here, in repairing the fort, and fitting up rooms, stores, etc., for accommodating the Continental and State Commissioners, which has injuring the clothing much."[6] What eventually turned out to be a seven-year building program had begun, and the American soldier suddenly found himself involved in a new facet of army life not covered by the Baron's instructions.

Eleven forts, including the restoration of two and the relocation of a third, were completed and occupied by Federal soldiers between December 1784 and October 1791.

FORT McINTOSH

Fort McIntosh had been built in 1778 by General Lachlan McIntosh. It was the typical stockaded frontier fort with four bastions and was defended by six pieces of artillery. Shaped in an irregular square, it was built of hewn logs.[7]

The thirty-mile boat trip from Pitt to McIntosh down the Ohio River during the winter months was a hazardous journey.

Mr. Evans, agent, and the Pennsylvania Commissioners [Samuel J. Atlee, Francis Johnson and Alexander Campbell] arrived. The boat in which they embarked with

[4] A Congressional committee studied the military situation in 1788 and submitted a written report October 2, 1788. They said Fort Pitt "Has only an officer and a few men to receive the supplies and dispatches forwarded to the troops by the secretary at war."
[5] *Journals of Congress,* Vol. 13, p. 119, October 2, 1788.
[6] *Harmar Papers,* Vol. 28, Letter Book A, January 15, 1785, Harmar to Dickinson.
[7] C. W. Butterfield, *Journal of Captain Jonathan Heart,* p. 47, Joel Munsell's Sons, Albany, 1885.

stores, having run aground, and being nearly overwhelmed with ice, they and the crew—almost frozen to death before the ice became hard enough to bear them—got on shore, landed the goods and brought them forward on packhorses.[8]

Harmar told Dickinson:

> This garrison is at length, by hard fatigue of the troops, put in tolerable good order. I beg leave to observe to your Excellency and the Honourable Council that unless some person is directed to remain here that immediately upon my marching hence, it will be demolished by the emigrators to Kentucky. Previous to our arrival, they had destroyed the gates, drawn all the nails from the roofs, taken off all the boards, and plundered it of every article.[9]

Later on, in June, Harmar wrote to one of the commissioners who had been exposed to winter conditions earlier that year, Colonel Francis Johnston, painting a different picture of McIntosh:

> I wish you were here to view the beauties of Fort McIntosh. What think you of pike 25 lbs.; perch of 15 to 20 lbs.; catfish of 40 lbs.; bass, pickerel, sturgeon, etc., etc. You would certainly enjoy yourself. It is very fortunate there is such an abundance of fish, as the contractor for this place, some time past, has failed in his supplies of beef.[10]

Four years later, Congress disposed of the fort. "Fort M'Intosh is ordered to be demolished, and a block-house to be erected in lieu thereof, a few miles up the Big Beaver-Creek, to protect the communication up the same and also to cover the country."[11]

Major John Doughty of the artillery, a subaltern officer, and fifteen privates were ordered to "old" Fort McIntosh on June 15, 1788: "to carry out the resolve of Congress of March 27, 1788, to dismantle and demolish the Fort and to erect a block-house in the vicinity."[12] Doughty was told to reconnoiter: "for an eligible position at or near the falls, which is about five miles from the mouth of the Big Beaver."[13] Harmar felt there would be some difficulty finding a proper position there: "in which case the block-house will be erected somewhere near the upper fording, about two miles up the Beaver."[14]

FORT FINNEY

A full company of infantry had been raised, with a great deal of difficulty, from the remains of the first year's Pennsylvania quota which had expired in June 1785. It was ordered to embark in September 1785 under the command of Captain Walter Finney to attend a treaty to be held at the mouth of the Great Miami River. Harmar wrote to Knox:

> After the treaty is concluded, I have given Captain Finney written orders to secure himself from insult at the Miami by fortifying his winter quarters, or if the commissioners should be of the opinion that it would be most eligible to assume any

[8] *Ibid.,* p. 51.
[9] *Ibid.,* p. 48.
[10] *Ibid.,* p. 47.
[11] *Journals of Congress,* Vol. 13, p. 112.
[12] *Harmar Papers,* Vol. 28, Letter Book C.
[13] *Ibid.*
[14] *Ibid.*

other position, as I conceive them acquainted with that part of the country, his orders are to obey their direction on that head.[15]

Ensign Ebenezer Denny commented in his journal:

> 22d—Arrive at Great Miami. Best ground for our station about a mile above the mouth, where the boats were brought and everything unloaded. All hands set to work chopping, clearing, etc., and preparing timber for block-houses and pickets; and on the 8th instant had ourselves inclosed. Hoisted the United States flag, and christened the place Fort Finney, in compliment to Captain Finney, the commanding officer.[16]

The fort was a square stockade with block-houses at each corner two stories high, 24 × 18 feet, connected by 100 feet of "stout" picket fence four feet under ground and nine feet above ground. It was situated 150 yards from the river on a rising second bank.[17] Within the confines of the stockade were an 18 × 20 foot building to accommodate the contractor's stores and Indian goods and a strong, small magazine directly in the center.[18] The commissioners and their parties pitched their tents, with wooden chimneys, within the walls of the fort. A council house, 20 × 60 feet, was constructed outside the walls but within gunshot. The brush and timber was cleared away for considerable distance around the fort.[19]

FORT HARMAR

Captain John Doughty and his company of artillery arrived at Fort McIntosh October 7, 1785, and were immediately ordered by Colonel Harmar to:

> take post at or near the mouth of the Muskingum, about one hundred and forty miles below M'Intosh and to stockade or pallisade himself for his own security as he would judge proper. Captain Jonathan Heart's company of infantry met on the 7th inst., upon the Laurel Hill, about four days march from Fort Pitt. I have given him orders to expedite his march, as he would be on time to go down the river with Captain Doughty, and to put himself under his command.[20]

Harmar instructed Doughty to burn cabins of squatters on his way down to the Muskingum. He thought the fort would be in an excellent position—at the mouth of the Muskingum—to prevent more squatters from settling on government lands and also permit soldiers to drive out those who had already settled in the area.[21] He also felt it would protect "the Continental surveyors, in some measure, in their laying off the seven ranges of townships and convince the Indians that Congress means to protect the legal settlers on the lands ceded to them by the treaty."[22]

Fort Harmar was described by the Congressional report of October 1788 as a "well constructed fort, with five bastions and three cannons mounted. It is at present [October 2, 1788] garrisoned

---

[15] Butterfield, *op. cit.,* p. 92.
[16] *Military Journal of Ebenezer Denny,* p. 263, Historical Society of Pennsylvania, J. B. Lippincott & Co., Philadelphia, 1860.
[17] *Ibid.*
[18] *Ibid.*
[19] *Ibid.*
[20] Butterfield, *op. cit.,* p. 92.
[21] *Ibid.,* p. 93.
[22] *Ibid.,* p. 94.

with four companies, and is considered as Headquarters, being conveniently situated to reinforce any of the posts, either up or down the Ohio."

Doughty picked a spot on the west bank of the Ohio River where the Muskingum River empties into the Ohio, across from present-day Marietta. The first legal settlers landed at Muskingum under the leadership of Rufus Putnam in April 1788 to establish the Ohio Company's new town, Marietta, directly under the watchful eyes of Fort Harmar. They proceeded to build four blockhouses

> of hewed or sawed timber, two Story high (erected at the expence of the Company) the upper stories on two sides projected two feet with loopholes in the projection to rake the sides of the Lower stories. Two of the block-houses had two rooms on a floor, and the other two three rooms—the block-houses so placed as to form Bastions of a regular Square and flank the curtains of the work, which was proposed to consist of private houses, also to be made of hewed or sawed timber and two Story high—Leaving a cleane area within of 144 feet square.[23]

The fortified settlement, Campus Martius, was located on "high ground 68 chains from the Muskingum."[24]

The last festivities to take place at old Fort McIntosh while it still remained as headquarters for the Federal corps were in honor of July 4th in 1785. Garrison orders read: "the men are to appear clean and orderly in every respect and are to celebrate it [the 4th] by firing three rounds of blank cartridges—after the parade [meaning muster] the commisary will issue one half pint of rum for each man."[25]

Regimental headquarters were moved to Fort Harmar less than a year later, and Harmar expressed his approval of the new fort in garrison orders of July 24, 1786:

> The commandant cannot but express the highest satisfaction with the police of the garrison. The construction of the Fort, the Cleanliness of the hutts, the good order of the troops, all bespeak the great attention of Captain Doughty and the officers under his command to discipline and regularity, which is highly commendable.[26]

THE NEW FORT FINNEY

Three days later, July 27, 1786, two companies were detached from Fort Harmar to the rapids of the Ohio (Louisville) to protect the government surveyors, as directed by a Congressional resolution of June 22, 1786, which read: "Resolved, That the secretary at war direct the commanding officer of the troops to detache two companies to the rapids of the Ohio, to protect the inhabitants from incursions and depredations of the Indians." Captains Finney and David Zeigler were told to stop at the Great Miami river mouth and evacuate old Fort Finney and take all the plank, nails, spikes, and other useful material with them in their "Kentucky boats" (large flatboats) to be used on the new fort. Harmar told them they did not have to demolish the old fort unless they thought the Indians would receive benefit from it if it were left standing. If so, they were to demolish it entirely.[27]

[23] Rowena Buell, *Memoirs of Rufus Putnam*, p. 105.
[24] *Ibid.*
[25] *Harmar Papers*, Vol. 32, Order Books 1784–88.
[26] *Ibid.*
[27] *Ibid.*, Vol. 28, Letter Book A.

The fear of Indian attack did not detract from the beauty and potential of the new land. Captain Jonathan Heart wrote to his friend, William Judd, in Farmington, Connecticut, January 8, 1786, from Fort Harmar: "I do not exaggerate when I declare the Soil in its present Situation is more Luxuriant than the best manured gardens in Wethersfield." And in the same letter he explained that "Deer, Buffaloe, Geese, Turkeys, etc., we have plenty."[28] He closed by saying:

> Agreeableness of situation, the Climate, Soil and Produce and I may add every consideration favorably invites the Eastern Emigrants to this Federal Territory their own Interest, the Happiness of Successors, their own importance in the Union, the Interest of the United States and I might almost add the Fate of the American Empire calls them from the barren Mounts of the North to these Luxuriant Fields.

The potential threat, however, was always present, and the men's hope for the future of the land was always dampened somewhat by the news of the scalpings. When Captains Finney and Zeigler completed their fort for the protection of settlers at the Rapids, Captain Finney wrote to Harmar requesting a name for the post. Harmar replied January 7, 1787:

> I very much approve of your conduct during your command at Fort Finney and have submitted to General Knox the substance of your letters—the position you have taken and the work which you have erected near the Rapids, appear to me to be very judicious—you will please to name your fort, Fort Finney—.[29]

FORT STEUBEN

In 1787 Major John Francis Hamtramck had been ordered to the Mingo Bottom (present-day Steubenville, Ohio) to erect a blockhouse for the protection of the surveyors and the geographer of the United States, Captain Thomas Hutchins, as well as for the ejection of squatters from government land. Harmar wrote Hamtramck, "I have not the least objection to your naming your fortress Fort Steuben."[30] Harmar described the position of the blockhouse to General Knox: "Captain Hamtramck's position (at Fort Steuben) about 45 miles below McIntosh—This position I judged most eligible in order to convince the intruders, that it is the determination of Congress to prevent their settling upon their lands."[31]

The following fall Major Hamtramck replaced Captain Finney at Fort Finney and subsequently the name of that fort was changed to Fort Steuben. The Congressional report mentioned earlier described Fort Steuben:

> At the Rapids of the Ohio, on the west side, is a well-constructed small fort with one cannon, and is garrisoned with a major and two companies. This post is established to cover the country from the incursions of the Indians and it also serves as a post of communications to Post Vincennes, on the Wabash.[32]

[28]Heart Letters, Guthman Collection.
[29]*Harmar Papers,* Vol. 28, Letter Book B.
[30]*Ibid.,* Harmar to Hamtramck, January 14, 1787.
[31]*Journals of Congress,* Vol. 13, October 2, 1788, p. 119.
[32]*Harmar Papers,* Vol. 28, Letter Book B.

FORT FRANKLIN

Orders to the officers directing them to construct forts were specific concerning location and time of departure but left the details of construction to the men in charge. Jonathan Heart received instructions from Commandant Harmar on April 9, 1787 to leave with his company for Venango (Pennsylvania) and take possession:

> You are to choose an eligible piece of ground for your works, to erect a block-house, and surround it with a parapet of earth, palisade the ditch, and fraze the parapet and provide water within—In short you must satisfy and establish yourself in a perfect Military manner, according to the strength of your command—.[33]

Harmar added that the reason for establishing a post at Venango was to check the Northern Indians on the frontiers of Pennsylvania along the Alllegheny River. "The United States are greatly embarrassed in their Finances and wish to avoid as much as possible an Indian war—nothing but unprovoked aggression on the part of the Savages on the troops or legal settlers should be an inducement to commence Hostilities—"[34] were his final instructions.

Writing from Fort Pitt where he was obtaining provisions for his march to Venango to construct a fort, on April 24, 1787, Heart sent Harmar a list of the tools he wished to take with him and asked the commandant's approval:

> Blacksmith's tools—
> 1 Bellows—1 anvil—1 sledge—1 tongs—1 hammer—1 vice
> Carpenter's tools—
> 1 whipsaw—1 cuttsaw—1 handsaw—2 broadaxes—20 falling axes—2 adz—10 fascine hatchets—15 spades—15 shovels—10 picks—iron square and compasses—frows—draw knives—beetle rings—iron wedges—1 jack plain—1 long plain—3 augers—2 hammers—2 spike gimblets—6 gimblets sorted—2 chisels—1 gouge—1 grind stone—2 fascine hooks—stone hammers—barrel tar—twine—[35]

Heart also listed items such as "old junk" and "iron, steel." Harmar was told by Captain William Ferguson that "I am fully of the opinion that they are all absolutely necessary to effect your orders to establish a Post at Venango."[36]

Again Captain Heart wrote to William Judd, this time from Venango (which was on French Creek, and Heart headed his letter "French Creek, 5th June, 1787").

> I left Muskingum the 10th of April with my compy (company) and small detacht (detachment) of artillery—am now building a Fort at this Place which is 150 Miles up the Alegany [Allegheny] and about the same distance from Niagra—am surrounded with Indians of the Six Nations particularly the Seneca tribes. All things are quiet and peacible in this Part. The Indians below we hear are doing some Mischief, I cannot vouch the truth—[37]

[33] Ibid., Harmar to Heart, April 9, 1787.
[34] Ibid.
[35] Letter Book of Captain Jonathan Heart, April 17, 1787–January 26, 1788, Record Group #94, National Archives.
[36] Ibid., Ferguson to Harmar, April 27, 1787.
[37] Guthman Collection.

Captain Heart closed his letter saying

> I have at present at least as handsome a command as I could wish—this place is nearly in the latitude of Hartford—about 5 days march from the Susquehanna by land—across by way of the great Island—and we are about 30 miles from the Connecticut Lands—I can't say much about this country arrived here only the 11th of May having a passage of 32 days from Muskingum which is 350 miles.[38]

Writing to Captain Heart December 19, 1787, Harmar said, "I very much approve the plan of your works, the neatness and accuracy of your drafts, the correctness of your returns, and all your transactions—"[39] He went on, "You wish a name for your fortress—as it is in the State of Pennsylvania, let it be named *Fort Franklin*."[40]

The Congressional report of October 2, 1788, described the fort:

> On French-Creek, near to the post formerly called Venango, is a small strong fort with one cannon, was erected in 1787, and garrisoned with one company. The excellent construction and execution of this work reflects honor on the abilities and industry of Captain Hart [Heart], who garrisons with his company, and who was his own engineer. This post was established for the purpose of defending the frontiers of Pennsylvania, which are much exposed by the facility with which the Indians can cross from Lake Erie, either to French-Creek, or to the Jadaghque Lake, and the Conneawango branch, and thence descend the rapid river Allegheny.[41]

Ensign Ebenezer Denny left Fort Harmar April 6, 1788, accompanying Harmar and the army contractor, Daniel Britt, to Fort Franklin. They traveled on a barge propelled by twelve oars, and Denny commented on the difficulty because of the rising and falling of the river, which made the "water remarkably hard."[42] When they arrived at Wheeling on the tenth, Britt left them and "took horse to go by land to Pitt."[43] They arrived at McIntosh on the thirteenth and "with extreme hard work" arrived at Fort Pitt on the fourteenth.[44] On the twenty-seventh Denny said:

> It was the General's intention to spend a day or two here, and proceed up the Allegheny River to Fort Franklin, but a continuation of heavy rains and consequent high water, induced him to delay for a more favorable time; but unwilling to be absent too long, we set out with high water and rising. This day we gained 15 miles.[45]

By the thirtieth Ensign Denny commented "last night the contractor's boat, from Venango [Fort Franklin] passed down on its way back to Pitt; had a passage of fifteen days up. Very hard water to-day; gained 20 miles."[46] Denny said on the first, "Current this day very rapid; made about 20 miles"; and on the third, "About eight o'clock this morning, after passing one island, we entered the

---

[38] *Ibid.*
[39] *Harmar Papers,* Vol. 28, Letter Book B.
[40] *Ibid.*
[41] *Journals of Congress,* Vol. 13, October 2, 1788, p. 119.
[42] *Military Journal of Major Ebenezer Denny,* p. 317.
[43] *Ibid.*
[44] *Ibid.,* p. 318.
[45] *Ibid.*
[46] *Ibid.*

mouth of French Creek. The fort stands half a mile up. Several miles below we were discovered by some Indians, who cut across and gave notice to Captain Heart of our approach."[47]

The commandant's arrival was announced by a seven-round salute from a six-pounder at the fort, and he was welcomed by Captain Heart and Lieutenant Ebenezer Frothingham. Heart's company was reviewed by Commandant Harmar, who then dismissed them and spent the rest of the day examining the new fort, the old British and French forts, and the countryside. Denny expressed disappointment in the new works:[48]

> Captain Heart's Fort, or Fort Franklin, as it is called, is built precisely after the one which had been erected by the British, called Venango. It is a square redoubt, with a block-house three stories high, in the centre; stands better than half a mile up French Creek, upon very good ground; but the situation, in my opinion, by no means so eligible as that of old Venango built by the English. This last work stood upon commanding ground pretty close to the bank of the Allegheny, half a mile below French creek, and a mile from Fort Franklin. The cellar wall and huge stack of chimneys of the block-house are of stone, and yet quite entire. The parapet and some other parts remain perfect, and the whole work might have been rebuilt with half the labor and expense of that build by Heart. The only reason the Captain could offer for taking new ground was the convenience of timber.[49]

However, in a letter to Commandant Harmar written the day after he had arrived at Venango, Captain Heart had explained that he had reconnoitered up the Allegheny for a considerable distance and found the most suitable spot to build his fortification on the south bank of French Creek about one-half mile from its junction with the Allegheny.[50] Heart observed that the old fort was not near any timber and the hills surrounding it were much higher, obstructing the view. He added that the old location was subject to flooding and there was an abundance of timber at his present location, and "I shall be able to perfectly cover my boats and obtain water without digging a well inside the works."[51]

Ensign Denny was not impressed with the Seneca Indians who lived along the banks of the Allegheny near the fort. "We saw several families of them; all appeared indolent, dirty, inanimate creatures; most so of any Indians I had seen."[52]

FORT KNOX

The Congressional Committee concluded their 1788 report with their résumé of Fort Knox:

> Post-Vincennes—On the Wabash, is a work erected during the year 1787, and has four small brass cannon. It is garrisoned by a major and two companies.
> It is established to curb the incursions of the Wabash Indians, into the Kentucky country, and to prevent the usurpation of the federal lands, the fertility of which has been too strong a temptation to the lawless people of the frontiers, who posted themselves there in force in the year 1786. Brigadier-General Harmar, by orders of

[47] *Ibid.*, p. 319.
[48] *Ibid.*, pp. 319–320.
[49] See page 57 for Heart's own description of the fort.
[50] *Letter Book of Captain Jonathan Heart,* Heart to Harmar, May 12, 1787.
[51] *Ibid.*
[52] *Ibid.*

Congress, formed an expedition, in August, 1787, for the purpose of dispossessing them, but previously to his arrival most of the intruders had abandoned their settlement.[53]

INDIAN TROUBLE

Vincennes had originally been settled by the French, who, as isolated traders, always had gotten along well with the Indians. However, as emigration of land settlers increased in 1786 and more and more Americans began to clear remote areas of the northwest, Harmar's small force could not possibly extend protection throughout the entire territory. The settlers were forced to take protective measures in their own hands. Locally organized militia raids from Kentucky occurred frequently as frontier Americans began to regard all Indians as hostile, killing them whenever they found the opportunity. The Indians, in turn, increased their raids upon the settlements and soon began to molest all whites, including the French.

All Indians were regarded as ignorant savages and were treated as such by the frontier settlers. There was no regard for human life or feeling on the part of white or red man. The *Vermont Journal* of November 13, 1786, carried the following story:

> On Saturday the 15th April last, a trading boat was proceeding up the Wabash for this place, which was attacked by savages, within five leagues of this place, when they were fired at from a thicket, and killed one man and wounded two; we felt for our country men, and were determined not to leave them to savage barbarity, and proposed to rescue them or fall in the attempt. We did so, a reinforcement of 23 brave fellows joined us and we rushed them with such impetuosity as drove them from their cover and totally routed them, leaving ten killed and 20 wounded. The King of the Kickapeans [Kickapoos] received a ball in his backside, and the Queen of the Piankeshaws miscarried of a prince, the firstborn of the family, and on whom the nation had placed great hopes. We have had council on council with them since this affair, they appear to be as abject as brutal; finding they could not rob us, they turned beggars; we are actually plagued with their solicitations and fair promises. While they behave peaceably, we are determined to treat them well, but they are a compound of deceit, and it would be folly in the extreme to trust them.

BRITISH INFLUENCE ON THE INDIANS

The following message addressed to Richard Butler, Superintendent of Indian Affairs, was sent by the Wyandot chiefs, illustrating the Indian point of view.

> Message from the Wiandot Chiefs. "We chiefs of the different nations, especially Wiandots, did inform you by your people, who went by here some time ago with cattle, that it was quiet and peaceable at that time; but since that time, there have been some of your people at the Shawnese villages and destroyed them, and likewise killed ten Shawnese, five of them principal chiefs and took a number of prisoners, women and children. We now acquaint that you be all means keep back your people from coming this way for or after any sorts of business and likewise you will inform the

---

surveyors to halt and not survey any more at present until we have had a great council with all nations at the Wiandot Towns."[54]

Scalpings, on the part of Whites and Reds, were common occurrences. An atmosphere of lawlessness prevailed, each side feeling it was wronged by the other. To make matters worse, British agents were constantly bombarding the Indian nations with propaganda against the United States, in hopes that the natives would never trust American treaties and would constantly remain at war, thus insuring continuing English occupation of their northwest forts and the safety of their fur trade.

Unscrupulous Americans, on the other hand, illegally seized land that belonged to the United States, as well as hunted and trapped on restricted lands which belonged to those Indian nations which had signed treaties with the United States. Those renegade Whites kept the frontier settlers nervous about future Indian depredations, by exaggerating incidents and inciting the Indians to attack the settlements.

PROBLEMS WITH SPAIN

Observing this hostility between American white and red men with great interest, the Spanish government was just as fearful of American expansion toward the Spanish possessions west of the Mississippi and south in Florida, as was the Indian in the northwest. Spain, therefore, closed the Mississippi River to American ships. The United States, without funds and in need of Spain's trade, agreed to the closing of the Mississippi, thus further antagonizing the frontier American settlers who were completely dependent upon the river to ship their goods to market at New Orleans. This increased lawlessness, and induced a complete lack of respect for the young nation among its own people in the northwest—an area without civil authority and beyond the governing reach of the weak Confederation. Congress finally passed a resolution on July 21, 1787, ordering Harmar to proceed immediately to Post-Vincennes and inform the Indians that Congress "is disposed to promote peace and friendship between their citizens and the Indians." He was to invite them to a friendly treaty with the United States to hear their complaints and learn the truth and causes of their quarrels with the frontier settlers.

LAWLESS BANDITTI

Commandant Harmar had written to Colonel Jean Le Gras, a resident of Vincennes, informing him that "Congress hearing of the robberies and outrages committed at Post Vincennes by a set of lawless Banditti, have ordered me to march with a body of regular troops there, and to assure the French inhabitants that they shall be protected in their rights."[55] Arriving at Vincennes a month later, Harmar immediately posted his orders and the resolve of Congress respecting intruders on public lands, having had them printed in both French and English.[56]

The inhabitants of Vincennes asked Harmar to take a petition to Congress requesting that the original French settlers be allowed to retain the land that had been theirs prior to the treaty. Harmar assured the residents that he would not expel them until Congress acted, "as I can not ascertain who are actually intruders."[57] Harmar did admit that many of the Kentucky militia who had participated in the unsuccessful raids on the Indian villages had taken up "tomahawk rights" on choice land.[58]

[54] *Vermont Journal*, January 15, 1787.
[55] *Harmar Papers, ibid.*
[56] *Ibid.*, Harmar to Knox, August 7, 1787.
[57] *Ibid.*
[58] *Ibid.*

His next order of business was to council with the Indians. He presented them with thirteen strings of wampum,[59] which represented the thirteen states, and advised them of the friendly intentions of the United States and also warned them against listening to the advice of "bad people."[60] Acting as representative of the United States, he asked them to send messages to the chiefs of all the Wabash tribes inviting them to assemble and listen to his message. In turn, the Indians presented the commandant with a handsome calumet ("peace pipe").[61]

While Harmar was in council with the Indians, Lieutenant John Armstrong and Ensign Cornelius Ryer Sedam, who had been detached with a party of forty-five men to bring up provisions and clothing in several perrogues (canoes made from hollowed tree trunks), were being attacked by Indians on the Wabash and lost one soldier, a French trader, one prisoner, plus all of the supplies.[62] Learning of this, Harmar immediately confronted the Indians at Vincennes, who vehemently denied any knowledge of the assault.

HARMAR'S GOOD-WILL MARCH

Deciding it would take too long to assemble all of the Wabash chiefs at Vincennes, Harmar set out for Kaskaskias, 160 miles away, with Ensign Nathan McDowell and twenty men, marching all the way accompanied by two Indian guides who continually supplied the party with fresh buffalo and deer meat.[63] From Kaskaskias the men marched to Prairie du Roche, La Belle Fontaine, Grand Ruisseau, and Cahokia and on the twenty-fourth crossed the Mississippi to dine with the Spanish commandant in St. Louis. Harmar then retraced his steps. He consulted the several stockaded towns on the proper placement of their militia and also warned them to obey the local magistrates until Congress "should be pleased to order a government for them."[64] Commandant Harmar observed that the inhabitants (French and American) were a people entirely unacquainted with liberty—trial by jury—and opined that a "commandant with a few troops is the best form of government for them."[65]

After his return to Vincennes in September, 120 Indians visited the post. Every precaution was taken against surprise attack. Two redoubts were thrown up on the right and left and the guard in front was entrenched. The troops were all dressed in new clothing "and put out a truly military appearance. The Indians saluted us by firing several vollies on the Wabash opposite our camp—there salute was returned by a part of ours firing several platoons."[66] Speeches were exchanged and gifts presented. The Indians were "Amazingly fond of whiskey and destroyed a considerable quantity of it."[67] The Indians presented Harmar with wampum and calumets which he in turn sent to on General Knox in "a rich otter skin."[68]

FORT KNOX ESTABLISHED

Commandant Harmar left Vincennes shortly thereafter and reported to General Knox. "I judged it expedient to leave a garrison at the post, as it would have been impolitic after the parade we had

[59] Ibid.
[60] Ibid.
[61] Ibid.
[62] Ibid.
[63] Ibid., Harmar to Knox, November 24, 1787.
[64] Ibid.
[65] Ibid.
[66] Ibid.
[67] Ibid.
[68] Ibid.

made, to entirely abandon the country."[69] Major Hamtramck was left behind with ninety-five men and ordered to "fortify himself, and regulate the militia, who are to join him in case of hostilities."[70] Major Hamtramck informed Harmar, in a letter dated April 13, 1788,

> My piquets are up and the block-houses are to their second story. If I have provision in time I am no way concerned, although one difficulty will existe the men [men's] time of Smith company being out so early and none of them have as yet inlisted, owing to the great fatigue they have had and have every day, indifferently victualed and no pay.

Fort Knox was located close to the Wabash at the foot of present-day Buntin Street, a rectangle 50×70, with four two-story blockhouses at the angles, built with platforms to accommodate cannon in the upper stories. It was completed by mid-1788. The palisades were eleven feet above ground and three feet below ground. The officers' barracks were two stories, placed along the seventy-foot palisade, facing the one-story-high soldiers' barracks on the opposite seventy-foot palisade. Another row of soldiers' barracks was placed along a fifty-foot palisade, opposite the blacksmith shop. A magazine, sunk into the ground to the eaves, was placed at the opposite end of the same palisade, a few feet from the wall.[71]

Major Hamtramck wrote to Harmar April 13, 1788, advising him that he had been told:

> our taking post at this place had alarmed the British in a very great degree; their fatigue parties employed at their fortification had been augmented and attended with an uncommon deligance. Mr. Brant and Indian officer had been last autum ordered to take post at the Miami which he did with four hundred families of the Six Nations. This man [Joseph Brant] had orders to prevent all communication with the Americans.

FORT WASHINGTON

Josiah Harmar was proud of the new fort being constructed by Major John Doughty opposite the mouth of the Licking River, 300 miles—roughly four days' passage—from Fort Harmar.[72] He told General Knox in a letter of January 14, 1790: "This will be one of the most solid substantial wooden fortresses when finished, of any in the Western Territory—it is built of hewn timber, a perfect square two stories high, with 4 block-houses at the Angles."[73] Erected on the site of an earlier blockhouse at a settlement called Losantiville, the fort stood between what are now Third and Fourth streets, Cincinnati.[74] The artificer's yard occupied a three-acre enclosure on the river bank with workshops, dormitories, and a two-story building for the quarter general, then known as the Yellow House.[75] Behind the fort, Colonel Winthrop Sargent, Secretary of the Northwest Territory, cultivated an expansive garden. A room in George Avery's tavern, near a large frog pond and marsh interspersed with elder bushes, was rented to accommodate the court-martial. This room was permanently equipped with pillory, stocks, and whipping post.[76]

[69] *Ibid.*
[70] *Ibid.*
[71] Northwest Territory Collection, William Henry Smith Memorial Library.
[72] *Harmar Papers,* Vol. 29, Letter Book G.
[73] *Ibid.*
[74] Benson J. Lossing, *The Pictorial Field Book of the War of 1812,* pp. 40–41.
[75] Clara Longworth de Chambrun, *Cincinnati,* p. 57.
[76] *Ibid.*

Fort Washington is remembered as the fortification at which the army made preparations for, and from which it embarked on, its first two campaigns—one unsuccessful, the other disastrous. It was from behind the walls of Fort Washington that Josiah Harmar wrote to General Knox March 24, 1790, a time when a confrontation with the Indians seemed inevitable. "No calculation will answer, but raising sufficient force to effectually chastize the whole of those nations, who are known to be hostile."[77] Jonathan Heart wrote to William Judd from behind those same walls on November 4, 1790:

> We yesterday returned from the expedition against the Miami Villages, that nest of murderers—which we have entirely destroyed. I suppose the History of New England that seat of Indian Wars scarcely affords an instance of such another bloody action. They fought with desperation, our loss was great and amongst the killed we have to drop a tear to the Memory of those good men Major John Palsgrave Wyllys and Lieutenant Frothingham.[78]

Exactly one year later, November 4, 1791, Heart was killed fighting the same Indians in an expedition from Fort Washington.

FRONTIER CRAFTS

Fort Washington housed facilities for every craft necessary to equip an army about to embark on a campaign—and whose supplies had not arrived on time. When he arrived at Fort Washington May 15, 1791, the new commander, General Arthur St. Clair, described the ordnance and other supplies as completely insufficient for the proposed campaign against the Indians. New carriages had to be made for the cannon, camp equipage had to be manufactured on the spot, all of the ammunition for the campaign had to be prepared (which meant establishing a laboratory in which to make the cartridges and shells), tools to make the equipment had to be forged, shops in which the tools and equipment were to be made had to be newly constructed, safe facilities to handle loose powder had to be created. Canteens, axes, camp kettles, knapsacks, kegs for musket cartridges, and spare cannon balls, splints used for wounded, all had to be made at Fort Washington.[79] "In short, almost every art was going forward and Fort Washington had as much the appearance of a large manufactory on the inside, as it had of a military post on the outside."[80] An armory had to be constructed since "the arms of the detachment were in bad order, also, and had nearly all to be repaired."[81] Even bells for the cavalry (militia) horses had to be made.[82] Artificers and fatigue men were required, but, as no corps of artificers existed, "draughts therefore had to be made from the corps of all that were to be found of that description, and they were required in a variety of branches, such as smiths, carpenters, harness makers, colliers, wheelrights, etc."[83]

TOOLS

The soldier learned to make or repair almost every article he used on the frontier. Tools listed in inventories, repair vouchers, and issue returns of the period give testimony to the many crafts involved in the maintenance of the Corps. Often orders to make something were carried out by recruits whose experience was acquired through their sudden exposure to whatever need was uppermost at the moment. Hammers, saws, axes, and other tools were as much a part of the soldier's

---

[77] *Harmar Papers, ibid.*
[78] Jonathan Heart to William Judd, November 4, 1790, Guthman Collection.
[79] Arthur St. Clair, "Campaign Against the Indians," pp. 10–13.
[80] *Ibid.,* pp. 12–13.
[81] *Ibid.*
[82] *Ibid.,* p. 13.
[83] *Ibid.,* p. 10.

equipment as musket, bayonet, and knapsack. The crafts, reflected in records of the tools used, include: cooper, blacksmith, armorer, harnessmaker, carpenter, turner, tinman, shoemaker, plasterer, lastmaker, brickmaker, stone mason, tool maker, gunsmith, painter, munitions worker, butcher, tailor, cook, rancher, baker, candlestickmaker, and sailor.

FORTS HAMILTON AND JEFFERSON

The last two forts were constructed by the corps during their march to the Indian towns in the disastrous 1791 campaign. Fort Hamilton was constructed on the east bank of the Miami River, thirty-five miles north of Cincinnati, "to cover the passage of the river, and to serve as a place of deposit for provisions, and to form the first link in the chain of communication between Fort Washington and the object of the campaign."[84]

The time-consuming and back-breaking method of constructing a frontier fort is described in detail by Arthur St. Clair on pages 152–154 of his *Narrative of the Campaign against the Indians,* as he tells about the errection of Fort Hamilton: "The circuit of that fort is about one thousand feet, through the whole extent of which a trench about three feet deep was dug to set the piquets in, of which it required about two thousand to enclose it; and it is not trees taken promiscuously, that will answer for piquets, they must be tall and straight, and from nine to twelve inches diameter." Trees of a larger diameter, he explained, were too unmanageable, and, in order to find those that were proper, searching a considerable area of woodland was required. The general went on to describe the construction:

> When found, they are felled, cleared of their branches, and cut into lengths of about twenty feet. They were then carried to the ground and butted, that they might be placed firm and upright in the trench with the axe, or cross-cut saw; some hewing upon them was also necessary, for there are few trees so straight that the sides of them will come in contact when set upright.

Continuing his description, St. Clair explained how the piquets were held in place:

> A thin piece of timber, called a ribband, is run round the whole near the top of the piquets, to which every one of them is pinned with a strong pin, without which, they would decline from the perpendicular with every blast of wind, some hanging outwards and some inwards, which would render them in a great measure useless.... The earth thrown out of the trench is then returned and strongly rammed to keep the piquets firmly in their places, and a shallower trench is dug outside about three feet distant, to carry off the water and prevent their being moved by rain; about two thousand piquets are set up in the inside, one between every two of the others; the work is then enclosed.

The site for the fort, he explains, was completely wooded:

> The ground for the site of the fort had to be cleared, and two or three hundred yards round it, which was very thickly wooded, and was a work of time and labour. The ground where the fort stands, is on the east side of the Miami river, on the first bank; but there is a second bank considerable elevated, within point blank shot, which

[84] *Ibid.,* p. 14.

rendered it necessary to make the piquets, particularly along the land side, of a height sufficient to prevent an enemy from seeing into the area, and taking the side to the river in reverse, and a high platform was raised in one of the bastions on the land side to scour the second bank with artillery. Another, made with the trunks of trees, and covered with plank as that was, was raised in one of the bastions toward the river, in order to command the ford, and the river for some distance up and down. Plank was sawed for the platforms and the gate, and barracks for one hundred men; a guard room, two store houses for provisions, and barracks for the officers were constructed within it, and all this was done in about fourteen days, almost entirely by the labour of men; though some use was made of oxen in drawing the timber, the woods were so thick and encumbered with underwood, it was found to be the most expeditious method to carry it.

The fort was finished in September 1791, the same month it was begun, and consisted of a stockade fifty yards square with four bastions. Platforms for cannon were constructed in two of them.[85] Barracks to accommodate 100 men and storehouses were added, and "on the thirtieth [September] the fort being nearly completed, so far at least, as to be in a condition to receive a garrison, two pieces of artillery were placed in it, and it was named Fort Hamilton."[86]

On October 13, having advanced forty-five miles beyond Fort Hamilton, a "proper place presented itself" for another fort.[87] The march halted and the army encamped in two lines, the artillery and cavalry occupied both flanks and the riflemen (militia) at right angles at each extremity.[88] An outline of a fort, thirty-five yards square with four bastions, was traced on the ground. Work began immediately, and by the twenty-fourth of the same month

it was in such forwardness, the houses being all covered, the platforms laid in the bastions, and frasing of those begun, that it was thought it might be completed by the troops which would be left in the garrison. A detachment was accordingly made for the purpose; two pieces of artillery were placed in it, and it was named Fort Jefferson.[89]

The fort was constructed of large timbers laid horizontally and the curtains formed the outer walls of the barracks.[90]

During the construction of Fort Jefferson a sizable number of the militia had deserted, weakening St. Clair's forces considerably.[91] The General felt that an intermediate fort should have been built between Hamilton and Jefferson but the nearness of the winter weather and unfavorable conditions prevented him taking the time for this.[92]

Here St. Clair's army was to meet defeat—twenty-nine miles from the fort on November 4.[93] The remnants of the army made their way back to Fort Jefferson, stragglers continuing to come into the forts for hours.[94] Most had not eaten a thing for the past twenty-four hours, and they found comfort and safety within the walls of the fort they had finished building several days earlier.

[85] Ibid.
[86] Ibid., p. 15.
[87] Ibid., p. 18.
[88] Ibid.
[89] Ibid.
[90] Ibid.
[91] Ibid., p. 19.
[92] Ibid.
[93] Military Journal of Major Ebenezer Denny, p. 373.
[94] Ibid.

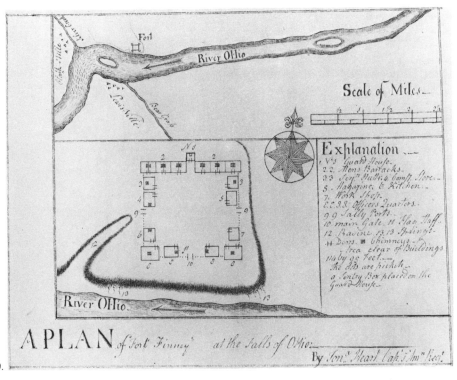

20. A plan of Fort Finney drawn by Jonathan Heart. Located near present day Louisville, Kentucky, the fort was built by two companies under Captains Finney and Zeigler in 1786.

In 1787, when Major Hamtramck replaced Captain Finney as commander of the fort, the name was changed to Fort Steuben.
Northwest Territory Collection, William Henry Smith Memorial Library, Indiana Historical Society

20.

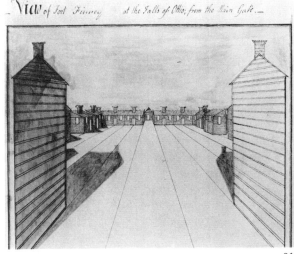

21. The interior of Fort Finney as viewed from the main gate, drawn by Captain Jonathan Heart, 1st American Regiment.

This is one of the few known sketches behind the exterior walls of an eighteenth-century frontier fort.
Northwest Territory Collection, William Henry Smith Memorial Library, Indiana Historical Society

21.

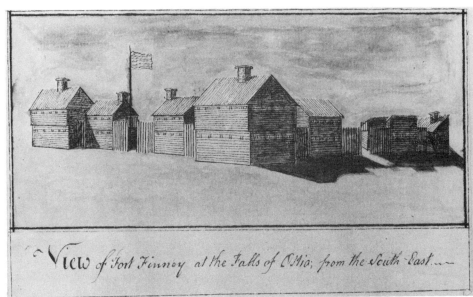

22. An exterior view of Fort Finney by Captain Heart. Note the change from windows, as seen on the interior view, to gun ports on the exterior view.

Since the American flag was relatively new at this time, Heart's interpretation of the Stars and Stripes is interesting.
Northwest Territory Collection, William Henry Smith Memorial Library, Indiana Historical Society

22.

23.

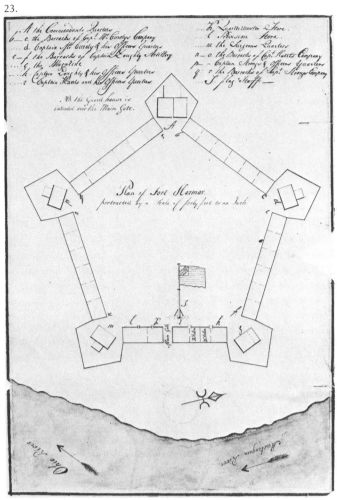

23. Manuscript ground plan for Fort Harmar, circa 1786. Another unusual interpretation of the American Flag was executed by the artist. The fort, with five bastions, was used as headquarters for the army until Fort Washington was built in 1790. *Harmar Collection, William L. Clements Library, University of Michigan; University of Michigan photo*

24. An overall view of Fort Harmar, from a nineteenth-century lithograph.

24.

25A.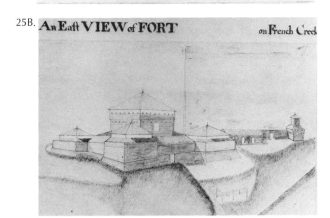

A PROFILE of the WORKS on French Creek.

Explanation.

Scale 10 feet to the Inch.

25B.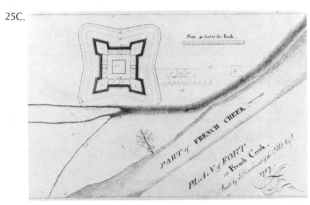

An East VIEW of FORT on French Creek

25C.

Scale 40 feet to the Inch.

PART of FRENCH CREEK.

PLAN of FORT on French Creek, 1787

25A. A pen-and-ink drawing of the profile of Fort Franklin on French Creek by Captain Jonathan Heart, who was sent to Venango, Pennsylvania, to construct the fort in April, 1787.
Heart enclosed this drawing in a letter he sent to Colonel Harmar June 1, 1787.
Harmar Collection, William L. Clements Library, University of Michigan

25B. An east view of Fort Franklin on French Creek, drawn by Captain Jonathan Heart, 1st U.S. Regiment.
This is a colored sketch that Heart sent to Colonel Harmar June 25, 1787.
Harmar Collection, William L. Clements Library, University of Michigan

25C. Topographical pen-and-ink plan of Fort Franklin and its adjacent area, by Captain Jonathan Heart.
This sketch was sent to Colonel Harmar by Heart June 1, 1787.
Harmar Collection, William L. Clements Library, University of Michigan

26. The original sketch of Fort Washington, drawn by Jonathan Heart in 1790, was discovered among a pile of photographic negatives at the Cincinnati Historical Society by the author.
Artist Don Troiani made the above drawing from the original sketch, which was in such poor condition it could not be successfully photographed.

26.

SOUTH WEST VIEW of FORT WASHINGTON

By Jon.ᵉ Heart, Capᵗ 1 U.S. Regᵗ 17.

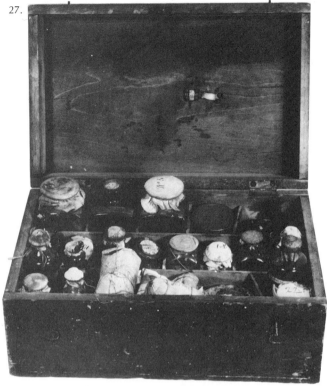

27.

28.

27. Eighteenth-century American medicine chest made of pine wood and painted red. The medicines are contained in bottles, paper packets and tin containers.

The contents are separated by thin, wooden dividers and the hardware is brass. Most of the medicines are for stomach disorders or fever.
Guthman Collection

28. Close-up views of two of the blown glass medicine bottles and three of the paper medicine packets. The bottles are covered with chamoislike tops that are tied with rope. Both the bottles and packets are marked with a number and the name of the medicine.
Guthman Collection

29. Accessories carried by soldiers and frontiersmen during the Federal period included many personal items. Leather wallets were often embossed with designs and patriotic words.

The folding pocketknife is made to look like a bird, and the folding fork, with horn handle, is delicately created.
Guthman Collection

30. This wooden-framed, leather-covered liquor chest, decorated with brass tacks, was typical of the baggage of eighteenth-century officers.

Most trunks, dining equipage, folding cots, medical kits, and document boxes were made similar to this chest, which contains four green liquor bottles.
Guthman Collection

29.

30.

Part II: Living in the Forts

CAPTAIN HEART AND HIS COMMAND

The physical description of the forts in no way reflects the thoughts of the men who built, lived, and died in them. The building of Fort Franklin is a good example of the human side of the army in those days.

"I make not the least doubt but you are Sufficiently impressed with the Importance of this Command—I wish you a pleasant march." Colonel Harmar told Captain Jonathan Heart April 9, 1787, as Heart left Fort Harmar for Venango, French Creek, Pennsylvania, with his command to build a fort. Heart, forty-three years old, was a native of Berlin, Connecticut, and had graduated from Yale and taught school in New Jersey. Serving during the Revolutionary war from May 4, 1775, until December 1783, Heart saw action as an officer at the sieges of Boston, Long Island, and White Plains and the Hudson River campaigns. He helped to build the fortifications of West Point and served in the Southern campaigns against Cornwallis, ending with the siege of Yorktown. He was mustered out as a captain, the rank he was reappointed to in 1785 when he marched with his company from Hartford to Fort Pitt to join the 1st American Regiment during its second winter at Fort McIntosh.

Heart's instructions, in 1787, were to pick up a sergeant and six privates from the artillery at Fort Harmar, and at his next stop, Fort McIntosh, he was assigned six artillery men. At Fort Pitt, Heart acquired a brass six-pounder, ammunition from ordnance supplies, and two months' supply of salted meat, flour, and other food provisions from the contractors. Tools necessary in construction work were to be issued from the supplies at Fort Pitt. Finalizing his orders, Harmar requested that Heart transmit monthly returns of his troops and "from time to time make me acquainted with the most minute Occurrences that happen in your quarter."[95] Reassurance was given that proper medical supplies would be available at the new post.

MEDICINE

"Doctor Sumner will take with him a proper proportion of Medicine for your detachment," Harmar added.[96] The demand for medicines always exceeded the supply, and, as the inadequately clothed soldiers were exposed to the most severe weather on the frontier, sickness was a constant major factor.

> When the weather is unsettled, cloudy, wet and rainy, the usual consequences are cold, attended with feverish and inflammatory symptom, especially Rheumatic, Pleuretic and Peripneumonic complaints, and if proper means are neglected they will soon generate into Consumptions, or Chronic Rheumatisms. In hot weather many diseases owe their origin to poisonous exhalations in the air and in this class are acute Fevers with Exanthemata of all kinds, as the Small Pox, Measles, Tertians, Quartans, double Tertians, Burning Fevers, Pleurisies, Opthalmias, Quinceys, Catarrhal Fevers, as well benign as malignant, Erysipelatious disorders, Rheumatisms, Gouts, diarrheas, Dysenteries, and Bastard Pleurisies. Those that wear dirty clothing and live an idle sedentry life and feed chiefly upon salt meat, old dry biscuit, farinaceous vegetables, Pease, Beans and old cheese, are very subject to many dangerous diseases and especially the Scurvy [warned Samuel Stearns's *North American Almanack* in 1776].

[95] *Letter Book of Captain Jonathan Heart,* Harmar to Heart, April 9, 1787.
[96] *Ibid.*

The diseases and the causes had not changed by 1787; however, Mr. Stearns did not list the most widespread disease, one which attacked every army throughout the Western world and was beginning to take its toll on the previously unaffected American Indian—venereal disease. This was a regiment reducer, and the only cures were ineffective ones occasionally advertised by quack doctors in almost every local newspaper in the major cities.

Wounds were slow in healing, and in many cases the men never recovered completely. John Elliot, surgeon's mate, reported January 1, 1789, that, of the men wounded in a skirmish with the Indians the previous July, one who was wounded in the right arm had lost the use of two fingers, another wounded in the shoulder had lost most of the movement of his right arm, another wounded in the arm had lost the use of two fingers. The latter "received a cut in 1785 at Fort M'Intosh and, in 1789, he had been rendered very lame and the leg and thigh considerably decayed."[97]

The lack of proper medication for the wounded is evident throughout the regiment's early history. The lack of "bark," or quinine, was particularly serious. Most of the men were afflicted with malaria, and the "Burning Fevers" Stearns mentions in his almanac are probably malaria.

Another commodity which was just as scarce as clothing, food, shelter, and medicine was vinegar, a necessary dietary balance when quantities of salt meats were consumed.

THE TRIP

Heart, assembling his provisions and supplies, found many articles unavailable in the public stores at Fort Pitt and these had to be purchased locally through the contractors. Ordnance did not have a brass six-pounder so Heart took an iron six-pounder, "which with very considerable repair I have now in order" and 100 rounds of ammunition.[98] Embarking on flat boats on April 27, the men proceeded up the Allegheny River, accompanied by a civilian well acquainted with the navigation of the river and a Seneca chief to inform the other tribes of the approaching detachment of Federal troops.[99] Heart expressed the hope that "I shall not find so many embarrassments with respect to a suitable place for erecting a Fortification and with the Indians at and near that Place as are apprehended by many."[100]

Venango was reached on May 11th, and the captain selected a spot half a mile from the Allegheny River on the south bank of French Creek on which to build his fort. He was pleased with his new command, located about 350 miles from headquarters at Muskingum and 150 miles up the Allegheny from Pittsburgh and about the same distance from Niagara.

Heart described the trip as strenuous because the boats were overloaded and his men were unacquainted with "polling."[101]

> The common current of the Allegheny is at least equal to the waters of the Ohio in the highest floods, in many instances the Men were under the necessity of being in the Water great part of the day; their unacquaintedness with polling in strong Water occasioned the loss of some half my Setting Poles in four Days, was oblijed to halt erect my Smiths Works and make a new sett.[102]

Finding that rotating the men for poling was not practical, he finally took the men best qualified for the task and retained them in the capacity throughout the trip, suggesting to Harmar that those men receive the same allowances of provisions and liquor allotted to men on water command.[103]

---

[97]Gayle Thornbrough, *Outpost on the Wabash,* Indiana Historical Society, Indianapolis, 1957, p. 147.
[98]*Letter Book of Captain Jonathan Heart,* Heart to Harmar, May 12, 1787.
[99]*Ibid.*
[100]*Ibid.*
[101]*Ibid.,* Heart to Harmar, May 12, 1787.
[102]*Ibid.*
[103]*Ibid.*

Most of the provisions were lost during the voyage, particularly the perishable sugar and coffee. Heart attributed the loss to: "the mode of transporting stores, particularly such as are liable to damage by water in such open Boats, is attended with great risque."[104]

BEGINNING THE FORT

As soon as a site had been selected, the men were put to work and were on "constant fatigue" erecting the fort. Since there was no provision for carpenters, smiths, men to work the sawpits, or artificers on the roster, those who had been selected for those jobs could not receive the extra allowances usually allowed, and Heart complained of this to his commander.

By June 1, he had written that in the detachment had the satisfaction of being under cover of their works, and later that month he wrote that the state of his works would present defiance to any open Indian assault. Heart asked Harmar for a name for the fort on June 25 in a letter in which he said the most important parts of the fort were already constructed and would soon be completed. Late in July the rains slowed down the construction and delayed completion, and by the end of October Heart admitted that he would not be able to complete work until spring, due to the summer rains and the severe winter ahead. He added that he hoped all that would remain to be completed would be the palisading of the ditch.[105] Not less than 100 Indian families had been hunting along the Allegheny near the fort, Heart wrote in December, and the precautions necessary during their visits impeded the construction work—another delay to completion.

> However, the works are perfectly defensable against any open attack and very few are sufficient against surprise—Vigilence is the only efficient Proof against that. The works are also in such situation as to afford convenient barracks and I hope comfortable winter quarters after a very laborious summer.[106]

Pleased with his progress, Heart reviewed his accomplishments in a letter to Harmar June 1, 1787.

> Having determined the spot [of construction] I made first point to conform to the Institutions in erecting my Works and in the next place to make them convenient for all the purposes of Defence Barracks and Stores with as little labour as possible—after trying every Figure Mode and Form I could invent there appeared none so eligiable as the One I have adopted; a five-sided figure would have been more defensible the line of Fire better and made more elegant appearance but the additional labour was too great—a Single Block-House with walls of Earth round it would have been much easier and quicker constructed but afforded no Room and appeared not a sufficient Cover for any out Works—in this Mode I have suffcient Room within the Walls for the Men. Stores and Artillery and the advantageous position of the ground under that Part between the Fort and the River, where my present Encampment is as perfectly covered as if within the Walls—
>
> The Block-House is compleated Breast high of the second story and the Line of Artillery mounted on it, the timbers of the surrounding Works laid up the Bomb Proofs covered with Logs the Bastions ready for putting on the Roofs and all the Stores under cover—the Smoke House is compleated, Armoreres Shop, Bake House and Hospital

---

[104] *Ibid*, Heart to Knox, October 29, 1787.
[105] *Ibid*.
[106] *Ibid.*, Heart to Harmar, December 5, 1787.

nearly finished a few Days will compleat them and the line of Pickets adjacent which will perfectly cover my present encampment—and having the trees cut and cleared off already to 150 yards distance round me, I considered my self so well posted as to allow the men a little rest after their excessive hard fatigues.[107]

THE FORT'S INTRUSION UPON THE INDIANS

Back at Fort Pitt, Heart had been informed by officers experienced in Indian affairs that it would not be wise to conceal the destination of his detachment, but rather to advise those Indians at Venango of his plans to establish a post there. Heart felt it was his duty as a soldier not to divulge troop movement information, but Colonel William Butler, acting for his brother General Richard Butler, Superintendent of Indian Affairs of the Northern District (Northwest Territory), and a Seneca Chief named Kayashuto, both of whom were at Pittsburgh at the time (April 1787), convinced him that if the natives at Venango saw the soldiers approaching unannounced they would all run away. This was a particularly poor time to create disfavor with those Indians since there was at that moment a treaty in session of six nations with the British at Fort Erie and Joseph Brant, the Mohawk chief and brother of Molly Brant, the mistress of the late Sir William Johnson.

Instead of maintaining military secrecy surrounding the detachment, Colonel Butler sent a Seneca Indian called Two Feet ahead with a message to the Seneca Tribes:

Brothers—In the absence of General Butler he had directed me to transmit any Business with the Indians in this Country. I therefore send you this Message by Two Feet. Kayashuto and myself have thought proper so to do least some ill designing people might misinform you of the truths of what we now write to you—

You must know Brothers that the great Congress of the United States have ordered Colonel Harmar their commanding Officer in this Country to send Captain Heart of his Regiment and a party of his troops to take post and build a Fort at Venango—at the same time Brothers you may rest assured he goes in the most Friendly manner and is ordered to protect your people from injury the same as his own—I am sure you will do the same, as what I tell you is truth and I am sure you will believe me and not the least harm will follow—Kayashuto goes with Captain Heart who will more fully inform you everything. William Butler, April 27, 1787.[108]

Heart arrived at Venango the eleventh of May and on the twelfth was confronted by the women and children of the nearby tribes who claimed they would all starve before the hunting season began if the army did not supply them with provisions. Heart told them that Colonel Butler was sending fifty bushels of Indian corn, but this did not satisfy the Indians, and on the fourteenth he was informed that chiefs of the Seneca, Mohawk, and Wyandot tribes wished a council. Heart felt that transacting business with Indians was not the duty of a junior officer, but since Colonel Butler's message announcing his arrival had been received, and since the Indians outnumbered the men in his command, he reasoned it unwise to deny them an audience.[109] On the fifteenth Kayashuto spoke for the Indians and said all the tribes were glad to see the safe arrival of their white brothers at that place and that they "now stroke you down, wipe off all the dust and sweat to make you well."[110] He

---

[107] *Ibid.,* Heart to Harmar, June 1, 1787.
[108] *Ibid.*
[109] *Ibid.*
[110] *Ibid.*

continued by saying that they were glad to have the protection of the army and would do whatever they were instructed by the United States. Heart replied, thanking the chiefs for their friendly assurances of peace and said the "Thirteen Fires" (the U.S.) had lit the pipe of peace and all were to smoke and

> I am glad to see that you hold the chain of peace the Thirteen Fires put into your hands. Be strong and hold it fast—I will hold one link with both hands, you must not lett it go. If you do it will fall out of my hands, it is a great chain and I cannot hold it alone you must help me—.

The captain continued, acting in the capacity of an American Ambassador, saying,

> You must not hear what bad men tell you—Brothers, tell your Old Men, your Women and Children they need not fear any injury from my young Men. You may all lie down and sleep in quiet your Young men may hunt without danger get meat to feed and skins to cover you; no bad Men will dare to hurt you while you hold the Chain of Peace which the Thirteen Fires have put around you and them—this Chain both ends of it are fastened together and binds us all in one tribe of Friends and Brothers.[111]

Heart gave them strings of wampum and Kayashuto made another reassuring speech of peace, ending the council.

At this time Heart was trying to learn what had transpired at the council at Fort Erie. The information he was given at that time was sparse, and all he could determine was that there had been only talk of peace and some of those attending had gone to Fort Niagara to receive gifts from the British. Heart did not feel the tribes in the vicinity of Venango were to be feared at that time because of the limited number of warriors, and he felt that they were sincere in their peaceful overtures.

He found that the Seneca tribes understood only their own language and was forced to hire a Cayuga who spoke both the Seneca tongue and enough English to act as interpreter. This Indian was given the military allowance of provisions, and Heart told Harmar that if the government disallowed the payment he would assume the support of the Indian himself rather than be without an interpreter.[112]

By mid-October Heart had learned more of the results of the council held at Fort Erie. The Indians had been given £6,000 in cash and the same amount in presents.[113] Joseph Brant left for Detroit with arms and ammunition, and was accompanied by warriors of the Mohawk, Onondagas, Mississinewa, Seneca, and some white men who fought with Brant during the Revolution. They were followed by sixteen bateaux of warriors. The warsong was chanted and Brant was heard to say, "If the White People want fighting I will give them enough of it."[114] Heart's informants were two—a white man who had come directly from Niagara and a "very trusty Indian" who spoke to a brother of Cornplanter, a Seneca chief who was at the council.[115]

Another Colonel Butler, a British officer, told the Indians that they must "be ready to take up the Hatchet whenever their Father [George III] called them which would be soon."[116] Cornplanter, the Seneca chief, however, would not allow his tribe to accept any British gifts, which consisted mostly

---

[111] *Ibid.*
[112] *Ibid.*
[113] *Ibid.*, Heart to Knox, October 18, 1787.
[114] *Ibid.*
[115] *Ibid.*
[116] *Ibid*

of arms and ammunition.[117] Heart relayed the information about Brant to Captain Ashton at Fort Pitt, requesting the commander at that post immediately relay the information to the other posts.

He continued to collect intelligence about the Indians and wrote to Harmar on December fifth telling him that the Indians were going to make war if Congress did not accede to their terms. Even though the Seneca tribes along the Allegheny River and the Munsee tribe gave him every assurance of peace, Heart was confident their connection with the other Indian nations and their young warriors would inevitably lead them to join the others in a war, especially "when the heart is open with Liquor." He prepared his post for an attack the following spring, even though the Indians displayed every mark of friendship.

Smallpox helped solve some of Heart's fears of Indian attacks. He told Harmar that the disease would leave very few Indians to make trouble: "only three Men five Women and a few Children are left of those who lived at this Place and the smallpox is spreading in the other Villages along the Allegheny."[118] So far, Heart said, he had kept it out of his garrison but did not see how he could possibly continue to do so since "Indians are constantly passing and repassing and dying around me. Humanity compells me to give some assistance."[119]

More Indians came into the area hunting later in the year, and in December Heart told of having to take the necessary precautions because over 100 Indian families had been in the vicinity within the past six weeks.[120]

EFFECT OF INDIANS UPON THE FORT'S SECURITY

Preparation for surprise attack was as necessary to the effectiveness of a fort and to its survival as the walls surrounding it. The ground surrounding a fort was always kept clear, and work parties were constantly formed to cut, pile, and burn brush, weeds, and fallen timber.[121] Tall tree stumps were never left standing. Sentries were ordered to be alert, especially at night, and the officer of the day was responsible for the guards and patrols. Soldiers were never to straggle from the garrison and always kept in readiness in case of an alarm. If, for any reason, a soldier had a pass to leave the garrison, he was always to carry his arms with him[122] and never to venture beyond hearing of the drum–beat[123]—an amazingly effective method of preventing soldiers from straying too far from the fort and also a means of guiding them back through unfamiliar forests. If, for any reason, soldiers did venture beyond hearing of the drumbeat, they were to return immediately upon hearing the firing of a cannon.[124]

A man was usually not allowed to go out of the fort unless accompanied by another. Gates of the fort were never opened until sunrise, and, if attack was expected, the troops were usually under arms at daybreak and remained so until half an hour after sunset. Ammunition, however, was not issued to anyone except the sentries, who kept their weapons continually loaded. When dismissed from guard duty, they were usually marched over to the laboratory where the old charge was withdrawn. A new cartridge was placed in the soldier's cartridge box and the old one delivered to the commanding officer of artillery.[125] Cartridges could only be withdrawn at the laboratory and those that could not be drawn from the barrels of the firearms were usually fired at a designated location in the camp, at a specified time in order to clear the weapon. Firing at random was never permitted.

---

[117] *Ibid.*
[118] *Ibid.,* Heart to Harmar, August 26, 1787.
[119] *Ibid.*
[120] *Ibid.,* Heart to Harmar, December 5, 1787.
[121] *Harmar Papers,* Vol. 32, Order Books, 1784–88, September 2, 1786, Garrison Orders.
[122] *Ibid.,* Vol. 32, June 3, 1788.
[123] U.S. Artillery Order Book, 2nd Regiment, May 14, 1790, USMA Library, West Point.
[124] *Ibid.*
[125] *Harmar Papers,* Garrison Orders, July 26, 1788.

A typical order given to secure the fort on the frontier was issued by Harmar October 10, 1788, at Fort Harmar, when Indian trouble had increased and surprise attacks were expected at any moment. Since Fort Harmar was the headquarters post, the number of men available for the alarm posts was larger than that of the smaller garrisons. When cutting winter firewood, the men were to start with those trees beyond the clearing, nearest the fort, always working away from the fort to widen the exposed area of cleared ground. Orders were to fell the trees low in order to minimize the height of the stumps and to retain all the straight poles for huts and barracks. Trees were never cut along the river banks because of subsequent erosion.[126] Working in the proximity of the fort while obtaining wood was a labor-saving procedure, as well as a defensive measure.

Whenever the troops were ordered under arms at the fort, banquettes were prepared for the men to stand on in order to fire over the top of the bastions and piquets.[127] They were usually three feet high, three feet wide, and roughly four and a half feet below the top of the piquets.[128] Wells dug inside the garrison were, of course, a major factor whenever the fort was under attack, and sites for the construction of forts were always chosen with an eye for available water supply within the walls. The "necessaries," or outhouses, were constructed outside the walls, but there were also "necessary facilities" inside the walls, for use at night and when under attack.[129]

Security within the fort was maintained with the help of a guardhouse that was usually built over the main gate. Violent prisoners, however, were secured in a dungeonlike cellar called "the black hole,"[130] usually in heavy irons.[131] Another important feature of camp security was the countersign, announced a day in advance of its use in the garrison orders.[132] The names of people or places were usually used.

RELAXATION AT THE FORTS

The fact that so many Indians had become afflicted with venereal disease proves that fraternization among soldiers and Indian women occurred frequently. Other than liquor—whenever it could be obtained—this was probably one of the few means of relaxation for the men. Each company, however, was allowed rations for four women,[133] a hardy breed of professional washerwomen which traveled with the army and did the washing for the men. Undoubtedly, some also served in the capacity of prostitutes. Others were married to men of the regiment. Theirs could hardly have been a lazy, luxurious life, since the men seldom paid and frontier living presented extreme hardship and deprivation. These women served along with the soldiers whenever there was need for extra hands, and their contribution cannot be underestimated, nor their activities belittled.

Life at the frontier garrisons was not at all monastic; some of the men were accompanied by their wives and children. Josiah Harmar ordered, and received, a set of two armed Windsor chairs and six Windsor sidechairs[134] so that he and Mrs. Harmar could enjoy some of the comforts of their Philadelphia home. Many of the men, and most of their children, trapped baby animals and domesticated them so that each garrison had an assortment of "wild" pets for amusement. Gardening and hunting helped pass the limited amount of free time the men might have had, and also served to supply whatever provisions the contractor failed to deliver.

[126] *Ibid.,* Garrison Orders, December 14, 1786.
[127] *Ibid.,* Garrison Orders, September 8, 1786.
[128] John Muller, *A Treatise of Fortification,* London, 1746, p. 211.
[129] *Military Journal of Major Ebenezer Denny,* p. 326.
[130] *Harmar Papers,* Vol. 28, Letter Book B, Harmar to Knox, March 18, 1787.
[131] *Ibid.*
[132] *Ibid.,* Vol. 32, Order Book, 1784–1788.
[133] *Ibid.,* Vol. 32, April 13, 1787.
[134] *Ibid.,* Vol. 29, Letter Book E, Harmar to Lt. Matthew Ernest, April 27, 1789.

CELEBRATIONS

Holidays and important visitors were always the occasion for an extra allowance of whiskey, and the men looked forward to these celebrations with enthusiasm. "Today being the Anniversary of American Independence the troops are to receive an extra gill of whiskey,"[135] Harmar told his men July 4, 1787, and on July 4, 1788, he said, "the troops are to appear clean and decent in every respect. The day is to be celebrated by a discharge of thirteen rounds at noon from the brass six-pounder—the troops are to receive an extra Gill of Whiskey per man—"[136] When the governor of the Northwest Territory (Arthur St. Clair) was expected at Fort Harmar in June, 1788, the men were told to "hold themselves in readiness to parade in a moment's warning and will appear with their arms bright and in good order and in perfect Soldier like condition in every respect."[137] Upon his arrival, St. Clair was saluted with thirteen rounds from the brass six-pounder, and the men presented their arms while the "officers and Colours are to salute him."[138] Blank cartridges were used to welcome the Fourth of July at Fort McIntosh in 1785.[139] At Fort Finney, on March 17, 1786, a special celebration was held.

> A majority of the men in the garrison are Irish. The soldiers requested to have the privilege of celebrating this day, as was customary. Accordingly the bung was opened and every man had permission to purchase and drink what quantity of liquor he pleased; and a pretty good portion did some of them take, for toward evening we had not six men in the garrison fit for duty, not even the guard excepted.[140]

One man died the next day from the effect of too much alcohol.[141]

The Fourth of July, 1786, at Fort Finney was celebrated by the officers in a grand manner.

> This day was celebrated with three round of small arms and three with the field-piece, after which the gentlemen all dined together. When dinner was over thirteen toasts were drunk, each accompanied with a round from the three-pounder, attended in the intervals by two drums, two fifes, and a couple of excellent violins. The evening was spent as well as circumstances would allow of.[142]

Jonathan Heart wrote from Fort Harmar in September, 1790 that "the fashion of eating is still in high vogue and there is enough whiskey to moisten the clay."[143] If Heart is any criterion, letter-writing consumed a large percentage of the spare time of the officers. Not only were they anxious to receive letters from friends back home who could tell them national and local news, but their own letter-writing gave them something constructive to do apart from their military lives. Newspapers were highly prized, and whenever one was delivered to the fort it was passed from man to man, even though the paper might be several months old.

Exploring became a fascinating pastime for some of the officers. The new country offered many opportunities to examine Indian burial grounds and the fortifications built by ancient tribes. Jonathan

---

[135] *Ibid.,* Vol. 32, Order Books, 1784–88.
[136] *Ibid.*
[137] *Ibid.*
[138] *Ibid.*
[139] *Ibid.*
[140] *Military Journal of Major Ebenezer Denny,* p. 283.
[141] *Ibid.*
[142] *Ibid.,* pp. 292–293.
[143] Heart to Judd, September 9, 1790, Guthman Collection.

Heart was fascinated with the ancient burial mounds on the Muskingum and, while stationed at Fort Harmar, wrote letters and articles, one of which was published in the *Columbian Magazine* in the summer of 1787. Another appeared in Gilbert Imlay's "A Topographical Description of the Western Territory of North America," published in London.

Land speculation was of great interest to those men stationed in the northwest, especially as they expected that army pension lands would be given to them for their past services during the Revolution. Not only did many of them furnish their friends at home with minute details of the new territory, but they schemed and contrived ways to obtain the best lands, knowing firsthand which were rocky and useless and which were rich in soil and minerals. Actually, land was one of the few paths to riches in those days of depression and disappointment.

Part III: Provisions

Feeding the Corps was a problem that was not solved as easily as securing their makeshift attire. There was no substitute for food, and there is nothing more morale-breaking than empty stomachs. Hunger was one of the most pressing problems that the regiment faced, and the major reason was, again, the weak financial position of the government. Advertisements were placed in newspapers by the Board of Treasury, similar to those placed for clothing contracts, requesting persons who desired to supply provision to the various outposts listed to submit their bids.

The first contract was placed in 1785 with James O'Hara, an Irish immigrant who served as a Captain under George Rogers Clark during the Revolutionary war and ended his colorful military service in 1783 serving as the assistant quartermaster for General Greene. O'Hara had married and moved to Pittsburgh, where he entered business. He won the first contract with his low bid of 13½ ninetieths of a dollar for supplying Fort Pitt, Fort McIntosh, and Fort Harmar. Harmar estimated the distance between Fort Harmar and Fort Pitt to be about 180 miles.[144]

"The contract was performed tolerably well; some complaints were made respecting particular posts, but the defects were perhaps inseparably connected with the state of the frontiers and of public affairs."[145] Thus, Congress summed up O'Hara's performance in thirty words in their study of the War Department. Josiah Harmar was not as brief. He told General Knox

> I am duty bound to represent the conduct of the contractor—For nearly two months past, the troops have received scarcely any meat, and what they have received has been of the very poorest quality—There is provision plenty in the country—he has no money to give for it, but depends entirely upon a Store of goods, which the country people will not take in payment—the consequence is the Troops have and still do suffer.[146]

[144] *Harmar Papers*, Harmar to Thomas Mifflin, March 19, 1787.
[145] *Journals of Congress*, Vol. 13, October 2, 1788.
[146] *Ibid.*, *Harmar Papers*, Harmar to Knox, Fort McIntosh, June 1, 1785, Letter Book A, Vol. 28.

Earlier that year Harmar had ordered the commissary to deliver a written report to him every Monday indicating the stock of provisions on hand, specifying the quantity and quality of each article and future expectations for supplies.[147]

Advanced preparation was a primary requisite for survival in the wilderness outposts, especially as the rivers froze over in the winter, precluding the transportation of supplies by boat from Fort Pitt to the various other forts along the Ohio River. The commandant made sure every precaution was taken on the part of the regiment to insure a safe supply of provisions, but he could not overcome the lack of funds available to the contractor, nor negligence, such as the time Mr. O'Hara went to New York for two months leaving the corps without an ample supply of beef.[148]

The contractor probably was trying to secure money to pay for the provisions during the period Harmar registered his complaint. O'Hara had offered to supply rations at an even cheaper rate if all the troops moved back to Fort Pitt, but Harmar felt that it was necessary for them to remain where they were.[149]

Bartering sometimes worked better than cash on the frontier. And the contractor could often obtain meat and other provisions from local traders if he offered them badly needed supplies in return. However, Mr. O'Hara did not have the proper trade items, according to Harmar's letter of June 1. Often the army and the contractor traded back and forth, with little or no money exchanging hands. Salt, vinegar, boats, medicines, and fresh beef were often worth more than money in the Northwest Territory. Fresh beef was a prime necessity, and, when an army moved into the wilderness away from supply depots, the men transported live cattle with them. Cattle and horses were transported on large flat boats—the "Kentucky boats"—[150] always under the vigilant "cattle guard," consisting of a noncommissioned officer and several private soldiers. Sometimes, when an attack seemed imminent, the guard was increased to as many as thirty men, under the command of an officer.[151] Cattle were properly fenced for grazing, and a strict accounting was kept for the commandant's monthly provision return. The beef would be slaughtered, if enough salt was available to preserve the meat during the hot weather. This meant a supply of vinegar had to be on hand, as that commodity was an absolute necessity with salt provisions.[152]

Ideally, the regiment should have a three-month supply of salt beef or pork continually available at the commissary. Hot weather and salt shortages, however, often made the curing ineffective, and much meat spoiled, creating severe shortages. Marauding Indians constantly attacked the contractors' supply boats, making off with supplies and cattle. A lack of government funds prevented purchasing fresh beef, and the army often went hungry and had to rely on the goodness of the village traders or on the talents of local hunters.[153]

Harmar told Hamtramck that, if salt provisions were not available, "hunters would be very useful, they might supply you with venison; there is a method of jerking it for its preservation."[154] He also told Hamtramck that Captain Heart or Ensign Bissel knew how to "jerk" meat and that they would be able to show him how to do it.[155]

During the summer months the principal supply of meat was fresh because cattle could be transported by boat to the various outposts and there properly penned under the watchful eye of the cattle guard. Usually the grazing area was sufficient to support a herd. However, in winter, if there

[147] *Ibid.,* Garrison Orders, Fort McIntosh, April 13, 1785, Vol. 32.
[148] *Ibid.,* Harmar to O'Hara, June 26, 1785, Vol. 28, Letter Book A.
[149] *Ibid.,* Harmar to Carleton, January 24, 1785.
[150] *Military Journal of Major Ebenezer Denny,* p. 261.
[151] *Ibid.,* p. 348. - Cattle Guard
[152] *Harmar Papers,* July 26, 1788, Letter Book A, Harmar to Hamtramck.
[153] *Military Journal of Major Ebenezer Denny,* p. 252.
[154] *Harmar Papers,* Harmar to Hamtramck, July 26, 1786.
[155] *Ibid.*

was no supply of salt meat, the men depended upon the hunters exclusively. "We should have starved had it not been for them[the hunters], as our winter supplies are not yet laid in," Harmar reported. Professional hunters had supplied Fort Harmar with venison in November and December of 1786[156] and Harmar told his men that "from the present dull prospect of receiving a supply of provisions on account of the navigation of the river, the commandant is obliged to order that the Bread which troops received this morning must last them for this day, Sunday and Monday, which will be the rate of half a pound per man."[157]

Harmar had told Secretary at War Knox that the failure of the contractors had created a "miserable situation" for his troops. He reported that the Muskingum River, which was 200 yards wide, was frozen over on November 23 with at least a foot of snow on top of that, and that "the Ohio full and driving with ice—boats can not go up or down it and he had not yet laid in his winter supplies."[158] The commandant added, in the same letter, that the men were desperate for clothing and those on duty protecting the surveyors were almost naked. During the winter of 1786 Harmar complained about the contractors, Messrs. Turnbull, Marnie & Company, who, along with contracting for the provisions, obtained a contract to furnish the clothing. Harmar told Knox that if "they did not better for clothing than they had done for provisions, I wished they had never secured the contract."[159]

Turnbull, Marnie & Company obtained their contract with their bid to supply the troops at Fort Pitt for 10⅓ ninetieths of a dollar and the troops at Forts McIntosh and Harmar for 11½ ninetieths of a dollar. The contract was "ill executed" and the contractors blamed this on the fact that they were paid in the currency of the state of Pennsylvania when that currency was greatly depreciated.[160] Commandant Harmar tried to raise morale when he told the suffering men at Fort Harmar that he was "very sorry the Contractor has so shamefully neglected his duty, as to suffer the garrison to be in want of provisions. Supplies may soon be expected, when every deficient Article shall be made up to the troops."[161] A few weeks later Harmar ordered the commissary to have a constant supply of 400-weight hard biscuit on hand for the use of the troops.[162] On November 8, 1786, General Harmar issued orders to the soldiers at Fort Harmar prohibiting them from individually purchasing flour from the commissary because of the small quantity left on hand and suggested each soldier be content with his daily ration.[163] On November 25 he cut the daily flour ration to one half pound per man and told the troops the deficiency would be made up as soon as a new supply arrived. He requested (not ordered) the officers to "be as economical as possible in the use of the article."[164]

In a letter to Major Doughty, Harmar said,

> You would have been surprised to see the Ohio when the Alleghany and Monongehala Ice came crushing down, sweeping all before it; Kentucky boats, canoes, etc., drifted by in great quantities but it was impossible to take them up—We should have starved had it not been for the hunters, who would frequently bring in fifteen hundred wt. of venison at a time and upwards of 200 wt. of turkey have been delivered at one time to the Troops. In short, my dear Sir, the name of Venison, Bear,

[156] *Ibid.,* Harmar to General Richard Butler, December 16, 1786, Vol. 32.
[157] *Ibid.,* Garrison Orders, Fort Harmar, December 16, 1786, Order Books 1784–88
[158] *Ibid.,* Harmar to Knox, December 7, 1786, Vol 28, Letter Book B.
[159] *Ibid.*
[160] *Journals of Congress,* Vol. 13, October 2, 1788.
[161] *Harmar Papers,* Fort Harmar, Vol. 32, Order Books 1784–88, July 24, 1786.
[162] *Ibid.,* Garrison Orders, Fort Harmar, August 17, 1786.
[163] *Ibid.*
[164] *Ibid.*

Turkey, Raccoon, Panther, etc., etc., became almost suspecting from their great plenty—I should like to be in your mess and have lobster for a substitute.[165]

Three days after Christmas a supply of flour was purchased from a local trader by the contractor. Harmar informed his troops at Fort Harmar that "there is at length a prospect of better times with regard to supplies of provisions, etc. . . . until further orders the troops are to receive one pound of flour per man daily and one gill of whiskey—the overplus due from the bakers is to be paid up immediately."[166] When the men fared well, so did the contractors. Ebenezer Denny said that whenever the men received their pay O'Hara sold whiskey and cheap goods to them and got most of the money that the paymaster brought on payday.[167] Money meant little to the men on the frontier, but the material articles that money could buy—to use, eat, or wear—meant much.

In 1787, James O'Hara submitted the lowest bid and again won the contract from the board of treasury, this time supplying five forts, two additional having been built by the army. Fort Pitt was supplied at 9¼ ninetieths of a dollar, McIntosh at 10¼ ninetieths of a dollar, Harmar at 11¼ ninetieths of a dollar, Rapids of the Ohio (present-day Louisville, Kentucky) at 13½ ninetieths of a dollar, and Venango (present-day Franklin, Pennsylvania) for 14 ninetieths of a dollar. Congress reported that this contract was executed better than the previous contracts. It stated that payment was made in warrants on the states of New Jersey, Pennsylvania, and Maryland.[168]

Harmar told Captain Finney that "my purse is drained in advancing money for the support of the troops at this post. I was obliged to do it, otherwise we should have starved through the mismanagement in the contractors' department." Harmar was referring to the meat he purchased from local hunters, and flour he was able to supply to the troops on December 28.[169] A week later Harmar wrote to Captain Ferguson, who was at Fort McIntosh,

> with respect to the contractor, if he does not furnish every part of the ration specified in the contract you will not sign his monthly abstracts, until he has done perfect justice to the troops—if the neglects were not so frequent, it would be well enough to accept of the deficiencies—for instance, if vinegar was not furnished in one week, and he could furnish it in the next, all would be well, but if at a longer period, endeavor to oblige him to pay the men at the current price vinegar sells for—I hope from my representation to the Secretary of War, and my determination to accept Mr. Duncan's[170] offer, that the contractors are a little alarmed and will supply us better in the future.[171]

Oftentimes Harmar had to compromise on the quality and quantity of rations. He rationalized that "ten ounces of bacon in this country I conceive to be an equivalent for the ration, etc."[172] The government specified the meat ration was to consist of three-fourths pound of pork or one pound of beef. When fresh cattle arrived by boat immediate protective measures were taken. A shipment arrived June 30, 1787, at the Rapids of the Ohio, and Harmar ordered the commissary to "pay particular attention to have the Cattle which are arrived turned into good pasture, and . . . have corn provided for them—Corporal Sheitz who has the Command of the Cattle Guard is to receive his

[165] Ibid., Vol. 28, Letter Book B, Harmar to Doughty, Fort Harmar, December 21, 1786.
[166] Ibid., Garrison Orders, Fort Harmar, December 28, 1786, Vol. 32.
[167] Military Journal of Major Ebenezer Denny, p. 282.
[168] Journals of Congress, Vol. 13, October 2, 1788.
[169] Harmar Papers, Harmar to Finney, January 7, 1787, Vol. 28, Letter Book B.
[170] Duncan was a Pittsburgh merchant who constantly kept Harmar informed of current news that he heard in Pittsburgh. When Duncan learned the contractors were failing, he offered to supply Harmar with 10,000 rations. (Ibid., January 9, 1787, Vol. 28, Letter Book B.)
[171] Ibid., Harmar to Ferguson, January 15, 1787.
[172] Ibid., Harmar to Knox, Fort Harmar, April 10, 1787.

directions from the Quarter Master respecting the penning and securing the Cattle at night."[173]

Toward winter, the situation became desperate again, and Harmar complained to Knox that he had to spend nearly £100 out of his own purse in order to keep the garrison supplied.[174] He found that provisions were cheaper and more abundant in Kentucky, and since O'Hara was unable to consistently keep the regiment provided he felt it wise to change to a Kentucky contractor, a Mr. Bradshaw.[175] An expedition to Vincennes was in the process of preparation at this time and Harmar could not afford to have the failure of the contractor hold up the timing of their departure. As usual, O'Hara ran into difficulties during the winter when the rivers froze. He was never able to keep the regiment supplied in advance, as Harmar would have liked. The lack of government funds at the time when the purchases were needed also aggravated this situation.

Conditions grew worse. Even after the new Constitutional government had taken office in 1789, and with an impending expedition against the Indians in 1790, the army's problem of an adequate supply of food never was solved. Money was the primary reason—the government's lack of it, and the contractor's need of it. Preparations for the expedition, which was to take place in the spring, were constantly postponed because of late deliveries. Harmar wrote to Knox and explained his position:

> I am sorry to inform you of the distressed situation that all the posts have been in, still are, and are likely to continue for want of provision—I am daily advancing money out of my own purse for the contractors' agent here, to purchase meat from hand to mouth—If force should be employed against the Savages some other mode of Supplies must be fallen upon, otherwise there is not the least prospect of Success in any expedition that may take place, or in establishing any new posts; this will positively be the case. Our boats are all nearly worn out; there are but 3 or 4 fit for service. If 2 or 3 boat builders were enlisted as artificers, and sent out to Head Quarters, it would be a saving to the Public—It is my duty to give timely notice of these matters. You will please to observe in my former letter that the Contingent money was nearly expended; further sum will be necessary, etc.[176]

A new contract had been placed in 1788 with the contracting firm of Elliot and Williams of Maryland. They were the lowest bidders and their prices were the lowest quoted of any of the previous contracts. They specified that payments should be made by warrants on their own home state, Maryland, and agreed to supply the forts at the following prices: Forts Pitt, McIntosh and Harmar for 7/90 of a dollar, Rapids of the Ohio for 7½/90 of a dollar, Venango 9/90 of a dollar and Post Vincennes for 16/90 of a dollar.[177]

In its report of October 2, 1788, Congress said public finances "would not admit of a further supply at present "[178] when it called attention to the inadequate supply and provision situation of the troops on the Ohio. The contractors were constantly trying to collect payment from the government either to buy much-needed supplies or to receive payment for those already delivered. Keen competition forced lower bidding each subsequent year and pointed to the fact that the contractor made his money selling liquor and cheap merchandise to the different garrisons on payday. Either contractors had to bid so low that there was no profit left in the contract and they were forced to make

---

[173] *Ibid.*, Order Books, 1784–88, Vol. 32.
[174] *Ibid.*, December 9, 1787, Letter Book B, Vol. 28.
[175] *Ibid.*
[176] *Ibid.*, Harmar to Knox, Fort Washington, June 9, 1790, Vol. 30, Large Letter Book A.
[177] *Journals of Congress,* Vol. 13, October 2, 1788.
[178] *Ibid.*

up their loss with sales of liquor and cheap merchandise to individual soldiers, or they took the contract purposely at a low figure in order to be able to take advantage of the soldiers' needs whenever they received their pay, knowing full well that as soon as a soldier received his money he would squander it on whatever material goods the contractor had to sell to him. As whiskey was cheap and there was plenty of it, the contractor made a constant debtor of the soldier.

Another avenue of profit was opened to the contractor when the quartermaster department was discontinued on the twenty-fifth of July 1785. In order to economize in personnel, the army set up a system whereby the contractor provided those provisions on the frontiers that would ordinarily have been handled by a quartermaster-general and his staff. The commanding officer of any of the garrisons, or the commanding officer of the regiment, submitted in writing an order to the contractor for whatever was needed and, upon receipt of the articles requested, gave the contractor a signed voucher. Upon submission of the vouchers to the Board of Treasury, every six months—along with his bills of sale for the articles procured for the army—the contractor was to be reimbursed for the cost plus a five percent commission. Harmar often cut through the red tape of this directive and purchased the supplies for the regiment from his own suppliers, finding their prices cheaper and their deliveries quicker.

Returns for the years 1787, 1788, and 1789 listed many articles received from the various contractors that were not specified on the official rations. Venison, brown sugar, bottled porter, Madeira wine, Lisbon wine, mutton, port wine, spirits, hyson tea, green tea, whiskey, and rum were among articles listed in Harmar's returns for those years. The army sold the contractors during those same years chests of carpenters' tools, Indian corn, candles, and salt, for which they received credit against future rations and supplies to be received.[179] The contractor would trade excess army supplies to the settlement merchants for things the army needed—or would sell the articles in the settlement for a profit. He was, when the boats were running and supplies getting through, in an enviable position: able to make a profit on surplus military material that he could barter away from the army and sell in town, and also supply the military with goods bought or bartered from the townspeople.

It wasn't a one-way street, however, and the various posts purchased many things from local traders and shopkeepers. Returns for those same years (1787, 1788 and 1789) list many articles which obviously were of local origin: cider, fowls, pigs, buffalo, turkey, mackerel, fishhooks, check (fabric), a pack of cards, potatoes, butter, calf, linen, beer, hair ribbon, eggs, raisins, bacon, cassimer, a lamb, three pounds of shot, a cheese, shelled Indian corn, rice, veal, bear meat, hogs' lard, onions, pepper, lump sugar, loaf sugar, allspice, and coffee. Many of the articles on the returns were grown in the soldiers' own gardens, for the use of the post, and many were brought in by local hunters or soldiers who hunted for the regiment.

Garrison gardening was a common practice, and, as soon as a fort was built, the men busied themselves gardening in their spare time. Each officer had his own private garden plot, tended by several enlisted men. The Ohio River valley was rich in vegetable products and wild game. It was either feast or famine, depending upon the season, the contractor, and the outpost.

The one consistent element about the provisions were their inconsistent availability to the regiment. The troops received only three-fourths pound of flour for rations during the winter of 1788,[180] and on Christmas day of 1788 the following order was issued: "The Commissary is to borrow and issue half a pint of whiskey this day to each man."[181] The commissary borrowed from a village trader or possibly gave tools or ammunition in trade for Christmas cheer. The orders for that

[179]*Ibid.,* Vol. 32, Order Books, 1784–88, Harmar Papers.
[180] *Ibid.,* January 16, 1788, Fort Harmar.
[181] *Ibid.*

day further stated "From the present dull prospect of supplies, the troops on the next drawing day which will be on Sunday the 28th, are to receive only ¾ pound of flour per man until further order—The Commandant calls upon the officers to be as economical as possible in the use of bread for their different messes."[182]

Messrs. Elliott and Williams, who were still the contractors in January 1789, were losing money, and Harmar told Secretary at War Knox that

> The Ohio must now be shut above, here it is impassable; we have about eight days meat on hand—the present Contractors have hitherto exerted themselves, and I believe still mean to do the best in their power to furnish the necessary supplies—I cannot see how they can possibly fulfill their contract, without a certain loss—I wish they may be able to go through with it, but am apprehensive they will not, as they have taken it on much too low terms, and must in my Opinion eventually be sufferers.[183]

In November 1790, a hunter called Miller was paid for delivering 160 pounds of venison to the fort. Harmar's expense book shows the entry to Miller for 1/6/8 at 2d per pound.[184]

On September 29, 1790, Harmar took the bull by the horns and sent a letter "To The New Contractors Whoever They May Be."[185] The government at that time was advertising for a new contract and the letter obviously was meant for Secretary at War Knox but was addressed through him to the new contractors. It specified the number of troops at each garrison to be supplied and added, "It will be necessary that you take the most effectual and speedy means for having at least three months' provisions at the several posts by the first of January next. . . ."[186]

NOTES:
Chapter 4,
Part I

GLOSSARY OF TERMS OF FORTIFICATION[187]

Banquette: is a kind of step made on the rampart of a work near the parapet for the troops to stand upon in order to fire over the parapet. It is generally 3 feet high and as many broad and 4½ feet lower than the parapet.

Bastion: is a part of the inner enclosure of fortification, making an angle toward the field and consists of two faces, two flanks, and an opening toward the center of the place called the gorge.

Battery: is a work made to place guns or mortars on; it consists of an epaulement, or breastwork about eight feet high and eighteen or twenty thick; when it is made for guns, openings or embrasures are made in it for the guns to fire through them.

Curtain: is the part of the body of the place which joins the flank of one bastion to that of the next.

Faces: of the bastion, are the two sides which meet in an angle projecting towards the field; of any work, are those parts where the rampart is made, making an angle pointed outward.

[182] *Ibid.*
[183] *Ibid.*, Harmar to Knox, Vol. 29, Letter Book E, Fort Harmar, January 13, 1789.
[184] *Ibid.*, Vol. 38, Expenses Receipts, 1789–1790.
[185] *Ibid.*, Vol. 29, Letter Book H.
[186] *Ibid.*
[187] Terms taken from Muller, *ibid.*

Fascine: is a kind of faggot made of branches, tied in two or more places, of about six or eight inches in diameter.

Flank: of a bastion is the part between the face and the curtain.

Fraise: stakes or palisades placed horizontally on the outward slope of the rampart made of turf to prevent the work being taken by surprise.

Loopholes: are square or oblong holes made in a wall, through which muskets can be fired.

Palisades: are a kind of stakes made of strong split wood of about nine feet long, fixed three feet deep in the ground in rows about six inches asunder.

Parapet: is a part of the rampart of a work, eighteen or twenty feet broad and raised six or seven feet above the rest of the rampart.

Platform: is a floor made of strong planks, laid upon joists, on a battery, to place the guns or mortars upon, in order to prevent the wheels or mortar bed from sinking in the ground.

Rampart: is an elevation of earth raised along the faces of any work, ten or fifteen feet high, to cover the inner part of that work against the fire of an enemy.

Salient angle: is that whose point turns from the center of the place.

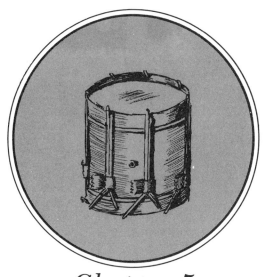

The soldier's duties were varied. His own survival in the wilderness and the protection of the settlers were obvious chores, but his all-important part in the surveying, mapping, and settling of the Northwest Territory is still not recognized today, yet it is one of the great contributions the army has made to this country.

Chapter 5

Part I: Duties and Deployment of the 1st Regiment

Soldiers of the 1st Regiment were required to build the barracks in which they lived and fabricate most of the tools, weapons, ammunition, and other necessities needed in the wilderness. Their duties, however, did not end with merely those crafts involved in frontier survival; their service in many other areas was required.

WITH THE SURVEYORS

One of the regiment's most important assignments was to protect the Geographer of the United States, Captain Thomas Hutchins, and his crew of surveyors and their assistants while they established boundaries that would eventually enable the United States to parcel out the new land and, it was hoped, collect desperately needed funds for the empty treasury. As result of the Land Ordinance of 1785 both the army and the surveyors in the northwest worked hand in hand, dividing and marking the land upon which frontiersmen later settled.

Congress resolved at that time that all of the land ceded to the United States after the war by the individual states, along with the land acquired from Great Britain as a result of the Treaty of Paris, was to be sold *after* surveys dividing the territory into townships six miles square had been completed. Each township was to consist of thirty-six plats (or lots), each of these containing 640 acres. The government considered well-regulated order more important than rapid settlement. The land would be sold to the public only as entire townships, half-townships, or sections of townships, costing $1 an acre plus surveying costs of $36 per township or $1 per section. As the average individual was unable to afford pieces of land this large, the eventual result was the formation of land companies (financial groups) that bought huge tracts from the government and, in turn, sold smaller plots to individual settlers at a profit. Unfortunately, the government was able to realize only partial payment from the more reputable groups and nothing from the highly speculative associations.

The precision of the survey, however, is a lasting monument to the Ordinance of 1785, the surveyors who carried out the work, and the soldiers who protected them. This system was continued through the nineteenth century, and the Midwest and the western portions of the United States were surveyed in exactly the same way. Today one can observe the rectangular pattern of farms, ranches, parallel roads and towns that forms a continuous grid extending to the Pacific Ocean. Monotonous but efficient, this unimaginative system of town planning and rural development is the most constant visual characteristic of the West. Although lacking in beauty, it allowed rapid settlement of the land and led to the tremendous growth and eventual financial stability of the United States.

The surveying was planned with military precision. Before surveying parties set out, each area to be surveyed was divided into seven ranges of townships. Out of each range, the government reserved four lots from every township and a fifth for the maintenance of public schools. The Secretary of War reserved certain lands which were promised to veterans for their service during the Revolutionary war, and in addition one-third of the mineral rights to all the land was reserved for the government. There were thirteen surveyors (one from each state), who were sent out in separate teams with their chain carriers, markers, and Indian guides. The entire program was under the direction of Hutchins, who personally supervised the survey of the important east–west line—the base upon which the entire survey depended. The other groups were each to survey one range (a projection of thirteen ranges whose completion was hoped for in 1785), and it was the corps' duty to supply adequate protection for each party.

Josiah Harmar wrote to Henry Knox and Thomas Hutchins July 13, 1786, telling them: "I am making my arrangements to be ready to cover the Surveyors as much as shall be in my power. The surveying and disposal of the Western Territory I take for granted to be the first grand object of Congress."[1] Harmar explained to Knox that he was going to detach two companies to the Rapids of the Ohio (Fort Finney) for protection of the surveyors against the Indians, detach three companies as a "flying corps" to the Mingo Bottom (Fort Steuben), where the "chief of the intruders[2] are,"[3] keep three companies at Muskingum (Fort Harmar), and an officer and small detachment at Pitt to guard the supplies, and a company at McIntosh.[4] His objective was to keep his small force as central as possible[5] and "I shall be able to take the field with near 300 men, if it should be found necessary, but an Indian war under the present embarrassed state of finance, as you will observe, must be avoided, if possible, consistent with the dignity of the United States."[6] Summing up his plan of deployment, Harmar said: "It shall be my study to pursue a plan best adapted to expedite the surveying of the Western Territory, and at the same time to avoid hostilities with the savages."[7]

Major John Hamtramck, at Mingo Bottom, had orders from Harmar which were more flexible: "I give you discretionary power to make your own arrangement—keeping your main body on the East and West line for the protection of the geographer himself, and detaching small parties with the surveyors whom he shall leave at every 6 miles."[8] A month later Hamtramck's detachment was cut up piecemeal, a few men deployed to each survey team. He was ordered to make certain every team was accompanied by a "trusty non-com" who could supervise the safe return of his group.[9] It was contemplated that as each of the thirteen ranges was completed, the parties would return to the main group, moving progressively westward, and Hamtramck would eventually find his command in a stronger position to resist an Indian assault.[10]

By the end of December, however, only four ranges had been surveyed. Further work was impossible because of the severity of winter and the hostility of the Indians,[11] and it was not until the

---

[1] *Harmar Papers,* Vol. 28, Letter Book A.
[2] By "intruders" Harmar was referring to squatters and renegade Whites working against the best interests of the United States.
[3] *Harmar Papers, ibid.*
[4] *Ibid.*
[5] *Ibid.*
[6] *Ibid.*
[7] *Ibid.*
[8] *Ibid.,* Harmar to Knox & Hutchins, July 13, 1786.
[9] *Ibid.,* Harmar to Hamtramck, August 20, 1786.
[10] *Ibid.*
[11] *Ibid.,* Harmar to Hamtramck, January 21, 1787, Vol. 28, Letter Book B.

following June that it was resumed when an ensign and his command left Fort Harmar to complete the fifth, sixth, and seventh ranges.[12] Hamtramck was recalled to headquarters with his command, leaving one company at Fort Steuben "to prevent intrusion and the preservation of the fort."[13]

Hutchins's next surveying expedition did not begin until the fall of 1788. Harmar detached forty privates, two corporals, two sergeants, one subaltern, and a captain to accompany the geographer, who was ordered to survey the lines of Dr. Manasseh Cutler and Winthrop Sargent who represented the Ohio Company's purchase.[14] Harmar complained that this deployment of troops weakened his command considerably.[15] The duty was so fatiguing that Harmar issued orders November 2, 1788, excusing those men who had just returned from the mouth of the Scioto, where the surveying had taken place, from duty for three days, during which time they had no other responsibility except to clean their arms.[16]

The surveyor and surveying instruments have long been neglected for their important role in American history. The surveyor was as colorful and brave as any of the legendary heroes of the frontier. These men with their wooden or brass scientific compasses, chains, and levels also carried rifles, tomahawks, and scalping knives, for their food and protection. They were Indian-fighters, professional hunters, and expert woodsmen.

During the military expeditions into the unchartered Northwest Territory in 1790 and 1791, surveying teams preceded the marching columns of troops and equipment by several miles. The surveyors were the first to be exposed to the danger of ambush and found the best course for the army to travel and the most likely spots to encamp, graze cattle, and obtain fresh water. The precise estimation of mileage and accurate sightings recorded by the surveyors provided the first maps, invaluable for subsequent expeditions, as well as vivid accountings of the size and wealth of the territory.

Surveying instruments have long been thought of only as implements of technical and scientific interest. In fact, they deserve a proper place along with other historic artifacts in museums and private collections for the significant role they have played in American history.

LAND COMPANIES

The Ohio Company was an outgrowth of an earlier land company. It was reorganized March 1, 1786, by a group of New Englanders, mostly Revolutionary war veterans, seeking one and a half million acres of land. In 1787 Dr. Manasseh Cutler and Winthrop Sargent represented the company in negotiations with Congress to purchase a tract on which they intended to form new settlements and develop the territory. During the course of the negotiations, the Northwest Ordinance was adopted by Congress and the highly speculative Scioto Land Company was formed by unscrupulous William Duer and his associates. Whether Cutler and Sargent added any constructive material to the Ordinance of 1787—and whether they had any financial interest in the Scioto Company—is questionable. Except for the ordinance which regulated the government of the settlers of both companies, the Ohio Company, the Scioto Company and the Northwest Ordinance had absolutely no connection with one another. However, their very nature and the timing of their creation point to a relationship, no matter how remote.

[12] *Ibid.,* Harmar to Ensign Spears, June 12, 1787.
[13] *Ibid.,* Harmar to Hamtramck, May 19, 1787.
[14] *Ibid.,* Harmar to Knox, October 7, 1788, Vol. 28, Letter Book D.
[15] Thornbrough, p. 138.
[16] *Harmar Papers and Order Books,* Vol. 32, 1784–88.

Whereas the Ohio Company was formed to sell and legitimately settle the land, the Scioto Company was a speculative organization, the purpose of which was to sell the land to capitalist interests abroad. Duer had undoubtedly used his Congressional influence as a wedge during the Ohio Company's negotiations with Congress, convincing Cutler and Sargent that Congress would be more receptive to the purchase of five million acres than to a million and a half. Duer, the contractor to the ill-fated St. Clair expedition, had recently been appointed secretary to the Board of Treasury of the United States, which was directly concerned with the Ohio Company's prospective purchase. In order to gain Congressional approval, the Ohio Company followed the advice of Duer, arranged for the purchase of five million acres, and then allowed Duer and his associates to acquire the rights to three and a half million of those acres from the Federal government, retaining one and a half million for themselves. Upon obtaining the rights to purchase the land, Duer and his associates formed the Scioto Company, which eventually swindled hundreds of unfortunate European emigrants who purchased acreage in the northwest from agents of the company. The Scioto Company never paid the government for the land and the newcomers, arriving in a foreign wilderness, were not able to obtain clear title to their purchases. This swindle was in contrast to the progress made by the Ohio Company, whose settlers moved into the new territory with clear title. Congress had provided for their welfare with the Land Ordinance of 1787.

ORDINANCE OF 1787 (JULY 13)

Called the Northwest Ordinance, the Land Ordinance of 1787 is one of the great documents in American history. It made provision for the government of that territory which later became the states of Michigan, Indiana, Ohio, Illinois, and Wisconsin. The ordinance provided for freedom of religion, habeas corpus and trial by jury, proportionate representation of the people in the legislature, judicial proceedings according to common law, encouraged schools and education, and supported the movement for the abolition of slavery and involuntary servitude. The government of the Northwest Territory was to consist of a governor (Arthur St. Clair), a secretary (Winthrop Sargent), and three judges (Samuel Holden Parsons, John Armstrong, Jr., and James Mitchell Varnum; Armstrong declined, and John Cleves Symmes was chosen to replace him). Congress appointed all of the officials.

St. Clair formally inaugurated the government in the territory in Marietta (Ohio), founded by the Ohio Company, July 15, 1788. Until that time the Federal corps acted as the territory's only form of government.

Under the protection of the government in the northwest, the surveyors were once again back to work, under the watchful eye of the 1st American Regiment.

One detachment that had been sent out with the surveying parties in mid-November 1788 was ordered down to the mouth of the Scioto River, the other from its mouth northward.[17] Harmar said of the latter party,

> I have some little apprehensions about safety, but I know of no more convenient opportunity to embrace than the present—when these two exterior lines are run, which (barring accidents) I hope be completed against the 20th instant, nothing will then be wanting but the presence of the Geographer, who shall have all the necessary guards in order that he may proceed and run the northern Boundary, which will finish the business and BRING THE MONEY FOR MESSRS. CUTLER & SARGENT'S PURCHASE INTO THE TREASURY.[18]

[17] *Ibid.,* Harmar to Knox, December 4, 1788, Vol. 29, Letter Book E.
[18] *Ibid.*

Harmar's comments illustrate the importance of the new government's position as landlord and stress what was probably the most successful role played by the regiment—that of enabling the surveyors to accomplish their job.

Confusing as the actual land negotiations were, that confusion must have been compounded tenfold for the soldiers on the frontier who heard rumors about land connivery from every corner of their limited world. Many were continually urged by their friends back home to identify the choicest pieces of land for them, particularly the officers whose former fellow officers from the last war were entitled to the newly reserved pension lands and most of whom had a financial interest in the land companies. Captain Jonathan Heart, through his correspondence with William Judd, kept most of his "brothers" in the Connecticut Society of Cincinnati informed about the good and poor lands, and offered his own ideas concerning future settlements. However, his letters were filled with questions about the men responsible for certain land transactions of which he was suspicious. He hoped more factual answers could be supplied by his friends at home who were closer to the political and economic situation than he was in the wilderness.

Heart's uncertainty about the economics of the country and the questionable integrity of many of the men who were influential and responsible for government policy was evidenced in his wordy letters and stood in contrast to his sincere belief in the eventual development of the Northwest Territory and the golden opportunity it presented to anyone who invested in its future. Familiar with most of the country from Lake Erie to Fort Pitt, Heart did not hesitate to offer his own suggestions about the best type of towns to establish and the quality of people to settle those towns. His prejudice against Virginians, particularly the Kentuckians, was almost as strong as his contempt for most of the Indian traders and trappers who he often referred to as "lawless banditti." Coupled with his intense dislike for British agents, who were continually creating trouble with the Indians, Heart made some profound observations pertaining to the settlement of the new land. In a letter from French Creek (Venango) July 8, 1787, he said,

> I am confident an active Man with his Ax and Gun to support him from April to October never need fear want afterwards—his Stock will live through the Winter without Forage, his Hogs will fat in the Woods and with his own Hands he may till four or five Acres of Corn and in many places he may clear it in as many Days as there are acres—Indeed I know of nothing to prevent a Man's living here but Laziness—of the Indians the latter will prove troublesome until the New England Mode of Settlement takes Place and the Ordinance for Sales of these Lands will not allow that, but I am persuaded the mode will be altered—at present the Prospects are not inviting.

He added observations about the surveyors' progress:

> The Surveys I believe are stopped. The Surveyors have no wish to loose [lose] their Scalps—you advise the locating a town on the Muskingum. I am now almost as far from it as I am from you—and I know very little what is going on in the Busy World being about 180 miles from Inhabitants except the Indians—of them have Neighbors plenty. The Whole Seneca Tribe around me—was not used to misfortunes. I would be vexed that the Public Securities are running to nothing as all I have in this world is vested in them—but I have too little even of that to vex myself about it.[19]

---

[19] Letter from Heart to William Judd, Guthman Collection.

Men like Heart were constant prey for certain of their friends back East who, with access to more up-to-date and accurate information concerning the disposal of lands, wanted to capitalize on it. Although Heart and his contemporaries knew the country and mapped, surveyed, and protected it—and were able to judge good and bad methods of settlement—they did not have an overall picture of the territory in which they lived. They could visualize its potential but became confused about its ultimate disposal when they received conflicting and misleading reports in letters or heard distorted versions of the truth from travelers passing through. Competition between the different states for land acquisitions created bitter rivalries, some of which had long been in existence, and nearly caused bloodshed between some states. Entrepreneurs, such as John Cleves Symmes and opportunists like William Duer and many others oftentimes overshadowed sincere land developers like Samuel Holden Parsons, Rufus Putnam, and Manasseh Cutler, thereby creating more doubt in the minds of the corps, whose job it was to protect *all* of the land companies.

Complications surrounding the disposal of state and Federal army pension lands, and the sale of federal lands—which was to go to whom first—all contributed to the uncertainty that Heart expressed in his letters. Many of his observations pointed to his strong feelings of confidence in the future of the new territory and for the entire country. In spite of the political and financial turmoil of the young United States, the unspoiled abundance of the northwest gave Heart and his fellow soldiers confidence for the future. The potential of the underdeveloped region with its natural treasure chest must have given them a sense of national unity that the thirteen squabbling states had yet to instill in their own citizens. Heart said: "The Fate of the American Empire calls the Eastern Emmigrants from the barren Mounts of the North to these Luxuriant Fields."[20]

Detailing his ideas about settlement in the same letter to Judd,[21] Heart added that the government ought to grant a certain number of ranges of townships (from the Ohio River to the Great Lakes) to all veterans of the Revolution, as was promised. "Those brave men whose toils have acquired these lands are best qualified to defend them," he said.[22] The grants should be made far enough west, he said, to form a protective barrier for other lands in the new territory. Since the veterans of the Continental army were best qualified to defend the territory, Heart suggested that Congress increase individual shares of pension land in order to make the idea more attractive, thus encouraging more ex-soldiers to settle along the frontier. If enough land were granted to accommodate only 150 men to each township of six square miles—thus guaranteeing adequate protection—Heart felt that the intermediate space between the frontier and the present thirteen states would immediately be filled with eager emigrants who would have no reason to fear Indian raids since the frontiers would be adequately settled by ex-soldiers, who would defend them.

Enthusiastically, he observed that "the situation of the Country with respect to Trade, etc., the great River Ohio, the Kenhawa, Miami, Wabash, etc., the vicinity of their Headwaters with the Lakes and the Great extent of the Mississippi will speak for themselves on the Map."[23] He added that the soil, climate, and produce of the territory were so agreeable to the welfare of the individual and the Union of the United States as to make the invitation to emigrate very appealing to the Easterner.[24]

Heart often emphasized the fact that the mode of settlement of the Southern colonists, particularly Virginians, was geared for the self-interest of the individual who picked, at random, the best lands for himself, thus scattering his acreage far from his neighbors and exposing his family to Indian depredations. The typical New England pattern of thickly settled townships, on the other hand, offered community protection and a solid barrier along the frontier that would discourage any ideas the hostile Indians might have about attacking the settlements. (The Ordinance of 1785 was predicated on the New England method of settlement.)

---

[20] Heart to Judd, Fort Harmar, January 8, 1786, Guthman Collection.
[21] *Ibid.*
[22] *Ibid.*
[23] *Ibid.*
[24] *Ibid.*

Realizing that the small Federal army could not adequately defend large numbers of settlers, Heart fervently wished that the government would distribute the pension lands to the veterans of the last war to whom "Congress are righteously indebted and wickedly withold Pay from,"[25] and who, he felt, "know the Terrors of War, will Cultivate Peace, and if necessary are calculated to defend the land."[26] Heart also feared the manipulation of unscrupulous schemers whose self-interest rose above any patriotic or nationalistic sacrifice. He told Judd, "The unstable situation of the Government under all Public Securities is of such uncertainty that it needs all the Knowledge of Law, Physie and Divinity to guard against Intrigues of Speculators."[27] Hastily, however, he added that "I am in a Territory of importance and flatter myself that my knowledge in it will not be to my disadvantage, but I wish it of advantage not only to myself but my friends."[28]

Their cooperation and influence back home was essential in whatever plans all might have in the future acquisition of land, and Heart added,

> My situation cannot be of much Service to me as an individual without my Friends and with their assistance I think it may and wish it devoted to their assistance, in whatever manner the future Plans of Congress must determine. Therefore, I only ask your influence there and please Communicate your command Wishes and Desires—[29]

It is impossible to separate land development, speculation, and military grants from any study of the Federal corps. Even though the states which held land in the Northwest ceded almost all of it to the Federal government prior to the adoption of the Constitution (not applicable to the Southwest), the Virginia Military tracts and Connecticut's Western Reserve played an important part in the lives of the men of the 1st American Regiment. Treaties with the Indians were attended by commissioners from some of the states as well as from the Federal government; and, obviously, those officers from the states represented at the treaties were involved in the proper settlements for their own states and the hope for military pension land.

The individual soldiers also witnessed the daily migration of families from the East to the new territory. Heart said:

> 5 to 10 Kentuck Boats pass in a Day each which carried three or four Families with their Cattle, Horses, Household Furniture and one hundred and three of those boats have passed since 1 Jany last—they will come from Fort Pitt to this Place 200 miles in 48 hours—[30]

Regional prejudice was reflected in a letter that he wrote to Judd. "A Settlement of Eastern People, I have once mentioned, this I wish on Principles for the Benefit of the Union."[31] He added in the same letter, "There is an insurmountable antipathy between Virginians and Indians, there is not the same with Eastern People and the Mode of their Settlements will form a more secure Barrier to our Frontiers."[32] In another, he said, "There can be no obstructions forming a Settlement in this Country provided they come in large Bodies and form their Settlements in towns according to the old New England mode—"[33]

[25] Heart to Judd, Fort Harmar, February 7, 1786, Guthman Collection.
[26] *Ibid.*
[27] Heart to Judd, Fort Harmar, March 3, 1786, Guthman Collection.
[28] *Ibid.*
[29] *Ibid.*
[30] Heart to Judd, Fort Harmar, June 5, 1786, Guthman Collection.
[31] Heart to Judd, Fort Harmar, August 9, 1786, Guthman Collection.
[32] *Ibid.*
[33] Heart to Judd, Grave Creek, November 15, 1786, Guthman Collection.

Heart offered these observations to his friends back home:

> There is plenty of bad and unprofitable lands and intermixed with the good, my opportunities on the different Ranges enables me to point out very nearly what towns are good and in many towns what particular lotts, and there are whole towns not worth a shilling in bulk, a few good farms amongst the hills, in others not a single Acre fit for improvement.[34]

The next sentence indicates the association he desired with some sort of profitable future. "Should a company for purchasing lands in this country I shall be happy to give them every information and more particularly to my friends."[35] Almost a year later, he wrote to Judd: "I received your Favor of the 31 March 87 approve the proceedings respecting Lands and shall be happy in partaking a Share in your adventures as far as my abilities will admit."[36] Heart proceeded to describe the country to Judd. He told about the good and bad tracts, the salt licks, the soil, trees, crops, topography, minerals, highlands and bottoms, giving an accurate early description of the territory.

Heart's correspondence with Judd continued until two months before the fatal massacre in 1791. His interest in land companies, speculation in the better lands, and everything connected with land, the treaties, commissioners, and government rulings concerning the disposition of the lands never ceased. Judd continued to receive descriptions of all the vital areas in which he and Heart had financial interests, along with those which they considered for future investment or pension lands. From the tone of his letters, and the enthusiasm of his associates back home, it is obvious that they thought the future hope of the Union—at least for many members of the regiment—lay in the development of the northwest[37] and not in the crowded seaboard that had left them so disillusioned and penniless after the Revolution.

The competition between the states for land acquisitions, both for pension lands to their veterans of the late war, and their own land companies, helped fan the flames of land fever within the corps. Officers who originally obtained their appointment through political patronage owed an allegiance to their native state and, therefore, information concerning the land they reconnoitered was given first to representatives of that state. Bitter feuds between states over land (such as New York and Massachusetts, the squatters in Vermont, the old Pennsylvania–Connecticut feud) had repercussions within the Federal corps, but the rich future that the territory promised to the United States overcame individual state jealousies. This hope, emanating from the new territory, helped strengthen the foundation of the United States army. It also fostered the pioneer spirit.

---

[34] *Ibid.*
[35] *Ibid.*
[36] Heart to Judd, French Creek, July 8, 1787, Guthman Collection.
[37] George Washington realized the immense wealth of the western territory as early as 1753 and 1754 when he served during the French–Indian War and undertook an expedition to the Ohio River. His observations are noted in *The Diaries of George Washington, 1748–1799* (edited by John C. Fitzpatrick for the Mount Vernon Ladies Association of the Union, Houghton Mifflin Co., Boston, 1925, Volume 1, pp. 43–102). In Volume 2, pp. 318–319, of the Washington diaries, he returns to the territory in 1784 to look after his holdings as bounty from Virginia for his French-Indian War service and he also purchased additional bounty lands from other officers and soldiers.

He said: "The Ohio embraces this commonwealth from its northern, almost to its southern limits. It is now our western boundary and lyes nearly parallel to our exterior, and thickest settled country."

"Into this river French Creek, Big Beaver Creek, Muskingum, Hockocking, Scioto, and the two Miamis and many others pour themselves from the westward through one of the most fertile countries of the globe."

He summarizes: ". . . All of these are so many channels through which not only the produce of the new states contemplated by Congress, but the trade of *all* the lakes, quite to that of the Wood, may be conducted according to my information and judgement—at least by one of the routes—thro' a shorter, easier, and less expensive communication than either of those which are now, or have been used with Canada, New York or New Orleans."

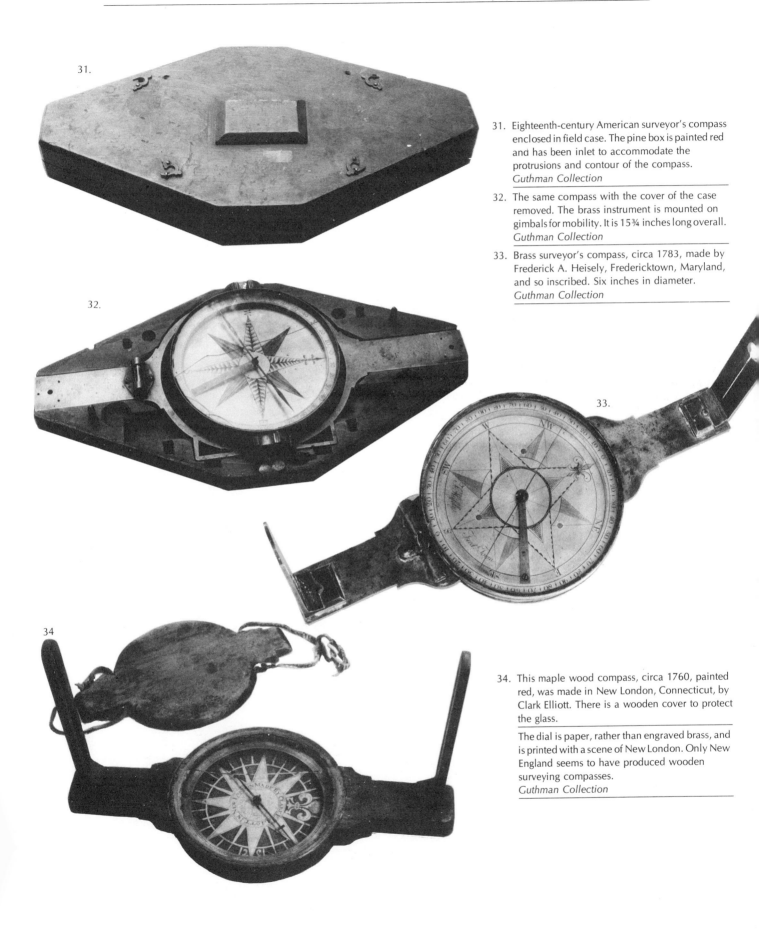

31. Eighteenth-century American surveyor's compass enclosed in field case. The pine box is painted red and has been inlet to accommodate the protrusions and contour of the compass. *Guthman Collection*

32. The same compass with the cover of the case removed. The brass instrument is mounted on gimbals for mobility. It is 15¾ inches long overall. *Guthman Collection*

33. Brass surveyor's compass, circa 1783, made by Frederick A. Heisely, Fredericktown, Maryland, and so inscribed. Six inches in diameter. *Guthman Collection*

34. This maple wood compass, circa 1760, painted red, was made in New London, Connecticut, by Clark Elliott. There is a wooden cover to protect the glass.

The dial is paper, rather than engraved brass, and is printed with a scene of New London. Only New England seems to have produced wooden surveying compasses. *Guthman Collection*

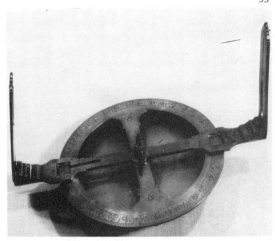

35

36.

37.

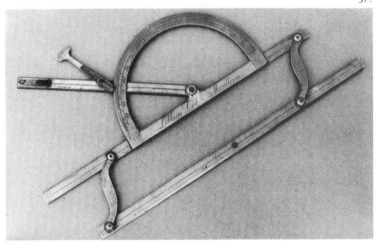

35. Brass circumferentor, circa 1785, made by Enos Doolittle, Hartford, Connecticut. The instrument measures 9½ inches overall length. Enos also made clocks and, later in life, bells.
Guthman Collection

36. Close-up of the dial of a beautifully engraved surveyor's compass made by Benjamin Rittenhouse, Philadelphia, circa 1785.
Guthman Collection

37. Unusual brass surveyor's combination parallel rule and protractor, made by Lebbeus Dod, Mendham, New Jersey, circa 1780.

Dod was in charge of an armory manufacturing and repairing weapons for the Continental Army during the Revolution.
Guthman Collection

38. Flat-bottomed river boat, from an old print. Probably much like the Kentucky boats described by Zadock Cramer.
Taken from The Ohio River, *by Archer Butler Hulbert, G. P. Putnam's Sons, 1906*

38.

Part II: Exploring, Charting, Mapping, Spying

The necessity for adequate maps and the handicaps suffered because they did not exist were expressed by General Knox in a letter to Josiah Harmar in June 1789. Knox explained that it was impossible at the time to raise additional troops to help guard the frontier and therefore "It is necessary to make the best possible disposition for covering the greatest extent of country."[38] He went on to say "Were we possessed of a *Map on which a perfect reliance could be placed* there would be less difficulty at this distance pointing out general positions than there is at present."[39] Knox severely criticized the inaccurate distances and other faulty details of the earlier maps drawn by Captain Hutchins, the geographer.[40] (Hutchins' maps of North America were published in 1755.)

Several months later, Secretary of War Knox sent Commandant Harmar secret instructions. He ordered two separate parties, consisting of an officer and non-commissioned officer accompanied by four or five Indians who were "well acquainted with living in the woods" to set off a month or two apart, in secret—and without official sanction—to explore the Missouri River.[41]

The Missouri River (at that time unexplored) emptied into the Mississippi River seventeen miles above present-day St. Louis. A gateway to rich fur country, the Missouri was a tempting target for investigation. The new government emphasized secrecy because this territory belonged to Spain, who jealously guarded her lands west of the Mississippi from the expanding infant nation. In addition, France, who had owned the territory prior to the French–Indian War, hoped to gain control of the Louisiana Territory (and did so in 1800 when Napoleon forced Spain to retrocede the land). Therefore, this other ally of the Revolution also restrained the United States from openly attempting westward expansion.

Harmar was ordered to send a detachment to investigate the river up to its source (little realizing in 1789 the vast extent of the great river) "and all navigable streams that run into the great north river which empties itself into the gulf of Mexico."[42] Knox was referring, of course, to the Mississippi, the mouth of which was controlled by Spain, who possessed Florida and West Florida. He said that these missions could not be undertaken with the sanction of public authority and that if the parties set off two months apart there would be a better chance of at least one returning, adding, "I say nothing about their equipment or the manner of their being furnished."[43] The Missouri was not actually explored until 1803 by Lewis and Clark, but Harmar's records do indicate at least two separate attempts took place along the waterways of the Northwest Territory.

---

[38] *Harmar Papers,* Knox to Harmar, June 10, 1789, Vol. 10.
[39] *Ibid.* (This points out the value of the surveys recorded in 1790 and 1791.)
[40] *Ibid.*
[41] *Ibid.,* Knox to Harmar, December 20, 1789, Vol. 11.
[42] *Ibid.*
[43] *Ibid.*

Harmar, preceding his campaign of 1790, told Lieutenant John Armstrong to explore the "Wabash" River and "give me a particular report of its communication with Lake Erie, the depth of the Waters, the distance, etc.—and if it can be done with safety proceed to the Miami Village, in which case it will be necessary to have an escort of Friendly Indians to accompany you."[44]

Harmar communicated with Armstrong two weeks later and told him that "the party employed on that business should be habited like Indians in all respects, *and on no pretense whatsoever* discover any connection with the Troops, of course they will not take any written orders with them. Acknowledge the receipt of this letter, and govern yourself accordingly; *you may then burn it."*[45]

Lieutenant Armstrong was partially successful, according to Harmar's letter of August 3, 1790: "Lieut. Armstrong's report with observations that he made whilst on the Mississippi, Maps, etc., etc., I also enclose by this opportunity, and a monthly return of the Corps dated the first inst."[46]

Some of the duties of an officer in the regiment were spelled out to Captain Jonathan Heart when Harmar told him the main objective at Venango was to explore the Big Beaver, ascertain practicability of navigation at different seasons of the year, ascertain the portage over the water of the Cuyahoga, and down the same river to Lake Erie, the general depth of the water, nature of the banks on the Big Beaver and Cuyahoga, and notice the nature of the grounds of the portage from the head navigation of one river to the other.[47] Emphasizing the importance of the mission, Harmar added, "It is a circumstance of great important to ascertain by judicious officers capable of giving clear and distinct accounts of the nearest communication from the Waters which run into the Ohio, with those which empty into Lake Erie."[48]

Heart was asked if he could secure some friendly Seneca Indians to accompany him, reminding him they would be well compensated for their trouble. Lieutenant Ebenezer Frothingham was ordered to go along with Heart also,[49] and their report was to be submitted to Harmar when the job was completed. Brief references to this mission were mentioned in several of Heart's letters to William Judd. "It is almost three months since I have seen Mrs. Heart as she is at Muskingum and I have been during that time in the woods, returned to this place [Fort Pitt] down the Alleghany only two days ago."[50] In another letter he told Judd that he had been detached on business at Lake Erie,[51] and in another said, "I have but just returned from a most fatiguing March up the Waters of Beaver across to the Head Waters of Cayahoga and down that River to Lake Erie and thence along the Lake to Cunneat and thence to Fort Franklin and down the Alleghany and Ohio to this place [Fort Harmar]."[52]

A fourth letter adds more detail:

> About the 20th of November, I left Muskingum and have since been up the Waters of Beaver across to the Cayahoga and down to Lake Erie and along the Lake to the Pennsylvania Line and from thence across to the Waters of the Alleghany and down those Waters to Pitt and from thence down the Ohio to this Place (Falls of the Ohio, present-day Louisville) which is 620 Miles from Pitt.[53]

Two years earlier Harmar had complimented Heart on his ability at mapmaking:

---

[44] *Ibid.,* Harmar to Armstrong, February 20, 1790, Harmar Papers, Letter Book G, Vol. 29.
[45] *Ibid.*
[46] *Ibid.,* Harmar to Knox, August 3, 1790, Vol. 30, Large Letter Book A.
[47] *Ibid.,* Harmar to Heart, July 13, 1789, Vol. 29, Letter Book F.
[48] *Ibid.*
[49] *Ibid.*
[50] Heart to William Judd, December 25, 1789, Guthman Collection.
[51] Heart to Judd, January 6, 1790, Guthman Collection.
[52] Heart to Judd, January 12, 1790, Guthman Collection.
[53] Heart to Judd, Falls of the Ohio, January 27, 1790, Guthman Collection.

> I want another large map of the country near Lake Erie, in order to send it to the war office—the one which you have been pleased to inscribe to me, being executed with such extreme neatness, I shall send to the supreme executive council of the State of Pennsylvania—the other view and profile of the Garrison I shall send on to the war office—when you can make it convenient you will please to send me a set to keep in my own possession—[54]

Exploring, charting, mapping, and, of course, reconnaissance of Indian movements was an essential part of the regiment's activities, and a major contribution to the future development of this country. The importance of this activity is reflected in Harmar's order to Ensign McDowell in February 1790: "It is the President of the United States' directions that you use unremitting means of exploring the navigation of all the waters of the Ohio, which may in the nearest degree communicate with the navigable waters of Lake Erie,"[55] he quoted from Knox's orders in a previous letter, relating the instructions to McDowell. Adding his own thoughts to those of Knox, Harmar said,

> In the spring, when the waters are in their ordinary state, proceed from the Falls of the Big Beaver to the highest navigation on it, and examine the distance from thence to the nearest Canoe waters of Lake Erie, and describe the nature of the ground between each, and ascertain the navigation down the Lake, estimating as accurately as possible, the distances from remarkable places in both waters, noting particularly all obstructions there in, that accurate judgments there of may be formed. . . .[56]

Warning McDowell to be alert, Harmar added, "You will continue to transmit me all the Indian news which you can gather in your quarter, and keep a sharp look out always to guard against surprise."[57] Information about the British posts was requested by Knox[58] and Harmar replied in December 1790, "You recommend my attention to obtaining intelligence from the British Posts—I had long ago impressed this kind of service as duty upon the officers commanding both Forts Franklin and Knox and whenever anything worthy of your notice may happen to transpire, it shall be communicated."[59] News of British violation of the Treaty of Paris was related in the same letter:

> Ensign Jeffers commanding at Fort Franklin informs me that some British traders from Niagara have established a valuable store of Indian goods at Cunniat, a village standing on a creek of the same name within the territory of the United States. Johnson [Sir John Johnson, Superintendent of Indian Affairs in British North America] is at the head of the house. There are ten men engaged as guards to the traders and their stores. The transaction is insulting to the authority of the United States and contrary to a law of the territory which will commence with the New Year.[60]

Although the army was in a position to spy on the British agents and their posts, it was not strong enough to enforce the terms of the treaty, confine Indian hostilities, or evict the British from American territory. The army did succeed, however, in constantly charting new travel routes in the territory.

[54] *Harmar Papers,* Harmar to Heart, Vol. 28, Letter Book C, March 28, 1788.
[55] *Ibid.,* Harmar to McDowell, Vol. 29, Letter Book G, February 4, 1790.
[56] *Ibid.*
[57] *Ibid.*
[58] *Ibid.,* Harmar to Knox, December 4, 1790, Vol. 30.
[59] *Ibid.*
[60] *Ibid.*

Lieutenant Armstrong relates such an incident to Harmar in a letter dated December 29, 1788: "I returned from Post Vincennes a different route from that I took in going there and from the observations I made by attention to my compass and watch with the difference of latitude between this place and the post I conceive the distance not to exceed 60 or 70 miles. In this opinion I am not alone."[61]

Armstrong goes on to recommend,

> It would certainly be a great advantage to the public if a road could be blazed not exceeding this distance and at the same time avoid Silver Creek knobs and some other hills which may be done by crossing Silver Creek about 6 miles west of this garrison, and crossing Blue River above the barrens, cross the present blazed way near the Lick, and strike White River below the Forks where the land is high on both sides and not subject to overflow. Here we crossed in returning from the Post.[62]

Ordered to serve under a militia officer, Armstrong felt humiliated[63] and compared the inability of the militia to the ability of the Federal troops. He was quick to criticize the route taken by the militia officer. His return (under his own command) was, as inferred in his letter, far more practical and much shorter.

Part III: Other Duties of the Regiment

RIVER TRAVEL

A most unusual type of reconnaissance was requested of officers commanding posts along the Ohio River when Secretary of War Knox directed Harmar to report on immigration down the Ohio from Pittsburgh into the new territory. An actual count was made of the number of boats (and of the people and cattle on board them) that passed by the outposts on their way to "Limestone and Rapids."[64] From his officers' tabulations Harmar made the following reports to Knox: From the officer of the day's count, kept daily, from June 1, 1787 to December 9, 1787, the number bound for Kentucky consisted of 146 boats, 3,196 persons, 1,381 horses, 165 wagons, 171 cattle, 245 sheep, and twenty-four hogs.[65] During the winter months travel on the river ceased, and the count began again the following March. Harmar's next letter totals the number from December 9, 1787, to June 15, 1788: 308 boats, 6,320 persons, 2,824 horses, 515 cows, 600 sheep, nine hogs, and fifty-one wagons "passed the garrison bound for Limestone and the Rapids."[66] Harmar added "the emigration is almost incredible."[67]

[61] Armstrong to Harmar, Thornbrough, *Outpost on the Wabash, op. cit.*, p. 144.
[62] *Ibid.*
[63] *Ibid.*
[64] *Harmar Papers*, Harmar to Knox, June 15, 1788, Vol. 28, Letter Book C.
[65] *Ibid.*, Harmar to Knox, December 9, 1787, Vol. 28, Letter Book B.
[66] *Ibid.*, Harmar to Knox, June 15, 1788, Vol. 28, Letter Book C.
[67] *Ibid.*

Volume dropped off from June to December 1788: 208 boats, 3,406 people, 1,655 horses, 394 cows, 407 sheep, and 123 wagons passed the post on their way to "Limestone and the Rapids."[68] In the *United States Gazetteer,* printed in Philadelphia in 1795, Joseph Scott describes Limestone as a post town of Kentucky, situated on a creek on the south side of the Ohio River and a "general place of landing for those emigrants to Kentucky who pass down the Ohio." Scott describes Louisville as a "port of entry and post town of Kentucky pleasantly situated on a rich elevated plain at the rapids of the Ohio."

Captain Jonathan Heart describes emigrant-laden flatboats traveling down the Ohio River as he viewed them from Fort Harmar:

> We are very agreeably situated; the beauties of an opening spring added to the prospect on a great river where 5 to 10 Kentucky boats pass in a day each which carries three and four families with their cattle, horses, household furniture and one hundred and three of those boats passed since January 1 last—they will come from Fort Pitt to this place 200 miles in 48 hours and in one instance a boat came in less that 36 hours.[69]

In his military journal, Ebenezer Denny made the following observation: "Our fleet now consists of twelve small keels and batteaux, besides two large flats called Kentucky boats. The flats carry cattle, horses, etc.; the other troops and goods for the Indians. Ohio remarkable low—two pilots employed to keep ahead and point out the channel; notwithstanding, some of the boats frequently ground."[70]

The Kentucky boat was still negotiating the currents of the Ohio River in 1811 when Zadock Cramer published *The Navigator,* a book written for the inexperienced traveler who planned to leave Pittsburgh to go down the Ohio River by boat. Cramer said that a comfortable family boat should be thirty to forty feet long and, at a cost of about $1.25 per foot, should total about $35.00, excluding the extra cost for fireplace, pump, and forty feet of cable. He suggested that these flat-bottomed boats be well boarded up on the sides and roofed to within seven or eight feet of the bow. He added that Kentucky boats were best suited for high waters and, after the winter ice had melted and the rivers had gone down late in the summer, the keel boat was more suitable for navigating the Ohio River.

Samuel Cummings indicated that the Kentucky, keel, and other small craft had largely disappeared from the Ohio River by 1833, when he wrote the *Western Pilot.* "The number of small boats have, however, rapidly diminished since the introduction of steam boats; and the singular race of men who navigated them have almost entirely been driven from these large rivers," he said. His reference to "singular race of men who navigated them" may aptly be applied to the men of the 1st American Regiment.

Since the food, clothing, ammunition, reinforcements, and almost every other necessity of the regiment had to be transported by water, a major duty of the soldier in the corps was to build, repair, caulk, navigate, and master the river boats, and the river upon which the boats traveled with those supplies. The dependence upon water craft and water communication by the regiment between 1784–1791 was so immense that, no matter how minor a soldier's duty in connection with boats might have been, its overall contribution to the operation of the Federal corps is too significant to overlook.

Marauding Indians discovered the army to be most vulnerable when traveling on the water while ascending the Ohio, Wabash, or other rivers in heavily laden boats moving slowly against

For seven and a half years the underfed force barely survived. The Indians were constantly on the warpath, and the army was ill equipped. Finally on November 4, 1791, near present-day Fort

---

[68] Letter of Jonathan Heart to William Judd, date missing, Fort Harmar, Guthman Collection.
[69] *Ibid.*
[70] *Military Journal of Major Ebenezer Denny,* p. 261.

strong currents. The number of casualties and loss of provisions—excluding the two campaigns of 1790 and 1791—resulting from Indian attacks on river craft far exceeded all the other losses incurred during land skirmishes. Referring to an attack by Wabash Indians upon two keel boats under the command of Lieutenant Edward Spear about 150 miles below the rapids of the Ohio River in the Spring of 1789, Harmar told Knox: "The Indians have an immense advantage in attacking boats ascending the river, indeed there can be no possible security unless our parties are strong enough to afford a flank guard on the shore."[71] This, of course, was impossible with the limited number of men in the regiment.

In spite of inevitable danger while traveling by water, the army still found it to be the most practical method of transportation because of the speed, directness, and low cost. While en route with the regiment to Post Vincennes in June 1787, Harmar told Knox: "Considering the immense expense which the public would sustain by Hiring pack horses, and indeed the uncertainty of procuring them, and the delay attending it; these circumstances have induced me to determine upon going to Post St. Vincent by water."[72] Explaining that the cattle would be taken aboard Kentucky boats to the mouth of the Wabash River and then disembarked and driven along the margin of the river, he said "ascending the Wabash and driving the cattle will be attended with some difficulty."[73] Even so, he calculated that it would require seventy packhorses at half a dollar a day if they were to march overland so that his method was "infinitely less expensive."[74]

Harmar's orders, as recorded in the order books, for the embarkation of the troops and supplies make an interesting sequence:

> Orders, Camp below the Rapids of the Ohio July 6, 1787. The cattle, horses, and cows are to be immediately put on board 8 of the Kentucky boats—the two large keel boats are to be loaded with flour and whiskey. One small keel boat is to be loaded with flour—one captain, one subaltern, 2 sergeants, 2 corporals and 62 privates (One of whom is to be Caulker furnished with Oakum and hIs intruments) supplied with five days provisions, two days fresh and three days smoked meat and hard bread in the following allowance—85 pounds for every 100 weight of flour, are for this command and are to embark on board this fleet, and are to sail as soon as the boats are loaded—the men are to be distributed as follows:

6 men on board each Kentucky boat	48
5 men in each of the large Keel boats	10
4 men in the small Keel boat	4
2 in each canoe	4
total	66

> One of the small canoes is for an officer to visit the boats and to attend strictly to their being baled—the other is for to carry corn to feed the cattle—great attention must

[71] Harmar Papers, ibid.
[72] Ibid., Harmar to Knox, June 15, 1787, Letter Book.
[73] Ibid.
[74] Ibid.

be paid that the cattle are fed and watered regularly—the troops are to be furnished immediately with 29 rounds of ammunition per man.

Jos. Harmar[75]

Prior to embarking from Fort Harmar on the trip to Post Vincennes, Harmar issued preparatory orders. In January, a lieutenant was placed in charge of the preservation, caulking and repairing of the boats.[76] A raft was ordered reconditioned at Fort Harmar in May "for the purpose of conveying the troops."[77] And the quartermaster was assigned to reconditioning it.

When the regiment arrived at the rapids of the Ohio, Harmar issued orders to have the keel boats immediately launched and taken to the old encampment (about fifty yards above the garrison—Fort Finney), "there to be filled with water for their preservation. The Officer of the Day will pay attention to this matter."[78] On July seventh Harmar issued the following orders from his camp below the rapids:

> The three Kentucky boats are to be filled with troops—One keel boat is to be loaded with the Commissioners goods and Quartermaster stores—Three keel boats for officers baggage—One keel boat for Major Wyllys and Major Hamtramck's luggage—Two keel boats for the ordinance and military stores—The very large canoe for shells, salt, soap, candles, etc. A lesser canoe for soap, candles, etc. Captain Strong's canoe for his own baggage. Another keel boat to be loaded with flour and whiskey—The keel boat which is so much out of repair is to be lightly loaded with pipe clay or any other articles of little consequence—The remainder of the canoes are to be taken along, to serve as tenders or lighters.[79]

At evening roll call Harmar ordered the troops to move out early the next morning, and told the officers to remain in camp that night unless they had "particular business in Louisville."[80] Major Wyllys and Hamtramck were placed in charge of the preparations and ordered the necessary fatigue parties. At six o'clock the following morning (July 8) the troops filed onto the boats. "On board of each of the Kentucky boats there must be an officer who must order a relief every half hour, that the men may exert themselves in rowing, and be able to keep up with the keel boats."[81] On the tenth, from camp eight miles above Green River on the Indian shore, Harmar issued orders to have "Two cattle put on board one of the Kentucky boats for the use of this command and all the women are to go on board."[82]

Besides Kentucky boats and keel boats (long, flat-bottomed boats) and canoes there were also skiffs, rafts, barges, and pirogues. These craft were as important to the survival of the settlers and soldiers in the Northwest Territory as food and clothing. However, these same vessels were a sign of danger to the Indians. The Miami tribes, carefully scouting the steady stream of Kentucky boats loaded with families, cattle, and household belongings traveling the Ohio from Pittsburgh, sensed

[75] Ibid., Vol. 32, Order Books, 1784–88, July 6, 1787.
[76] Ibid., May 17, 1787.
[77] Ibid., May 23, 1787.
[78] Ibid., June 12, 1787.
[79] Ibid., July 7, 1787.
[80] Ibid.
[81] Ibid., July 10, 1787.
[82] Ibid.

the encroachment into "their" wilderness. British agents continually reminded them that these boats were bringing a type of people into their hunting grounds who would soon cut down the forests and drive away the wild herds. Although the British had ceded the Indian land to the United States at the Treaty of Paris, without consulting the tribal chiefs, agents of King George III continued to arouse hatred for the settlers among the tribes. The warriors sought to plunder and destroy as many of the boats as they could, singling them out because they alone were responsible for the influx of emigrants who would eventually bring an end to their native, uncultivated homeland of virgin forests.

OTHER CRAFTS

Army life in the wilderness required varied and unusual skills of the soldier, many of which have been touched on in other chapters. An order was issued by Josiah Harmar July 1, 1787: "Each company is to make and deliver to the Quarter Master fifty fathom of bark rope—the Quarter Master will give directions how to make it strong and substantial."[83]

Ropemaking, although serving an important need, can be taken in a light vein whereas "friendmaking"—making friends of the Indians—was a function of the highest importance. Undoubtedly many soldiers antagonized, mistreated, and brutally tormented the natives, thereby creating hatred rather than respect for the United States. The official policy was aimed at making allies rather than enemies. Harmar commended a subordinate officer August 7, 1790:

> You acted very properly in sending the soldier to instruct the cornplanter, and his people in the planting their fields of corn; I am very happy to hear that you did it and that they are so peaceable and well disposed towards the United States, and as I mentioned in my last two letters, you must use all your endeavor to cultivate friendship and harmony with them; but at the same time never be off your guard.[84]

Their mission as ambassadors of good will encompassed more than the Indian tribes as the army attempted to bring the good will of the United States into the interior settlements habited by new emigrants and long-established French-Canadian traders. Lawlessness was rife in many of the frontier villages, such as Kaskaskia, a southern Illinois settlement on the Mississippi River. Congress ordered the Secretary at War in 1786 to inform the inhabitants (who had complained about lawlessness) that a plan for a temporary government for the district was under consideration.[85]

Troops were ordered to Post Vincennes (Indiana) April 24, 1787, "to take immediate and efficient measures for dispossessing a body of men, who have, in a lawless and unauthorized manner taken possession of Post St. Vincent's, in defiance of the proclamation and authority of the United States."[86]

Not until October 5, 1787, did the Northwestern Territory have a government; at that time Arthur St. Clair became governor.[87] In the interim Spain was competing with the United States for emigrant settlements and promised many rewards to those settlers who purchased Spanish land west of the Mississippi River. The army was the government's only available instrument with which to

[83] Ibid.
[84] Ibid., Harmar to Jeffers, August 7, 1790, Vol. 29, Letter Book H.
[85] Journals of Congress, Vol. 11, August 24, 1786.
[86] Ibid., Vol. 12, April 24, 1787.
[87] Ibid., October 5, 1787.

preserve law and order on the frontier. The small force was dispatched and whenever possible squatters were dispossessed of the lands they had illegally seized, their huts were burned,[88] and lawless gangs of bandits were driven from the territory.[89] Describing his visit to Kaskaskia, Harmar said:

> On the 26th, at the request of the inhabitants, I assembled them and gave them advice to regulate their militia and obey their magistrates, etc., until Congress should be pleased to order a government for them. I have to remark that all these people are entirely unacquainted with what Americans call liberty. Trial by jury, etc., they are strangers to. A commandant with a few troops to give them orders is the best form of government for them; it is what they have been accustomed to.[90]

Major John Francis Hamtramck, whom Harmar left in charge at Post Vincennes, reported April 13, 1788:

> The government of this country has been in the Legras and Gamelin family for a long time to the great dissatisfaction of the people who presented me a petition some days ago where in they complained of the injustice of their court, in consequence of which I have dissolved the old court, ordered new magistrates to be elected and established new regulations for them to go by. Copy of which I have the honor to enclose. My code of laws will no doubt make you laugh but I hope you will consider that I'm neither a lawyer or a legislator.[91]

Harmar answered Hamtramck's letter three months later. "I observe that you had a total change of government at Post Vincennes. The copy of your regulations for the court has been perused, which as far as my knowledge extends in civil matters, I think to be very proper."[92]

Establishing and maintaining civil law and order, and acting in a diplomatic capacity with both Indians and settlers, were major tasks of the corps. Indian treaties were another area in which the army played a major role. This part was actually spelled out in the Congressional resolve of June 3, 1784—the same day Congress established the army: "Whereas it is necessary to expedite the holding of treaties with the Indian nations, *which it appears cannot be done but under the protection of an armed force.*"[93] Protection was only a portion of the army's contribution to the series of treaties that were held from 1784 to 1791. Five Indian Commissioners had been elected March 4, 1784,[94] and they were ordered to summon those units of the army assigned to them to the site where the treaty was going to be held[95] and allotted $15,000 to purchase rations and trade goods for the treaty. The army transported and protected the trade goods, as well as restored old Fort McIntosh, the site of the treaty (January 1785).

On August 7, 1786, Congress ordered the Indian department divided into two districts: southern (all nations south of the Ohio River) and northern (all other nations within the said territory and west of the Hudson River).[96] A superintendent was appointed for each district who was to "*regularly*

[88] *Harmar Papers,* Harmar to Carleton, April 23, 1785, Vol. 28, Letter Book A.
[89] *Ibid.,* Harmar to Doughty, October 3, 1785.
[90] Thornbrough, *op. cit.,* p. 51.
[91] *Ibid.,* p. 71.
[92] *Ibid.,* p. 96.
[93] *Journals of Congress,* Vol. 9, June 3, 1784.
[94] *Ibid.*
[95] *Ibid.*
[96] *Ibid.,* Vol. 11, August 7, 1786.

correspond with the secretary at war through whom all communication respecting the Indian department shall be made to Congress; and the superintendents are hereby directed to obey all instructions, which they shall, from time to time, receive from the said secretary at war."[97]

On July 21, 1787, Congress resolved that "the superintendent of Indian affairs for the northern department, and *in case he be unable to attend, then Colonel Josiah Harmar immediately proceed* to post St. Vincent's or some other place more convenient, *in his opinion,* for holding a treaty with the Wabash Indians, the Shawanese and other hostile tribes."[98] Harmar was instructed to tell the Indians that

> Congress is sincerely disposed to promote peace and friendship between their citizens and the Indians that, to this end, he is sent to invite them in a friendly manner to a treaty with the United States, to hear their complaints, to know the truth and the causes of their quarrels with those frontier settlers, and having invited those Indians to the treaty, he shall make strict inquiry into the causes of their uneasiness and hostile proceedings, and form a treaty of peace with them, if it can be done on terms consistent with the honor and dignity of the United States.[99]

Arriving at St. Vincent, September 5, 1787, Harmar reported:

> The troops were all new clothed, and made a truly military appearance. I was determined to impress upon the Indians as much as possible the majesty of the United States, and at the same time that they were informed that it was the wish of Congress to live in peace and friendship with them, likewise to let them know that if they persisted in being hostile that a body of troops would march to their towns and sweep them off the face of the earth.[100]

To the regiment, "treating with the Indians" also meant building council rooms,[101] escorting contractors' boats laden with provisions for the treaty,[102] or transporting the commissioners and provisions on their own boats. To some of the officers, it meant participating in the conferences as witnesses and signing the treaties in that capacity. In effect, the Indian Department worked under the supervision of the War Department. It could not have functioned without it. In fact, the Indian department was another branch of the small American military force. Ineffectual, functioning at times more for the benefit of the various states than for the Federal government, the Indian Department nevertheless did serve a constructive purpose. The army learned it had to deal with Indian problems, not as diplomats, but as a physical force, better equipped and more knowledgeably trained in Indian tactics. Unfortunately, the lesson was not learned until after the defeat of St. Clair. However, in 1794, Wayne was able to utilize the experience of the 1st and 2nd regiments plus the maps of the surveyors—and this time win a victory.

[97] *Ibid.,* Vol. 12, July 12, 1787.
[98] *Ibid.*
[99] *Ibid.*
[100] Thornbrough, *op. cit.,* p. 51.
[101] *Harmar Papers,* Garrison Orders, Vol. 33, June 12, 1788.
[102] *Ibid.*

Army weapons are of particular interest, as are accouterments and other accessories. Carefully documented material from records of the period present an extremely interesting and new and revealing insight into the arms of the 1st Regiment. This chapter, with the profuse illustrations of actual material, will be of particular interest to the weapon-collecting fraternity.

Chapter 6

Part I: Small Arms

Although America's manpower was limited, its source of firepower was overwhelmingly unlimited. On January 3, 1784, Henry Knox proudly told Congress that his mind was "filled with rapture" to think of the large quantities of cannon, which he labeled "War trophies," that had been "wrested by the hand of virtue from the arm outstretched to oppress it."[1] The United States had inherited a huge supply of weapons from the Revolution. It is logical, therefore, that the Federal corps was equipped with the same weapons that their Continental army predecessors had been issued several years earlier.

During the Revolutionary war many thousands of these weapons had been purchased in Europe, with the aid of France and Holland, and either shipped directly to the United States or to ports in the West Indies where they were then transferred to ships bound for America. Hundreds of English and Hessian weapons had been captured during the war and reissued to American troops. Early in the war contracts were given by the various branches of the Committee of Safety to their local gunsmiths to manufacture muskets patterned after the British Brown Bess. Continental armorers and local gunsmiths continued to manufacture new muskets or reassemble old weapons from existing parts until the end of the war. Teams of officers were dispatched throughout the countryside periodically during the war to purchase privately owned local firearms.

This heterogeneous group of muskets, rifles, fusils, carbines, pistols, fowling pieces, etc., all requiring different caliber ammunition and different sized bayonets, ended up, after the war, stacked like cordwood, in various arsenals scattered throughout the thirteen states.

As the last remaining troops were discharged at New Windsor and West Point in 1783, their arms were gathered and stored in wooden shacks high above the Hudson River along with thousands of other weapons and accouterments that had never been issued, but had remained in storage throughout the war. In addition to West Point, the makeshift repositories at Springfield and Rhode Island and the several throughout upper New York state, Philadelphia, Virginia, Fort Pitt, Carlisle, Pennsylvania, and the Carolinas were bulging with war surplus materials when the Revolution ended.

---

[1] *Knox Papers,* Knox to Congress, January 3, 1784.

In his report to Congress in 1784 Henry Knox said that the storage facilities at West Point were not adequate. "The small arms have been selected and an arsenal is preparing," he continued, "in which such of them as are in good repair may be placed in the manner best tending to their preservation." He went on to point out that "the many defective arms demanding repair want attention, but the arms general do not want much labor to put them in perfect order."

Knox urged Congress to take measures to preserve the vast store of weapons. "They are," he said, "too valuable to remain neglected, viewed from a political or commercial medium." He asked for twenty armorers to clean and restore the weapons, estimating they would be able to complete their job in six months. He then proudly suggested that Congress, after studying his tabulation of artillery, small arms, and accouterments, "review this ample return of war-like stores and compare it with the scanty one of 1775."[1a]

Congress could not afford to properly maintain that vast arsenal of war surplus materials. Deposited in dilapidated, temporary repositories, they were unprotected prey to vandals, thieves, and the weather; and tons of shot and shell rusted in neglected idleness at the various furnaces in which they were cast. Ironically, the bankrupt nation, so wealthy in armament, could not afford sufficient personnel to maintain its treasure, thus allowing time and the elements to achieve what the British army could not—the destruction of an immense accumulation of eighteenth-century firepower.

Even so, the supply of Revolutionary war weapons lasted and was used by American troops well past General Anthony Wayne's victory at Fallen Timbers. Captain John Doughty, in command at West Point after the Revolution ended, summed up the War Office attitude toward caring for the weapons when he was unsuccessfully requesting coopers and materials to repack the powder at that repository in 1784: "The war office has favored me with four premises but no performance."[1b]

As early as 1785, Henry Knox had urged that permanent arsenals be established throughout the United States. Using the vast quantities of war surplus as his illustration, Knox said that the United States "had the opportunity to make a perfect arrangement of the means upon which their independence may ultimately depend." However, the establishment of national armories was not ordered until April 2, 1794, and the purpose at that time was primarily the manufacture of new weapons, not the preservation of surplus arms.

Congress realized its problem and admitted so in its study of the Department of War in 1788. "The ordnance department," the report read, "is important and interesting to the union. The ordnance, arms, ammunition and all the numerous appendages and complex apparatus belonging thereto, in possession of the United States, are highly valuable and require an incessant attention to their preservation."[1c]

All of this background material points to the fact that it would be virtually impossible today, unless absolute documentation accompanied a particular specimen, to identify any weapon as one that had been *used* during the Revolution. Available records listing military weapons that were owned by the United States and subsequently issued between 1784 and 1795 clearly reveals that most specimens classified by collectors today as having been carried during the Revolution actually remained unissued in racks in one of the many repositories in the United States during the war. This includes only those weapons actually purchased by the various government agencies during the course of the war—not those owned privately.

Thousands of French, English, and Hessian muskets remained in storage, without U.S. surcharge, until *after* 1784 when a Federal armorer cleaned, possibly repaired, but most assuredly stamped or branded "US," "United States," or "U States" (to indicate government ownership) on them before they were issued to the troops. An advertisement that appeared in the *New York Gazetteer and Country Journal,* June 21, 1785, illustrates the point:

[1a] *Journals of Congress, op. cit.,* Vol. 13, p. 123.
[1b] Doughty to Knox, Oct. 9, 1784, Knox Papers.
[1c] *Journals of Congress, op. cit.,* Vol. 13, p. 121.

Wanted, a number of regular bred armorers, to be employed at West Point, in repairing, cleaning and STAMPING the arms belonging to the public. Any person disposed to engage, may know the terms by applying to the subscriber, at the War-Office or at No. 60 Cherry Street. Samuel Hodgdon, Commissary Military Stores.

Invoices to the United States from gunsmith Joseph Cranch, who was working at West Point in March 1791, charged 2¢ to stamp locks and 2¢ to stamp barrels on guns he was cleaning and repairing from the storage racks.

Approximately 15,000[2] muskets, rifles, smooth rifles, carbines, pistols, rampart arms, wall pieces, blunderbusses, and other small arms were cleaned and repaired at West Point between 1785 and 1792. Connecticut, New Jersey, and New York enlistees were issued their weapons at that highland arsenal on their way to the frontier. Additional quantities of that same supply of weapons were packed in cases marked "US," insulated against damage by pieces of unusable tentage which were tucked securely around the packed pieces inside the wooden crates. They were then shipped by boat down the Hudson River to New York where they were transferred to other vessels and delivered to the quartermaster at Philadelphia. At this juncture they were either forwarded to the troops already stationed at the frontier in the northwest, who for one of many reasons needed new firearms, or to those troops in the Southwestern Territory guarding against the Creek Nation.

West Point also supplied the Revenue cutters and coastal fortifications which guarded the Atlantic shoreline. Recruits from Pennsylvania and garrisons on both the southwestern and northwestern frontiers were also supplied by the repositories in Philadelphia. Both arsenals, whenever there was need, supplied volunteer militia and levy groups from Pennsylvania and Virginia (Kentucky) during the Indian campaigns. Fortunately, the supply was large as the loss of weapons was extremely high during the 1784–1791 period. During the St. Clair campaign alone, approximately 1,200 muskets[3] or more had been lost. Over this seven-year period, quantities were stolen by marauding Indians raiding supply boats on the Ohio River or attacking isolated parties of regulars escorting supplies overland, guarding surveyors, etc. Many of the Federal recruits had never owned guns prior to their enlistment in the corps and their lack of care and misuse rendered hundreds of muskets unserviceable. Many others were stolen, along with clothing and other military articles, by the scores of men who deserted into the wilderness to escape the balance of their military commitment. Few were recovered. Those who were apprehended had usually sold their government property before their captors could bring them back to the post for court-martial. Often, although they had stolen and sold government property, the men were treated with leniency and retained in service to fulfill quotas.

In addition, cases of muskets and ammunition were lost overboard, or sank with the flatboats, during the fall and spring seasons when, although the Ohio River was high and its water turbulent, the army was forced to ship badly needed supplies. A further drain on the supply was the ordnance and small arms issued to often defenseless settlements in the remote Illinois and Indiana country. Local frontier militia units were frequently armed with government property when they undertook Indian reprisal raids. Friendly Indians were given small arms as token of friendship and often, when they agreed to ally themselves with the United States against unfriendly tribes, were completely equipped by the government.

The above demands, combined with the staggering loss of weapons inadequately stored and cared for, had by 1792 considerably diminished the tremendous arsenal inherited after the Revolution. During that same year the Uniform Militia Act was passed. It required white male American citizens between the ages of eighteen and forty-five to equip themselves with a musket, a bayonet, a belt, two spare flints, a knapsack, and a cartridge box. The cartridge box was to contain at

[2]*West Point Waste Books* No. 1, 2, and 3, 1784–1792, USMA Library, West Point.
[3]*Diary of Winthrop Sargent,* p. 265, *Ohio Archeological and Historical Society Publications,* Columbus, Ohio, Vol. 33, 1924.

least twenty-four cartridges, "suited to the bore of his musket or firelock." While those who owned rifles could appear for muster with them instead of muskets, they were required to carry a powder horn, a shot pouch containing twenty balls "suited to the bore of his rifle," and a knapsack. The law projected that within five years the bores of all muskets would have to become standardized: "they shall be of bores sufficient for balls of the eighteenth part of the pound." The projection did not include rifles for the militia five years hence.

Congress, looking ahead to 1797, saw the end of the Revolutionary war arms surplus and wisely demanded standardization. Although the law clearly specified each man was to provide his own equipment, it is probable that most states requisitioned weapons and accouterments from the Federal arsenals.

RIFLES

The rifle was one of the most valuable frontier tools. Armed with muskets, the American soldier fought a losing battle against the Indians in guerrilla warfare. He fought, as he was taught, from the pages of Steuben's manual.

The frontiersman, on the other hand, had learned the value of the rifle and with it not only procured food for his family, but made the Indian fear his deadly aim. Men of the Kentucky and Pennsylvania frontier settlements along the Ohio River had not only been able to survive the angry depredations of the Indians but could retaliate with equal ferocity and capabilities in the art of woodland warfare.

The rifle was the frontier settler's prime requisite to successful combat. Rifles conformed as a weapon to the Indian-style tactics. Musketry did not.

Lewis Nicola said in his "Treaties of Military Exercise Calculated for the Use of the Americans," published in Philadelphia in 1776: "—there is a species of war, with which I am unacquainted, that is, bush-fighting; but as this may be very necessary in so woody a country as this, all the troops should be instructed therein." Nicola further said that riflemen should be substituted for grenadiers in each battalion. About the rifle he said:

> Using rifles in war is certainly savage and cruel, but the Americans may alledge in their defence the law of absolute necessity, which supersedes all other obligations; for they, undisciplined and unused to arms, are compelled to make use of every advantage Providence has put in their power, in order to effectually resist regular and well-disciplined troops.

Nicola was preaching guerrilla warfare with rifles as the combat weapon early in the Revolution. Rifle battalions were used successfully against the British, but unfortunately these successful lessons were never applied to the Federal corps in its fight against the Indians. The proven success of the rifle during the Revolution, and by those settlers living on the Ohio River frontier settlements, was completely overlooked by Knox, Harmar, and St. Clair.

West Point returns indicate that there were only six rifles on hand at that post after the Revolution ended. Fort Pitt returns of 1785 show 104 rifles in store, and Henry Knox's inventory of U.S. repositories in 1792 indicates there were 5 rifles and 20 smooth rifles at West Point, 110 rifles in store at Philadelphia, 64 rifles (plus 4 damaged rifles) at Fort Washington, 41 rifles (plus 11 damaged rifles) at Fort Hamilton, 34 rifles at Fort Pitt, and 16 rifles at Fort Franklin. The number of rifles listed on the returns, in comparison to muskets, and even fusils, reflects the negative attitude of the military mind in the eighteenth century about the effectiveness of the rifled long arm. Even though the rifle was successful as a combat weapon during the Revolution, particularly at Kings Mountain and Saratoga, the American military tactician did not assign it a prominent role in the Federal corps.

Prior to his expedition in 1790, Harmar was told by Knox that "as it is probable most of the militia may be armed with rifles,[4] *which are certainly not good arms in a close fight,* it may perhaps be proper for you to attempt to persuade some of them to arm themselves with the spare muskets you have in store."[5] Rifles were not considered adequate weapons for close-range warfare (the type carried on against Indians). Anthony Wayne told Knox, when it was feared that Spain was arming the Southern Indian tribes in 1790, that the Creeks had demanded from the Spanish 6,000 of "that kind of smooth bore arms that *suited* the Indians."[6]

One year earlier, Wayne told Knox that even though the British attributed the loss of Burgoyne's army largely to rifles, he felt that they were an improper arm for the army.[7] He said, "Maybe a few of them in the hands of expert marksmen might occasionally be serviceable for small desultory parties when covered by thick woods and behind works, and supportd by troops *properly* armed."[8] He suggested at that time that the Creek Indians were convinced that smooth bore muskets were superior in war and had applied to the Spanish government for them.[9] Knox replied that "my opinion entirely coincides with yours as to the utility of rifles."[10]

The approximate number of rifles in the possession of the 1st Regiment is difficult to determine. A private was court-martialed in 1785 for stealing a rifle at Fort McIntosh.[11] Complaining about the difficulty of filling the New Jersey quota of recruits in 1786, Harmar suggested to Knox: "I beg leave to submit to your consideration whether it would not be advisable to recommend to Congress that the corps should be augmented by recruiting 200 or 250 riflemen."[12] He added that it would not be difficult to enlist these riflemen on the frontiers, and "if the Indians should incline to be hostile, the nature of the service I would suppose would require a number of expert woodsmen attached to the corps."[13]

Knox, in a letter to Harmar in 1786, agreed: "As it is important almost in any event to have riflemen attached to the troops who shall act on the frontiers—could you not pick out a sufficient number of good marksmen from the several companies of your regiment and form them into one company of light infantry or riflemen? I request your opinion on this subject."[14]

Comparing the opinions of Wayne and Knox, in their letters of 1790, to those letters between Harmar and Knox in 1786, it seems that rifles and riflemen served a special purpose only under special circumstances during a campaign; but that the infantryman, in close-quarter or open field fighting, was thought to be much more effective with his faster, easier-loading musket. The lack of government rifles was further evident when Harmar wrote to Knox about raising riflemen for the

---

[4] Instructions from President Washington to the Governor of the Northwest Territory, October 6, 1789. Congress called on the Militia September 29, 1789 for the protection of the frontiers, to act in conjunction with federal troops: "The militia are to arm and equip themselves, but to be furnished with public ammunition if necessary." (*American State Papers,* Vol. 1, Indian Affairs.)
[5] *Ibid.,* Knox to Harmar, August 24, 1790.
[6] *Knox Papers,* Wayne to Knox, March 20, 1790.
[7] *Ibid.,* December 25, 1789.
[8] *Ibid.*
[9] *Ibid.*
[10] *Ibid.,* February 7, 1790.
[11] *Harmar Papers,* Orders, Fort McIntosh, August 13, 1785, Vol. 32, Order Books 1784–88.
[12] *Ibid.,* Harmar to Knox, March 6, 1786, Vol. 28, Letter Book A.
[13] *Ibid.*
[14] *Ibid.,* Knox to Harmar, March 11, 1786, Vol. 3.

regiment: "They are wanting rifles."[15] Harmar told Ensign John Armstrong, who was recruiting in Philadelphia in July, 1785, for "30 stout able-bodied men," to fill the Pennsylvania quota: "My ideas respecting riflemen are these—I should wish to have not more than twenty-five rifles in the corps—and to draft from the infantry that number of men, who understood the use of them."[16] Qualifying this statement, he went on to say, "You'll observe in the first place, the corps should be all infantry—but I would have the rifles at hand, and occasionally use them, in which case you would stand a good chance to have the command."[17] In almost the same words, he wrote to John Dickinson a week later: "If about five-and-twenty rifles could be obtained to occasionally arm that number of infantry, I should think it advisable. I have ordered Ensign Armstrong to receive your Excellency's instructions, and when he has recruited thirty stout, able-bodied men to rejoin the corps."[18]

There were about 342 experienced riflemen under St. Clair during his campaign: 300 militia and forty-two in the levies.[19] Those particular militia riflemen, from the district of Kentucky, consisted for the most part of frontiersmen whose survival depended upon their ability as hunters and therefore came armed with their own hunting rifles. On March 3, 1791, Congress called for 2,000 levies to be raised from the different states for six months to supplement the regular army—if St. Clair were unable to enlist enough levies by July 10, 1791, he was then to call upon the militia of Pennsylvania, Virginia, and the Kentucky district. There were forty-two riflemen in one battalion of levies, under the command of Lieutenant James Rhea of New Jersey.[20] Many of those rifles were private property (and were in need of repair when the men reported for duty at Fort Washington).[21] That the rifles were the individual property of the militia is further borne out in correspondence between Knox and Richard Butler in preparation for St. Clair's campaign: "Arms and equipment for the additional battalion are at Fort Pitt," Knox told General Butler. He went on, "I leave the 100 riflemen to your judgment. The arrangement you make of paying for the rifles in case of being lost, and also of their being repaired is right; but *each person ought to have something for the use of it.*"[22]

During the 1790 Harmar campaign the militia riflemen were issued a half a pound of powder and one pound of lead, and the infantrymen carrying muskets were issued twenty-four cartridges.[23] Returns indicate, also, that riflemen carried powder horns, bullet molds, and shot pouches. Few references indicate that rifles did belong to the government. One example, however, states that Ebenezer Denny, Harmar's adjutant, sent Lieutenant Thomas Doyle a "new rifle, complete,"[24] on March 6, 1787, from Fort Harmar. (Doyle was then stationed at the Rapids of the Ohio.)

Knox changed his mind about the effectiveness of a rifle corps after the defeat of Arthur St. Clair in 1791. Proposing a newly organized military establishment, Knox suggested in December, 1791, an army consisting of 4,168 noncommissioned officers and privates including one regiment of infantry to consist entirely of riflemen (912 men).[25] Washington followed the suggestions of Knox; on December 27, 1792, he ordered the reorganization of the army. Called "the legion," it was divided

---

[15] *Ibid.*, Harmar to Knox, Vol. 28, Letter Book A.

[16] *Ibid.*, Harmar to Armstrong, July 25, 1786, Vol. 28, Letter Book A.

[17] *Ibid.*

[18] *Journal of Captain Jonathan Heart,* edited by Consul Willshire Butterfield, Joel Munsell's Sons, Albany, 1885, Harmar to Dickinson, August 1, 1785, p. 82.

[19] St. Clair, op. cit., p. 197.

[20] *Ibid.*

[21] *Ibid.,* p. 199.

[22] *American State Papers, ibid.,* Knox to Butler, June 30, 1790, p. 190.

[23] *Military Journal of Major Ebenezer Denny,* p. 347.

[24] *Ibid.,* p. 301.

[25] *American State Papers, ibid.,* Knox to Washington, December 26, 1791, p. 199.

into four sub-legions, and consisted of 4,120 noncommissioned officers and privates. Each sub-legion was composed of one company of artillery, two battalions of infantry, one battalion of riflemen and one troop of dragoons.[26] Riflemen continued to become more acceptable as tactical units and proved themselves at the Battle of New Orleans on January 8, 1815.

Rifles were given to the Indians as gifts. Infrequent references in the records indicate that they were not given to arm the friendly tribes, as were muskets, but were placed in the category of a luxury item, such as a silver arm band, soap, jewelry, etc. Ensign Kingsbury was given permission by Harmar to give provisions, one "public rifle," a little powder, and a light boat or canoe to the Chicasaw and Choctaw chiefs from New York visiting Post Vincennes in 1787.[27] Listed on the returns for sundry articles "being the residue of what were purchased for the Indian treaties in the years 1785 and 1786" are 100 flints, twenty-six gunlocks, and two "best *brass* bore rifles."[28] It is difficult to imagine rifles, which required much more attention in cleaning than smooth bore muskets, surviving for any length of time in the hands of the Indians, who were notorious for their lack of care of firearms.

FUSILS

Fusils were in use during the period of the 1st American Regiment. Not popular with American forces during the Revolution, these weapons were not even prescribed by Baron von Steuben in his regulations of 1779 and only occasionally show up on returns of surplus Revolutionary war materials after the peace of 1783.[29] They do show up in company returns of the 1st American Regiment[30] and in Harmar's orders: "Captain Ferguson is to deliver up the short fusees of his company and to receive the *long French muskets* in lieu of them. The officers are to be armed with these short fusees and parade with them instead of the espontoon."[31]

When Colonel Henry Jackson was organizing the Massachusetts quota of additional troops authorized by Congress in 1786, he asked Knox: "Are the company officers to be armed with fusees or espontoons? If fusees I wish they may be supplied with them out of the public store than paying for them."[32] The former Revolutionary war commanding officer added, "the fusee is much more material and military I think than the *espontoon*."[33]

Prior to St. Clair's expedition, Knox wrote to General Richard Butler, second in command of the campaign: "There are no light fusees for the levie officers. The French arms which have been forwarded are not heavy; and I should presume would answer the purpose of all the officers very well."[34] He added in the same letter an interesting sidelight: "The colours for levies have not been deemed essential; but at your request they shall be forwarded."[35]

The fusil was merely a lighter version of the standard military musket and would have weighed roughly twenty-five percent less. Possibly Secretary at War Knox was referring to the French carbines that were listed on the returns.[36]

---

[26] *Ibid.*, p. 41, Knox to Congress, December 27, 1792.
[27] *Harmar Papers,* Harmar to Kingsbury, Vol. 28, Letter Book B, Post Vincennes, Sept. 23, 1787.
[28] *Ibid.*, Return of Indian Articles, Knox letter of Aug. 2, return dated July 22, 1786, signed George Nixon.
[29] *American State Papers,* Vol. 1, Military Affairs, pp. 44–60.
[30] *Harmar Papers,* Inspection Return of Captain Jonathan Heart's company, French Creek, May 27, 1787, Heart Letter, June 1, 1787.
[31] *Ibid.*, Garrison Orders, Fort McIntosh, July 19, 1786, Vol. 32, Order Books 1784–88.
[32] *Knox Papers,* Colonel Henry Jackson to Knox, February 25, 1787.
[33] *Ibid.*
[34] *American State Papers,* Vol. 1, Indian Affairs, June 9, 1791, Knox to Butler, p. 188.
[35] *Ibid.*
[36] *Ibid.*, Vol. 1, Military Affairs, *West Point Waste Books*, No. 1, 2 and 3, pp. 44–60.

FIREARMS OF THE INDIAN

Reporting to Secretary at War Knox after an unsuccessful peace mission with the Indians of the Northwest, former Revolutionary war Artillery Colonel (now Government Emissary) Thomas Proctor told of an incident at a council meeting of the chiefs of the Turtle tribe of the Seneca Nation. When he arrived at Buffalo Creek, thirty-five miles from Niagara, where Red Jacket and other chiefs resided, Proctor and his party were saluted with a two-pound swivel gun. The gun, however, was overloaded and upset with its carriage when fired.[37]

It has already been noted that Spain was arming the Southern Indian tribes with smooth bore muskets[38] and the British were supplying the Northern tribes with all the necessities of war.[39] Indians had become accustomed to using the white man's weapons (but not his tactics) in warfare. Thomas Rhea, an American who had been taken captive by the Indians and was confined at Sandusky, Ohio, made a point of this fact in his testimony to Congress June 30, 1791. He told of the British agents, Captain Elliott and Colonel Mckee of the Indian Department, Colonel Joseph Brandt (a Mohawk Chief and British Ally), and British Army officers Captain Banbury and Silvie having "stores of goods with arms, ammunition and provisions, which they issued to the Indians in great abundance."[40] He said the Indians set off "fully equipped to head off the forces of the United States near the upper Miami Towns."[41] However, Rhea observed, there was a large body of "wild" Indians that had bows and arrows and refused to accept guns, preferring their own weapons.[42] Rhea said that Simon Girty, a renegade American, who supplied the Indians with supplies in trade for furs, was also there. An eleven-year-old boy, captured by the Indians in 1792, described Girty as wearing a silver-mounted pistol stuck in his belt on each side and at his left a short, broad dirk.[43]

The misuse of Indian firearms is understandable since Indian philosophy entailed no thought of the future—no hoarding of food, no preservation of clothing or weapons. As long as the musket fired, most Indians would not have given any thought to preserving its mechanical capabilities for the future. This attitude did not change throughout the Indian wars of the nineteenth century.

The British must have supplied many thousands of Brown Bess muskets to their Indian allies. Stolen and captured weapons and those obtained in trade for furs also added to the Indian arsenal.

Fur companies distributed hundreds of cheaply made fowling pieces to the Great Lakes Indian in exchange for their valuable furs. These weapons resembled the finer European fowlers of the period except the traders specified that the guns for the Indian trade should be as cheaply made as possible. Long and slender, these nonmilitary muskets were often decorated with a silver or brass escutcheon on the wrist of the stock (just behind the barrel on the upper portion of the stock). Later, in the nineteenth century, Indian weapons were highly decorated with brass tacks, beadwork, and other ornate applications.

[37] *American State Papers,* Proctor to Knox, June 7, 1791, Vol. 1, Indian Affairs, p. 155.
[38] *Knox Papers, op. cit.,* roll 26—No. 3.
[39] *Ibid.,* roll 18, David Duncan to Thomas Hutchins, March 28, 1786.
[40] *American State Papers, ibid.,* Testimony of Thomas Rhea, June 30, 1791, p. 196.
[41] *Ibid.*
[42] *Ibid.*
[43] Consul Willshire Butterfield, *History of the Girtys,* Robert Clarke & Co., Cincinnati, 1890, p. 269.

Part II: Edged Weapons

Both the Indian warrior and the American Federal soldier carried weapons other than guns into battle. Unlike firearms, these other lethal tools of war were designed for close contact and, depending upon which weapon was used, were meant to effect mortal puncture, cut, or contusion wounds. When Congress resolved on July 18, 1775, that the United Colonies of North America would form militia companies consisting of all able-bodied men between the ages of sixteen and forty-five, it specified that each infantryman would be furnished with "a good musket, that will carry an ounce ball, with a *bayonet,* steel ramrod, worm, priming wire and brush, fitted thereto, a *cutting sword or tomahawk*, a cartridge box containing twenty-three rounds, twelve flints and a knapsack."[44]

In 1776 Massachusetts resolved that its infantry soldiers would arm themselves thus: "Each man furnish himself with a good firearm and *bayonet* fitted to the same, or instead of a bayonet, a *hatchet or tomahawk*, a cartouch-box, knapsack and blanket."[45] (It is interesting to note that in 1775 the men were to "be furnished" and in 1776 they would "furnish themselves"; and that by 1776 the sword was no longer required.)

Steuben's regulations stipulated, in 1779, that "the arms and accoutrements of the officers, noncommissioned officers, and soldiers should be uniform throughout. The officers who exercise their function on horseback, are to be armed with *swords,* the platoon officers with *swords* and *espontoons,* the noncommissioned officers with *swords, firelocks* and *bayonets,* and the soldiers with firelocks and *bayonets.*"[46]

Connecticut's General Assembly passed a resolution November 29, 1780, raising 575 able-bodied men who were to furnish themselves with their own equipment. Each recruit was to be allowed fifteen shillings for each gun with a bayonet, four shillings for each cartouch box, six shillings for each knapsack, and four shillings for each blanket.[47]

West Point returns of 1783 indicated that there were, in surplus storage, spears, swords, horsemen's sabers, tomahawks, bill hooks, bayonets, cutlasses, and espontoons.[48] It is interesting to note that there were 10,455 good bayonets, 2,719 damaged bayonets, compared to only 474 swords, 114 horsemen's sabers, forty-five tomahawks, thirty damaged swords, and 1,023 sword blades.[49] The West Point returns of 1793 indicated that there were, in storage, only 1,743 bayonets and *still* 389 swords, only 2,617 damaged bayonets, and *still* sixty-two damaged swords.[50]

The infantryman's sword had given way, early in the Revolution, to the bayonet. Recruiting specifications seldom mentioned swords as a part of the infantryman's equipment after 1775. However, the importance of the bayonet as both a tactical and defensive infantry weapon became more prominent as officers such as Steuben and Anthony Wayne taught its efficiency and required its service as a major weapon. Wayne had said, before the Battle of Brandywine: "I also wish to exchange a number of rifles for muskets and bayonets—I don't like rifles—I would almost as soon face an enemy with a good musket and a bayonet without ammunition as with ammunition without a

---

[44] *Journals of Congress,* Vol. 1, p. 159.
[45] *Resolves of the General Assembly of Massachusetts Bay,* Boston, 1776, B. Edes, Printer.
[46] Steuben, Baron von, *Regulations for the Order and Discipline of the Troops of the United States,* Styner & Cist, Philadelphia, 1779.
[47] "At a general assembly of the Governor and Company of the State of Connecticut, Holden at Hartford, on the 29th day of November, A.D. 1780," printed by Hudson & Goodwin (Hartford) (broadside).
[48] *West Point Ordnance Return,* December 28, 1783, USMA Library.
[49] *Ibid.*
[50] *American State Papers,* Vol. 1, Military Affairs, pp. 47–48.

bayonet."[51] General Washington suggested precisely this to Wayne when planning the strategy for the assault upon Stony Point: "This party is to be preceded by a vanguard of prudent and determined men well commanded, who are to remove obstructions, secure the sentries and drive in the guard. *They are to advance (the whole of them) with fixed bayonets and muskets unloaded.*"[52]

Steuben did not even mention the sword as part of the infantryman's equipment in his regulations, and Josiah Harmar used those regulations faithfully for the training of the Federal corps.

Major Jonathan Heart, who, during the Revolution, had participated in those engagements in which the bayonet played a major role, was killed leading a bayonet charge in a rear guard action of the 2nd U.S. Regiment who were attempting to protect the retreating forces of Arthur St. Clair during the disastrous defeat November 4, 1791. Consul Butterfield said, "During the engagement, Major Heart handled his men with consummate skill and bravery. He led them in person against the enemy, and put a number to flight through the energetic use of the *bayonet.*"[53] Denny described the use of the bayonet in that same engagement: "The battalions in the rear charged several times and forced the savages from their shelter, but they always turned with the battalions and fired upon them back; indeed they seemed not to fear anything we could do. They could skip out of reach of the *bayonet* and return, as they pleased."[54] An accounting of the battle that appeared in the *Columbian Centinel* published in Boston, December 24, 1791, described events during the battle more vividly:

> The Indians charged our troops, tomahawk in hand, and must have suffered considerably from the bayonets of our troops.... After Major Heart, of the 2nd U.S. Regiment was killed, Captain Phelan became commanding officer of the regiment with which he made a third charge; but fell in it, as did both of his subaltern officers.

In conclusion, we can say that the bayonet was the primary edged weapon of the U.S. infantry soldier during the period 1784–1791.

SWORDS

Infantry officers and noncommissioned officers, unlike the men they commanded, carried swords, as did artillery officers and noncommissioned officers. Artillery and infantry swords were both shorter than those of the dragoon. Private soldiers in the artillery carried muskets, or if available, swords, carbines or light muskets, spears, and pistols.[55] Officers, noncommissioned officers, and enlisted personnel of the militia cavalry all carried long-bladed swords in preference to firearms. The sword, the eighteenth-century dragoon discovered, was a much more effective weapon than a firearm, although, when available, mounted soldiers carried carbines or musketoons[56] and heavy pistols. Cavalry officers also carried long-barreled pistols.

Since most fashionable eighteenth-century gentlemen carried handsomely crafted small swords

[51] Charles J. Stille, *Major General Anthony Wayne,* J. B. Lippincott Co., Philadelphia, Pa., 1893, p. 118.
[52] *Ibid.*
[53] *Journal of Captain Jonathan Heart,* Biographical Sketch.
[54] *Military Journal of Major Ebenezer Denny,* p. 370. This passage indicates the poor choice of weapons for Indian warfare—the rifle and tomahawk would have been more effective.
[55] *West Point Waste Book,* #2, April 5, 1790, USMA Library.
[56] *Harmar Papers,* Garrison Orders, Fort McIntosh, July 19, 1786, Vol. 32, Order Books, 1784–88.

(called court swords) as part of their attire and when hunting carried even smaller edged weapons, just as elegant, called hunting swords, they brought these same fashionable weapons to war with them in 1775. Possibly because he attended a Quaker school as a boy, Josiah Harmar did not purchase his sword until 1775 when he enlisted as a captain in the 1st Pennsylvania Battalion. His 1794 ledger contains an entry: "An old silver-mounted small sword bought in the year 1775 worth now about 10 pounds to be added to the account of military furniture."[57]

TOMAHAWKS

War clubs and tomahawks had fulfilled the requirements of the Indian warrior's surprise and ambush tactics for centuries. Remaining almost constant in style from the seventeenth through the nineteenth centuries, the war club gradually degenerated by 1840, into a highly decorated ceremonial object and is rarely mentioned or pictured in battle accounts of the late eighteenth century. Tomahawks, on the other hand, remained important sidearms to the Indian until the mid-nineteenth century when open plains and repeating rifles superseded them as tools of war. Battleaxes (roughly fashioned stones fastened to wooden handles) had been useful weapons and tools even in prehistoric times. These heads (or "celts") eventually became more refined by shaping and polishing. The American Indian began to utilize crudely shaped pieces of native metals as well as stone while the medieval European had already evolved a more sophisticated metal hammer–axe combination tool and weapon.

When white men first made contact with the Indians they discovered one of the most valuable trade items to the Indians was the steel axehead; it remained an important barter implement throughout the history of the fur trade. Styled after the European axe hatchet,[58] these forged iron and steel tools resembled smaller versions of European felling axes. Ranging in size from two to three pounds to lightweight axes, called belt axes, they served as both tool and weapon and were invaluable in the wilderness. Excavated examples are plentiful,and this type of tool–weapon has been found in Indian burial grounds all over the United States.[59] Its efficiency as a weapon cannot be better proclaimed than contemporary accounts of battles that relate the obvious terror its victims felt toward the tomahawk.[60]

As noted earlier in the chapter, American soldiers were armed with tomahawks or swords early in the Revolution. Shortly after the war was under way, the sword was dropped from the requirement of the enlisted man in the infantry, but the tomahawk was optional—along with the bayonet. Undoubtedly, many infantrymen carried belt axes, probably identical to those carried by the Indians. These were used as both weapons and small axes around camp. Whether belt axes were issued to the U.S. infantryman during the period 1784–1791 is not known. The returns of West Point ordnance in December 1783 list forty-five tomahawks,[61] while those at Fort Pitt in 1785 list 380 tomahawks.[62] It is possible that some of these tomahawks at Fort Pitt were trade articles for friendly Indians. They do not

[57] *Ibid.,* Vol. 34, Waste Book, Journal & Ledger MNO, 1792–3–4.
[58] Henry C. Mercer, *Ancient Carpenter Tools,* Bucks County Historical Society, 1960, pp. 92–94.
[59] Harold L. Peterson, *American Indian Tomahawks,* Heye Foundation, Museum of the American Indian, 1965, p. 18.
[60] The terror in which the tomahawk was held is illustrated in the three wood cuts (Chapters 8 and 10), each depicting Indians with tomahawks in the act of violence against soldiers and settlers (*Death of Gen. Butler, A Scene on the Frontiers,* and *The Columbian Tragedy*).
[61] *Knox Papers,* West Point Ordnance Return, December 28, 1783.
[62] *Ibid.,* Fort Pitt Ordnance Return, July 25, 1785.

show up on the returns of 1793 at Fort Pitt, but the Fort Washington returns of that year indicate 236 tomahawks and sixty-eight scalping knives and scabbards,[63] while the returns at Carlisle, Pennsylvania, for that same year list over 2,000 tomahawks.[64]

Fort Pitt was a point of embarkation for both men and supplies destined for the Northwest, as well as being a storehouse for provisions and a magazine for ordnance. It is not unlikely that the tomahawks which were listed at Fort Pitt in 1785 had been dispersed either to the troops or to friendly Indians by 1793. However, those listed at Carlisle in 1793 could have been of new manufacture. Over half did not have hafts (handles); and the implication is that newly made heads had been shipped to Carlisle, which was a repository of military stores, and the heads would either be affixed to handles by artificers at Carlisle before issuing them to the troops or, more likely, would be distributed as trade axeheads to the friendly Indians.

Riflemen did use tomahawks, and those few militia volunteer frontiersmen from Kentucky, who fought under Harmar and St. Clair, and those who fought in the militia raids, carried belt axes or pipe tomahawks, not only into battle, but as part of their daily accouterments into the wilderness. Since the riflemen did not utilize the bayonet, the tomahawk was a necessary accessory. Along with his knife, which was used for cutting patches when loading his rifle, the rifleman depended upon his tomahawk for defense and offense and as a utility ax in the woods. The knife was used also for utility, for taking scalps, and as a weapon.

Part III: Accouterments and Ammunition

THE SOLDIER'S ISSUE

Standard issue, although the records indicate constant deviation, apparently consisted of the following allotment per man in the Federal corps:

> 1 stand of arms (musket and bayonet)
> 1 gun sling
> 1 bayonet belt
> 1 bayonet scabbard
> 1 cartridge box
> 3 flints
> 4 cartridges (more under combat conditions)
> 1 gun worm
> 1 brush and wire (for cleaning the barrel vent)
> 1 screw driver for every 5 men (for disassembling muskets)
> 1 knapsack (either painted linen or animal hair left on hide) or 1 haversack
> 1 canteen (either wooden or tin)
> canteen straps
> fifes[65]

[63] *American State Papers*, Vol. 1, Military Affairs, pp. 44–60.
[64] *Ibid.*
[65] *West Point Waste Book*, #1, May 12, 1786, USMA Library.
[66] *West Point Waste Book*, #2, April 5, 1790, USMA Library.
[67] *Ibid.*
[68] *West Point Waste Book*, #1, October 31, 1788, USMA Library.

In addition the artillery was issued, when available, pistols, spears, powder horns (cannon priming horns),[66] and swords.[67] Each company of both infantry and artillery was also issued the following articles for daily maintenance of the troops:[68] camp kettles, axes, ax slings, buckets, bowls, orderly books, ink powder, portmanteaux, steel yards, firewood, straw (for bedding), bed jacks, and tents, both wall and common.[69] Typical issue for a company of seventy men and officers consisted of:

2 camp kettles for the captain
2 camp kettles for the subalterns
1 camp kettle for the sergeants
1 camp kettle for the corporals
12 camp kettles for the privates and musicians
16 axes
16 wooden bowls
16 wooden buckets
70 bundles of straw (for 2 months, then burned and reissued)
1 pair of steel yards (scales)
shovels
andirons
1 company book
orderly books
quivers
paper
paper ink powder
blankets, etc.[70]

The amount of firewood estimated for the garrison at West Point October 31, 1791, amounted to one foot per man per month for six months, while at an outpost the amount was doubled to two feet per man per month.[71] The wood was usually hauled in the winter months on sleds. The outposts obtained their supplies when cutting trees and clearing the areas surrounding the newly built forts.

A return of Jonathan Heart's company dated French Creek, May 27, 1787,[72] indicated that there were on hand for fifty-four men and three officers:

2 fusees	45 bayonet scabbards
56 muskets	10 swords
56 bayonets	1 sword belt
56 bayonet belts	1 drum
56 cartridge boxes	56 flints
46 gun slings	336 cartridges

The return also had spaces for fifes, worms, screwdrivers, brushes, and picks, but none were listed in the possession of Heart's company. Possibly they had been lost, as Heart wrote a notation at the bottom of the return that the men had just completed a long and tedious march through the woods to their new post. Their clothing, knapsacks, and haversacks were almost worn out; and the tents were in bad condition.[73] Heart did mention that the arms and accouterments were in good order.[74] The return also lists:

[69] *Ibid.,* April 5, 1790.
[70] *Ibid.,* October 31, 1791.
[71] *Ibid.*
[72] *Harmar Papers,* Vol. 5, French Creek, May 27, 1787, Heart's Company of Infantry.
[73] *Ibid.*
[74] *Ibid.*

1 wall tent	no mess axes
11 common tents	no spades
5 camp kettles	no picks
45 knapsacks	1 company book
34 haversacks	54 men's books
no canteens	1 quire of paper
3 axes	2 portmanteaus
8 axe slings	

Indicating the lack of many necessary pieces of equipment, the company return serves as an excellent record of the amount of gear in the field during actual service accounted for by one detachment of the Federal corps.

Improvisation occurred as much in the repair and substitution of accouterments as it had in weapons. Captain Ashton received orders at the Rapids of the Ohio from General Harmar at Fort Harmar: "Knapsacks we have none that are worthy to be issued. You will receive 30 haversacks by this conveyance—the quartermaster sends also 10 camp kettles for the use of your company and two for the officers." Harmar went on to tell Ashton to improvise: "Captain Bradford will deliver you 53 cartridge box belts and 24 damaged bayonet belts, which is all that is in store—the cartridge box belts will answer for bayonet belts and the bayonet belts you can convert into gun slings."[75]

West Point returns continually indicated improvisation for materials that were lacking with stores on hand: May 12, 1786, sixty-four hame strings[76] were issued to be made into canteen straps,[77] and on that same day forty-two more hame strings issued for canteen straps;[78] August 9, 1788, 70 hame strings and two back bands were issued for canteen straps;[79] April 5, 1790, an artillery company, received ninety waist belts to make sixty-eight shoulder bayonet belts and an infantry company received ninety waist belts to make seventy-four shoulder bayonet belts;[80] and 3,000 canteen straps made out of old belts were shipped to the Secretary at War from West Point, April 16, 1791.[81]

Buff waist belts for bayonets were preferred to black ones[82] and the linen knapsacks were usually painted on the top[83] (the outside flap usually Spanish brown or red). Cartridge box belts were buff also, as were the gun slings.[84] General Harmar testified that he had the knapsacks of the first regiment covered with bearskin, which increased the martial appearance of the troops.[85] He said that the bearskins cost about $2 each, and each would cover five or six covers.[86] Compared to the knapsacks of the levies, which were small, they looked much more military: "The levies with clothing of no price, by the side of the regulars who were well clothed and accoutred."[87]

Often equipment was shipped incomplete because of the urgent need. Knox explained to General Richard Butler just prior to St. Clair's expedition, when supplies were delayed and expected momentarily, "The knapsacks were neither painted or strapped, but the quarter master was to

[75] Ibid., Vol. 29, Letter Book E, February 15, 1789.
[76] Horse artillery equipment.
[77] West Point Waste Book, #1, USMA Library.
[78] Ibid.
[79] Ibid., #2.
[80] Ibid.
[81] Ibid.
[82] Letter Book, #2, West Point, June 26, 1788, USMA Library.
[83] Ibid., February 26, 1790.
[84] Ibid.
[85] St. Clair, Expedition against the Indians, p. 205.
[86] Ibid., p. 206.
[87] Ibid.

forward both paint and straps. But in order to remedy this matter entirely, I have directed a sufficiency to be painted and strapped here [Philadelphia], and they will be forwarded in a few days."[88]

A few weeks later Knox informed Butler that 200 powder horns, and 200 "bullet or shot pouches," which Butler had requested, would be forwarded immediately.[89] These were intended for the militia and levie rifle companies. Knox added that "the four bugle horns have gone forward."[90] These would have been issued to the militia and levie cavalry units enlisted for the forthcoming campaign. Rifle pouches were listed on the Fort Pitt returns of 1785,[91] as were powder horns and dragoon belts at West Point on the 1783 returns.[92]

That same return listed 1,337 clasps for cartridge boxes, indicating that the metal-type fastener was used during the Revolution, as well as the Federal Period. The 1783 West Point return also lists 403 tin canteens.[93] Few canteens are listed on any of the returns and the tin containers must have been obsolete during the Federal Period. *Old* tin canteens (six) are listed on the 1793 returns at Carlisle, while seventeen canteens (no descriptive adjective) are listed at Fort Hamilton that same year.[94] Since tin was used as something out of the ordinary during the post-Revolutionary period, it is assumed wooden canteens were used exclusively by the Federal corps.

The regiment observed orderliness about the arms and accouterments, as well as the men and their clothing. Although many times makeshift implements were used, everything that was part of the soldier's equipment was strictly recorded in the company and regimental books and returns, and a system for everything was demanded by the commander.

Arms were neatly stacked, whether barracks had been built, tents pitched, or the men had nothing but open sky for a roof.[95] Ammunition was carefully issued and never given to the men without strict orders and exact count. If the cartridges were carried fixed, the boxes usually contained 836 cartridges each.[96] A wooden box was used to transport the cartridges. When leaving on special details, the men were usually issued one cartridge for every day of detached duty (unless the situation required more). While stationed at camp, the troops were issued six cartridges to be kept in their cartridge boxes.[97] Muskets were never loaded, except on specific orders; and, if an attack was expected and the men told to load their muskets but the attack never occurred, then the pieces were unloaded at the laboratory and the old cartridges turned in to the officer in charge. If for some reason the charge could not be withdrawn, a specific time and place was usually appointed near the camp where the muskets could be discharged.

Firing muskets for practice was the exception rather than the rule, because of the short supply of gun powder on the frontier. Hamtramck advised Harmar that "if you thought proper to allow me some ammunition for the purpose of practicing the artillery and infantry I am well persuaded that it would be of great service, for the men appear to me to be unacquainted with firing."[98] When powder was issued for target practice, it was usually poor quality. "Bradford took with him a barrel of damaged

[88] *American State Papers*, Knox to Butler, June 9, 1791, Vol. 1, Indian Affairs, p. 188.
[89] *Ibid.*
[90] *Ibid.*
[91] Fort Pitt Return, July 25, 1785.
[92] West Point Return, December 28, 1783.
[93] *Ibid.*
[94] *American State Papers*, Ordnance Return, Vol. 1, Military Affairs, pp. 44–60.
[95] *Harmar Papers*, Vol. 32, Order Books 1784–88, Orders, Fort Harmar, September 22, 1788.
[96] *West Point Waste Book*, #2, August 9, 1788, USMA Library.
[97] *Harmar Papers*, Vol. 32, Order Books 1784–88, December 18, 1787, May 19, 1787, October 3, 1788, June 2, 1787.
[98] Thornbrough, *op. cit.*, p. 125.

powder which will answer the purpose for practicing the artillery and infantry,"[99] was Harmar's answer to Hamtramck's earlier request for practice.

Pre-cast musket balls were usually shipped to the frontier.[100] However, balls were made at the outposts: "You will also forward to this post, ten barrels of gun powder fit to make musket cartridges, and as much lead as you can spare with cartridge paper and *moulds,* etc.,"[101] Harmar instructed Major Doughty while en route to Vincennes in 1787. Cartridge paper was used exclusively on the frontiers and the East Coast magazines and different qualities of paper and powder were used for muskets, rifles, and pistols—depending on which arm the cartridges were destined for.

Cartridges were prepared at magazines in the East and shipped in wooden boxes that were made specifically to house the cartridges.[102] More often than not, however, the cartridges arrived too late, or not at all, and laboratories at the various posts on the frontier had to be established to manufacture fixed ammunition for the Federal corps. Riflemen, of course, carried powder horns and shot pouches, as well as the riflemen's knives to cut patches for loading. At times, infantrymen melted down the larger 69- or 75-caliber lead balls into small shot for close-quater fighting. "Your running up part of your lead into buck shot was very proper, as they are exceedingly useful in close quarters."[103]

NOTES:
Chapter 6,
Part I

Returns submitted by the upstate New York garrisons at the end of the war reflect accurately the size of the ordnance used at frontier forts.

Listed on those returns (dated 1783), Fort Rensselaer possessed three-, four-, six-, and twelve-pounders and a 4 2/5-inch brass mortar. Fort Herkimer had six- and 9-pounders. Schenectady still retained four and six-pounders, and Albany accounted for iron and brass six-pounders and a brass three-pounder.[104]

Although it is dated a year later, a Fort Pitt return[105] indicates the type of ordnance contained at that Post which, in July 1785, was a storage depot and point of embarkations for the frontier. Whether the ordnance listed was left over from the Revolution or whether it was newly arrived in storage awaiting transfer to one of the outposts is not important. The caliber of weapons listed is an indication of those pieces supplied to Josiah Harmar and his 1st American Regiment, and the type used there during the Revolution:

1 brass eight-inch howitzer
1 brass royal howitzer
2 brass six-pounders
field carriages for the brass ordnance damaged
5 iron six-pounders on damaged garrison carriages
1 wrought iron six-pounder on damaged field carriages
1 wrought iron three-pounder on damaged field carriages
2 cast iron four-pounder on damaged field carriages

During the Indian campaign of 1790, General Harmar told General Knox that he took with him on the expedition a six-pounder, a three-pounder and a 5½-inch howitzer.[106] St. Clair's defeat in 1791 might not have been as disastrous if the 5½-inch shells had arrived on time, Henry Knox said afterward in a complaint to Quartermaster Hodgdon.[107] Records do indicate, however, that St. Clair took 600 three-pounder-round shot with him on the expedition.[108]

[99] *Ibid.,* p. 155.
[100] *West Point Waste Book, #2,* December 29, 1791, USMA Library.
[101] *Harmar Papers,* Vol. 28, Letter Book B, Harmar to Doughty, July 1, 1787, Rapids of the Ohio.
[102] *West Point Waste Book, #1,* November 12, 1786, USMA Library.
[103] *Harmar Papers,* Vol. 29, Letter Book G, Harmar to Jeffers, Fort Washington, February 11, 1790.
[104] *Knox Papers,* Ordnance returns, December, 1783.
[105] *Ibid.,* Ordnance returns, Fort Pitt, July 25, 1785.
[106] *Harmar Papers,* Harmar to Knox, November 23, 1790, Vol. 28A.
[107] *American State Papers,* Indian Affairs, Vol. I, Knox to Hodgdon.
[108] *Ibid.,* Returns of August 4–9, 1791.

The Congressional report in 1788 stated that the frontier forts possessed the following cannon: Fort Harmar—three cannons mounted; Fort Steuben—one cannon; Post Vincennes—four small brass cannons; Fort Franklin—one cannon.[109] When Jonathan Heart was ordered to build a post at Venango, he was given the choice of picking up a brass six-pounder or a howitzer, whichever he thought could be transported most conveniently.[110] Several months later, a howitzer was placed aboard a Kentucky boat laden with ordnance and military stores destined for an island in the Ohio river opposite Clarkesville, in the vicinity of the Rapids of the Ohio. The island was to be a temporary encampment for this advanced detachment while waiting for the rest of the regiment to catch up on its trip to Vincennes in 1787, and a single howitzer was chosen to guard the supplies.[111]

Small bore ordnance was the accepted artillery for aggressive troop movements. Described as field batteries, or field artillery, the eighteenth-century military tacticians in Europe, England, and the United States specified light pieces which would be moved in different directions, according to circumstances and the position of the enemy troops on which the fire was to be directed.[112] "In common traveling days, and in bad roads, artillery in general required nearly twice the time of the infantry in marching the same distance . . . ,"[113] said Louis de Tousard, explaining why European tacticians earlier in the eighteenth century had changed their old-fashioned theories and replaced their heavy field artillery (batteries that accompanied infantry) with light, maneuverable pieces.

In 1757, John Muller said "Whoever consults the oldest authors, will find that guns are made at present nearly in the same form as they were at first: for since Dilichius, a German, who wrote about 200 years ago, scarce any alterations have been made..."[114] However, Muller went on to say, "Our field pieces are made lighter today, though, and have been found to answer better in the field than any others we ever had..."[115] Continuing, he emphasized the need for lighter artillery and said that "even lighter pieces than the present would do."[116]

The two artillery companies that originally were formed in the 1st American Regiment, and the additional two formed in 1786, faced exactly the same conditions that Muller and Toussard describe. The artillery had to keep up with the infantry on their expeditions, maneuver with the provisions caravans on land and water, and be "light and maneuverable" in every sense of the phrase. Josiah Harmar suggested "two or three grasshoppers would be serviceable against the Savages,"[117] after the experience of his unsuccessful expedition. Grasshoppers are described in contemporary references as "small, light cannon"[118] and the European description would probably be likened to Muller's "galloper" carriage. "There is one carriage more, which is called Galloper; it serves for a pound and half gun. This carriage has shafts so as to be drawn without a limber..."[119] Toussard describes a Galloper as "a piece of a small caliber,"[120] the same definition given by others to the Grasshopper.

The ordnance returns submitted to Congress in December 1793 indicate the sizes of the artillery pieces at the different northeastern garrisons:[121]

FORT WASHINGTON
3 brass 6-pounders
5 brass 3-pounders
1 8" brass howitzer

FORT HAMILTON
1 iron 6-pounder
1 iron 1-pounder
1 iron 5½" howitzer

FORT PITT
1 brass howitzer, mounted
3 iron 6-pounders
2 5½" brass howitzers
1 iron 4-pounder
2 iron coehorns

FORT JEFFERSON
1 iron 6-pounder
1 5½" howitzer

[109] Journals of Congress, Vol. 13, October 2, 1788.
[110] Harmar Papers, Vol. 28, Letter Book B., April 9, 1787.
[111] Ibid., Vol. 32, Order Books 1784–88, June 18, 1787.
[112] Louis de Tousard, American Artillerist's Companion, Philadelphia, 1809, Vol. 1, p. 1.
[113] Ibid., Vol. 2, p. 5.
[114] John Muller, A Treatise of Artillery, London, 1757, p. 10.
[115] Ibid.
[116] Ibid.
[117] Harmar Papers, Harmar to Knox, January 25, 1791, Large Letter Book A.
[118] Dictionary of Americanisms.
[119] Muller, op. cit., pp. 185–186.
[120] Tousard, op. cit., Vol. 2, p. 639.
[121] American State Papers, Vol. 1, Military Affairs, p. 59.

Ammunition returns indicate that none of the above-mentioned forts had anything larger than a six-pounder except Fort Pitt. Although the 1783 returns list quantities of assorted types of fixed and unfixed ammunition, the 1793 returns for the forts in the northwest are fairly consistent for the assortments at the various outposts:[122]

FIXED AMMUNITION—FORT WASHINGTON
6-pound grape shot
6-pound strapt shot
3-pound strapt shot
6-pound case shot
3-pound case shot

UNFIXED AMMUNITION—FORT WASHINGTON
3-, 4-, and 6-pound shot
6-pound grape shot
3-pound strapt shot
3-pound case shot
8½-inch howitzer case shot
5½-inch howitzer case shot
loose grape shot
hand grenades

[122]*Ibid.,* pp. 57–59.

39.

40.

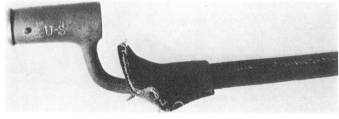

39. Wrist of surcharged British musket neatly repaired by a Federal gunsmith. The break has been clamped with sheet brass, then bound with strong cord.
Guthman Collection

40. French bayonet (in scabbard) surcharged "US".
Guthman Collection

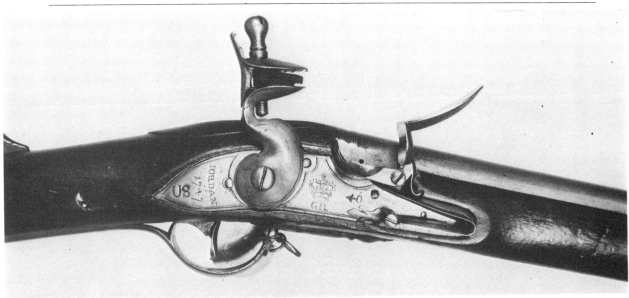

41.

42.

41. Lock of a British musket, captured by the Americans during the Revolution, and surcharged "US". The other markings are English.
Collection of the United States Military Academy West Point Museum

42. Eighteenth-century cartridge box consisting of a sewn, leather cover and flap containing wooden box with twenty-one drilled holes, each to hold a paper cartridge. Carrying strap is suspended from the back of pouch. Bayonet and sling are attached.

43. Close-up of three paper cartridges, each containing ball and powder.
Guthman Collection

43.

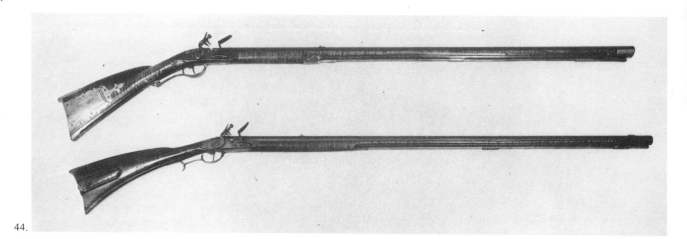

44.

45.

46.

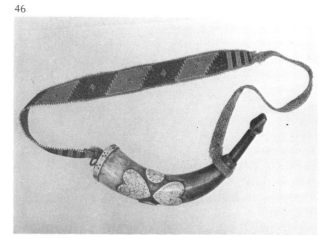

44. Two eighteenth-century Pennsylvania rifles, both curly maple stocks. Upper, by Wolfgang Haga, Reading area, unsigned, brass patch box. Lower, by Herman Rupp, Allentown area, unsigned, wooden patch box.

45. Close-up of a beautifully executed brass patch box by John Young, Easton, Pennsylvania, unsigned, late eighteenth-century. Butt of rifle only is shown.
Guthman Collection

46. Eighteenth-century rifleman's powder horn with typical Pennsylvania raise-carved decoration. Attached is the original Indian-made, moose hair carrying strap, edged with white beads.

Attached to the plug (or base) is a wrought iron ring to which the strap is secured. The original wooden stopper is still in the spout.
Guthman Collection

47.

49.

48.

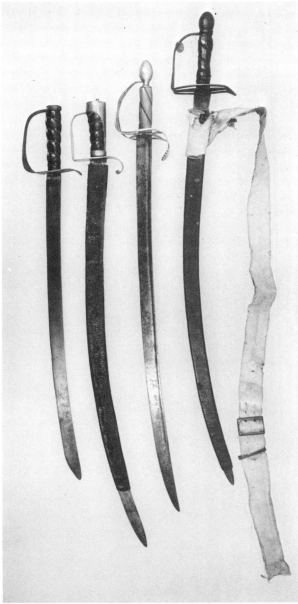

47. Partial view of an eighteenth-century sword with Federal period decoration. The United States' Arms and "American Light Horse" are engraved on the blade, which is imported.
Guthman Collection

48. Four eighteenth-century American-made sabers. From left to right, signed Potter (New York), iron hilt; Potter (New York), brass hilt; blade marked GW, brass hilt; signed Potter (New York), iron hilt. The saber on the right has a buff leather frog (attachment of belt to scabbard) and belt with brass buckle.
Guthman Collection

49. Cased set of artillery instruments in silver made by Thomas Wright, instrument maker to George II, circa 1750. Every artillery unit required a similar set, although usually made of brass. Top, plotting scale or protractor; left, parallel rule; center, case; right, sector; bottom, gunner's calipers.
Guthman Collection

50.

51.

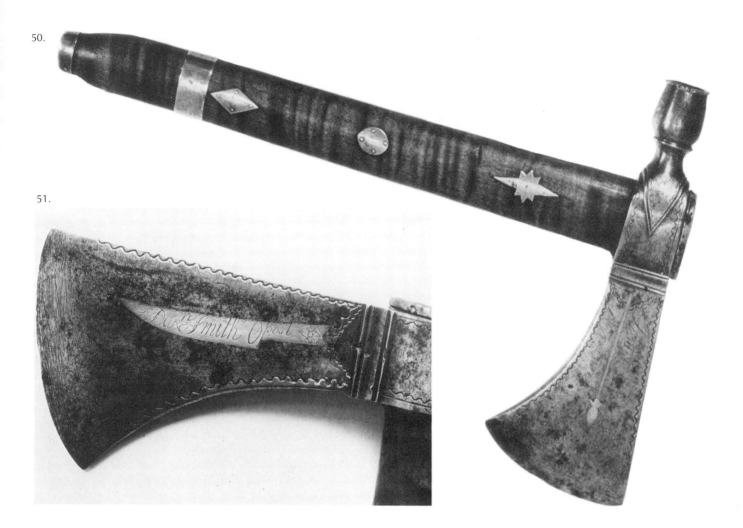

50. Surveyor Daniel Smith's pipe tomahawk lost on the expedition to mark the Virginia–North Carolina boundary in 1779. Haft, maple; bowl and blade, iron and steel; inlays, silver.

The name "James Stephenson" is crudely engraved on the reverse side of the blade. He was a Kentucky militia rifleman with the expedition. He later served with St. Clair.
Guthman Collection

52.

51,
52,
53. Close-ups of three tomahawks by the same maker.
51. Obverse of Daniel Smith blade marked "OPOST," early name for Vincennes (Indiana).
52. Almost identical tomahawk made for Smith after he lost the above. 53. Inscription "H KNOX" on blade of tomahawk engraved by same man as above two pieces.
51. *Guthman Collection;*
52. *The City Museum, Bristol, England;*
53. *Smithsonian Institution*

53.

54.

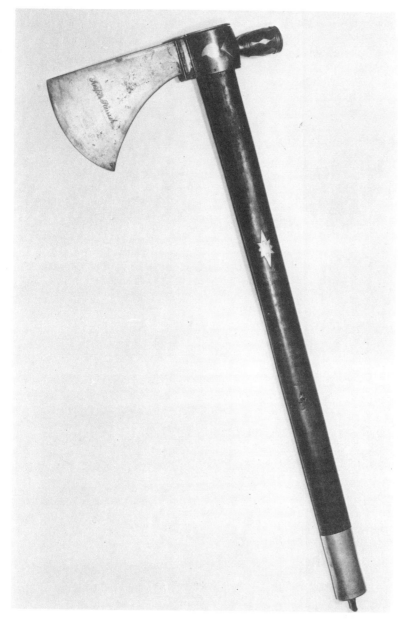

54. Pipe tomahawk of Jasper Parrish, whose name is engraved on the blade. Captured by Delaware Indians in 1778, he remained prisoner until 1784.

Released at the Treaty of Fort Stanwix, he became an interpreter for the United States in 1790 and remained in the Indian Service for many years.
Guthman Collection; Helga photo

55. White man's scalping knife, circa 1785, that was made for a prosperous woodsman. The curly maple haft has four silver inlays and a silver cap and ferrule. All silver is engraved, one piece with a fine Federal eagle. The hand-forged blade is 7½ inches long.
Guthman Collection

55.

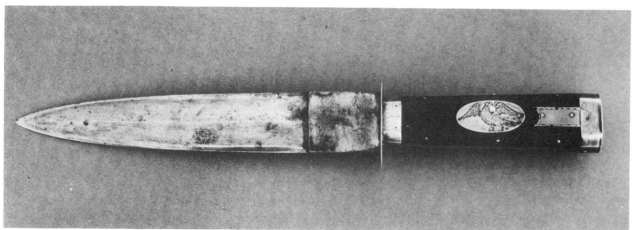

Chapter 7

The Miami Indian of Ohio was the enemy. Supplied by the British, used by the fur trader, hated by the Kentuckians, he was a formidable foe, thanks to his training, his thinking, his ambitions, his weapons, and his capabilities in combat. He was "one of the greatest infantry in the world," and his eventual downfall was caused by the white man's disease and alcohol, not military inability.

Military tactics of eighteenth-century Europe did not apply to backwoods warfare. In most instances, moreover, the wrong tactics were used at the wrong time. Lessons were never really learned from previous failures, such as Braddock's defeat during the French–Indian War.

Part I: The Indian–A Skillful Soldier and Underrated Enemy

America's newly acquired independence marked the beginning of the end of the Indian's freedom to roam the woods and plains wherever and whenever he chose. Prior to the boundary lines devised by civilization, he was barred from new territory only by unfriendly tribes or because it lacked natural resources. The American aborigine hunted when he needed to eat and traveled to where the game was most plentiful.

Although his day-by-day existence contributed nothing to the land upon which he lived, it did not extract more from the forests and soil than was required to support his meager requirements, so the face of North America did not change—except for nature's own elements of destruction and production. Man, beast, and vegetation remained constant, balanced by nature. Depending completely upon the harvests of the wilderness, the American Indian's nomadic life followed a pattern similar to that of a tree bending through the darkness of the forest toward the direction of the opening that would allow the most sunlight to reach its leaves. Unlike the trees, which offered shade, shelter, and even food or fuel, the Indian gave nothing back in return for the nourishment he received from the land.

During the period of discovery, and the trade era that followed, European and British monarchs, through the daring achievements of their adventurous subjects in the new land, extracted as much as they could of whatever natural resources they were able to turn into profit and returned little more than the natives did back to the land. Traders taught the Indians the effectiveness of the white man's implements, and the seeds of dependency that eventually destroyed the aborigine were sown.

Colonization followed, and the civilization from across the water began to create towns and provinces in the former wilderness world of the American aborigine, driving him away from the Atlantic Ocean and westward across the continent. The retreating tribes conquered, or were conquered by, the Indian nations onto whose land they had been driven. The basis for those territorial claims was the strength of the various tribes.

European nations claiming territory in the new land based their claims on the concept that they were contributing to the growth of this land through the establishment of their culture and economy.

Ever since explorers first began to investigate unknown parts of the world, titles to undeveloped wilderness occupied by savages had been established on the basis of discovery followed by settlement and development, allowing the original natives the right of occupancy but not ownership of the land.

In 1783 Great Britain ceded Northwest Territory lands that had been wrested from the control of the French at the conclusion of the French–Indian War to the United States. During both English and French control of those lands, the Indians who had occupied the territory traded with the sovereign states who claimed their region, and fought beside them against their enemies. Although clothed, fed, and armed by the ruling empire, the savage never felt the encroachment of civilization as the only permanent settlers were traders and trappers who had no ambition to build and develop the country, merely extracting its furs in exchange for cheap trinkets and whiskey. Many of these men lived almost as the natives, and those small primitive settlements that arose did not pose a threat to the world of the Indian. On the contrary, they became centers of supply and refuge during severe winters for those natives, who soon came to depend on the profiteers for their food and clothing (in addition to arms and whiskey). Working with the agents of European monarchs, the traders and trappers were encouraged not to create any change in the Indian world. Status quo was essential to the fur trade.

Colonists settling in the vicinity of the Ohio River valley in the territory of Kentucky and Pennsylvania presented a threat to the aborigine who soon found that his freedom to hunt where he pleased—and his supply of game—were in jeopardy. Therefore, the frontiersmen and their families were subjected to the brutal wrath of the savages. This hatred and mistrust was inherited by the thousands of new emigrants who swarmed down the Ohio River to the newly acquired Northwest Territory after the Revolution. In contrast to the French and English, who had only collaborated with the Indian in the lucrative fur trade, the American settlers were competing with him for his land, his game, and his pride.

At the conclusion of the French–Indian War, after the French ceded the territory to the British, the Indian's life remained unchanged. Most of the French traders continued to live in the territory; the only difference was that the trade was controlled by England, instead of France—a remote detail that did not concern the natives, who still received gifts and supplies from the controlling crown.

When the British ceded the territory to the United States, however, after the Revolution and settlers began to migrate into the territory with their farm tools, fences, domestic animals, and household furnishings, the savages realized that a change in their way of life was about to occur. Compounding the deceit England had already imposed upon the northwest tribes by ceding their territory, the agents of the British Empire told the unsuspecting aborigines that the Americans had no right to the land upon which they were settling. More experienced in diplomacy, and much less honest with the Indians than were the poverty-stricken thirteen colonies, Great Britain continued to wield a mighty influence over the tribes she had betrayed in her land cessions to the United States.

Important as the fur trade was to the economy of the United States, equally important were the sale and settlement of the Northwestern Territory. Wealth, growth and the ability to strengthen the nation were contemplated by the Union in the settlement of its new territory. Unfortunately, this same land was the hunting ground of the powerful Western Confederacy of Indian tribes, including the Wyandots, Miamis, Shawnees, Delawares, Ottawas, Chippewas, and Potawatomi.[1]

SOME OF WASHINGTON'S VIEWS ON INDIANS

Four days after the definitive treaty of peace was signed on September 3, 1783, the soon-to-retire George Washington wrote to his friend James Duane, noted New York jurist and expert on Indian

---

[1] Elmore Barce, "The Land of the Miamis," *The Benton Review Shop*, 1922, p. 44.

affairs, and he gave his opinion about the terms of the peace. The general said, "The settlement of the Western Country,[2] and making a peace with the Indians, are so analogous, that there can be no definition of the one, without involving considerations of the other. . . ."[3] He pointed out the necessity of forming a "distinct and proper" government for the new territory in order to impose heavy restraint upon those persons who were illegally surveying, land-jobbing, and monopolizing territory that did not belong to them. "It would," he said, "people the country progressively, and check land-jobbing and monopolizing, which are now going forward with great avidity,"[4] and with proper government to supervise the boundaries it would prevent improper possession by whites of Indian lands and preserve the peace.

"Our settlements would be compact," he continued, "government well established, and our barrier formidable, not only for ourselves, but against our neighbors."[5]

Referring to the Indian problem, he continued,

> The Indians will ever retreat as our settlements advance upon them, and they will be as ready to sell, as we are to buy. That is the cheapest, as well as the least distressing way of dealing with them, none who is acquainted with the nature of an Indian warfare, and has ever been at the trouble of estimating the expense of one, and conspiring it with the cost of purchasing their lands, will hesitate to acknowledge.[6]

The Indians, he said, should be told that, since they had joined arms with Great Britain and committed hostilities against the United States during the prosecution of the war, they should be forced, along with Great Britain, according to the terms of the peace treaty, to withdraw beyond the Great Lakes. However—since Americans were more generous than other nations, and since the United States preferred peace with the Indians to a state of warfare and considered the Indians a deluded people convinced of their error in taking up arms against the Union—a veil would be drawn over the past and a boundary line established between Indian and settlers' land. Trade and friendship should be established between the two peoples "as the country is large enough to contain us all."[7]

Warning that "in establishing the line, care should be taken neither to yield nor to grasp at too much; but the endeavour to impress the Indians with an idea of the generosity of our disposition to accommodate them," he prophesized that since the future might well dictate that the new land would produce a population that would become dissatisfied with the original boundaries "compensation should be necessary for their claims within it."[8] "If the government," he added, "did not control the new territory, the western territory would be over-run by 'banditti' who would defy the authority and dispose of the cream of the land and probably precipitate an Indian War."

Indian agents, he admitted, might be necessary, but he was not certain. If they were appointed, the United States should *not* follow the policy of Great Britain where the self-interest of the agents "was the principle by which they actuated."[9] Using the British Indian agents as examples, he said, "By accumulating lands and passing large quantities of goods through their hands, the Indians were

[2] Washington was owner of huge tracts in the Western Country which he offered for settling to the public.
[3] W. C. Ford, "The Writings of George Washington," New York, G. Putnam, 1891, Washington to James Duane, September 7, 1783.
[4] *Ibid.*
[5] *Ibid.*
[6] *Ibid.*
[7] *Ibid.*
[8] *Ibid.*
[9] *Ibid.*

made to speak any language they pleased by their representation, and were pacific or hostile as their purposes were most likely to be promoted by one of the other."[10] Strict regulations over the agents should be maintained by the government, and no purchases of Indian land or trade should be permitted to those appointed. An ample fixed salary would be adequate compensation, he said.

Washington felt trade with the Indians should be carried on only by those persons who had been properly licensed by the government. He felt that this Indian trade should not lead to excessive profit. It should, he pointed out, benefit the Indians, and make just enough profit to defray expenses and risks, adding but little to the trader's pocket. This would enable the United States to secure the loyalty of the Indians in its interest "and is a better mode of treating with them than that of giving presents, where a few only are benefited by them."[11]

By the time of his presidency, the Indian situation had deteriorated. Washington, however, still believed the natives should be treated with humanity and understanding. He wrote to Timothy Pickering in January 1791 expressing his thoughts about the American red men:

> Humanity and good policy must make it the wish of every good citizen of the United States, that husbandry, and consequently civilization, should be introduced among the Indians. So strongly am I impressed with the beneficial effects, which our country would receive from such a thing, that I shall always take a singular pleasure in promoting, as far as may be in my power, every measure which may ensure it.[12]

In April of the same year he told Alexander Hamilton that every expedient measure was being taken to insure peace with the hostile Indian tribes. But was not convinced that a peace could be effected; even if it were, he felt it would only last a short time. Blaming "land jobbers" and the "disorderly conduct of our borders," along with the "intermeddling" of the various states in matters of Indian affairs which "belong to the general government," Washington said, "To sum the whole up into a few words, the interference of the States, and the speculations of the individuals, will be the bane of all our public measures. . . ."[13]

The Indian nations had been told that the United States was the only authority with the power to negotiate with them. Washington had seen an extract concerning a treaty about to take place between the New York legislature and those same Indians and referred to this in his letter to Hamilton.

Just prior to St. Clair's ill-fated expedition, Washington told Edmund Randolph, his attorney-general, to examine the existing laws governing Indian affairs—the security of their lands, restraining states and individuals from purchasing their lands and forbidding unauthorized private intercourse with them. He told Randolph that auxiliary laws should be suggested to supplement defects in the existing ones and thus enable the President to enforce obedience. The President said:

> If Congress expects to live in peace with the neighboring Indians, and to avoid the expenses and horrors of continual hostilities, such a measure will be found indispensably necessary; for, unless adequate penalties are provided, that will check the spirit of speculation in lands, and will enable the execution to carry them into

[10] *Ibid.*
[11] *Ibid.* The practice of giving presents was later revived by Knox, however, and thousands of dollars were spent on trade goods for treaties between 1785 and 1790.
[12] *Ibid.,* Washington to Pickering, January 20, 1791.
[13] *Ibid.,* Washington to Hamilton, April 4, 1791.

effect, this country will be constantly embroiled with and appear faithless in the eyes not only of the Indians, but of the neighboring powers also.[14]

Sometimes after St. Clair's defeat, Washington wrote to Benjamin Hawkins,[15] the North Carolina United States Senator, Indian commissioner, and negotiator of treaties, suggesting in retrospect that the Indians found it more profitable to plunder than hunt because they had been stimulated to do so by the British traders and by the withholding of the western posts by Great Britain from the United States. He pointed out that, since the United States was at war with several tribes, the only measure to take was the offensive. A defensive operation was costly and impractical. Offensive steps into the heart of the Indian country should be taken, preceded by pacific overtures.

These steps were taken in the last campaign (St. Clair's) he said, but many obstacles prevented either a peaceful settlement or a military victory. The defeat of November fourth, he continued, could be ascribed to several causes. Short enlistment of the troops (levies and militia) was a prime factor for the defeat. Short enlistments have an uncontrollable influence on all operations, he said, while long enlistments enable one to take advantage of time and circumstance. Under long enlistment terms, he pointed out, men grow more valuable every month, at half the expense of new men, while under short terms, just as soon as they are trained, they are discharged and new troops are enlisted to take their place.

Another factor responsible for St. Clair's defeat, according to Washington, was inadequate army intelligence. Speculating that the number of hostile Indians was greater than the 1790 estimate of 1200, and that not only were the Miami and Wabash tribes involved in the battle, but also the Wyandots, Delawares, and others, Washington proved that army intelligence had been inadequate for the expedition—and far less effective than the intelligence of the Indian scouts.

JOHN MARSHALL'S SUMMATION

Although the United States was the final cause of the deterioration and subsequent disappearance of the powerful Indian nations in North America, this was merely the end result of 300 years of ambition, curiosity, and the desire to progress generated by every civilized society. The previously unwritten laws exercised by European powers to control the territories they seized through discovery or conquest in North America were formalized by the United States Supreme Court in 1823.[16] Chief Justice John Marshall's summation was, in fact, an accurate history of the events that had occurred from the beginning explorations in the fifteenth century up to the eventual claim of ownership by the United States of its territory. Marshall pointed out that monarchs gave commissions to explorers (Cabot, Hudson, DeSoto, Cartier, etc.) to discover territories then unknown to the Christian World. He said:

> On the discovery of this immense continent, the great nations of Europe were eager to appropriate to themselves so much of it as they could respectively acquire. Its vast extent offered an ample field to the ambition and enterprises of all; and the character and religion of its inhabitants offered an apology for considering them as a people over whom the superior genius of Europe might claim an ascendency.[17]

[14]*Ibid.,* Washington to Randolph, October 10, 1791.
[15]*Ibid.,* Vol. 12, pp. 71–73.
[16]*Johnson and Graham's Lessee vs. Wm. McIntosh* (8 Wheaton, 543), 1823.
[17]Joseph P. Cotton, Jr., *The Constitutional Decisions of John Marshall,* G. P. Putnam & Sons, 1905, Vol. II, pp. 1–3.

The Justice went on to say that "The potentates of the old world found no difficulty in convincing themselves that they made ample compensation to the inhabitants of the new, by bestowing on them civilization and Christianity, in exchange for unlimited independence."[18]

Pointing out the principle of the right of acquisition between competing European nations in the new world, he continued: "Discovery gave title to the government, by whose subjects, or by whose authority, it was made, against all other European governments, which title might be consummated by possession."[19]

While the original inhabitants were admittedly the rightful occupants of the land, Marshall pointed out that they had less right to complete sovereignty, as an independent nation, and no right to dispose of the land to whomever they wished, since this right was based on the principle "that discovery gave exclusive title to those who made it."[20]

The point that bears directly to America's claim to the land was contained in his following observation:

> While the different nations of Europe respected the right of the natives as occupants, they asserted the ultimate dominion to be in themselves; and claimed and exercised, as a consequence of this ultimate dominion, a power to grant the soil, while yet in possession of the natives. These grants have been understood by all to convey a title to the grantees, subject only to the Indian right of occupancy. The history of America, from its discovery to the present day, proves, we think, the universal recognition of these principles.[21]

Further along in the opinion he came back to the point:

> The United States, then, have unequivocally acceded to the great and broad rule by which its civilized inhabitants now hold this country. They hold and assert in themselves the title by which it was acquired. They maintain, as all others have maintained, that discovery gave an exclusive right to extinguish the Indian title of occupancy either by purchase or conquest; and gave them also a right to such a degree of sovereignty as the circumstances of the people would allow them to exercise.[22]

Referring to the legacy left by the British, he said: "The British government, which was then our government, and whose right have passed to the United States, asserted a title to all the lands occupied by the Indians within the chartered limits of the British colonies."[23] Almost apologizing, and yet proudly asserting the historical facts that led to the bloody wars which humbled the Indian tribes, Marshall explained the position of the United States, which had to assert itself physically in order to control a land which it had, and was in 1823 very much in the process of, improving and developing.

[18] *Ibid.*
[19] *Ibid.*, pp. 4–5.
[20] *Ibid.*, p. 3.
[21] *Ibid.*
[22] *Ibid.*, p. 18.
[23] *Ibid.*

The title of conquest is acquired and maintained by force. The conqueror prescribes its limits. Humanity, however, acting on public opinion, has established, as a general rule, that the conquered shall not be wantonly oppressed, and that their condition shall remain as eligible as is compatible with the objects of conquest. Most usually, they are incorporated with the victorious nation and become subjects or citizens of the new government with which they are connected. The new and old members of the Society mingle with each other; the distinction between them is gradually lost, and they make one people. Where this incorporation is practicable, humanity demands, and a wise policy requires, that the rights of the conquered to the property should remain unimpaired; that the new subjects should be governed as equitably as the old. . . .[24]

Putting his finger squarely on the reason for all of the Indian wars in the past, and unknowingly predicting many more bloody battles in the future, the great jurist painted a simple, but extremely accurate character description of the American Indian:

But the tribes of Indians inhabiting this country were fierce savages whose occupation was war, and whose subsistence was drawn chiefly from the forest. *To leave them in possession of their country was to leave the country a wilderness;* to govern them as a distinct people was impossible, because they were as brave and high spirited as they were fierce, and were ready to repel by arms every attempt on their independence.[25]

Sadly drawing a conclusion to the impossibility of absorbing the Indian nations into the civilized system of government of the United States, he said: "As the white population advanced, that of the Indian necessarily receded. The country in the immediate neighborhood of the agriculturists became unfit for them. The game fled into thicker and more unbroken forests, and the Indians followed. . . ."[26] Marshall added: "The law which regulates, and ought to regulate in general the relations between the conqueror and the conquered, *was incapable of application to a people under such circumstances.*"[27]

Although in 1823 Marshall's opinion summarized the reasons for failure that finally forced the Indian culture to succumb to the increasing demands made by Western civilization in North America it was Little Turtle, the great Miami chief who, almost thirty years earlier, had predicted the eventual downfall of his own people. Commenting after the victory of Wayne's Legion at Fallen Timbers, the wise leader astutely pointed out that the Indian, who did not plan for the future, was no match for a civilized society that made preparations during the present for whatever achievements it hoped to accomplish in time to come.

The difference between a civilized society and a savage society is a simple one: The savage lives for the present, sacrificing everything which he has prepared for tomorrow in order to satisfy that which he desires today, while civilization plans always for the future, storing flour during the summer so that it might have bread during the winter. Thousands of Indian families starved during severe winter months because their entire year's harvest of furs had been traded for whiskey which was

---

[24] *Ibid.,* pp. 20–21.
[25] *Ibid.*
[26] *Ibid.*
[27] *Ibid.,* p. 22.

available only so long as the Indians had furs to exchange. Compounding this common tragedy of the eighteenth and early nineteenth centuries was the squaws' neglect of crops during drinking orgies, so that the tribes lost not only their valuable furs but also their food. Left with only their pride, and the hypocritical promises of the British army and traders, eventual war between the United States and the Western Confederacy was inevitable.

Another factor that contributed to the eventual downfall of the Indian was the fateful mistake that he made in his choice of allies. As Justice Marshall pointed out, he could not become a part of the society that was conquering him, and therefore, because of his high spirit and determination not to give in, he chose allies (British agents and French, English, and renegade American fur traders) who caused the most harm to his society. These treacherous men lived in the Indian towns of the Western Confederacy, traveling back and forth from Detroit and Canada with propaganda from the British government, whiskey, rum, weapons, ammunition, and false hopes to exchange for valuable furs.

In his declining years Little Turtle, who had fought with the British during the Revolution and under their influence during the Federal Period Indian Wars, finally saw through the veil of propaganda that had been spread over the Indian nations by the British agents and unscrupulous traders. He realized that they were deliberately hiding the truth that would, if exposed, ruin their profitable fur trade. His vigorous protests to his fellow tribesmen against alcohol and the destructive effect it would have upon the future of the entire Indian people were proof of his professions of peace with the United States after the defeat at Fallen Timbers. He was responsible for the first legislation prohibiting traffic in liquor to the Indians in the United States[28] and made many speeches before his own people, Congress, and the legislatures of Kentucky and Ohio espousing his cause.[29] He said that liquor was more to be feared than the gun and tomahawk.[30]

Unfortunately, few of the other Indian leaders possessed either the insight or the foresight of Little Turtle. However, there were many others who were capable leaders, military strategists, and, although of an uncivilized society, their mental capacity was as great or greater than the leading military minds of Western civilization in terms of their profession—war—in a warfare that was contained within their own environment.

General William Henry Harrison described the warriors of the Western Confederacy as the finest light troops in the world.[31] The hero of Tippecanoe, whose military experience began with the 1st Regiment in August 1791 and matured as aide-de-camp to Anthony Wayne in the Legion, said that from 1785 to Tippecanoe the confederacy of northwest tribes could not have placed more than 3,000 warriors in combat against the United States at any one time.[32] This statement is corroborated by another Indian fighter, Colonel James Smith, who said that the Indians could not have fielded more than 3,000 warriors at any one time from the French–Indian War until 1799.[33] An Indian prisoner during the French–Indian War who served as an officer for both the British and later, during the Revolution, the American militia, Smith commented that it was unfortunate the military tactics of New Englanders, who had become expert Indian fighters during the thirty years war of the early settlement, had become obscured in history.[34]

[28] Calvin M. Young, *Little Turtle,* Greenville, Ohio, 1917, p. 148.
[29] *Ibid.*
[30] *Ibid.,* p. 149.
[31] Barce, p. 61.
[32] *Ibid.,* p. 60.
[33] *Ibid.*
[34] Colonel James Smith, *A Treatise on the Mode and Manner of Indian War,* Joel R. Lyle, Paris, Kentucky, 1812, p. 2. An interesting comparison of the mode of Indian warfare is given in William Smith's *An Historical Account of the Expedition Against the Ohio Indians, in the Year 1764. Under the Command of Henry Bouquet, Esq.*

INDIAN WARFARE

A treatise on Indian warfare was published by Smith in 1812, written shortly after Harrison's questionable victory at Tippecanoe. Smith said, stating his reason for writing the treatise, "I am now a poor old man; my contemporaries are chiefly all gone; and the only thing I can now do to serve my country as a patriot, is to lay before the public something of the nature of the Indian War."[35] The aged veteran continued, "I make no doubt (if only attended to), this may be a means of saving many lives, if an Indian war cannot be prevented."[36]

"I have often heard the British officers call the Indians undisciplined savages—but this is a capital mistake,"[37] Smith said, as he commenced his treatise. Indians had, he pointed out, all of the requisites of discipline: They had competent commanders, they were quick to obey orders, they had unity of action, achieving almost perfect harmony when moving (by observing the movements of the warrior on his right, each brave communicated the motion from right to left and could therefore march abreast, quickly even though in scattered order in columns over a mile wide keeping perfect pace and unison for considerable distances without confusion or disorder).[38] They could maneuver, he continued, as fast or slowly as they ran, and could form a circle to surround the enemy or a semi-circle, if the enemy had a river on one side. If, on the other hand, the enemy was about to surround them, they would form a hollow square in order to prevent from being shot from either side of the trees.[39]

Unlike their civilized opponents, the warriors were not burdened with cumbersome uniforms and equipment. They often fought naked, except for their breechcloth, leggings, and moccasins. Corporal punishment was not a part of their discipline; degrading was effective and the only chastisement necessary to effect their obedience.[40]

"Their officers plan, order and conduct matters until they are brought into action, and then each man is to fight as if he were to gain the battle himself,"[41] Smith observed. He went on to say that general orders were given in battle either to advance or retreat, by a shout or yell that was understood by all, and the orders were followed immediately with complete harmony.[42]

Arms supplied to the Indians were usually excellent, and the warriors were expert in the use of their weapons. They were just as expert in determining the kind of force they were about to meet in combat. Smith tells that they used every means available to them to detect the size of the approaching army and the mode of its marching and encampment. Usually the best runners were sent out as spies when the wind was high, enabling them to slip past the enemy sentries without being heard. Not only did they reconnoiter the troops in camp or marching, but the Indian spies carefully examined campsites after the troops had pulled out in order to determine the size of the encampment. If they found that the army had camped on a small piece of ground, in close order, it signified that it would be the proper procedure to attack while the men were encamped.[43]

[35] *Ibid.,* p. 2.
[36] *Ibid.*
[37] *Ibid.,* p. 4.
[38] *Ibid.*
[39] *Ibid.*
[40] *Ibid.*
[41] *Ibid.*
[42] *Ibid.*
[43] *Ibid.,* pp. 4–5.

Smith claims that the principal cause of defeat of every army that was unsuccessful against the Indians, from the time of Braddock during the French–Indian War on, was the fact that they camped or marched in close order. While marching, or encamped in close order, the Indians can kill twenty to one, and in Braddock's defeat, says Smith, the Indians killed 100 to one. "If," the Colonel points out, "they [the soldiers] had only encamped on a large hollow square and marched in an oblong square, and the orders had been in case of attack to face out and take trees, it would I think have taken the Indians some days to have killed as many as they did in comparatively a short time."[44] The Virginians, said the colonel, fought that way, and won. At the mouth of Kanawha (the Kanawha River, cite of Battle of Point Pleasant, October 10, 1774), they fought the Indians from sunrise to sundown, gained the battle, and lost about 100 men.[45]

Interrogation of prisoners was a major factor in the methods of Indian warfare. Colonel Smith relates that the Indians took prisoners in order to obtain information and that the prisoners would be threatened with death unless they talked. Prisoners were also warned that, if they did not tell the truth, their captors would find out afterwards and would then subject the captives to a painful end. Another trick was to pretend friendship up until the time of battle, such as the Delawares did just before the defeat of Braddock when they deserted to the side of the French. Learning the enemy's plans helped the tribal strategists formulate their own plan of attack or defense. They received little, if any, help from their English or French allies, Smith said, other than provisions, arms, and ammunition. The battle plans were their own, and usually prepared with a great deal of skill and in most cases were highly successful.[46]

There had been twenty-two major Indian engagements since Braddock's, recalled Smith, and in all except where the white men fought the same type of warfare as the Indians the red men had been successful—with very little loss to their own warriors. "The Indians do not regard the number of white men," he relates, "if they can only get them in a huddle they will fight them ten to one, and frequently defeat them."[47] He goes on to say "the Indians are the best disciplined troops for a wooded country in the known world."[48] Comparing the Indian tactics to the British, he says, "I apprehend that the Indian discipline is as well calculated to answer the purpose in the woods of America as the British discipline in Flanders; the British discipline in the woods is the way to have men slaughtered, with scarcely any chance of defending themselves."[49]

America's success during the Revolution, Smith contends, was due in great measure to the tactics our frontier soldiers had learned from their combat with the Indians. Burgoyne's defeat, he says, was accomplished by Indian tactics, and Morgan's riflemen learned their skills in the same manner. Kentucky, he goes on, would not have been settled during the period that it was had not the frontiersmen learned to combat the Indians by using their own method of warfare. Some of the small Kentucky scouting parties, Indians had told Smith, were as capable as any Indians in a fight in the woods. Because they act together, Smith surmises, small parties, according to their number, fare better in Indian warfare than do large armies under a general.[50] "It is easier," he points out, "for a small party to learn to act in concert in scattered order without running into confusion, than a large army; also because most of the generals never attempted marching or encamping in scattered order."[51] General Wayne, however, "contrived a discipline of his own in scattered order, that answered the purpose."[52]

---

[44] *Ibid.,* p. 5.
[45] *Ibid.*
[46] *Ibid.,* pp. 5–6.
[47] *Ibid.,* pp. 8–9.
[48] *Ibid.*
[49] *Ibid.*
[50] *Ibid.,* p. 10.
[51] *Ibid.,* pp. 10–11.
[52] *Ibid.,* p. 11.

Summing up his theories about Indian tactics, the Colonel enumerated the basic procedures practiced by the warriors:

> The business of the private warriors is to be under command or punctually to obey orders, to learn to march abreast in scattered order so as to be in readiness to surround the enemy or prevent being surrounded, to be good marksmen, and active in the use of arms, to practice running, to learn to endure hunger or hardship with patience and fortitude, to tell the truth at all times to their officers, but more especially, when sent out to spy the enemy.[53]

Pointing to further practices of the Indian war strategy, he said that the leaders[54] never allowed their men to group in close quarters because, if surrounded by the enemy, they would be exposed to fire from every side. They never attacked unless they could fire from every side. They never attacked unless they had a considerable advantage, "or without what appeared to them the sure prospect of victory, and that with the loss of few men."[55] If, at any time, they find they were mistaken and the victory would be too costly in the loss of their men, "it is their duty to retreat, and wait for a better opportunity of defeating their enemy, without the danger of losing too many men."[56] From Braddock's defeat until the battle of Point Pleasant, he points out, the Indians hardly ever made an unsuccessful attack. "The Indians will commonly retreat if their men are falling fast," he said. "They will not stand cutting like the Highlanders or other British troops, but this proceeds from a compliance of their rules, rather than cowardice."[57] On the other hand, he pointed out, if they were surrounded, the savages would fight until the last man dropped rather than surrender.[58]

Moving on to suggestions for marching and encamping when planning to attack the Indians, he stipulated that the army:

> march in an oblong square—
> the square to be at least 40 to 50 yards broad—
> light horse and light infantry inside the square—
> at front and rear in order to "sally out" and surround the enemy—
> baggage in the center of the square—
> in case of attack the men face out in each direction of the square, each man to a tree—
> light horse and light infantry "sally out" and surround the enemy—
> since Indians want to kill anyone acting like an officer, the officers must keep moving about within the square giving their orders—
> when encamped, the army should pitch their tents in a large hollow square, with light horse and light infantry in the center, front and rear, and baggage, horses and bullocks in the middle—[59]

---

[53] *Ibid.*
[54] He said the Indians never relied on a single leader, but rather a council of officers who make the plans—these officers appointed by their merit.
[55] *Ibid.*, p. 12.
[56] *Ibid.*
[57] *Ibid.*
[58] *Ibid.*
[59] *Ibid.*, p. 13.

If, he went on, an army consisted of 2,000 men, then the hollow square should be thirty or forty acres, so that the men would not be encamped in close order, rendering them vulnerable to an attack. The horses and bullocks should be in the center. Lacking room for both, the horses should be kept in the square, since the Indians always sought them in an attack and constantly made away with great numbers. They did not drive away the bullocks because these animals were too slow.[60]

When attacked the men were to face out on every square, standing behind a tree and keeping well concealed. Until they sight the enemy and take good aim at their mark, they were not to fire, since a large number of guns fired at one time encourages the Indians "to advance on empty guns."[61]

Smith wrote this treatise in 1811 and, even at that late date, pointed out that almost precisely the same political situation that existed during the period of the Federal corps was reoccurring: "I am of the opinion that nothing but fear will cause the Shawanoes [Shawnees] and their confederates to stand a treaty, *while they have the British to supply and encourage them.*"[62]

Some additional pointers of the wise Colonel were:

> Indians do not attack where there has recently been an alarm and the people are alert—
> Indians always spy before the final attack—
> they spy when the wind is blowing so the dogs can not smell them—
> Indians usually attack at day break—
> Scouting parties should march Indian (single) file, one or two rods behind the other, with flankers on the outside—
> if attacked, the front wheels to the right, the rear to the left, taking to trees and scattering—
> if attacking Indians at night (if moon is bright enough), slip up and only half the men fire, the other half rush with loaded guns and tomahawks—
> Never attack in a dark night—the Indians never do, because they might get confused and kill each other—[63]

Smith sums it all up by saying the government, in the past, had always sent an insufficient number of men against the Indians with "commanders unacquainted with Indian warfare."[64] Both Bouquet and Wayne "carefully taught their men how they should proceed in scattered order before they marched into Indian country."[65] He continued, "I do not know one instance, in the aforesaid two and twenty campaigns, where a commander went against the Indians in close order but what was defeated."[66]

Smith's account fairly accurately details the tactics that should have been, but were not, used by Braddock. "The glittering army of redcoats with drums beating and flags flying so much admired by Washington, forded the Monongahela and ascended the banks of the river between two hidden ravines. Suddenly they were greeted by a terrible fire on the front ranks, which almost immediately spread to the right flank, and then followed a hideous massacre of huddled troops."[67] The Indians

---

[60] *Ibid.,* p. 17.
[61] *Ibid.*
[62] *Ibid.*
[63] *Ibid.,* p. 19.
[64] *Ibid.,* p. 21.
[65] *Ibid.*
[66] *Ibid.*
[67] Barce, *op. cit.,* p. 63.

who attacked "went into battle stripped to the skin, and with bodies painted with horrible stripes of vermillion."[68] Smith's description is more colorful: "I saw numbers running towards me stripped naked, except breech-clouts, and painted various colors, though the principal color was vermillion or a bright red; yet there was annexed to this, black, brown, blue, etc."[69]

Piamingo, a Chickasaw chief who accompanied St. Clair on his disastrous expedition, told the general afterward, said Winthrop Sargent,

> that the armies of Britain had been formerly opposed to his nation [Piamingo's] and that the officers were at first distinguisable among the soldiers, as among our troops, by cocked hats, plumes, etc., and were soon killed—whereupon confusion ensued and the men fell easy victims of their prey. [This happened to St. Clair's army, also.] But, grown wiser by experience, they dressed their forces all alike [the British] and became victorious. He [Piamingo] recommended strongly to the General to fight the Indians in their own way from behind logs and trees, and be continually changing the ground of action. This is their manner and they seldom fire twice from under the same cover, but as soon as they have discharged their pieces from behind one tree, shift themselves to another; so that it is almost impossible to find them out, or to know whither to direct your fire.[70]

This is exactly the style used by the Indians when they defeated St. Clair.

In contrast to Braddock's defeat (and Harmar's and St. Clair's), Wayne did not use patrols or picket guards. He would have been cut off. Instead of these, his men were always kept alert, ready for action.[71] "The greatest object of Indian tactics," said General Harrison, "was always to flank the enemy. In fighting Indians, there was no shock to be given or received and a very open order was therefore attended with two advantages; it more than doubled the length of the lines and, in charging, gave more facility to get through obstacles in the woods."[72] He added, "The old European system of fighting men shoulder to shoulder was entirely impracticable in a wilderness woods for it invited too great a slaughter."[73]

The type of warfare that had been proven successful against the Indians in the amazingly few Colonial- and Federal-period victories was precisely the guerrilla tactics used by the frontier settlers in the Kentucky territory of Virginia in their frequent encounters with Indians. Learning through heartbreaking and painful experience, these men and women acquired the woodland tactics of their savage foes and used them with the weapon best suited for their all around needs.

The rifle, underrated by eighteenth- and early-nineteenth-century military tacticians, and even today not credited by modern military historians for its many frontier achievements, was the weapon chosen and used almost exclusively by the hardy settlers in the untamed territory. Requiring accurate aim at a target he was able to see clearly, the rifleman had to use trees or brush as comouflage in order to secure time to sight a victim. If, after firing, he found himself in close combat with the enemy, his tomahawk and scalping knife were far more maneuverable in trees and thick underbrush than the bayonet.

[68] *Ibid.,* p. 65.
[69] Smith, *op. cit.,* p. 24.
[70] Winthrop Sargent, "Dairy," *Ohio Archeological & Historical Society Publications,* Vol. 33, pp. 255–58, Columbus, Ohio, 1924.
[71] Barce, *op. cit.,* p. 67.
[72] *Ibid.,* p. 66.
[73] *Ibid.*

The rifled weapon lent itself to individual combat rather than the close order formation of squads of men. No given command could direct each soldier whenever a target appeared in his sights. A bayonet charge, of course, could be effective after the enemy had been repulsed in guerrilla-type warfare and the only objective left was to force his retreat—or in desperate attempts to flush concealed foes into the open at tremendous loss of troops.

In retrospect, the weapons and tactics that had repeatedly proven successful and which, in effect, preserved the frontiers from complete annihilation and actually opened the doors for America's westward expansion, were not adopted by the United States Army except in isolated instances. A long record of unsuccessful Indian campaigns bears pathetic testimony to this fact.

In order to survive, the lone frontiersman learned to think like the savage warrior when he entered combat or traveled through Indian-infested woods. Unfortunately, European-oriented military minds commanding troops in the North American wilderness throughout the eighteenth and early nineteenth centuries expected the successful methods of Windham, Steuben, Vauban, Muller, and Simes to work against the savage who had never read their celebrated military books of instruction and tactics.

TORTURE

Indian fighters and frontier settlers faced the prospect of a slow death if they became captives of the enemy. Just as he was an expert in guerrilla warfare, so was the Indian an expert in savage torture. This barbaric treatment of prisoners was not a device aimed against the white man exclusively, but a custom that had been practiced against enemy Indian tribes for centuries in the past.

Excluding his involvement with white man's politics, trade goods, or land seizure, the Miami Indians waged intertribal warfare for honor rather than land acquisition: "the acquisition of prisoners or scalps as tokens of the bravery and skill of the warriors was very important to them."[74] Early in the eighteenth century Louis Deliette recorded the Miami ritual of torturing a captive:

> When he is condemned to die, it is always by fire. I have never seen any other kind of torment used by this nation. They plant a little tree in the earth, which they make him clasp; they tie his two wrists, and with torches of straw or firebrands they burn him, sometimes for six hours. When they find his strength gone, they unfasten him and cut his thumbs off, after which they let him, if he wishes, run after those who are throwing stones at him, or who wish to burn him. They even give him sticks which he holds with great difficulty. If he tries to run after anybody, they push him and he falls on his face, at which they hoot. He sometimes furnishes a whole hour's diversion to these barbarians. Finally he succumbs under the strains of his torments, and sometimes drops down motionless. The rabble run to get firebrands, which they poke into the most sensitive parts of his body; they trail him over hot embers, which brings him back to life, at which they renew their hootings, as if they had performed some fine exploit. When they are tired of their sport, an old rascal cuts his flesh from the top of the nose to the chin and leaves it hanging, which gives him a horrible appearance. In this state they place a thousand tricks on him and finally stone him or cut open his stomach. Some drink his blood. Women bring their male children still at the breast and place their feet in his body and wash them with his blood. They eat his heart raw.[75]

---

[74] W. Vernon Kinietz, *The Indians of the Western Great Lakes,* University of Michigan Press, Ann Arbor, Michigan, 1940, p. 196.
[75] *Ibid.,* p. 201.

Lieutenant John Armstrong sent the following account to the commander of his detachment at Fort Knox in 1789:

> From appearances at this place the enemy was in force and after making my encampment secure, sent a detachment for the corpse of a soldier killed a few hours before who had been sent express to meet me. He was shot in two places with balls, had two arrows sticking in his body, was scalped, his heart taken out and his privates cut off.[76]

Denny reports in his Journal that, in 1788, "The Indians have lately killed a soldier in the vicinity of the fort at the Rapids, and not content with scalping him, cut him in four quarters and hung them upon the bushes."[77] However, during Harmar's campaign of 1790, Denny reports an atrocity performed by members of the militia.[78]

The frontiersmen had acquired many customs derived from the Indian's culture. Although the material culture of the Indian had changed because of his great dependence upon the white man's weapons, clothes, and food, which altered his more primitive, although secure way of life, the frontiersman on the other hand had acquired many more of the Indians' living habits. It was the trapper and trader who had become more savage and drifted away from the customs and mores of his society while the Indian, accepting the more advanced tools of civilization as well as its vices, did not deviate from his religion or tradition. He remained an Indian.[79]

A perfect example is the white American renegade, Simon Girty. Heading a large force of savages attacking Dunlap's Station in February 1791, Girty ordered a prisoner tortured within sight and hearing of the fort, hoping that the commander, Lieutenant Kingsbury, would surrender the garrison rather than watch the unfortunate captive, Abner Hunt, suffer a painful death. Realizing that if he capitulated, all of the occupants of the fort would no doubt suffer the same treatment, Kingsbury and his detachment were forced to witness helplessly the following ordeal:

> They stripped him naked (says William Wiseman, who was inside the fort), pinioning his outstretched hands and feet to the earth, kindling a fire on his naked abdomen, and thus, in lingering tortures, they allowed him to die. His screams of agony were ringing in our ears during the remainder of the night, becoming gradually weaker and weaker till toward daylight, when they ceased.[80]

There is no doubt that many of the white settlers on the frontier practiced just as cruel atrocities as did the Indians. Living far from their own civilization, and learning that in order to survive they had to acquire the cunning and ferocity of their enemies, those men fought fire with fire.

---

[76] Thornbrough, *op. cit.*, p. 174, Armstrong to Hamtramck, June 11, 1789.
[77] *Military Journal of Major Ebenezer Denny,* p. 331.
[78] See page 192.
[79] George Irving Quimby, *Indian Life in the Upper Great Lakes,* University of Chicago Press, Chicago, Ill., 1960, p. 151.
[80] Consul Willshire Butterfield, *History of the Girtys,* Cincinnati, Robert Clarke & Co., 1890, Reprint Long's College Book Co., Columbus, October, 1950, pp. 250–55.

Part II: Southern Indian Tribes

President Washington ordered Captain Henry Burbeck's company of artillery to accompany the commissioners treating for the newly installed constitutional government of the United States with the Creek Nation. The negotiations for the treaty were conducted at Rock Landing on the Oconee River in the State of Georgia, September 15, 1789. Unsuccessful and frustrated, the commissioners returned to Henry Knox in New York on November 20, 1789, but the artillery company remained, establishing headquarters at St. Mary's River, Georgia. Although the activity of the Federal Corps in the Southwestern Territory is insignificant during the period 1784–1791, three companies[81] of troops were stationed there,[82] and a review of the Indian situation in the Southern district[83] is therefore pertinent to the history of the United States Army. An investigation of the theories and procedures of Washington and his secretary of War in these matters gives the reader a better understanding of the similar causes and events that led to the fatal expeditions in the Northwest Territory during the same period.

Secretary of War Knox described most of the Indian nations within the boundaries of the United States as "discontented, and some of them turbulent." He then divided his discussions into three reports confining himself to the northern and southern Indian districts, exactly as the Ordinance of August 7, 1786, had geographically divided the tribes in setting forth the specifications for Indian affairs. Knox related that the Creek Nation was separated into two divisions, the Upper and the Lower Creeks. The Upper Creeks resided in about sixty towns or villages located along the Alabama River, while the Lower Creeks inhabited about forty towns or villages along the Apalachicola River. Most of the Creeks lived within the borders of the United States except for the southernmost tribes, the Seminoles, who lived in Spanish Florida. The fighting strength of the nation was estimated to be 6,000 warriors or "gun-men," as they were described by Knox. Each town had its headman or chief, but the central leader of the nation was Alexander McGillivray, a half-breed who wielded great influence over the Creeks. His father, Lachlan, was an inhabitant of Georgia who, during the Revolution, remained loyal to the Crown. Lachlan's property was confiscated by the victorious Americans and he returned to his native Scotland after the war. Alexander, who had received an English education, served the British cause during the Revolution against the United States and returned to the home of his mother, a high-ranking woman of the Upper Creeks, at the close of the hostilities.

Living among his mother's people he prospered in the trading business, controlling the Creek trade with the outside world and creating a monopoly which he enjoyed financially with his British partners in the loyalist firm Panton, Leslie & Company. His trade communication with the outside world was protected by the Spanish through whose territory his imports and exports had to be sent. Although he was receiving a pension from the Spanish government to enforce Spain's trade monopoly with the Creeks, the profits of the enterprise centered in Great Britain, and one of the Bahama Islands was an intermediate place of deposit.

McGillivray's resentment toward the State of Georgia for confiscating his father's property after the war, as well as the property belonging to other loyalist friends, was probably the cause of the war between the Creek Nation and that state, which Knox felt would require the interference of the United States. The Secretary of War related the events that precipitated the hostilities: Two treaties

---

[81]Captain Burbeck's company was stationed at St. Mary's River. Captain Smith's company was stationed at Beard's Bluff on the Altamaha River. Captain Savage's company was stationed at Oconee, the north branch of the Altamaha River. (*Harmar Papers,* Vol. 12, Knox to Harmar, April 12, 1790.)
[82]*American State Papers,* Vol. 1, Indian Affairs, p. 113.
[83]*Ibid.,* pp. 12–18.

had been promulgated between Georgia and the Creeks, the first in 1783 and a second in 1785. Both treaties defined boundaries and gave concessions of Creek lands to the state. A third parley was held in 1786, at which time the Creeks acknowledged that some of their warriors had violated former treaties; they also ratified former boundaries. Knox pointed out that now McGillivray—and the Creeks—were objecting to the validity of the three former treaties. They claimed, he said, that the entire Creek Nation wasn't represented at the negotiations. Since just a few towns were represented when the land was ceded, and since this land belonged to the entire Creek nation the chiefs now maintained the treaties were invalid.[84]

Summing up the incidents that caused the situation of the moment, Knox said that the treaties were made in the more ancient form recognized by the Indians but were not formalized according to legal procedures practiced by civilized governments. The treaties, however, were made and observed by the Indians and, actually, these were of the type of treaties common among the tribes. The Indians, however, now regretted the treaties and felt that if they made demands against Georgia for a revision of the concession that the United States would not interfere. Georgia, on the other hand, wished the United States to reaffirm that state's position and make it clear to the Creeks that the government would back up the provisions of the earlier treaties. North Carolina and Georgia appointed commissioners and, in November 1788, invited the Creeks to a treaty the next June 1789; but instead of accepting the Indians increased their depredations and alarmed not only the frontiers but the entire state of Georgia.

Prior to the invitation for a treaty, the late Congress of the Confederation, Knox said, passed a resolution July 15, 1788, ordering the superintendent of Indian affairs of the southern department to warn the Creeks that, if they continued to persist in their refusal to enter into a peaceful treaty, the arms of the United States would be brought against them for the protection of the frontier. Knox was ordered to report to Congress with a plan for effecting the resolution. Knox first responded to the resolve with the submission of a plan July 26, 1788. He pointed out that the resolve stipulated that the plan for the southern tribes agree in principle with the Congressional resolve of July 21, 1787, which was initiated in response to the hostility of the Wabash tribes in the Northwest Territory. That resolve called for a treaty to be held at Post-Vincennes in order to communicate to the Indians the desire of the United States to promote peace and friendship between its people and the Indian tribes then hostile to the frontier settlers on the Wabash and the Ohio Rivers. Also specified was the stationing of troops in the Northwest Territory and permission for the Federal corps to call on up to 1,000 Kentucky militia, if necessary, to serve under the direction of the Federal commanding officer. If the Indians did not agree to hold a peaceful treaty, Knox asked that "rigorous exertions be made in the first instance, calculated to terminate effectually the contest, in one campaign." Otherwise, he added, the United States would be drawn into a tedious, costly, and inglorious war. He compared the strength of the Wabash tribes for whom the resolve of July 21, 1787, was adopted, to the strength of the Creeks. There was a vast difference. The Creeks were superior in numbers, far more united as a nation, better regulated and headed by McGillivray, whose capabilities had insured him the confidence of all the Creek tribes. Also, Knox pointed out, the resolve of 1787 involved troops already stationed on the Ohio. The Kentucky militia was to act only as an auxiliary under the command of the officer in charge of the Federal troops.

The situation of the southern Indians, he said, was entirely different, since there were no Federal troops on the frontiers of Georgia and it would not be practical to remove any from the Ohio country and transfer them south. Because of different circumstances, use of the militia from the Southern states would not be practical for the protection of their exposed borders. A large body of militia, called upon whenever the need was urgent, to protect the extensive Georgia frontier would be far

[84] The Western Confederacy used the same logic, rejecting the treaties of 1784, 1785, and 1786.

more costly, Knox felt, than raising a body of Federal troops. Knox suggested that 2,800 infantry, cavalry, and artillery would be sufficient, and that the enlistment should run for nine months: the amount of time, he estimated, required to train and equip the men and to invade the Creek country and defeat the enemy. A well-regulated force of that size, he stipulated, was necessary and suggested that the soldiers be drawn from Georgia, North Carolina and South Carolina. Knox figured the total cost at roughly $450,000. (By 1789 he tripled that figure.)

Reciprocal depredations were inflicted upon women and children of both the southern Indian nations and the inhabitants of frontiers of Georgia and North and South Carolina. All attempts of the United States commissioners to negotiate with the Creek nation were frustrated by the Southern states, who had been taking matters into their own hands. North Carolina had not, as yet, even consented to become a member state under the new constitutional government. Encouraged to retaliate against depredations of the white men along the borders, the Indians made scattered attacks on settlements along the frontiers, all individual acts of terror and destruction being coordinated under the talented leadership of McGillivray.

Following his résumé of July 6, 1789, Knox sent Washington a lengthy report the next day further discussing the Southern situation and emphasizing that the state of affairs between Georgia and the Creeks was critical. In the event of war, he said, it was probable that all the other Southern Indian nations would unite with the Creeks against the Whites living on the frontiers. His reason: Although the various tribes might quarrel with each other because of intertribal boundary disputes, they would join in a union as strong as the Six Nations of the North because of their common fear of oppression and loss of lands. Already, he went on to say, the Cherokees had taken refuge from the violence of the frontier settlements of North Carolina within the boundaries of the Creek lands. The Choctaws and Chickasaws, under McGillivray's persuasion, would soon follow, he thought, even though they were farther from the hostile settlers.

Another problem, he said, involved the jealousy of the Spaniards toward the expansion of the United States. Knox felt Spain would endure great expense to build up and cement the union of the Southern tribes in order to present an impassable barrier to the United States. As Spain claimed a considerable part of the territory ceded by Great Britain to the United States, McGillivray had asserted that Spain was bound by treaty to protect the Creeks in their hunting grounds.

Knox then made two recommendations: first that the United States raise an adequate army. His estimates differed from those he submitted in the first report of July 26, 1788. Now the Secretary of War suggested a force of 5,000 men (2,800 in 1788), which, he said, would be reduced to 3,500 fighting effectives due to the normal necessities of operation, sickness, and positioning of guards at supply depots, guard stations, etc. The operation, he thought, would last two years (his guess was nine months in 1788), and the entire project would cost $1,500,000 annually (compared to his $450,000 estimate for nine months in 1788). A lesser army, Knox said, would be a useless expense and end in disgrace to the nation.

His second recommendation was for Congress to appoint three commissioners to negotiate an amicable peace between the United States and the southern Indians. The commissioners should be authorized to examine the pathetic case of the Cherokees (who had been subjected to brutal incursions and extermination at the hands of the frontier settlers) and be given power to renew the treaty made at Hopewell in 1785.

All treaties with the Indians would be worthless, he pointed out, unless they were backed up by a body of troops that could enforce the terms of the treaties on the part of both Indians and Whites. "The angry passions of the frontier Indians and whites, are too easily inflamed by reciprocal injuries, and are too violent to be controlled by the feeble authority of civil power," he said. Furthermore, he continued, "There can be neither justice nor observance of treaties, where every man claims to be the sole judge in his own cause, and the avenger of his own supported wrongs."

If an amicable treaty were concluded, said Knox, the boundaries between the frontier whites and the Indians must be protected by at least 500 troops. The post which they would occupy should not be within the jurisdiction of any individual state, but within the territory assigned to the Indians. If all offenders of treaty provisions should be tried by a court-martial, the Indians would soon be convinced of the justice and good intentions of the United States. They would learn to venerate the power which protected them from the lawless Whites.

In either case, an army would be necessary—for an expedition against the Southern Indians or to back up a successful treaty.

The Secretary of War went on to say that the disgraceful action of the lawless whites who violated the treaty of Hopewell should be given serious consideration by Congress. He said that the direct and manifest contempt of the authority of the United States by those frontier Whites, if allowed to remain unpunished, would hinder the attempts of the government in establishing itself with authority along the frontiers. The Indian tribes would have no faith in the worthless promises of the United States and the lawless whites would ridicule a government who made treaties and attempted to regulate boundaries *on paper only*. Washington was influenced by Knox's profound understanding of the Indian situation.

After studying the Knox reports, Washington submitted the following recommendation to Congress August 7, 1789:

> While the measures of government ought to be calculated to protect its citizens from all injury and violence, a due regard should be extended to those Indian tribes whose happiness, in the course of events, so materially depends on the national justice and humanity of the United States.
>
> If it should be the judgment of Congress that it would be most expedient to terminate all differences in the Southern district, and to lay the foundation for future confidence, by an amicable treaty with the Indian tribes in that quarter, I think proper to suggest the consideration of the expediency of instituting a temporary commission for that purpose, to consist of three persons, whose authority should expire with that occasion.

Again, on August 22, 1789, the President appeared before the Senate, and this time he was accompanied by his Secretary of War (who was not officially in office until September). Washington presented the legislature with the awesome facts about the powerful Southern tribes who, he said, had a combined fighting strength of 14,000 warriors. "Your serious attention should be given," he said, "to all efforts to conciliate these tribes and attach them firmly to the United States."

He went on to summarize previous treaties between the United States, and the Choctaws, Chickasaws, and Cherokees, stating that North Carolina and Georgia protested the legality of the results of the negotiations. Those two states claimed that the treaties infringed upon their legislative rights and were contrary to the Confederation. Washington went on to say that the Cherokee treaty had been violated by disorderly white people on the North Carolina frontier and that no treaty had been formed with the Creeks. After pointing out the delicate situation in which the United States found itself, between the Indians and the Southern states, the president stated that it was essential to conclude peaceful negotiations with those tribes in order for the United States to form a friendly barrier against the encroachment of European colonies which might some day become the enemies of the United States.

After studying the report of the commissioners, Knox submitted his own report to President Washington, January 4, 1790. He told the President that "The assurances given by some of the chiefs of the peaceable intentions of the Creek nations, are too uncertain in their nature, even if sincere, for the United States to rely upon." Knox added that, after the solemn offer of peace had been made by the United States and rejected by the Creeks, it was incumbent on the United States to be in a situation to punish all unprovoked aggression. He said that an army "of sufficient strength should be raised to march into their country and destroy their towns, unless they should submit to an equitable peace."

Knox again repeated his previous suggestions for an army of 5,000 men, enlisted for the duration of the expedition. Whether there would be negotiated peace, or an army to coerce the Indians into peace, the establishment of military posts on the southwestern frontier was required. He added, "No peace with the Indians can be preserved unless by a military force." He went on, "The lawless whites, as well as Indians, will be deterred from the commission of murders when they shall be convinced that punishment will ultimately follow detection." He went on to say that it was up to the United States to protect the Cherokee Nation, and this could only be accomplished by sufficient troops. The Cherokees looked up to the United States for protection in consequence of the treaty at Hopewell, and friendship and trade with the Choctaws and Chickasaws could not be cultivated without adequate troops.

The present permanent force, he said, was entirely inadequate to prevent usurpation of the lands of the United States, to facilitate the surveying and selling of these lands in order to reduce the public debt and to protect the frontiers from Georgia to Lake Erie. At that time the standing army consisted of one battalion of artillery, composed of 240 noncommissioned officers and men, and one regiment of infantry, which totaled 560 noncommissioned officers and men. In order for the United States to accomplish the three long-range objectives he had outlined, Knox recommended a permanent army of one battalion of artillery (240 men) and two regiments of infantry (700 men each), totaling 1,640 noncommissioned officers and privates.

He also recommended a reduction of pay for the noncommissioned officers and privates and a raise in pay of the commanding officers of the regiments and battalion on the grounds that this would promote the economy and good of the service. These recommendations of Knox's were, he emphasized, for the permanent army and not the expeditionary force.

After studying both Knox's report and the report of the commissioners President Washington advised Congress on January 11, 1790, that the situation on the Southern frontier was critical, and on the twelfth of September he told them he was going to submit to them the commissioners' confidential reports of the Secretary of War.

A few months later, with the consent of Congress, Washington sent Marinus Willett to treat with the Creek Indians. Through Willett's persuasive efforts McGillivray came back to New York, along with other chiefs of the Creek nation, to treat with the United States. Entertained by President Washington, Governor Clinton, the Tammany Society (whose ceremonies and costume copied those of the American Indian), and prominent officials, the Creeks appeared ready to enter into a treaty with the United States. Before the Senate on August 4, 1790, Washington advised that the articles of the treaty were being prepared.

"As *the trade of the Indians is a main means of their political management,* it is therefore obvious, that the United States cannot possess any security for the performance of treaties with the Creeks, while their trade is liable to be interrupted or withheld, at the caprice of two foreign powers," he said. He carefully pointed out how the British merchants—McGillivray and his partners—brought in goods from England through the Spanish ports and sold them to the Creeks. This company of British merchants, he said, had an exclusive trade with the Creeks under the arrangement with Spain.

For that reason, he continued, new channels of trade between the Creeks and the United States had to be established. This, he added, would take time in order not to suddenly break the present arrangement causing many repercussions. A secret article of the treaty was therefore presented to the

Senate, after a statement that any trade carried on through the Spanish territory and at the consent of the Spanish government could, at any time, be stopped. The United States, in the event her trade routes were restricted, should designate, through the President, certain persons who would be able to bring into Creek territory through the territories of the United States any quantity of goods not exceeding $60,000 a year, and these persons would be free from duty but subject to regulations guarding against abuse.

The Senate accepted the secret solution to the delicate trade situation with the Creeks. Washington then nominated Henry Knox on August 7, 1790, to negotiate a treaty with the Creek chiefs. Within twenty-four hours Washington presented a treaty, *agreed to by the Creeks for ratification* by himself with the *consent of the Senate*. Basically, the treaty was sound. In it, boundaries were specified, law and order was established between the United States and the Creek Nation pertaining to violations of those boundaries, and new modus vivendi was established between the United States and the Creeks. The United States would teach the Creeks to cultivate their lands and domestic animals. United States citizens would be sent to live with and help the Indians to achieve those new modes of civilization, and to establish trade with them.

"That the Creek nation may be led to a greater degree of civilization and to become herdsmen and cultivators, instead of remaining in a state of hunters," said Washington, "the United States will, from time to time, furnish gratuitously the said nation with useful domestic animals, and implements of husbandry." He added:

> And further, to assist the said nation in so desirable a pursuit, and at the same time to establish a certain mode of communication, that the United States will send such, and so many persons, to reside in said nation, as they may judge proper, and not exceeding four in number, who shall qualify themselves to act as interpreters. These persons shall have land assigned them by the Creeks for cultivation for themselves and their successors in office; but they shall be precluded from exercising any kind of traffic.

This last paragraph established the practice of Indian agents of the government living in the territory, and later on reservations, of the Indian tribes in the United States. The British had observed this procedure for years, but by not restricting these agents commercially, men like Sir William Johnson became powerful and wealthy through the office. Thus, Washington and Knox were sincerely trying to help the Indians, whereas the British monarch used the office as a political plum to reward a loyal subject with the opportunity to expand his fortune in the new world.

The boundaries settled upon in the treaty swept away all Indian claims to the land in exchange for which they received gifts, quantities of "Indian goods" and $1,500 paid annual to the Creek Nation. McGillivray was given a pension of $1,200 a year and an honorary commission of brigadier-general. Six other Creek chiefs were to receive $100 annually, and the negotiations ended successfully for the United States and the Creeks.

As the United States was still not enough of a world power to maintain its position, and McGillivray being the opportunist he was, the treaty was short lived. When McGillivray returned home, the Spanish government raised the pension he received from them. Then, under pressure from the Yazoo company of land speculators and their British partners, and stung by the resentment of some of the other Creeks, the Creek leader signed a treaty with Spain in 1792 repudiating the treaty with the United States. McGillivray died in 1793, but further trouble between the Creeks and the United States began to foment and, by the time the War of 1812 broke out, the Creeks allied themselves with Great Britain and Tecumseh to become once again bitter enemies of the United States.

Moravian missionary David Heckewelder, who lived among the Ohio Indians during the priod of the 1st and 2nd regiments, recounted a more human and loving aspect of the people whom he tried to help and convert. He said that "the eloquence of the Indians is natural and simple; they speak what their feelings dictate without art and without rule."[85] Indians, he continued, are proud but not vain.[86] Vanity was considered unworthy of the character of a man and was degrading.

The hunter never boasts of his skill or strength, nor the warrior of his prowess. It is not right, they say, that one should value himself too much for an action which another may perform as well as himself, and when a man extols his own deeds, it seems as if he doubted his own capability to do the same again when he pleased. Therefore, they prefer in all cases to let their actions speak for themselves.[87]

White men, he went on, were believed by the Indians to have been created by the same Great Spirit which created them. Each race was assigned a different employment; the white man to till the soil, the Indian to hunt—which was a nobler profession.[88] Indians, they said, were a race that remained unchanged from the beginning of time (called *Lenape*), whereas the white race was mixed and therefore troublesome. "The Great Spirit, knowing the wickedness of their disposition, found it necessary to give them the Great Book and taught them how to read it," Heckewelder said,[89] "that they might know what the Great Spirit wished them to do and what to abstain from." Heckewelder added: "But the Indians have no need of any such book to let them know the will of their Maker; they find it engraved on their hearts."[90]

Describing their dress, Heckewelder said, "The present dress of the Indians is well known to consist in blankets, plain or ruffled shirts and leggings for the men, and petticoats for the women, made of cloth, generally red, blue or black."[91] The more wealthy Indians adorned themselves "with ribands or gartering of various colors, beads, and silver broaches. The ornaments of the men consist of principally in shaving themselves and painting their head and face, and wearing silver arm spangles and breast plates, and a belt or two of wampum hanging from their necks."[92] The women, he went on, lined their blue or scarlet blanket and petticoat with choice various color ribands on which they fixed a number of silver broaches or small round buckles. Their "mocksens," he said, were embroidered with colored porcupine quills and had little bells and brass thimbles fixed around their ankles so that they might jingle when they walk.[93] Another Moravian missionary, David Zeisberger, for whom Heckewelder worked as an assistant, said that

the men rarely let their hair grow long, and it is common practice among them, that they root out the hair from the forehead backward so that the head is bald up to the crown and only a hand-breadth of it in a circular form is suffered to remain, whence in the case of savages generally depend long braids, one on either side, plaited and bound by bracelets, etc., etc.[94]

Zeisberger also said that the Indian had both the capacity and skill for work but did not have the inclination.[95] They were, he said, proud and haughty, "even a miserable Indian, capable in no respect, imagines himself to be a great lord,"[96] which is unlike the description given by his colleague, Heckewelder. He went on to say that they are much encouraged by dreams which they held to be very significant, and the missionaries found a difficult task to thoroughly humble those Indians that came to church in order that they give up "the vain imaginations concerning themselves."[97]

[85] Reverend David Heckewelder, *History, Manners & Customs of the Indian Nations,* Historical Society of Pennsylvania, 1876 (originally published in 1818), p. 132.
[86] *Ibid.,* p. 170.
[87] *Ibid.*
[88] *Ibid.,* p. 187.
[89] *Ibid.*
[90] *Ibid.*
[91] *Ibid.,* p. 203.
[92] *Ibid.*
[93] *Ibid.*
[94] David Zeisberger, *History of the North American Indians,* Ohio State Archeological and Historical Society, edited by A. B. Hulbert & Wm. N. Schwarze (1910) in German, 1779 and 1780, p. 12.
[95] *Ibid.,* p. 21.
[96] *Ibid.,* p. 18.
[97] *Ibid.,* pp. 18–19.

56. Ancient Indian mounds and fortifications on the Muskingum River drawn for the *Columbian* Magazine by Captain Jonathan Heart and republished by a French magazine.

Heart was fascinated with archeological explorations of ancient Indian sites and wrote many papers on the subject, several of which were published.
Guthman Collection

57. Michikiniqua, or Chief Little Turtle, chief of the Miami tribe, 1752–1812. Taken from a lithograph based on the original painting attributed to Gilbert Stuart, 1797.
Bureau of American Ethnology Collection, Smithsonian Institution

58. Pacane, the Miami chief who accompanied Harmar on his goodwill trip to Kaskaskia in 1787. The drawing was made by the wife of Colonel John G. Simcoe, who was Revolutionary commander of the Queen's Rangers and, in 1791, was appointed first lieutenant-governor of Upper Canada.
The Public Archives of Canada

56.

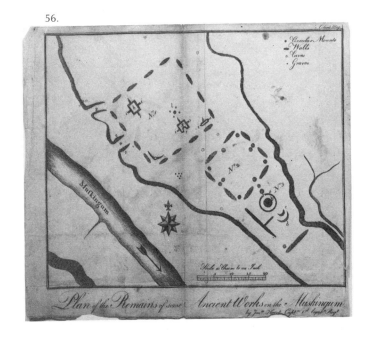

Courtesy of Smithsonian Institution.

LITTLE TURTLE, OR MICH-I-KIN-I-QUA
Miami War-Chief, Conqueror of Harmar and St. Clair

Eight

57.

Pacane. a Miamis Chief

by Mrs Simcoe
1794

58.

59.

59. Joseph Brant, the Mohawk chief, taken from an old print. Brant, whose sister Mollie was the mistress of Sir William Johnson, was schooled in England and became a powerful agent for the British amongst the Six Nations. He united the tribes that defeated St. Clair.
Guthman Collection

60. Cornplanter, the Seneca chief, who was a faithful friend and ally of the young United States. He was one of the chiefs who tried to help Colonel Thomas Proctor on his unsuccessful peace mission in the Spring of 1791. From a lithograph published by McKenney and Hall.
Smithsonian Office of Anthropology, Bureau of American Ethnology Collection

61. Tecumtha, better known as Tecumseh, the Shawnee warrior who scouted St. Clair's march for Little Turtle. His brilliant reconnaissance was partially responsible for the Indian victory. During the War of 1812, as a chief, he was a powerful foe of the United States. From an old print taken from a sketch by Pierre Le Dru in 1808.
Smithsonian Office of Anthropology, Bureau of American Ethnology Collection

TECUMTHA.

60.

61.

62.

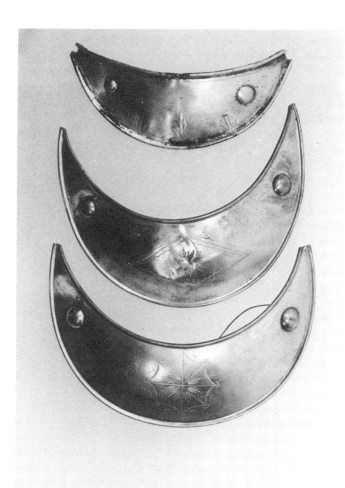

62. Three silver gorgets, circa 1780, made by American or Canadian silversmiths for the Indian trade. Special gorgets were made for treaties, with the arms of the United States, or of the state conducting the treaty with the Indians. British treaty gorgets had the British arms inscribed. *Guthman Collection*

63. Various examples of eighteenth-century Indian trade silver made for the fur trade and peace treaties by Canadian and American silversmiths. The trinkets were worn on clothing and in the hair. *Guthman Collection*

64. Wampum belt that was given to General Anthony Wayne at the Treaty of Greenville in 1795. The belt remained in the possession of Wayne's descendants until purchased by the author. *Guthman Collection*

63.

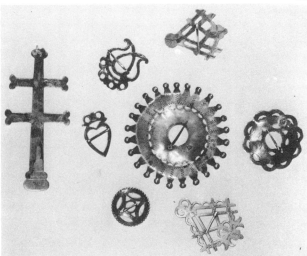

64.

65.

65. Ceremonial pouch, late eighteenth-century, Creek, made of red homespun cloth, white and green beads, and lined in print cloth, obtained from white men in trade.
Guthman Collection

66,67. Several Creek chiefs, including Alexander McGillivray, traveled to New York City in 1790 to attend a treaty. They were entertained by President Washington, Governor Clinton, the Tammany Society, and others.

The two chiefs were sketched by artist John Trumbull during this visit.
Smithsonian Institution

66,67.

The prelude to the campaigns of 1790 and 1791, highlighting the deteriorating situation on the frontier, as shown in the letters of Jonathan Heart, an officer in the Federal corps.

Background on those treaties leading up to the warfare in the northwest, and a discussion of the lawless Whites and frontier militia, precede the story of the ill-fated expedition.

Chapter 8

Part I: Prelude to the Indian Campaigns of 1790 and 1791

The Jonathan Heart correspondence discloses his observances, chronologically, while he was serving in the Federal corps on the frontier, as the Indian–United States relations deteriorated between 1786 and 1791. He was a part of the army as the form of government evolved from the Confederation to the Constitution. Pertinent excerpts from his letters presage the tragedy that climaxed the period.

His first letter[1] expresses hope for peace with the Indians through the efforts of Samuel Holden Parsons, one of the three United States commissioners treating with the tribes. "Prospects as to Peace with the Tribes in general," Heart said in January 1786,

> are more favorable, too much credit cannot be given to him [Parsons] for this, and the Events will Show, others may have the credit; that if we have peace with the Indians, General Parsons' Policy in counteracting British Emissaries and treating the Indians in a manner perfectly conformable to Honor, Fair, open plain and honest Dealings and agreeable to the feelings of unpolished Nature has done it.

An incomplete, undated[2] letter shows Heart's complete faith in the ability to overcome the hazards that existed in the new territory. Disregarding the twofold danger, Indians and the elements, Heart expressed optimism and enthusiasm for the new land:

> I was in hopes before this time I should hear of larger Parties [of settlers] moving this way. I hope reports of Indian Wars will not prevent. I cannot see sufficient grounds to determine that the Tribes who have been treated with unfriendly—*while the British troops keep possession of the Western Garrison*, their Emissaries will keep up jealousies and quarrels will ensue, but very little danger is to be apprehended by four or five hundred Families settled in any part of this Country.

[1] Heart to William Judd, Fort Harmar, January 8, 1786, Guthman Collection.
[2] A postscript is dated Fort Harmar, June 4, and there is a reference to a newspaper article dated February 7, 1786; therefore the assumption is this letter was written June 4, 1786.

He continued, expressing his greatest concern over an insufficient number of troops guarding against *squatters* on government land rather than hostile Indians.

Heart went on:

> —there has been some little appearances of War. Those who are better acquainted with Indians say they are common—the Western Tribes who have not been treated with still hold the Hatchet, and a few Banditti of the Cherikees [Cherokees], we hear, they have been to the Kentucke Settlements, where their Chief and 7 or 8 others have been kill'd—*but the Possessions of the British Garrisons Detroit, etc., is the most important Object with the United States. That will give us possession of this Country at Once*—until that time we must expect enimies and submit to Such Impositions as their Emissaries, the Indian traders, please to impose upon us. The Benefits of the Indian trade are at present great, but none can do anything at it but under British protection—.

Writing in August, Heart said: "Indian Affairs are very silent at Present—the trade uncertain it affords great profit but has great Risques—"[3] A year later he pointed out that "all our Expectations and indeed *almost every thing depends on the Northern Posts*."[4] He, of course, was referring to the Great Lakes forts which the British had refused to relinquish to the United States.

American soldiers had little communication with the rest of the world, as Heart indicated in a letter to Judd in July, when he told his friend that he had not even heard from his commanding officer "in a long while." He apologized for his limited letter: "I would be willing to fill up the sheet if I knew what to write but so long an absence and so little connections with the Eastern States I have lost all Political issues of conversation and fear I might commit some capital blunders and make up of ecclesiastical terms on civil subject—."[5] A few weeks later the news-hungry Captain told Judd: "I hope you will not fail of writing me all the Political, Foreign and domestic Intelligence in your quarters—you may believe me, we are almost starved for News—Indians is all we see, know or hear of—."[6] Heart wrote again two weeks later and reaffirmed the isolated situation: "—at this distance I know so little of the Politics, that I can form no Opinion,"[7] he said, referring to his lack of knowledge about the Ohio Company in which he hoped to own an interest.

"As to Indian news," he said, for the first time showing pessimism over any peaceful settlement, "you will have the whole in Public Papers and probable more than true—the Mohawk with Brant at their head I believe are gone to assist the Western Nations—."[8] Heart went on to say, "—the Virginians are continually killing and plundering—I am certain we shall forever have War with Indians until a different set of Inhabitants are settled on our Frontiers—."[9]

Squabbling between the states over boundary lines and territorial claims was a major factor that contributed to the disorganization of the thirteen states during the post-Revolutionary Period. These antagonisms were greatly magnified along the frontier, where disputes over land were living realities to those persons forced to cling to each other for survival in a strange and unfriendly wilderness. Blaming the Southerners (Virginians living in Kentucky—the latter a part of Virginia's land reserve) for all of the Indian trouble, as Heart had said, was typical of the lack of the cooperation that was needed on the frontier.

[3] Heart to Wm. Judd, Fort Harmar, August 9, 1786, Guthman Collection.
[4] Heart to Wm. Judd, French Creek, July 8, 1787, Guthman Collection.
[5] Heart to Wm. Judd, French Creek, July 21, 1787, Guthman Collection.
[6] Heart to Wm. Judd, French Creek, October 14, 1787, Guthman Collection.
[7] Heart to Wm. Judd, French Creek, October 30, 1787, Guthman Collection.
[8] *Ibid.*
[9] *Ibid.*

Not at all bashful about the skilled diplomacy with which he claimed the New Englander dealt with the natives, Heart boasted he had a certain manner that enabled him to get along well with his savage neighbors. It would be wise, he said, before making any land purchase to send an intelligent man to reconnoiter the country first. In contrast to the problems precipitated by the Virginians, he told Judd, "I have sufficient influence with the Indians here[10] to procure some trusty young men [braves] who will go with him and I should apprehend very little danger in going over the whole country."[11]

Two years later Heart indicated that a definite lack of communication still existed within the corps stationed along the frontier and the men were faced with an uncertainty about the status of Indian affairs that rendered their duties of diplomat and protector that much more difficult to execute. He wrote to Judd asking about General Parsons, who "with two others are appointed commissioners, I hear, to hold a treaty with the Indians and purchase the land of them—when is it to be held?"[12] Parsons, who had been appointed the first judge of the Northwest Territory in 1787, was also a director of the Ohio Company and very much involved in land speculation. Heart undoubtedly was referring to a treaty for the State of Connecticut to negotiate with the Indians who resided on the lands in the Connecticut reserve.

Simultaneous negotiations with the same tribes, *by both the Federal government and the State governments,* worked against the interests of the United States and helped to fan the flames of war by creating unrest among the tribes. This also served to add to the frustrations of the soldiers, whose interests, as revealed by Heart, were obviously twofold. Ending his letter on a note of optimism, Heart told Judd that "I hope by this time you begin to experience the Benefits of the New Government. We are anxiously awaiting the Events and to know whether anything will ever take place to our advantage."[13]

His next letter exhibits the kind of thinking that divided the Union; and yet Heart, whose final sacrifice two years later was for his country, is now responding like his contemporaries to the feudal roles played by the states. This feudal attitude, indeed, was one of the great causes for the easy victories of the Indian tribes over the United States Army. Explaining the complexities of a state-held treaty, Heart said:

> You Sir are too well acquainted with Indian Affairs to need any information with respect to the expenses of Public Treaties—the sending our messingers, delays in coming, in length of time they must be fed previous to business and etc.—in particular in the present instance than Connecticut will think proper to advance, and as for taking advantage of any public treaty if will make very little difference. The more an Indian receives the more he expects and unless you find out and acquaint them with the business previous to their coming, they will not finally conclude it—besides it is not probable there will be another general treaty very soon—therefore in answer to your Queries, how, where and when will it be best to hold a treaty with the Indians, etc.,

[10] Heart was probably referring to lands in the Connecticut reserve when he suggested Judd obtain a man to reconnoiter the territory before making any purchases. Judd acted as Heart's business representative back East. Reciprocating the favors of Judd and other associates in the land ventures back home, Heart sent all of the information he could gather about the most desirable lands: where they were located, which had minerals, where the best soil was located and the type of terrain and timber. He also drew maps and attempted to send surveys.
[11] Heart to Judd, French Creek, October 30, 1787, Guthman Collection.
[12] Heart to Judd, Fort Franklin, May 18, 1789, Guthman Collection.
[13] Heart to Judd (Referring to the new Constitutional government), Fort Franklin, May 18, 1789, Guthman Collection.

permit me to say I would recommend a Private and separate Treaty with the different Nations at their different hunting Grounds or Villages and as soon as possible.[14]

(Heart was referring to the state of Connecticut holding a private treaty with the Indians in hopes of extinguishing their claims to the Connecticut—Western Reserve—Lands.)

The reasons for holding a Private Treaty are partly assigned above and in addition calling them together will look like a tacit acknowledgement that the lands have not been ceded and will give them an opportunity of consulting together, forming plans and of receiving the advice of the Western Indians (whose interest it is that those lands should not be relinquished) not to consent to any extinguishing of claims whereas those Lands have long since been ceded, ratified and confirmed by the Delawares who were the actual proprietors and the Indians who now reside and hunt on those Grounds have no just claims; yet, as from long usage they have hunted on those Grounds and by possession have attended a kind of claim; it will be good Policy to make them a compliment for obtaining their friendly concurrence and this I presume may be done by holding our Proper Terms—which leads to an Answer to your Query what kind of terms will be best calculated to gain their Confidence and Friendship—I should adopt a System very ["different"? he omits the word] from any as yet held out—the Indians now residing on that tract are a small village of the Six Nations at the Northeast corner a few Delawares at the south and southeast, Chippeways, Ottaways and Potowattamis on the North and West—These, particularly the three last, are in small parties from different families and their respective nations who live at a great distance from those Grounds. Then in the first place I would give a general invitation to those who are now, have been accustomed to or even wish to hunt on those Ground to come and sett themselves down and then reside and encourage them to do it in the first instance grant to them their Heirs and assignes forever a certain tract or tracts (to the different nations, Tribes or families as they would wish) sufficient for them for towns and Corn Fields, and guarantee them a full right to pass and repass, cut timber, build hunting Camps, hunt and fish in any and all parts of said Tract forever—and also make them some Presents not as a Purchase of the Lands, but as an assurance and in Testimony of the Contract—as to the Querie respecting the Lands I am not able to determine—from general information that there is much good and also large Tracts of very indifferent Lands and the present mode will oblige the purchaser to take so much bad lands with the good and the risque whether the Tract you wish for and purchase may not finally fall even in a different Town. That there is not sufficient encouragement to the purchaser. Thus, I have endeavored to answer the main part of your Letter. I expect soon to have the pleasure of seeing you at Muskingum and shall be happy in giving every assistance in my Power, for carrying the wishes of the State of Connecticut into Execution. . . .[15]

By June 1790 Heart was discouraged about the prospects of the United States ever attaining a strong, well-trained army to combat the hostile tribes. The Indian situation, which had deteriorated

---

[14] Heart to Judd, Fort Franklin, August 20, 1789, Guthman Collection.
[15] *Ibid.*

swiftly, was critical and the new Congress had just passed an act[16] which lowered the basic pay of the Federal army, thus demoralizing the infant corps when it was faced with its most critical chore. Heart's letter imparts his sarcasm and disgust over the new military act and exposes the cold reality of the undeclared Indian war in which they were involved.

He also discredited a false report he had heard was circulating in Connecticut: "I am informed that Captain Heart is taken by the Indians as report says in Connecticut—it is not true. Neither is Majour Doughty kill'd. He lost Seven Men kill'd and four wounded of our fifteen[17]—I was with

[16] The act of April 30, 1790, although raising pay of the commanding officer, lowered the pay of all of the other officers and enlisted men. The effect of this act upon the men is clearly defined in the bitterness that Heart expressed in his letter to Judd. The act stated:

Lieutenant–Colonel Commandant	$60 per month
Major–Commandant of artillery	45 " "
Majors	40 " "
Captains	30 " "
Lieutenants	22 " "
Ensigns	18 " "
Surgeons	30 " "
Surgeons' Mates	24 " "
Sergeants	5 " "
Corporals	4 " "
Privates	3 " "
Senior Musicians	5 " "
Musicians	3 " "

The act further provided for the following deductions:
    monthly from sergeants and senior musicians—$1.40 for uniform
    clothing and .10 for hospital stores.
    monthly for corporals—$1.15 for uniform clothing and .10 for hospital stores.
    monthly for privates and musicians—.90 for uniform clothing and .10 for hospital stores.

[*Acts Passed at a Congress of the United States of America*, Begun and Held at the City of New York, on Wednesday, the Fourth of March, in the Year M, DCC, LXXXIX, Hartford: Reprinted and Sold by Hudson & Goodwin, M, DCC, XCI, pp. 173–75.]
    Forage and rations were reduced for the officers. Clothing allowance was as follows for noncommissioned officers and privates annually:

1 hat or helmet	1 coat
1 vest	2 pair of woolen overalls
2 pair linen coveralls	4 pair of shoes
4 shirts	2 pair of socks
1 blanket	1 stock and clasp
1 pair buckles	

The following daily rations for noncommissioned officers and privates:

    1 lb. of beef or ¾ lb. of pork
    1 lb. of bread or flour
    ½ gill of rum, brandy or whisky [liquor ration cut in half, and from a morale point of
    view, probably just as disturbing as the cut in pay.]
    1 quart of salt, 2 quarts of vinegar, 2 lbs. of soap, 1lb. of candles—every 100 rations
                                                                                                   [*Ibid.*]
[17] Major Doughty was ordered on a peace mission to the Cherokee by Secretary of War Knox. They had been attacked March 22 on the Tennessee River and his force of 15 men was whittled down to four actives. The battle lasted four hours and Doughty's surviving group of five wounded, four actives, escaped, and were given aid by the Spanish commander at New Madrid (a Mississippi River town in Spanish territory and today located in the state of Missouri). (Thornbrough, *op. cit.*, p. 231 footnote.)

him—."[18] (The news in the letter clearly illustrates the severity of the Indian problem.)
Heart's displeasure over the pay decrease was obvious when he told Judd:

> Yesterday we returned to this Place—after having been absent five months—I
> have not time to particularize my route; at some other time—are you all determined to
> brake up the Army—on what Principles is pay reduced; is it to compell Americans to
> act the villinous Part of cheating the Public—I believe there is yet virtue enough
> remaining to induce them rather to resign—It is said the whole is done by the influence
> of the New England Members [of Congress]—I do not believe it—."[19]

Several days later Heart enlightened his friend with a more detailed letter.[20] "I forwarded a few
lines some days since to acquainte you that I am neither Dead or a Prisoner as report has informed—I
have had a most Fatiguing Command a small detail of which I wrote the Doctor—it is impossible for
me to give the least conjecture what will be the Consequence of our troubles here—,"[21] he said,
referring to the Indian situation. Referring to the forthcoming Indian campaigns, Heart prophesied
quite accurately:

> —if Congress wished to support any Dignity in this Country their measures must be on
> a Scale well enlarged. If this Country is of no importance, let Congress leave to the
> people here to defend; the sale of the land is doubtless of consequence, but the
> forming of settlements will be granted is of infinite detriment to the Present Federal
> States by opening such a door for migration—but land so valuable cannot be kept in a
> State of nonimprovement [he bears out the reasoning of a civilized nation versus a
> savage nation in claiming the rights of the soil]—then this single question will arise,
> will it be best to have the Territory settled under the auspices, Aid and Assistance of
> Congress by People attached to republican governments who have Friends and
> connections in the Atlantic States or will it tend to strengthen the Cords of Government
> by which we even now scarcely hold the territory West of the Mountains—for
> Congress to oppose the Settlements leave it without Law or support opens a Door for its
> becoming an Asylum for a Banditti without Principles of Law attached to no
> Government and never having had an assistance in its defence will think themselves
> under very little obligation to the Mother States—.[22]

Changing the subject, Heart went on:

> But no more of National Politics—I perceive the State of Connecticut have lost
> their Lands—as the Indian Claims cannot be extinguished except at Public Treaty.
> There never will be another treaty nearer than Detroit or the Kaskaskias. The
> attendance of your commissioners (Connecticut), etc., at that distance is more than the
> Territory is worth at 20 cents the acre and certainly you must sell as low as Congress
> sells their Lands—I think the State justly punished tho I pitty some of the
> Individuals—Jealousy and fear have cost them their State Debt—.[23]

[18] Heart to Judd, June 16, 1790, Fort Harmar, Guthman Collection.
[19] *Ibid.*
[20] Heart to Judd, June 20, 1790, Fort Harmar, Guthman Collection.
[21] *Ibid.*
[22] *Ibid.*
[23] *Ibid.*

Centralization of the Constitutional government was beginning to take effect, and the passing of states' autonomy is reflected in Heart's reference to the impracticality of an individual state treaty with the Indians. His reference to individual losses due to jealousy and fear and the exclusion of individual treaties except under the auspices of the general government are an indication of strengthening of the Union and the lessening of the power of the state in matters of national importance. Heart actually contradicts himself in the letter, wishing on one hand that the national government would take a strong position, as far as the army is concerned, against the Indians, but expressing bitterness over the central government's control of policymaking with the Indians and excluding the prerogative of the individual states to act in this capacity. Failing to recognize the seriousness of the Indian situation, and unable to evaluate the capabilities of the tribes, Heart reported to Judd in July, 1790, stating that the settlement at Marietta was progressing as well as could be expected[24] and that the Indian danger would not be a problem to those settlers "by another Season."[25]

Commenting about the new military arrangements, he said, "We are waiting to hear whether Congress intend to put up with Insults [Indian] or with proper Dignity resent their insolence—."[26] He injected sarcasm, as he said: "—the new arrangement of the Army does not look like any great military operation and savours too much of what we would call *Penny Wise*—but as Congress knows all things doubtless it must be right—."[27]

Writing again on September 9, 1790, Heart complained about the impracticality of the system of the land division that the Ohio Company had instituted[28] and the conflict of interest of those directors of the Ohio Company who also served as directors of the Scioto Company.[29] Critical of the land company in which he had a financial interest (The Ohio Company), Heart then turned his criticism to the treaty just concluded between the United States and the Creek nation: "Alexander McGilvrey [the Creek Chief] has cheated Congress—as Indians always do white people—it is better to be a Doorkeeper in the House of the Lord than to dwell in tents of Wickedness for Congress give their Doorkeeper 730 Dollars a year, a Lt. Col. Commandant has only 720 Dollars a year—."[30] (Heart was referring to McGillivray, who was given a pension of $1,200 a year and the honorary rank of brigadier-general.)

Returning from the Harmar expedition on November 4, 1790,[31] Heart wrote: "We yesterday returned from the expedition against the Miami villages, that nest of murderers—which we have entirely destroy'd, etc."[32] Heart led Judd to believe the expedition was highly successful. It was not. However, his statement underscores the illusion that existed. Heart and his contemporaries, used to permanence in both fortifications and dwellings, burned the evacuated villages of the Miami tribes along with their winter corn supply. But the Indian's dwelling was a temporary affair; its loss of little importance to him. His winter corn was an important asset, but he might have lost it many other ways, for the savage did not take proper precautions to preserve and provide for the winter months. He was used to this kind of an emergency, and the Miamis had the British at Detroit to depend on for supplies during the winter.

[24] Heart to Judd, Fort Harmar, July 29, 1790, Guthman Collection.
[25] *Ibid.*
[26] *Ibid.*
[27] *Ibid.*
[28] Heart to Judd, For Harmar, September 9, 1790, Guthman Collection.
[29] *Ibid.*
[30] *Ibid.*
[31] St. Clair's defeat (November 4, 1791) was exactly one year from the date of this letter of Heart's.
[32] Heart to Judd, Fort Washington, November 4, 1790, Guthman Collection.

Heart's letter went on:

> I suppose the History of New England, that seat of Indian Wars (Pequot), scarcely affords an Instance of such another Bloody action. They fought with desperation. Our loss was great and amongst the kill'd we have to drop a tear to the Memory of those good men Major Wyllys and Lieutenant Frothingham. I have not time to enter into further particulars.[33]

The December 28 letter[34] was entirely concerned with business of the Ohio Company and land speculation. Heart said there was nothing new but severe weather and "peace." On September 2, 1791, he wrote his last letter to Judd. It was pathetic and prophetic. Heart told of the unprepared state of the new troops recruited for the expedition. Heart was killed, along with most of the regulars, on November 4 of that year.

Part II: The Events Leading Up to the Hostilities

Included with his January 4, 1790, report on the Southern Indians, Henry Knox submitted to President Washington a brief résumé of the northwestern Indian–frontiersman controversy. Those people living Northwest of the Ohio River did not get the proper protection from military posts, he said; they therefore employed their own militia at the expense of the United States. "The economy of disciplined troops is always superior to militia," he continued, "while their efficacy is at least equal; hence, if troops are employed within the district of Kentucky, as patrols or otherwise, they ought to be detachments from the regular troops of the United States, under orders of the commanding officer on the Ohio." Unknowingly, Knox's views on disciplined troops as opposed to militia were a prophecy of the unfortunate campaigns that followed, when the undisciplined militia, along with regulars, were defeated. He continued: "About four companies, acting as patrols or scouts, would afford all the satisfaction to the settlements which could be derived from defensive measures; *but it is only from offensive measures that full security can be obtained.*"

Pointing out that the tribes situated on the Wabash River extending up to the Miami village (present-day Fort Wayne) frequently attacked the settlements of Kentucky, Knox said that those Whites who received injury from the Wabash Indians often made incursions into the Wabash country Northwest of the Ohio River, indiscriminately taking revenge against all Indians. This, then, was the problem that existed in 1790 that required immediate attention of the United States.

"That the people of Kentucky are entitled to be defended, there can be no doubt," Knox said, "But, as there seems to have been such a prevalence of hostilities as to render it uncertain who are wrong or who are right, the principles of justice, which ought to dictate the conduct of every nation, seems to forbid the idea of attempting to extirpate the Wabash Indians, until it should appear that they cannot be brought to treat on reasonable terms." He continued, "If, after a treaty should be effected with them, it should be violated, or, after an invitation to treaty, it should be refused, and followed by hostilities, the United States will clearly have the right to inflict that degree of punishment which may be necessary to deter the Indians from any future unprovoked aggressions."

---

[33] *Ibid.*
[34] Heart to Judd, Fort Harmar, December 28, 1790, Guthman Collection.

General St. Clair, the governor of the Northwest Territory, should be instructed to effect a general treaty with the Wabash tribes, Knox said, and, if the Indians refused, the United States should chastise them. Discussing the proper preparations for the treaty, the Secretary of War emphasized that Congress should provide gifts to the Indians as well as provisions.[35] "It seems," he said, "to have been the custom of barbarous nations, in all ages, to expect and receive presents from those more civilized, and the custom seems confirmed by Modern Europe, with respect to Morocco, Algiers, Tunis and Tripoli." Continuing, "The practice of the British government and its colonies, of giving presents to the Indians of North America is well known. They seem to have been convinced that *it was the cheapest and most effectual mode of managing the Indians.*" Knox suggested that "the idea of fear, in purchasing a peace, is not to be admitted, in the cases above stated, but the conduct appears to have been dictated by wise policy. A comparative view of the expenses of a hostile or conciliatory system towards the Indians, will evince the infinite economy of the latter over the former."

If the United States discontinued the custom of distributing presents to the Indians, he continued, this would only tend to push them closer to those European colonies that continued the practice. Estimating the number of gifts needed, Knox figured that there were 20,000 Indian warriors in the United States, and 60,000 old men, women and children—a total Indian population for 1790 of 80,000. Knox added,

> Since the United States became a nation, their conduct, and the conduct of some of the states, towards the Indians, seems to have resulted from *impulses of the moment.* Until the treaty effected at Fort Harmar January 9, 1789, it seemed a prevailing opinion that the Treaty of Peace with Great Britain, instead of the preemption only, actually invested the United States with the absolute right to the Indian territory. In pursuance of this idea, treaties were made and boundaries allotted to the Indians. But by the direction of Congress, of the 2nd July, 1788, to the Governor of the Western Territory, to extinguish the Indian claims to lands they had ceded to the United States, and to obtain regular conveyance of the same, *it would appear that they conceded the Indian right to the soil.*

Comparing that which had already taken place with what he thought should take place, he continued:

> The various opinions which exist on the proper mode of treating with the Indians, require that some system should be established on the subject. That the Indians possess the natural rights of man, and that they ought not wantonly to be divested thereof, *but in* consequence of open treaties, made under the authority of the United States, the foundation of peace and justice would be laid.

Suggesting that the states' perogative to individual treaties with the Indians was a severe detriment to the Union (as Heart had commented), he continued: "The individual states claiming or possessing the right of preemption to territory inhabited by Indians, would not be materially injured by such a declarative law; the exercise of their right would be restrained only when it should interfere with the general interest."

---

[35] See Notes for return of sundry articles of Indian treaties in 1785 and 1786, dated New York, July 22, 1786, *Harmar Papers* (in *Knox Papers* of August 2, 1786).

Spotlighting one of the major problems facing the United States, he came to the point: "Should any state, having the right of preemption, desire to purchase territory, which the Indians should be willing to relinquish, it would have to request the General Government to direct a treaty for that purpose, at the expense, however, of the individual state requesting the same." Proving himself an excellent analyst of the Indian situation, he continued: "But as Indian wars almost invariably arise in consequence of disputes relative to boundaries or trade, and as the rights of declaring war, making treaties, and regulating commerce, are vested in the United States, it is highly proper *they should have sole direction of all measures for the consequence* [of] *which they are responsible*."

Part III: Militia

When President Washington requested Congress for aid from the militia, most of the regular troops were offended. The Federal corps had been recruited mainly from Eastern states; the militia were the Virginia and Pennsylvania frontiersmen, living along the Ohio River and there were enough differences in backgrounds of the men to create antagonism.

Congress passed a resolution July 21, 1787, providing that, in case the Indian situation worsened, "The executive of Virginia be requested to give orders to the militia in the district of Kentucky, to hold themselves in readiness to unite with the federal troops, in such operations as the officer commanding them may judge necessary for the protection of the frontiers—."[36] Again, on August 12, 1788, Congress passed a resolution requesting that

> the Executives of Virginia and Pennsylvania, be requested to give orders to the militia of their respective frontiers, to hold themselves in readiness to unite with the Federal troops in such operations as the governor of the western territory may judge necessary for the protection of the inhabitants; and that on application of the said governor, the said executive be requested to give orders that parts of their said militia, not exceeding 1,000 for Virginia and 500 for Pennsylvania, be embodied and take such positions *as the commanding officers of the federal troops shall direct* for acting in conjunction with the said federal troops—.[37]

The resolve went on to say that the militia shall be "paid, supported and equipped by the states from which the same may be respectively called, and that such state be credited for the same out of the existing specie requisitions so far as such expenditures shall be for pay and rations, which are to be computed on the federal establishment for similar service, etc.—."[38]

Commandant Harmar told Secretary of War Knox, in a letter written September 14, 1788, that the resolve of August 12, 1788, requisitioning militia from Pennsylvania and Virginia would defeat all the plans of the regular army if militia colonels should "take command of the Majors of the

[36] *Journals of Congress,* Vol. 12, July 12, 1787.
[37] *Journals of Congress,* Vol. 13, August 12, 1788; and *St. Clair Papers,* manuscript letter of Charles Thompson, Guthman Collection.
[38] *Journals of Congress,* Vol. 13, August 12, 1788.

regiment."[39] He went on to say: "It is lamentable circumstance that instead of calling for Militia, the Government is so feeble as not to afford three or four Regiments of national troops properly organized who would soon settle the business with these perfidious Villains upon the Wabash."[40]

One day later, Governor St. Clair told Secretary at War Knox that if something happened during an expedition against the Indians to the commanding officer, rather than let the command go to a militia officer of a higher rank, it would be best to promote regular officers, like Hamtramck and Wyllys.[41] "If the ragamuffins of the Militia were to command," St. Clair said, "I have seen few in my life that would be fit for it."[42] St. Clair was placing his finger squarely on the problem—the officers of the Federal corps rebelled against serving under senior officers in the militia.

Lieutenant John Armstrong sent a letter to Commandant Harmar December 29, 1788, that began, "Dear Sir, By Captain Beatty I informed you of an Injury done me by being ordered to march to Post Vincennes *under the command of a militia officer* on state affairs, etc.—."[43] Armstrong wrote about the inadequate soldiering, lack of routine on the march, and poor reconnaissance of the territory on the part of the militia.

As early as 1786 the Federal troops resented the participation of organized militia groups entering into military activities. Harmar criticized the expedition in 1786 of Kentucky Militia Colonel Benjamin Logan. He returned to Limestone, Harmar told Henry Knox, with 900 militia, having met very little opposition as all of the warriors had gone to meet General George Rogers Clark. Burning towns, taking a few scalps and women and children prisoners, Logan was severely criticized for shooting a friendly Shawanee chief, Melanthy. "Melanthy, the Shawanese chief, would not fly, but displayed the thirteen stripes and held out the articles of the Miami treaty, but all in vain; he was shot down by one of the party, although he was their prisoner. I am sorry that this disgraceful affair should have happened as Melanthy had always been represented as a friend to the United States."[44] Harmar added that Clark's own expedition was a failure, as 400 of his 1,100-man expedition deserted.[45]

In a letter to surveyor general Hutchins, Harmar said that the shooting of Chief Melanthy "was a breech of faith on the part of the United States."[46] From militia expeditions in 1786 through expeditions in 1788, the retaliation of the frontier settlers continued to antagonize the Federal troops as well as the Indians—possibly because the troops were not strong enough to contain either the Indians or the retaliating Kentuckians. Harmar told Knox, in a letter dated December 9, 1787, that "It is a mortifying circumstance, that while under the sanction of federal authority, negotiations and treaties are holding with the Indians, that there should be such presumption in the people of Kentucky as to be forming expeditions against them."[47]

Writing to Major Wyllys December 9, 1788, Harmar said: "It is a mortifying affair that you were obliged to call upon the Militia for the Cattle Escort—It is my wish that not a single officer of the Regiment may ever have the humiliating disgrace of being subjected to Militia Command, but suppose in the present case you found it unavoidable."[48]

[39] *Harmar Papers,* Vol. 28, Letter Book D, Harmar to Knox, September 14, 1788.
[40] *Ibid.*
[41] *Knox Papers,* St. Clair to Knox, September 15, 1788, Roll 22.
[42] *Ibid.*
[43] Thornbrough, *Outpost on the Wabash,* pp. 143–44.
[44] *Harmar Papers,* Vol. 28, Letter Book B, Harmar to Knox, November 15, 1786.
[45] *Ibid.*
[46] *Harmar Papers,* Harmar to Hutchins, Vol. 28, Letter Book B.
[47] *Harmar Papers,* Harmar to Knox, Vol. 28, Letter Book B.
[48] *Harmar Papers,* Harmar to Wyllys, Vol. 29, Letter Book E.

Reporting to the President September 14, 1789, the Governor of the Western Territory summed up the events of the past years:

> The constant hostilities between the Indians who live upon the river Wabash, and the people of Kentucky, must necessarily be attended with such embarrassing circumstances to the Government of the Western territory, that I am induced to request you will be pleased to take the matter into consideration, and give me the orders you may think proper.
>
> It is not to be expected, sir, that the Kentucky people will, or can, submit patiently to the cruelties and depredations of those savages; they are in the habit of retaliation, perhaps without attending precisely to the nations from which the injuries are received. They will continue to retaliate, or they will apply to the Governor of the Western country (through which the Indians must pass to attack them) for redress; if he cannot redress them (and in present circumstances he cannot), they also will march through that country, to redress themselves, and the government will be laid prostrate. The United States, on the other hand, are at peace with several of the nations; and, should the resentment of those people fall upon any of them, which it is unlikely enough may happen, very bad consequences will follow.[49]

St. Clair went on to say that the Indians would soon feel the United States had no regard for any of the treaties it had made in the past and they would unite against the government. This, he said, would place his office in a bad position, in which he could neither redress nor protect the Indians, nor the white settlers. Therefore, St. Clair asked Washington to request Congress to call upon the militias of Kentucky and Pennsylvania to "act in conjunction with the continental troops and carry war into the Indian settlements."[50] He said this resolution would then conciliate the Western people, showing them that the government had not forgotten them, and would also be used as a threat to the Indians.[51] It would, he thought, possibly eliminate the need for an expedition against the Indians. He closed by saying that "The handful of troops, sir, that are scattered in that country, though they may afford protection to some settlements, cannot possibly act offensively by themselves."[52]

St. Clair was wrong. The threat to the Indians by Congress ordering up the militia to supplement the regular army did not deter them from further depredations. Pitted against the Indian in man-to-man combat, protected by brush and trees in his familiar woodlands, the frontiersman was an incomparable fighter. Ohio River valley farmers, also serving in the militia, stood to the death when fighting off the vermilion-striped savages who were burning their homes and torturing their women and children.

But the frontier trappers and hunters and the men who tilled the soil found themselves in a frightening circumstance when they faced the hated enemy, in the vulnerable exposed ranks of a formal military expedition whose demanding discipline they despised. Bewildered and frightened, they ran, leaving the regulars to stand and protect them until death. If the army had deviated from tradition and learned, in humbleness, the guerrilla methods of the woodsmen, the outcome might have been entirely different.

---

[49] *American State Papers,* Vol. 1, Indian Affairs, p. 58.
[50] *Ibid.*
[51] *Ibid.*
[52] *Ibid.*

Part IV: Treaties with the Northwest Tribes

Shortly after negotiations with Great Britain had been concluded, and a treaty of peace agreed upon, the United States began a series of separate negotiations with the various tribes of the Northwest Territory. Commissioners Plenipotentiary for the United States Oliver Wolcott, Richard Butler, and Arthur Lee held a treaty with the Six Nations (the Mohawks, Oneidas, Onondagas, Tuscaroras, Cayugas, and Senecas) at Fort Stanwix on October 22, 1784, at which time the western boundary line of the Six Nations was agreed upon and drawn.

Those same commissioners for the United States held a second treaty at Fort McIntosh on January 21, 1785, with the Wyandot, Chippewa, Delaware, and Ottawa nations, at which time the boundary line South of Lake Erie was agreed upon. A third treaty was held at the mouth of the Great Miami River January 31, 1786, between the United States Commissioners Richard Butler, George Rogers Clark, and Samuel Holden Parsons and the Shawnee Nation; and a boundary line was drawn between that nation and the United States.

Maintaining that the above tribes were the defeated allies of the British, and accepting the principle of the right of the transfer of ownership of the land that Great Britain ceded according to the terms of the Treaty of Paris, the United States pushed the northwestern tribes back far enough to quickly cause them to become alarmed and join into a confederation which renounced the past treaties. Aided and abetted by Great Britain, the Confederate Council, consisting of the Five Nations,[53] Hurons, Ottawa, Twightwees,[54] Shawnese, Chippewas, Cherokees, Delawares, Potawatomis, and the Wabash Confederates met at the Huron Village near the mouth of the Detroit River November 28 through December 18, 1786. Persuaded by the British agents, and the Mohawk leader Joseph Brant, the confederation called for an end to individual treaties. "You kindled your council fires where you thought proper, without consulting us, at which you held separate treaties, and have entirely neglected our plan of having a general conference with the different nations of the confederacy."[55] A halt to all surveying "and others that mark the land" was demanded, as well as a stop to surveyors and settlers crossing the Ohio onto "our side," until a treaty could be held in early spring.

Reviewing the past situation in a report to President Washington May 23, 1789,[56] Henry Knox said that the Indians were exceedingly tenacious of their land and did not generally relinquish title except upon the principle of purchase. When the United States was a British colony, the Crown had established the practice of purchasing Indian lands, and, he said, because of this long-continued practice, it would in 1789 be difficult to violate this custom without causing an Indian war that would be far more costly than the original purchase price.

Because the treaties of Fort Stanwix and Fort McIntosh did not state that the boundaries agreed upon were defined by purchase from the Indians, he continued, the Indians at the council held in 1786 at the mouth of the Detroit River considered the past treaties null and void.

Congress then passed a resolution, on October 5, 1787, ordering a general treaty held with those tribes residing within the limits of the United States northwest of the Ohio River and in the vicinity of

---

[53] The six Iroquois-speaking nations were sometimes referred to as the the Five Nations—the Tuscaroras, who were admitted last, were never given full status by the original five other tribes.
[54] Twightwees, or "naked Indians," was the name given to the Miamis by the English. (W. Kinietz, *The Indians of the Western Great Lakes,* University of Michigan Press, 1940, Ann Arbor, p. 167.)
[55] *American State Papers,* Vol. 1, Indian Affairs, p. 9.
[56] *Ibid.,* pp. 7–9.

Lake Erie. The treaty was to be held as soon after April 1, 1788 as weather permitted, at the time and place selected by Arthur St. Clair, the governor of the Northwest Territory. Congress instructed the Superintendent of Indian Affairs of the Northern department to inform the tribes of the resolution.

That resolution was repealed October 12, 1787, and another resolution was passed appropriating $20,000 for the purpose of Indian treaties whenever Congress judged them necessary. Congress resolved on October 22, 1787, that the governor of the Northwest Territory was empowered to hold a general treaty the following spring, if he judged it necessary, and was authorized to draw $14,000 of the $20,000 appropriation allotted October 12 of that year. An additional $20,000—plus the $6,000 remaining from the original $20,000 appropriation—was authorized by Congress to be used exclusively for extinguishing Indian claims to land which they had already ceded to the United States at previous treaties since the termination of the Revolution.

The Northwest Ordinance was passed three months earlier that year. It has already been noted that this ordinance set up the territorial government for the ownership of land which the United States was about to renegotiate with the Indians. Provision was made for a governor to head the territory, and he was almost immediately called upon to treat with the Indians in order to secure ownership for that same territory to which he had already been appointed to govern.[57]

A letter of instruction from Congress, written October 26, 1787, by Charles Thomson, secretary of the Continental Congress, was sent to the governor of the Northwest Territory ordering him to examine the "real temper" of the Indians inhabiting the northern district.[58] If the governor found the Indians hostile, and the welfare of the frontier inhabitants demanded a treaty, then, in conjunction with the superintendent of Indian affairs of that district, a general treaty with all of the tribes was to be held.[59] (This is exactly what the confederation of tribes, influenced by the British Indian department, had demanded in 1786.)

The primary object of the treaty, Congress said, was to remove all causes of controversy between the United States and the Indian tribes, settling the boundaries and regulating trade with the Indians. Congress told St. Clair that "For this purpose you will do everything that is *right* and *proper*."[60] He was also told that the treaties made in the past might be examined but must *not* be departed from unless a beneficial change in a boundary was derived for the United States.[61] "Although the purchase of the Indian right of soil is not a primary object of holding this treaty, yet you will not neglect any opportunity that may offer, of extinguishing the Indian rights to the westward, as far as the river Mississippi."[62] He was further ordered to stipulate that the east–west boundary line, ordered to be run by the ordinance of May 20, 1785, should be the boundary between the United States and the Indian tribes, as long as the Indians agreed that it should run "throughout unto the river Mississippi."[63] Any white person, he was told, who trespassed over that boundary without a proper license would be subjected to whatever manner of punishment the Indians wished to inflict upon the lawbreaker. St. Clair was also instructed to ascertain who were the "real head men and warriors" of the different tribes—and also those who had the greatest influence over the tribes. "These men," he was told, "you will attach to the United States, by every means in your power."[64] In conclusion, the letter stated that every exertion was to be made to defeat the "confederations and combinations among the tribes" and to conciliate the white settlers living along the frontiers toward all the Indians.[65]

[57] The treaty was not held, however, until January 9, 1789, at Fort Harmar.
[58] *American State Papers,* Vol. 1, Indian Affairs, pp. 7–9.
[59] *Ibid.*
[60] *Ibid.*
[61] *Ibid.*
[62] *Ibid.*
[63] *Ibid.*
[64] *Ibid.*
[65] *Ibid.*

A second letter from Thomson was written to St. Clair July 2, 1788, with additional instructions. A sum of $26,000 had been appropriated by Congress for the sole purpose of "obtaining a boundary advantageous to the United States."[66] It went on to say that the sum was to be used, also, "for further extinguishing by purchase Indian titles, in case it can be done on terms beneficial to the Union."[67]

Thomson emphasized that further purchases were not to be made unless "on terms evidently advantageous to the United States."[68] The boundary line, stipulated in the letter of last October, was to be changed from the east and west line to a new east and west line as far north "as the completion of the 41st degree of north latitude."[69] St. Clair was told to make payments for the purchase of lands immediately, as long as he had money in hand; but, if he found it necessary to use the additional funds appropriated, those payments should be delayed as late in the year 1789 as possible.

Preparations for the treaty were first recorded in the copybook of the 1st American Regiment on March 1, 1788. Commandant Harmar sent a letter from headquarters at Fort Harmar to Major Wyllys, who was stationed with his detachment at Fort Finney, instructing the major to turn over to Ensign Spear all of the commissioner's goods for the forthcoming treaty.[70] Food, presents, and supplies for the Indians who were to attend the treaty had been stored in Fort Finney, and Ensign Spear had been detached with twelve privates and a corporal and ordered to proceed by boat to Fort Finney to transport the supplies.[71]

Garrison orders at Fort Harmar on March 6, 1788, instructed the troops to treat visiting Indians with courtesy:

> Captain Pipes the Chief of the Delaware nation with some of his young men may be expected the day after tomorrow at the garrison—the Soldiery are strictly ordered to use those Indians in the most Friendly manner—the hunters are forbidden to go up the Muskingum, any where near their Encampment—if they should presume to menace or ill treat any of these Indians—the Military Law shall certainly take place.[72]

Private Lewis Leach was sentenced to receive 100 lashes at morning roll call on April 3, 1788, for stealing "three belts of wampum."[73]

Even though the army was trying to maintain cordial relations with all the Indian tribes, some of the Miamis living along the Wabash who were in constant communication with the British at Detroit could not be influenced by the overture of the intended treaty. Ensign Spear's party, returning with the provisions for the treaty, was

> fired upon by some vagabond Wabash Indians—he lost only two men—Mr. Melchior[74] was on board the boat. The fire was returned from the troops, they fired two rounds instantly, but the Savages have great advantage over boats ascending the River—I sincerely hope the New Government will shortly be adopted, and that the

[66] *Ibid.*

[67] *Ibid.*

[68] *Ibid.*

[69] *Ibid.*

[70] *Harmar Papers,* Vol. 28, Letter Book C, Harmar to Wyllys, March 1, 1788.

[71] *Harmar Papers,* Vol. 28, Letter Book C, Harmar to Spear, March 7, 1788.

[72] *Harmar Papers,* Vol. 32, Order Books 1784–88, Fort Harmar, March 6, 1788.

[73] *Ibid.,* April 3, 1788.

[74] Jacob Melcher was a cadet from Pennsylvania. He joined the regiment in 1787 and was commissioned an ensign Sept. 29, 1789.

next Treaty (provided the present intended one has not the desired effect) may be held with the Savages with 1,500 or 2,000 Troops—,[75]

Josiah Harmar told Governor Mifflin of Pennsylvania.

Another incident occurred a short time later when Ensign McDowell's detachment of twenty privates, escorting more provisions for the treaty, were attacked and several killed. On their way to the falls of the Muskingum with the trade goods, and under orders to build a council room there for the ensuing treaty, they were attacked by Ottawas and Chippewas. Harmar, furious over the audacity of the Indians, said, "The loss of the men is not so great as the insult offered to the dignity of the United States."[76] He added, "I hope the time is not far distant when an augmentation of the troops will take place, and that we may be enabled to sweep these perfidious Savages off the face of the Earth—."[77]

St. Clair requested Harmar to have the men and provisions return to Fort Harmar and he deferred the treaty, demanding an apology from the Indians. Another officer, Ensign Sedam, and his detachment were also attacked on their way from the Miami River to the falls of the Ohio—and the frequency of incidents at a time when the United States was trying to create a peaceful negotiation with the Indians was humiliating the small force of soldiers whose detached forces each consisting of a handful of men bore the brunt of the Indians' hostility.

Less than a month later Harmar issued an order that reflected the other side of the picture of the assignment that the small Federal corps was faced with and entrusted to secure. In a letter to Captain David Zeigler he said:

> The Six Nations are on their way by water to the treaty, which is to be held at this Post—I am informed that several Vagabonds [white settlers] in the Neighborhood of Wheeling meant to fire upon these Indians on their passage down the Ohio to this Post—such a step might be attended with Ruinous Consequences—You are hereby ordered to take the said Indians under your protection and safely escort them to this Garrison—Treat them kindly, and if any of these lawless Rascals should presume to fire upon them, you are ordered to land and attack them in Return for their insolence and defiance of the Supreme Authority. . . .[78]

The 1st American Regiment was little more than an understaffed police force trying to maintain peace between savages, who, born into a culture that trained them for war, were fearful of losing their hunting grounds and embittered Whites, filled with the desire for revenge, who had suffered the ravages of those Indian tribes and who had lived on the governmentless frontiers so long that law and order was something they read about—whenever they were fortunate enough to obtain a newspaper. The intended treaty was, in retrospect, only wishful thinking on the part of the United States government—a government that was not respected by its citizens on the frontiers because it could neither protect them nor prevent them from attacking the savages. At stake were the valuable lands of the Northwest Territory and the fur trade, all depending upon the results of the forthcoming treaty. Interested spectators were the foreign governments who had thousands of dollars of trade to lose if

---

[75] *Harmar Papers,* Vol. 28, Letter Book C, Harmar to Mifflin, Fort Harmar, June 9, 1788.
[76] *Ibid.,* Vol. 28, Letter Book D, Harmar to Wyllys, Fort Harmar, July 16, 1788.
[77] *Ibid.*
[78] *Ibid.,* Vol. 28, Letter Book D, Harmar to Captain David Zeigler, Fort Harmar, August 7, 1788. (Zeigler was stationed at Fort Pitt.)

the United States negotiated a peaceful settlement with the Indians. Their "passive" interest was actually a vigorous and active propaganda campaign and the supplying of war materials to the tribes through their agents and traders.[79]

There is no doubt that the British high command in North America knew of every detail that transpired between the Indian Department and the tribes, both in the physical exchange of gifts to verbal intercourse. Sir John Johnson said, "Indian accounts shall be first examined by a board of Accounts, if any can be formed in the district where the expenditures have been made, or stores purchased, and forwarded by the first convenient opportunity to Head Quarters, Quebec for the inspection of the Commander in Chief."[80]

The British policy was no secret to the Americans. The War Department was aware of the British influence over the Indians, and the officers of the 1st Regiment were kept continually informed by their own confidants within the northwest tribes. Fort Detroit was the key to the Indian problem, and the military men on the frontier, almost from the moment they arrived at Fort McIntosh in the fall of 1784, realized that as long as the British refused to evacuate the post their obligation to protect the frontier would be almost impossible to fulfill.

Before answering St. Clair's invitation to attend the treaty at Fort Harmar, the tribes assembled in council together at the Detroit River and awaited instructions from Joseph Brant. In August 1788 Josiah Harmar told Henry Knox, "The intelligence is, that the Indians are councilling in great numbers at the Detroit River and are only waiting for the arrival of Brant, when they mean to attend the grand treaty—the Governor has yet received no answer to his message."[81]

On the fourteenth of September 1788 Harmar again wrote to Knox, telling him that Captain Zeigler and his company of fifty-six men arrived at Fort Harmar escorting "Cornplanter the Seneca Chief, Half Town, an Oneida Chief, and several of the Six Nations, amounting in the whole to about 50 including men, women and children in order to attend the treaty—."[82] Continuing on a grimmer note, he said: "I have the mortification to inform you that on the 27th July last, a Party of 35 men under the command of Lieutenant Peters, who were detached by Major Hamtramck to bring up Provisions, was attacked on the Wabash near its mouth by Savages—10 of the Party were killed and 8 wounded—etc."[83] He continued, taking an affirmative attitude: "—this transaction shows that the Wabash Indians are for War—and its high time they were severely chastised—."[84]

St. Clair received word that the Wyandots, Delawares, and several other of the Indian nations were on their way to the treaty, Harmar told Knox in December, but that they were moving very slowly.[85] He said that "I believe Mr. Brandt has been using all his influence to prevent their coming to this Post—."[86] A week later Harmar wrote to Thomas Mifflin, reporting the progress of the coming treaty to the executive head of the state of Pennsylvania: "Brandt has decamped and drawn off as many as he could, but notwithstanding, his influence is not so universal as was imagined—It is a difficult matter for our yellow Brethren to enter into a general Confederacy and to preserve it—they are much divided in their Councils—."[87]

[79] Notes to Chapter VIII, Part III.
[80] Sir John Johnson to Alexander McKee, December, 1786, Guthman Collection.
[81] *Harmar Papers,* Harmar to Knox, Fort Harmar, August 17, 1788, Vol. 28, Letter Book D.
[82] *Ibid,* September 14, 1788.
[83] *Ibid.*
[84] *Ibid.*
[85] *Harmar Papers,* Harmar to Knox, December 4, 1788, Vol. 29, Letter Book E.
[86] *Ibid.*
[87] *Harmar Papers,* Harmar to Mifflin, Fort Harmar, December 12, 1788, Vol. 29, Letter Book E.

Overtures of peace and vigilance against attack were both evident in a letter that Harmar wrote to Lieutenant Frothingham[88] at Fort Franklin less than a month prior to the treaty, sending the following instructions: "I have directed Ensign Denny to send you by this conveyance One thousand white wampum,"[89] said Harmar, suggesting a peaceful gesture toward the tribes surrounding that fort in Pennsylvania. Cautioning the lieutenant in the next sentence, the commandant said:

> I must impress upon you the Strongest terms the absolute necessity of the utmost vigilance at Fort Franklin in order to guard against Surprize—I observe that great harmony still subsists between troops, and the Senecas, who are hunting in the vicinity of the Garrison; but our yellow brethren seem to be perfidious; I would have you therefore never to be off your Guard.[90]

The impossible situation that confronted the Federal corps in 1788 in regard to the forthcoming treaty may best be illustrated by the following correspondence. A twofold task—containing the hostile Indians, and containing the belligerent whites—faced the small force commanded by Harmar before the proper climate to hold a treaty could be reached. William Knox sent a letter to his brother Henry in September 1788[91] describing the uncertainty, according to Arthur St. Clair, of gathering the Indians together at Fort Harmar for a treaty. Many of the Indians, he said, were on their way to Detroit where the British were going to hold a treaty. In March 1787 Josiah Harmar told General Knox: "It is the prevailing feeling of the people in general upon the frontiers that it is no harm to kill an Indian—."[92]

The passionate hatred of the Indians—any Indians—felt by the frontier Whites was an extremely important factor inadvertently aiding the British trade interest in the Northwest, and working against the peaceful intentions of the United States toward those same Indians. An excellent example, typical of the feelings of the frontier Whites and a perfect instance of the many incidents that faced the Federal corps, is shown in a letter written by Hamtramck at Post-Vincennes to Harmar in the summer of 1788: "On the 18th of this month one Patrick Brown[93] who calls himself a major and from Nelson County arrived on the other side of the river with about 60 men and informed me that he was after Indians and had killed nine that morning."[94] Hamtramck continued the narrative: "I asked him by whose authority he came into the territory of the United States to make war? He told me that it was by order of his governor."[95] Asking him for his commission and orders from the governor, Brown told Hamtramck that "he had them not with him or about him."[96] Major Hamtramck replied to the Kentucky raider that he did not believe he had any orders to follow Indians into the territory of the

[88] Ebenezer Frothingham (Conn.) was in charge while Captain Heart was on detached duty.
[89] Harmar to Frothingham, Dec. 15, 1788. Harmar Papers, Vol. 29, op. cit.
[90] Harmar to Frothingham, Dec. 15, 1788, Letter Book E, Vol. 29, Clements Library.
[91] Knox Papers, William Knox to Henry Knox, September 16, 1788, Roll 22.
[92] Harmar Papers, Harmar to Knox, Vol. 58, Letter Book B, March 18, 1787.
[93] Patrick Brown fought with the Virginia troops and George Rogers Clark during the Revolution and later, under St. Clair in 1791, was a justice in the first court held in Hardin County, Kentucky. He was also active in politics and fought ardently against slavery. Brown was one of the outstanding citizens of the Kentucky community. He was not a lawless citizen. His outrageous attacks upon the Indians represented the release of emotion, revenge, and what obviously was a sense of potency that the Federal government had not been able to produce on the part of the average frontier settler.
[94] Harmar Papers, Hamtramck to Harmar, August 31, 1788.
[95] Thornbrough, op. cit., p. 115.
[96] Ibid.

United States to make war on them. He said that it was possible Brown had been following a regulation of the Kentucky assembly which called for a body of troops to follow any groups of Indian warriors "who might come into their settlement to commit depredations."[97]

Explaining to Brown that there was a difference between hostile Indians on the warpath and peaceful Indians under the protection of the United States, Hamtramck ordered the Kentuckian and his group to depart immediately. "I also insisted," Hamtramck said,

> on his returning such horses as belonged to the French, Americans and Indians under my protection. He promised that he would but did not comply. He also contrary to my orders broke the padlocks which fastened the canoes and crossed the river at the town. I could have presented him with the canon at the fort, but did not think the affair of sufficient consequence to spill blood, beside I wanted to get the horses which could have been done but by gentle means, not having sufficient force to compel him.[98]

Making certain that there was no cause for misunderstanding between Brown and himself, Hamtramck continued:

> The magistrates and people in town after he had crossed the river waited on him and painted to him the mischief he had done, the consequences of his conduct and forbided him to pass t[h]rough the village. I also sent Captain Ferguson twice to him to demand the horses he had belonging to Pakan[99] and dire[c]ted Captain Ferguson to inform him that Pakan and his Indians were employed in the service of the United States, which is the case, for all the true intelligence [I] have been able to collect from different places has been by those Indians who have given me convincing proof of their fidelity and have now Pakan at the Miami to know the result of a counsel which is to be held at LaRoche du Bout by the British Commissioner of Indian Affairs.[100]

Continuing, Hamtramck pointed up the futility of his position to handle the situation:

> All those reasons would not do. Six horses were too great a price to be return'd, and I was forced to the humiliating necessity of letting him keep the horses. Never was my feeling so much wounded before. But what could I do? I had but nine men fit for duty, the American militia would not have fought them if I had been able to march 50 men, what French there was in town at that time would have joined me cheerfully and would perhaps persuaded Mr. Brown to accept my propositions.[101]

Emphasizing the great damage that Brown and his men had inflicted ubon the goodwill atmosphere the United States was trying to establish with the Indians, Major Hamtramck continued: "The Indians they have killed were of LaDemoisel's band, and of Pakan. Perhaps you may recollect LaDemoisel. He had your protection and Pakan was one who went with you to Illinois."[102] Describing the steps he had taken to counteract the damage that Brown and his men had caused, he said:

[97] *Ibid.*
[98] *Harmar Papers, ibid.*
[99] A Miami chief.
[100] *Harmar Papers, ibid.*
[101] *Ibid.*
[102] *Ibid.*

The next day I called in to consel all the Indians in town and explained to them who those people were, and took every possible measure to persuade them that it was not done by any lawfull authority, and that I disapproved of their conduct. Some concluded to stay in the vicinity of the village, others are gone to the Weeya and Pakan Indians are at Terre Haute waiting for the return of Pakan. What will be the consequences of the incident time will determine. I am in hopes that I have persuaded them not to revenge on us. Our garrison is very sickly and no medicine.[103]

Although Hamtramck's command of the English language was poor (he was born in Canada of French-Canadian and European parents), his observations and reports were explicit and to the point. His letter to Harmar portrayed the true plight of the army.

Just as disturbed over the behavior of the Indians as he was over that of the Kentuckians, he wrote to Harmar in November 1788 telling him that:

The hostile disposition of the Indians appears to me to be in a great measure released in this quarter, but for all that I do not flatter my self that they will be at a perfect peace with us, for vengeance is their darling passion and forever will have some old or new grudge to satisfy. They have no doubt during last war and perhaps since, lost some of their relation in some of the excursion. Those lives must be paid for, as no length of time ever closes their wounds, let them be ever so slight, and altho' the nations should determine to be at perfect peace with us, their young warriors in my opinion will always in a secret manner commit depredations unless prevented by a good chastisement.[104]

Knox actually repeated the same concept to President Washington in a letter July 7, 1789, six months after the peace treaty at Fort Harmar: "The angry passions of the frontier Indians and whites are too easily inflamed by reciprocal injuries and are too violent to be controlled by the feeble authority of civil power."[105] He was referring to what he felt was an inadequate body of troops accompanying St. Clair at the past treaty. The general felt at least 500 troops were needed to protect the frontiers and back up the decisions of the governor of the territory, in respect to both lawless Whites and hostile Indians.[106]

A year earlier Hamtramck told Harmar that Alexander McKee had warned the Indians not to attend the treaty at Fort Harmar.[107] Hamtramck said that he had been told by two Shawnee Indians that McKee said the treaty would serve no purpose at all. Whatever St. Clair promised the Indians in the way of peace would be broken immediately by the "Kentuck people."[108] Hamtramck also said, shortly after the treaty, that the British had directed the Indians to agree to nothing unless the north side of the Ohio River was made their boundary and that, if that request was refused, to immediately attack the American garrisons and settlements.

An example of the ineffective position of the United States is demonstrated by an incident that happened to Hamtramck in October 1788:

[103] Ibid.
[104] Harmar Papers, Hamtramck to Harmar, November 28, 1788.
[105] Knox Papers, Knox to Washington, July 7, 1789, Rolls 24–81.
[106] Ibid.
[107] Harmar Papers, Hamtramck to Harmar, August 31, 1788.
[108] Ibid.

About a month ago, a large party of Shawnese passed through the village and had with them three prisoners. I have made out to rescue them at the moderate price of little provision. One of the prisoners is the son of one Major Hay in Kentuck, the other two are the one woman and a girl taken at the same time which is seven years ago.

What else could the residents of Vincennes and the Indian tribes have thought but that the new government was forced to use bribery rather than military might to accomplish its goals? What was the army's position if turned down by the Indians and the small detachments were faced with a confrontation with a larger force of Indians? Harmar answered this question in a letter to Hamtramck, in October 1788: "At present the appearance is dull indeed, no treaty has yet taken place, neither do I believe one will. The savages are in my opinion hatching a great deal of mischief."[109] He added, looking ahead to the adoption of the Constitution, that: "The new government I hope will soon operate, and expect in the course of the next year we shall not tamely suffer the subjects of the United States to be murdered by these perfidious savages; a proper force must be certainly raised to chastise them."[110]

Circumstances surrounding the approaching treaty made its failure seem an almost certainty. The pessimism of the officers of the Federal corps, however, did not deter the private soldiers from enjoying whatever vices existed within the confines of the Indian camps: "The officer of the day reports that the Soldiers get drunk in the Indian Encampment and are very disorderly," read the Fort Harmar Order Book.[111] It was a common occurrence, and Harmar soon forbade the soldiers from going into the encampment again. The treaty was concluded January 9, 1789, at Fort Harmar,[112] and the earlier treaties reconfirmed.

"The Grand Treaty is at last concluded; the articles were signed yesterday and the day before, by 27 chiefs—,"[113] Josiah Harmar wrote in a letter to Henry Knox, January 13, 1789. "The Nations assembled," he continued, "were the Wyandots, Delawares, Chippeways, Ottaways, Pottwatemies, Munsees and Sac and part of the Six Nations; total near 600—the Governor writes fully upon the subject, to which I beg you to be referred—."[114]

St. Clair reported to President Washington that "The negotiations were both tedious and troublesome, and for a long time had an unpromising aspect, but it came at last to as favorable an issue as could have been expected; and I trust will be attended with consequences friendly to the frontier parts of the United States."[115] Continuing in a grimmer vein, he said:

There are, however, several nations on the Wabash, and the rivers that empty themselves into it, that are ill disposed, and from whom there is reason to expect, that a part of the frontier of Virginia [Kentucky], and the settlement forming on the Miami [Marietta], will meet annoyance; indeed, that they have not been disturbed during the winter was not expected, either by me or the chiefs of the nations, who met me at Fort Harmar.[116]

---

[109] *Ibid.*, Hamtramck to Harmar, October 13, 1788.
[110] *Ibid.*
[111] *Ibid.*, Vol. 32, Order Books, 1784–88.
[112] *Ibid.*, Vol. 29, Letter Book E, Harmar to Knox, January 13, 1789.
[113] *Ibid.*
[114] The earlier treaties were reconfirmed by those tribes present in consideration of additional payment for the land by the United States. Two separate treaties were formed: one with the Six Nations, the other with the Wyandot, Delaware, Chippewa, Ottawa, Pottawatomie, and Sac nations.
[115] *American State Papers,* Indian Affairs, Vol. 1, p. 10.
[116] *Ibid.*

Cooperation from the Wyandots was producing some tranquillity, he added, but the Wyandot claim to lands reserved to the Shawnese was a problem that he resolved by inserting a memorandum at the bottom of the treaty.[117] St. Clair said the claim was insisted upon the Wyandots because they predicted the Shawnese and the Cherokee would continue to give the United States trouble. If, he said, the United States could not cope with these troublesome tribes, the Wyandots themselves claimed they would drive them out. A post established at the Miami village, the Wyandots told St. Clair, would be an effective means of overawing the Indian nations on the Wabash.[118] "It is certainly well situated for that purpose," they told him, "and would command the greatest part of the Indian trade."[119]

A post that far inland, St. Clair commented, would be difficult for the United States to support. He added that he doubted a post could be established at the Miami village without a conflict with the Indians who lived there, and he told the Wyandot chiefs that even the younger braves of the Wyandot tribes would become involved on the side of the Wabash tribes, or as he termed it, "the ungovernableness of their young men."[120] The Wyandot chiefs said there was a danger of this, but that they would send their principal men to the Miami village to prepare them to receive the U.S. post and would report back to St. Clair in the Spring.[121]

The reason, he continued, that the treaties were made separately between the United States, the Six Nations, the Wyandots, and the more westerly tribes was "a jealousy that subsisted between them, which I was not willing to lessen, by appearing to consider them as one people—they do not so consider themselves: and I am persuaded their general confederacy is entirely broken: indeed, it would not be very difficult, if circumstances, required it, to set them at deadly variance."[122]

Commandant Harmar told Major Hamtramck, in a letter written February 15, 1789, "You will observe that none of the Western Indians attended the treaty. My opinion of the effects of the treaty is, that it will have this good tendency at least, to divide the savages in their council, and to prevent the General Confederacy taking place, which [Joseph] Brandt was so anxious to establish."[123]

By June 15, 1789, Knox had a full report prepared for the President about the troubled situation on the northwest frontier. Several murders of the inhabitants had been committed, Harmar told him, by small parties of Wabash Indians. Since some of the murders had been perpetrated on the south side of the Ohio River, the inhabitants on the waters of that river, he said, are exceedingly alarmed for the extent of 600 or 700 miles.[124] He added that since the conclusion of the war with Great Britain "hostilities have almost constantly existed between the people of Kentucky and the Wabash Indians."[125] No treaty, he said, had ever been formed between the United States and those Indians.

"Some of the inhabitants of Kentucky," he continued, "during the past year, roused by recent injuries, made an incursion into the Wabash country and, *possessing an equal aversion to all bearing the name of Indians,* they destroyed a number of peaceable Piankeshaws, who prided themselve in their attachment to the United States."[126] Politely saying that the situation was a mess, he continued:

[117] *Ibid.*
[118] *Ibid.*
[119] *Ibid.*
[120] *Ibid.*
[121] *Ibid.*
[122] Thornbrough, *op. cit.,* p. 152.
[123] *American State Papers,* Vol. 1, Indian Affairs, p. 10.
[124] *Ibid.,* p. 12.
[125] *Ibid.*
[126] *Ibid.,* p. 13.

Things being thus circumstanced, it is greatly to be apprehended that hostilities may be so far extended as to involve the Indian tribes with whom the United States have recently made treaties. It is well known how the passion for war exists in the mind of a young savage, and how easily it may be inflamed, so as to disregard every precept of the old and wiser part of the tribes who have more just opinions of the force of a treaty.[127]

Prophesizing, and wisely so, Knox continued: "Hence, it results that, unless some decisive measures are immediately adopted to terminate those mutual hostilities, they will probably become general among all the Indians Northwest of the Ohio."[128]

Offering two different methods to solve the problem, he went on to say:

In examining the question how the disturbances on the frontiers are to be quieted, two modes present themselves, by which the object might perhaps be effected; the first of which is by raising an army, and extirpating the refractory tribes entirely, or secondly by forming treaties of peace with them, in which their rights and limits should be explicitly defined, and the treaties observed on the part of the United States with the most rigid justice, by punishing the whites who violate the same.[129]

However, by the first method, if a force large enough to defeat the hostile tribes were easily available, would the United States have a clear right compatible with the laws of nature and the principles of justice to carry out the expulsion of the savage on the Wabash? Knox's answer followed in the next sentence: "It is presumable, that a nation solicitous of establishing its character on the broad basis of justice, would not only hesitate at, but reject every proposition to benefit itself, by the injury of any neighboring community, however contemptible and weak it might be, either with respect to its manner or power."[130] Referring to the vulnerable key to the Indians' existence, he went on:

When it shall be considered that the Indians derive their subsistence chiefly by hunting and that according to fixed principles, their population is in proportion to the facility with which they procure their food, it would most probably be found that the expulsion or destruction of the Indian tribes have nearly the same effect; for if they are removed from their usual hunting grounds, they must necessarily encroach on the hunting grounds of another tribe, who will not suffer the encroachment with impunity—hence they destroy each other.[131]

"The Indians, being the prior occupants, possess the right of the soil," he continued, and "the land cannot be taken from them unless by their free consent, or by the right of conquest in the case of

[127] *Ibid.*
[128] *Ibid.*
[129] *Ibid.*
[130] *Ibid.*
[131] *Ibid.*

a *just war."*[132] Dispossessing them in any other manner, he said, was a gross violation of the fundamental laws of nature. Even if it were considered a just cause to remove by violence the Wabash tribes from their present territory, the financial status of the United States, Knox warned, was not adequate to support an armed expedition.[133]

There were, Knox estimated, between 1,500 to 2,000 warriors amongst the Wabash tribes and it would take an army of at least 2,500 men to undertake any military operation against them. There were less than 690 regular troops on the frontiers—and of those not more than 400 could be taken from their present stations and participate in the expedition. "To raise, pay, feed, equip and arm 1,900 additional men, with their necessary officers for six months, and to provide everything in the hospital and quartermaster's line, would require the sum of $200,000; a sum far exceeding the ability of the United States to advance, consistently with a due regard to other indespensable objects,"[134] he said. Descrbing the position of the United States at that time with respect to the Wabash tribes, he continued: "Were the representations of the people of the frontiers (who have imbibed the strongest prejudices against the Indians, perhaps in consequence of the murders of their dearest friends and connexions) only to be regarded, the circumstances before stated, would not appear conclusive—an expedition, *however inadequate,* must be undertaken."[135]

Proving how important a factor public opinion was to the American government in 1789, Knox went on: "But when the impartial mind of the great public sits in judgment, it is necessary that the cause of the ignorant Indians should be heard as well as those who are more fortunately circumstanced. It well becomes the public to inquire before it punishes; to be influenced by reason, and the nature of things, and not by its resentments."[136] Policy and justice dictated an attempt to hold a treaty with the Wabash tribes before making war, Knox said, so that all parties could try to amicably adjust their differences. If, after attempting to solve the problem through negotiation, the Wabash Indian continued their depredations against the frontier people, then it would be proper for the United States to inflict whatever punishment it thought necessary.[137] War would incur a tremendous national expense, but if no treaty were held and incidents, which were occurring in rapid succession along the frontier, were allowed to continue, "their progress and issue will deeply injure, if not utterly destroy, the interest and government of the United States in the Western territory."[138] Knox went on to say that it was time the United States adopted a liberal system of justice for the various Indian tribes within the limits of the United States. Congress appeared to be of the opinion, he said, that the Treaty of Paris with Great Britain in 1783 had invested them with the fee of all the Indian lands within the limits of the United States, and that they had the right to assign or retain whatever portion they thought proper.[139]

However, Knox continued, it had been evident ever since the consideration was formed at the Huron village in 1786 that the Indians were of a different opinion and that they thought themselves the only rightful proprietors of the soil. Congress concurred with this idea, Knox continued, when it passed the resolve of July 2, 1788, by which Congress had appropriated money solely for the purpose of paying the Indians for claims to lands they had already ceded to the United States. The Treaty at Fort Harmar had accomplished this, and Knox pointed out that the future administration of justice toward the Indian should be based on the same principle.[140]

Approximately 14,000 Indian warriors resided south of the Ohio River and east of the Mississippi River, while approximately 5,000 Indian warriors resided north of the Ohio River and south of the Great Lakes. Old men, women, and children were estimated at a ratio of three for each warrior, making a total Indian population of roughly 76,000. It would cost, Knox estimated, about

[132] *Ibid.*
[133] *Ibid.*
[134] *Ibid.*
[135] *Ibid.*
[136] *Ibid.*
[137] *Ibid.*
[138] *Ibid.*
[139] *Ibid.*
[140] *Ibid.*

$15,000 a year to attach the Indians to the United States and manage them, as opposed to a cost of much more to pursue a course of coercion and oppression from time to time and the cost of blood and injustice "which would stain the character of the nation, would be beyond all pecuniary calculation."[141]

Appealing to the logic of reality, Knox continued: "As the settlements of the whites shall approach near to the Indian boundaries established by treaties, the game will be diminished, and the lands being valuable to the Indians only as hunting grounds, they will be willing to sell further tracts for small considerations."[142] He predicted that within fifty years the Indians, because of the above circumstances, would probably be reduced to a small number. The Secretary of War was emphatic about one point, however, and that was that "the United States *must* soon possess the posts within their limits on the lakes. This circumstance will either awe the Wabash Indians, or in case of their continuing refractory, enable the Union to operate against them with a much greater prospect of success than at present."[143] Depredations continued, and no treaty with the Wabash was held.

NOTES: *Chapter 8, Part II*

Return of the sundry articles being the residue of what were purchased for the Indian treaties in the years 1785 and 1786 and delivered by the Commissioners for Indian Affairs to the following persons—etc., etc.—

40 Silver Arm bands	461 Match Coats
24 gorgetts	269 Ruffled Shirts
38 3/4ths doz. scolloped broaches	252 plain shirts
20 doz. heart broaches	96 callic shirts
50 doz. shirt broaches	3 childrens shirts
5 lockets	10 ps. of white ½ thicks
27½ pairs ear bobs	½ ps. purple thicks
17 shells or Moans	2½ ps. blue stroud
12 large crosses	1 ps. red stroud
37 3/4th doz. small crosses	1 ps. printed lin. handkerchief
16 Hiar pipes	4 black silk handkerchiefs
4 Sham Cutteau	7 1/3 groc. bed lace
1 Gross of Jews-harps	15 gros. gartering
3 Groces of Rings	6 doz. of [course] Combs
2 Rings brass wire	4 doz. Ivory Combs
2 Bunches Barley-corns	12 ps. of Ribbands
6 Hatchets	1 3/4ths lbs. of fine thread
1300 needles	1 lb. sewing silk
160 lbs. of Vermilion	1 laced hat
310 lbs. of tobacco	22 plain hats
1 box of soap	1 nest of gilt trunks
1 doz. quart pots	27 doz. pistol cap'd Knives
18 wine glasses	1 doz. Scissors
2 tea pots	12 doz. cutteaux Knives
30 lbs. of chesse	2 doz. pen-Knives
332 lbs Muscovado sugar	2 doz. small fram'd glasses
6 lbs. Hyson tea	2 dozen looking glasses
5 lbs. of peppers	210 wt. lbs. of powder
32 Galls. of Spirits	430 lbs barr lead
19 Bells	100 flints
27 Bridles	26 Gun locks
5 boats	2 Best Brass bore Rifles
3 oars	800 Black Wampum *
1 groce steel thimbles	28.750 White Wampum *

[*Harmar Papers*, dated New York, July 22, 1786.]

[141] *Ibid.*
[142] *Ibid.*
[143] *Ibid.*

Black Wampum was considered more valuable than white wampum. White wampum belts were a sign of peace, black of war. Black wampum was actually the purple part of the shell. Wampum was made from both sea and fresh water clam, mussel, and spiral shells. Because of the great difficulty of shaping and polishing wampum, it was considered valuable and used as currency.

Some wampum belts had a mnemonic use. The history of each tribe was retained by one member of that tribe who, as he grew older, passed the history onto a younger member. This occurred each generation, and the wampum belts served as the only record of significant events, each belt representing a specific incident in the tribe's history. These belts were retained by the tribe.

Other wampum belts were given as tokens of peace and friendship, or as a declaration of war. All formal Indian affairs were conducted with the use of wampum belts and/or strings of wampum. These represented official documents to the tribes and were given and received as such.

NOTES:
Chapter 8, Part III

A study of the orders entitled "Instructions for the good Government of the Branch of the Indian Department within the District of Detroit,"[144] written by Sir John Johnson, superintendent general and inspector general (British) of Indian Affairs in 1786, and intended for Alexander McKee, deputy agent for Indian affairs (British) at Detroit, reveals the active participation of the British government in the affairs of the Indians within the territory of the United States. Johnson told McKee to "continue to emply your utmost endeavors to promote his Majesty's Indian Interest in general by keeping up a friendly intercourse and Communication between all the Indian Nations assuring them of the King's paternal care and regard as long as they continue to merit them by acting as good and obedient Children ought to do—."[145]

McKee was ordered to govern himself by the following instructions: "As these people consider themselves free and independent, and are in fact unacquainted with Controul and subordination, they are alone to be governed by address and persuasion, and they require the utmost attention to ceremonies and all external appearances, with an uncommon share of patience, good temper and forbearance; in all which you will instruct the interior officers under your direction—."[146]

Carefully avoiding any direct reference to tribes that had no connection whatever with the British in Canada, the next paragraph ordered:

> Upon the arrival of distant parties of Indians at your post, you shall report the same to the officer commanding who, with the officers of the Garrison are to assist in receiving them, which is to be done with every mark of solemnity and friendship; and, as after the usual ceremonies, they will make known their wants, their requests if reasonable are to be complied with: Should they, as is customary on these occasions lay down presents of any kind, they are to be taken with thanks, and in return presents exceeding the value of theirs are to be given them, in which case the Chiefs are always to be distinguished.[147]

---

[144] Manuscript instructions, 7 pages, written by Sir John Johnson to Alexander McKee, December 1786, or shortly thereafter; the official instructions of the British Indian Department to their agent at Fort Detroit, Guthman Collection.

[145] *Ibid.*

[146] *Ibid.*

[147] *Ibid.*

Sir John, son of the famous Indian agent, Sir William Johnson, went on to instruct about treaties: "When public conferences are held between you and the Indians, the commanding officer shall preside, attended by all the officers of the Garrison, to whom due notice is to be given, on all such occasions; but he is not under pretense of this regulation to interfere with you in the Management of the Indian Department."[148]

Point four, the next phase of the instructions, is extremely important because it was through the spoken word—British propaganda—that so much damage was inflicted upon the American cause and which, in effect, aroused and incited the Indians to battle against the United States. Johnson said,

> As Indians are in general curious and wish to carry news to their Villages, the officers should be very cautious not to relate any to them but what they know to be facts, and these should be very distinctly told, for the mistaking, or not properly understanding a piece of news has been known to alarm and estrange whole Nations from a Post, for which and other reasons, you should endeavor to make one or two sober and intelligent Chiefs of the Indian Nations, living at or near your Post your friends and Confidents, and on any occasion of calling together a Council, to have them present, and make one of them your Speaker, having him prepared for the Meeting, and when met, you are to have the Interpreter to prompt him in what you intend to say, which is a custom among themselves, their speakers having commonly Prompters—and Speeches so delivered will always have more influence than coming from an interpreter being delivered in their own way—.[149]

Sir John Johnson had the advantage of being taught by probably the most knowledgeable Englishman about Indian customs and ceremony—his father, whose acuminious tact was acquired during the French–Indian Period. McKee was an extremely successful agent for the British Crown and his name was mentioned often by members of the American military force and legislature whenever they discussed the serious Indian problem that confronted the United States. He, with his colleague Matthew Elliot, and his confidants Simon Girty, the renegade trader, and the Mohawk chief Joseph Brant, probably were responsible for most of the propaganda that was disseminated to the northwestern tribes.

Although humanity was seldom shown by the Indians toward their prisoners, and little was done by the British to prevent brutalities, Sir John Johnson's instructions contained the following: "You are at all times to inculcate into the minds of the Indians, principles of humanity and tenderness to prisoners, particularly upon the departure of all parties during a War from your Post, or while there is a probability of retaliating or resenting injuries sustained."[150] It is extremely interesting to note the

---

[148] *Ibid.*
[149] *Ibid.*
[150] *Ibid.,* See page 168.

words "Particularly upon the departure of all parties during a war from your post"; the reference to war probably applied to American settlers, militia, and the American army. Sir John goes on to instruct McKee that all provisions, presents, and supplies given to the Indians had to be turned over to them in front of the officers at the Fort and never in private. The army was in charge of all gifts, supplies and provisions and had to account for them. He went on to say,

> The General Orders of the 6th of December, 1786, directing "that all persons attached to the Army in North America, or belonging thereto, entrusted with the receipt and expenditure of public Money, the receipts and issues of public stores, shall make up, state and settle their respective accounts at the end of every quarter, the first quarter to commence from the 25th December, 1786."[151]

The irony of instructions to inculcate humanity in the minds of the Indians can be seen in the following article that appeared in the *Connecticut Courant and Weekly Intelligence,* January 14, 1783:[152]

> Extract from a letter from Captain Gerrish, of the New England militia dated Albany, March 7. 'The peltry taken in the expedition will, as you see, amount to a good deal of money. The possession of this booty at first gave us pleasure; but we were struck with horror to find among the packages, eight large ones, containing scalps of our unhappy country folks, taken in the three last years by the Senneka Indians, from the inhabitants of the frontiers of New York, New Jersey, Pennsylvania and Virginia, and sent by them as a present to Colonel Haldimand, Governor of Canada, in order to be by him transmitted to England. They were accompanied by the following curious letter:
>
> "Teoga, January 3, 1782
>
> May it please your excellency,
>
> At the request of the Senneka Chiefs, I send herewith to your Excellency, under the care of James Boyd, eight packs of scalps, cured, dried, hooped and painted with all the Indian triumphal marks, of which the following is invoice and explanation:
>
> No. 1, 43 scalps of congress soldiers, killed in different skirmishes; these are stretched on black hoops, 4 inch diameter; the inside of the skin painted red, with a small black spot to note their being killed with bullets. Also, 62 farmers, killed in their houses; the hoops red; the skin painted brown, and marked with a hoe; a black circle all around to denote their being surprised in the night; and a black hatchet in the middle, signifying their being killed with that weapon.
>
> No. 2, containing 98 farmers killed in their houses; hoops red; figure of hoe, to mark their profession; great white circle and sun, to show they were killed in the day time; a little red foot; to show they stood upon their defense, and died fighting for their lives and families.
>
> No. 3, containing 97 of farmers; hoops green, to show they were killed in their fields; a large white circle with a little round mark on it for the sun to show that it was in the day time; black bullet mark on some, hatchet on others.

---

[151] *Ibid.*
[152] Archives of the Connecticut Historical Society.

No. 4, Containing 102 of farmers, mixed of the several markers above, only 18 marked with a little yellow flame, to denote their being prisoners burnt alive, after being scalped, their nails pulled out by the roots and other torments; one of these latter supposed to be of a rebel clergyman; his band being fixed to the hoop of his scalp. Most of the farmers appear by the hair to have been young or middle-aged men; there being but 67 very grey heads among them all; 17 others, hair very grey; black hoops; plain brown colour; no mark but the short club or the passetete, to show they were knocked down dead, or had their brains beat out.

No. 5, [Text Missing]

No. 6, containing 193 boys' scalps, of various ages; small green hoops, whitish ground on the skin, with red tears in the middle, and black bullet marks, knife, hatchet, or club, as their deaths happened.

No. 7, 211 girls scalped, big and little; small yellow hoops; white ground, tears, hatchet, club, scalping, knife, etc.

No. 8, the package is a mixture of all the varieties above mentioned, to the number 122; with a box of birch bark, containing 29 little infants' scalps of various sizes; small white hoops, white ground; no tears, and only a little black knife in the middle, to show they were ript out of their mothers' belly—

With these packs the Chiefs sent to your excellency the following speech, delivered by Coneiogatchie, in council, interpreted by the elder Moore, the Trader, and taken down by me in writing.

Father,

We send you herewith many scalps, that you may see we are not idle friends.

A blue belt.

Father,

We wish to send these scalps over the water to the Great King, that he may regard them and be refreshed; and that he may see our faithfulness in destroying his enemies, and be convinced that his presents have not been made to ungrateful people.

A blue and white belt with red tassels.

Father,

We have only to say further, that your traders exact more than ever for their goods; and our hunting is lessened by the war, so we have fewer skins to give them. This ruins us. Think of some remedy. We are poor; and you have plenty of everything. We know you will find us powder and guns and knives and hatchets; but we also want shirts and blankets. A little white belt.

James Craufurd.''

Unofficial approval and subversive ''payoff'' on the part of the British government to their Indian allies for the atrocities performed on the American settlers is a sad chapter in the heroic and constructive story Englishmen played in the development of North America. It was not the savage mind that reduced itself to a lower level of mankind when it resorted to tortures that barbaric custom had always prescribed. However, those highly civilized white men who consorted with their savage allies, and under the protection of the monarch for whom they were paid agents, lowered their standards to the uncivilized practices of the Indians, in many instances for their own pleasures as well as the benefit reaped by the mother country.

68. Camp and field equipment and accouterments.
   Drawing by Don Troiani

68.

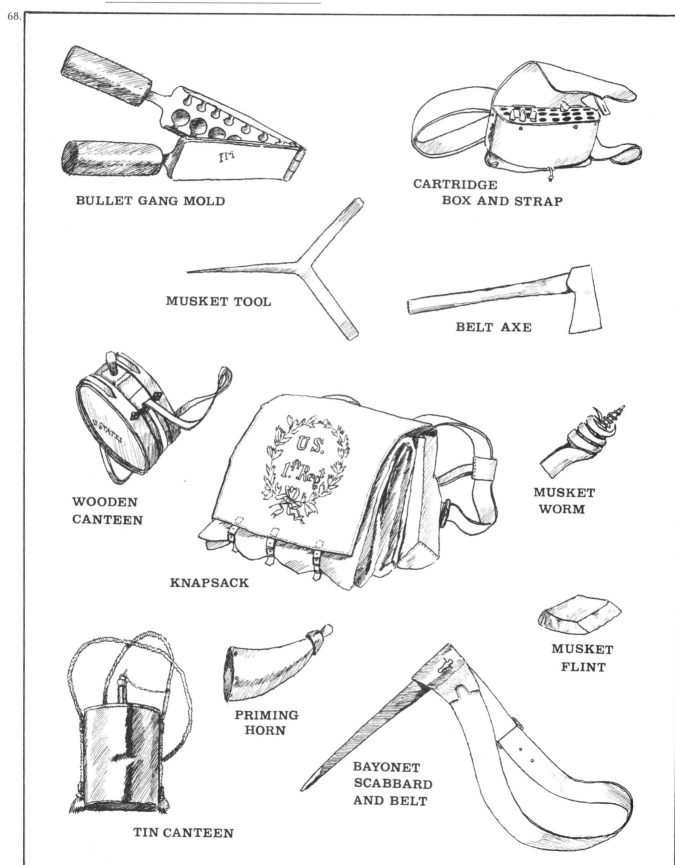

BULLET GANG MOLD

CARTRIDGE
BOX AND STRAP

MUSKET TOOL

BELT AXE

WOODEN
CANTEEN

KNAPSACK

MUSKET
WORM

MUSKET
FLINT

TIN CANTEEN

PRIMING
HORN

BAYONET
SCABBARD
AND BELT

A SCENE ON THE FRONTIERS AS PRACTICED BY THE HUMANE BRITISH AND THEIR WORTHY ALLIES!

*Bring me the Scalps
and the King our Master
will reward you*

*Reward for
16 — Scalps*

*Arise Columbia's Sons and forward press
Your Country's wrongs call loudly for redress
The savage Indian with his scalping knife
Or tomahawk may seek to take your life*

*By bravery aw'd they'll in a dreadful fright
Shrink back for refuge to the woods in flight
Their British leaders then will quickly shake
And for those wrongs shall restitution make*

70.

69. A late eighteenth-century woodcut depicting the British paying the Indians along the frontier for American scalps. The guns, knives, and tomahawks are all labeled "GR", denoting King George.
Guthman Collection

70. Militia horseman or dragoon helmet, circa 1794, bearing maker's label of Norman Smith, Hartford, Connecticut. This is typical of the headgear of mounted troops during the Federal period.
The crown is hard leather and a bearskin comb and a red velvet band, secured with silvered brass buttons and silver cord. Visor is softer leather with a silvered brass rim.
Guthman Collection

71.

General Wayne's Trace Marker
85 miles from Cincinnati on the
Auglaise River, 1794

71. Rare wooden trail marker from the Wayne campaign, 1794. Similar markers were used during Harmar and St. Clair's expeditions in 1790 and 1791. They were placed along the trail marking distances from the starting point of each campaign. This is marked "W" (Fort Washington), "85" (miles from Fort Washington), and "94" (1794).
Cincinnati Historical Society, Guthman Photo

72. General George Washington's field tent with the field cot of Brigadier-General Peter Gansevoort inside, to the right. Both pieces of field equipment are similar to those used by Harmar and St. Clair.
Smithsonian Institution

73. Major General Arthur St. Clair, from an old print after the original painting by C. W. Peale.
Guthman Collection

72.

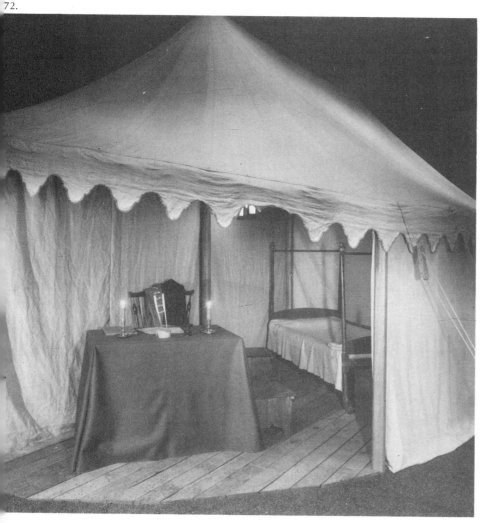

73.

The Indians had to be taught a lesson. Josiah Harmar and the 1st American Regiment set out during the fall of 1790 to show the mischievous savages that the United States government was not to be challenged by frontier hostilities. The Miami villages were burned, their corn destroyed—but the enemy had retreated long before the army approached. Harmar unwisely deployed several detachments that were ambushed by the Indians.

Chapter 9

The First Campaign

On September 16, 1789, President Washington told Congress that "The Governor of the Western Territory has made a statement to me of the reciprocal hostilities of the Wabash Indians, and the people inhabiting the frontiers bordering on the river Ohio."[1] Washington asked Congress to pass an act enabling the President to call upon the militias of Virginia and Pennsylvania to supplement the strength of the Federal corps in an effort to contain the hostile Indians.[2] He pointed out that circumstances were exactly the same as they were previously when Congress passed similar acts July 21, 1787, and August 12, 1788.

On the last day of the first session of the first Congress the newly installed Constitutional Congress passed an act legally recognizing the military establishment that had been authorized by the late Congress of the Confederation by an act passed October 3, 1787. In addition, the new Congress also gave the President, as commander-in-chief, "for the purpose of protecting the inhabitants of the frontiers of the United States from the hostile incursions of the Indians," the power to call into service "from time to time, such part of the militia of the states respectively, as he may judge necessary."[3]

At last the fruits of centralization were beginning to take effect. In 1789, therefore, the President was given the authority by Congress to call upon the state militia to supplement the small Federal force without asking permission of Congress. The pay and subsistence of the state militia, while they were in the service of the United States, was to be the same as that of the regular troops.[4]

President Washington told the Congress on December 9, 1790, that the constant depredations made upon the frontier settlements by the Wabash Indian tribes from the northwest side of the Ohio river, and also those of the neighboring Indian nations that could be "seduced to join in their hostilities," had made it necessary for him to call forth militia to act in conjunction with the regular troops. He said an expedition was in the process of preparation[5] and that the Secretary at War had been directed to give Congress details of the expenses and particulars of the forthcoming campaign.

[1] *American State Papers,* Indian Affairs, Vol. 1, p. 57.
[2] *Ibid.*
[3] "Acts Passed At A Congress of the United States of America," Hodge, Allen and Campbell, New York, 1789.
[4] *Ibid.*
[5] *American State Papers,* Vol. 1, Indian Affairs, p. 83.

Knox then presented a list of events that had occurred during the past nineteen months, in spite of the treaty of peace held at Fort Harmar, January 9, 1789. This ineffectual treaty, which had been completely ignored by the Wabash tribes, was actually the beginning of a series of Indian campaigns that ended in the defeat of the United States army and militia.

The bold attempts of the hostile Wabash Indians to prevent the treaty supplies from arriving at Fort Harmar, and the inability of the Federal troops to protect either supplies or men from those attacks had turned the treaty into a farce. The officers on the frontier, and Henry Knox in the War Office, knew that an eventual showdown was inevitable. All of their hopes were placed in the new government's ability to build a more substantial military machine, but there was still the strong resentment against a large standing army that existed at the end of the Revolution. One of the staunchest opponents was William Maclay, senator from Pennsylvania, who said in March 1790 when a bill was introduced into Congress for enlarging the army: "The first error seems to have been the appointing of a Secretary of War when we were at peace, and now we must find troops lest his office should run out of employment."[6]

The Secretary of War had submitted a plan for an organized militia to President Washington on January 18, 1790. The president in turn submitted the plan to Congress January 21, 1790, endorsing Knox's ideas, which incorporated many of his own expressed a half-dozen years earlier. Knox maintained that

> A small corps of well-disciplined and well-informed arillerists and engineers, and a legion for the protection of the frontiers and the magazines and arsenals, are all the military establishment which may be required for the present use of the United States. The privates of the corps to be enlisted for a certain period, and after the expiration of which to return to the mass of the citizens.[7]

Pointing out that "An energetic National Militia is to be regarded as the Capital Security of a free republic; and not a standing army, forming a distinct class in the community,"[8] Knox told Congress to reject a standing army and establish a "well-constituted militia."[9] Every man of proper age (eighteen to sixty) and ability, according to the plan, was firmly bound to perform, personally (no substitutes) his proportion of military duty. This would not only defend the country against its enemies, but create "a glorious national spirit."[10] As Congress, however, did not approve of the plan, the need for a larger military establishment for the protection of the frontiers was still unresolved. The Indian hostilities which continued along the northwestern borders were almost too remote to make any impression upon many of the Congressmen—particularly anti-Federalists, such as Maclay, who bitterly opposed the administration. Lengthy debates followed and the emotion and political sentiment of those opposing a stronger military force appeared to be winning the contest.

In the meantime, Governor St. Clair forwarded to Major Hamtramck at Fort Knox speeches containing peace proposals for the Wabash tribes. He instructed the major to select a messenger from Vincennes, and, since the person chosen would probably be French, the governor ordered the

---

[6] Edgar S. Maclay, ed., *Journal of William Maclay, 1789–1791*, D. Appleton & Company, New York, 1890, p. 227.

[7] Henry Knox, "A Plan for The General Militia of the United States," printed by Francis Childs and John Swaine, New York, 1790, pp.6–7.

[8] *Ibid.*, p. 7.

[9] *Ibid.*

[10] *Ibid.*

speeches translated into that language. St. Clair said that an attempt to make peace with the Indians must be made, but that if it failed the tribes must be chastised.[11]

Antoine Gamelin,[12] who carried on trade with the Indians and was always well received,[13] was selected to carry the messages to them. He departed April 5, 1790,[14] conferring with tribes along the way and, upon reaching the Miami town (Fort Wayne), he found that prospects for peace were discouraging. Gamelin's report stated that British Fort Detroit was wielding too great an influence over the Wabash tribes for any overtures of peace offered by the United States to be favorably received and young warriors could not be stopped from going off to war. Gamelin was told by an old chief that the English at Detroit, the place "where the fire was first lighted," were arming and encouraging the young men to force the Americans back across the Ohio.[15] Joseph Brant, the Mohawk chief, and British agent Alexander McKee were the chief agitators for the British government.

Increasing hostilities along the frontiers, and the unsuccessful peace mission, made it obvious to Knox and St. Clair that a military expedition had to be planned. After bitter opposition, Congress passed a bill April 30, 1790, increasing the strength of the army to 1,216 noncommissioned officers and privates for a term of three years. The Federal corps was to consist of one regiment of infantry and one battalion of artillery. Although the manpower was increased, the morale of the military establishment was severely injured because, as noted in the last chapter, the pay of everyone except the commanding officer was decreased.

Having enlarged its military force, the United States moved toward a showdown with the hostile Wabash tribes, and public opinion on the frontier helped to accelerate the plans. In a letter to the Secretary of War July 7, 1790, Kentucky Judge Harry Innes pointed out that over 1,500 people had been killed, 20,000 horses stolen, and property valued at over 15,000 pounds destroyed by plundering Indian raids into the territory over the preceding seven years.[16] Innes told Knox that, unless the Federal government expressed intent to furnish relief to the frontier inhabitants who faced further Indian depredations, he feared local expeditions would be carried out against all tribes, friendly as well as hostile, creating a war in the territory that would take many more lives and destroy much more property.[17] He said the Indians would no longer have faith in the United States, and government regulations for law and order would no longer be effective on the frontier.[18] Judge Innes wrote to General Knox again the following day, July 8, telling him that St. Clair had sent him a letter dated July 5, from the Rapids of the Ohio, admitting that any hopes for peace were lost, and that he had come back to the territory sooner than he had expected to prepare for operations against the Indians.[19] Governor St. Clair asked Innes to appraise the field officers of the Kentucky militia as, per orders from the president, they were going to be called out according to the previous acts of Congress to operate in conjunction with the Federal troops against the Indians.[20]

St. Clair wrote to General Knox August 23, telling him that there was no longer any hope of attaining a peaceful settlement with the Indians along the Wabash and Miami Rivers.[21] The governor arrived at that conclusion as soon as he received the report from Major Hamtramck about the

---

[11]William Henry Smith, *The St. Clair Papers*, pp. 130–131, Vol. II., Robert Clarke & Co., Cincinnati, 1882.
[12] His cousin, Pierre, had failed to carry out a similar mission previously.
[13] William Henry Smith, *op. cit.,* p. 164.
[14] *American State Papers,* Vol. 1, Indian Affairs, pp. 93–94 (refers to Gamelin here as Anthony).
[15] Smith, *op. cit.,* pp. 167–168; *American State Papers,* Vol. 1, Indian Affairs, *op. cit.,* p. 4.
[16] *American State Papers,* Vol. 1, Indian Affairs, p. 88.
[17] *Ibid.*
[18] *Ibid.*
[19] *Ibid.*
[20] *Ibid.*
[21] *Ibid.*

unsuccessful peace mission of Antoine Gamelin, along with accounts of more recent Indian incursions along the Wabash River. At the time of Hamtramck's dispatch, St. Clair was busily engaged in setting up local governmental and militia systems at Kaskaskias (on the Mississippi) and other remote settlements in Illinois, whose impoverished inhabitants had been suffering from a lack of any sort of civil or military authority. Leaving the secretary of the Western Territory, Major Winthrop Sargent, to carry out his plans for installation of local government officials, St. Clair hurried to Fort Washington to confer with Harmar at army headquarters.[22]

St. Clair acted quickly, fearing that preparations for the campaing would consume most of the best time of the year for carrying out a successful operation. He brought Robert Elliot,[23] the contractor, to confer with Harmar about receiving supplies in time for the operation up the Wabash. Supplementing the Federal troops with local militia was the next step, and St. Clair drew upon the maximum number allowed—1,000 from Virginia and 500 from Pennsylvania. He told Knox that 300 of the Virginia militia had been instructed to rendezvous at Fort Steuben and were to march, with the garrison at that Fort, to Fort Knox and join forces with Major Hamtramck's garrison.[24] This combined body of troops was to march up the Wabash, attacking villages along that river while the remaining twelve hundred militia, who were instructed to rendezvous at Fort Washington, marched under the command of Harmar with the Federal troops stationed at that post (300, making a combined force of 1,500) across country directly to the Main Miami villages.[25]

St. Clair felt that, although it might be better to operate as a single force, time would not allow a practical junction of the troops at a proper place, and probably the coordinated attacks upon the tribes at separate places would, in turn, prevent them from joining forces with each other.[26] A larger force, St. Clair said, would prove to be additional insurance for a victory and would put the success of the expedition out of chance of accidents, for a failure would be attended with the very worst consequences.[27] He advised Knox that if President Washington approved enlarging the militia force it was not too late, because many more men might be obtained on short notice, he thought, from that part of Virginia that was supplying the original 1,000 men. The rendezvous was set for September 15, at Fort Washington, but St. Clair said he did not expect the militia to arrive before the twentieth, and they would be ready to march by October 1.[28] Robert Elliot, the contractor, told General Harmar that there would be no difficulty obtaining provisions in time, except for flour. However, corn, which was plentiful in Kentucky at that time, could be substituted, and this satisfied Harmar.[29]

Pessimism was expressed over the enlistment of the Pennsylvania quota of militia as St. Clair explained that half the counties from which troops were to be drawn (four counties) had not had an officer for over two years,[30] and, he added, there was a general complaint about a lack of arms in those counties. Presenting his complaints to the executives of Pennsylvania, St. Clair said they hoped to overcome the manpower shortage by voluntary enlistment and that a quantity of arms had been ordered forwarded for their militia troops. St. Clair told Knox that a disappointment would be fatal, and that President Washington might make conditional provisions in case Pennsylvania failed its

[22] *Ibid.*
[23] Robert Elliot and Eli Williams received contract for provisions and supplies after James O'Hara's contract expired.
[24] *American State Papers,* Vol. 1, Indian Affairs, pp. 92–93.
[25] Miami villages were located at present-day Fort Wayne, Indiana.
[26] *American State Papers,* Vol. 1, Indian Affairs, pp. 92–93.
[27] *Ibid.*
[28] *Ibid.*
[29] *Ibid.*
[30] *Ibid.*

quota.[31] He urged that General Knox relay his apprehensions about the Pennsylvania quota to President Washington before St. Clair returned to Fort Washington, which he hoped to do almost immediately. The Pennsylvania quota was due to rendezvous on September 3, and begin their march to Fort Washington by the tenth.[32]

It is understandable that many of the soldiers in the Federal corps—newly recruited under the resolution of April 30, 1790—would have barely enough training to embark upon a major expedition against seasoned warriors of the Miami and other Wabash tribes the following October, and the 1,500 militia that were to march in conjunction with the Federal force would have even less (if any) training by that time. But an immediate reprisal against the Indian hostilities seemed to outweigh the practical factors: an untrained force marching into strange country to face keen, angry, superbly trained Indian foes supplied by the British.

St. Clair had sent a circular letter to the militia county lieutenants July 15, 1790, telling them that there were no prospects of achieving a peaceful settlement with the Indian nations on the Wabash. The letter went on,

> The commanding officer of the troops and myself have, therefore, concerted a plan of offensive operations against them, and in conformity with the above recited instructions, I now call upon you in the name of the President of the United States for_____men, rank and file, properly officered according to the legal establishment of the militia in your state, to act in conjunction with the Federal troops, against the said Indians; and they be at_____on the_____day of September next, armed, accoutred and equipped, for service of sixty days or more, after they shall have joined the troops, unless the object in view shall be sooner accomplished.[33]

St. Clair was thus acting under direct orders from President Washington, who according to the Congressional act of September 29, 1789, was authorized to call into service, in conjunction with the Federal troops, such part of the militia as he thought necessary for the protection of the frontiers. The counties in Virginia called upon were: Nelson, 125 men; Lincoln, 125 men; and Jefferson, fifty men. All of these were to rendezvous at Fort Washington September 12. Those Virginians ordered to rendezvous at Fort Washington September 15 were from the following counties: Madison, 125 men; Mercer, 125 men; Fayette, 200 men; Bourbon, 125 men; Woodford, eighty-five men; and Mason, forty men.[34] The counties in Pennsylvania were: Washington, 220 men; Fayette, 100 men; Westmoreland, 110 men; and Alleghany, sixty men. These were to rendezvous at McMahon's Creek, four miles below Wheeling, on September 3, 1790.[35] (All of the Virginia counties that were called upon are today part of Kentucky.)

St. Clair instructed the senior officers of the Pennsylvania militia to make certain no injury came to any of the friendly Indians in the vicinity of McMahon's Creek.[36] He said, in his letter addressed to the senior officer, that many Indians with whom the United States had treaty commitments hunted in the vicinity of the rendezvous place at McMahon's Creek. They were Wyandots and Delawares, and were to be treated, he said, with kindness.[37] On the other hand, St. Clair instructed that every security

[31] *Ibid.*
[32] *Ibid.*, p. 93.
[33] *Ibid.*, pp. 94–95.
[34] *Ibid.*, p. 95.
[35] *Ibid.*
[36] *Ibid.*
[37] *Ibid.*

precaution was to be taken while at the rendezvous camp, to guard against a surprise attack from hostile tribes.[38]

A good relationship with friendly Indians was in order throughout the Federal corps during the troublesome period. Harmar had instructed the commander at Fort Franklin to "cultivate a good understanding with the Cornplanter in order to counteract the designs of Brand and his adherents."[39] He also began to make preparations for the forthcoming campaign, telling Major Doughty "—all prospects of peace with the hostile Indians, are at an end—We Therefore are planning an expedition against them—"[40] Harmar told Doughty to order the blockhouse at "the Beaver"[41] to be evacuated and the troops stationed there to be in readiness, along with Major Doughty's command to join Harmar at Fort Washington.[42]

Knox, in the meantime, had forwarded St. Clair's pessimistic report concerning the hostile intentions of the Indians to President Washington.[43] The President, he told St. Clair, approved of the forceful measures to be taken by the governor; and, Knox added, "The offers of peace which have been made on principles of justice and humanity to the Wabash Indians and refused, will fully justify the conduct of the United States in the operations which have been directed for the prevention of future murders and robberies."[44]

President Washington, said the Secretary of War, was fully confident of St. Clair's ability and judgment to estimate the force of the Indians and the nature of their mode of operation. He felt, Knox continued, that St. Clair would be able to evaluate, thereby, his own forces, and if, after deliberating his analysis, he found he needed to strengthen his army, he was authorized by the President to requisition additional militia.[45] They should be drawn from the frontier counties of Virginia, he continued, because of their proximity to Fort Washington, the rendezvous point. Knox told St. Clair the President was apprehensive about the reactions of the British, who would certainly become alarmed when they discovered an armed force was marching toward their stronghold at Detroit,[46] even though the English were supposed to have evacuated long ago.

Naively, Knox suggested that a messenger be dispatched to the British commandant at Detroit assuring him of the real objective of the expedition.[47] Assurances of a pacific disposition of the United States toward Great Britain and its possessions should be given, he said, and it should be carefully pointed out that retaliation was aimed at the Shawnese and the others who had joined with them and committed hostile offenses against the United States.[48] Just as important, he added, the friendly Indian tribes should be assured of the United States' good intentions toward them, as well as the objectives of the expedition.[49]

Following Knox's orders, St. Clair dispatched a civilian messenger to Major Murray, the British commandant at Fort Detroit, on September 19, 1790.[50] He said that an expedition to chastise the hostile tribes was under preparation by that the United States harbored no hostility toward any British

[38] *Ibid.*

[39] *Harmar Papers,* Vol. 29, Letter Book G, Harmar to Jeffers, February 1, 1790.

[40] *Harmar Papers,* Vol. 29, Letter Book H, Harmar to Doughty, July 15, 1790.

[41] A blockhouse near the old Fort McIntosh

[42] *Harmar Papers,* Vol. 29, Letter Book H, Harmar to Doughty, July 15, 1790.

[43] William Henry Smith, *op. cit.,* Vol. II, p. 162.

[44] *Ibid.*

[45] *Harmar Papers,* Vol. 29, Letter Book H, Harmar to Doughty, July 15, 1790.

[46] William Henry Smith, *op. cit.,* p. 163.

[47] *Ibid.*

[48] *Ibid.*

[49] *Ibid.*

[50] *American State Papers,* Vol. 1, Indian Affairs, p. 96.

post. On the other hand, the Governor said that the United States did not expect the British to aid the Indians against whom the campaign was going to be conducted.[51] He went further, requesting the commandant to restrain those British traders "from whose instigation there is good cause to believe, much of the injuries committed by the savages has proceeded."[52]

By notifying the British, Harmar played right into the hands of Brant, McKee, Girty, and British policy to retain control of the Great Lakes fur trade. Both Knox and St. Clair, as well as many of their contemporaries familiar with the unsettled situation in the northwest, had pointed out many times in the past that the British were behind the Indian uprisings and that, until the key posts in that region were relinquished by Great Britain, the situation would never be resolved peacefully. How either one—particularly Knox—could have been so naive as to expect the commandant at Detroit to honor their secret is difficult to understand. Even Washington expressed apprehension over St. Clair's communication to the British. He wrote to Knox November 4, 1790,[53] stating that the message should not have been dispatched until after the troops had begun their march toward their objective. Washington knew that the British were both encouraging and supplying the Indians, and told Knox that the untimely message would only serve as a warning—through the British—to the Indians.[54]

Knox either misunderstood Washington, or sent the orders to St. Clair entirely on his own.[55] At any rate, Harmar's expedition was no surprise to the intended victims. Unaware of British betrayal, Knox and St. Clair were highly optimistic. St. Clair suggested that, upon the successful defeat of the Indians, the United States should establish a military post at the Miami villages, the place selected as the main objective for the expedition. The Miami villages were located at the headwaters of the Miami River, where the St. Mary's and St. Joseph rivers formed a junction. This was the Indian's most important stopover place in the Northwest territory, since it was the point of portage connection between the Great Lakes and the Ohio River.[56] It was known by the Indians as "the Great Carrying Place"[57] and was the vital connection between British Detroit and the Indians on the Ohio.[58]

Secretary at War Knox replied to Governor St. Clair's letter September 12, 1790, telling him that a post at the Miami village presented a better strategic position that any of the other locations excepting the posts occupied by the British that rightfully belonged to the United States.[59] The idea was relayed to President Washington, who not only agreed, Knox said, but had expressed the same opinion in 1784.[60] To maintain such a post however, he said, would require a force of 2,000 men with three months' provisions at least, plus supplies and artillery—none of which were, at the moment, compatible with either public finances or public sympathy. Besides, it might complicate the delicate negotiations with the British for the release of the frontier posts ceded to the United States at the peace treaty and might also alienate some of the friendly tribes with whom treaties had already been concluded.[61] Therefore, he reasoned, the establishment of the post, at that time, was not to be undertaken. "The expedition," he went on to say, "will either incline the Indians to treat for peace, or it will induce them to wage open war in the Spring."[62] Knox continued, "A further time is also

[51] *Ibid.*
[52] *Ibid.*
[53] William Henry Smith, *op. cit.,* p. 186.
[54] *Ibid.*
[55] Barce, *op. cit.,* p. 47.
[56] *Ibid.*
[57] *Ibid.*
[58] *Ibid.,* p. 51.
[59] William Henry Smith, *op. cit.,* Vol. II, p. 181; *American State Papers,* Indian Affairs, Vol. 1, p. 100.
[60] *Ibid.*
[61] William Henry Smith, *op. cit.,* Vol. II, pp. 182–183; *American State Papers,* Indian Affairs, Vol. 1, p. 100.
[62] *Ibid.*

required to know the intentions of the British respecting the delivery of the forts at Niagara and Detroit." The decision at this point, he emphasized, "has an intimate connection with the peace of the frontiers."[63] The President, he said, closing the letter, expressed the anxiety that the proposed expedition be rendered entirely effectual. Harmar, in the meantime, was making preparations at Fort Washington and in Lexington, Kentucky where he told Colonel John Hardin he was pleased he had been selected to command the Kentucky militia and told Hardin he expected him to be with the 700 Kentucky militia at Fort Washington, together with the Volunteer Horse, "who should be well mounted, and equipped to act as cavalry."[64] He asked Hardin to bring along five or six trusty men who were acquainted with the country to act as guides.[65] The commandant also told the militia colonel that he hoped to be able to march at least 300 Federal troops with three pieces of cannon.[66]

The militia were in high spirits for the intended expedition, Harmar wrote to Major Wyllys, but "Captain Ferguson reports to me that the Iron for Mounting the Artillery, making spades, the hemp for cordage and files for the armourers, which were to have been sent up by the first boat from the Rapids, have not yet arrived at Headquarters."[67] Critical of Elliot and Williams, he added, "This is a most unpardonable neglect in the Contractors, as those ARTICLES are immediately wanted—"[68]

Major Ebenezer Denny reports in his journal that every day was employed in the most industrious manner making preparations for the expedition; every officer was busily employed, particularly Captain William Ferguson, with his company of artillery, and Lieutenant John Pratt, the quartermaster.[69] Kentucky militia began to arrive September 18, and Denny commented that they were not the type of men he had been accustomed to seeing on the frontiers. "They appear to be raw and unused to the gun or the woods; indeed, many are without guns, and many of those they have want repairing."[70] Commandant Harmar, he said, was greatly distressed over the kind of people sent from Kentucky. "One half," Denny continued, "serve no other purpose except to swell their number. If the leading patriots of Kentucky don't turn out rascals, then some men that I know are greatly mistaken."[71] Instead of experienced woodsmen, the militia were the misfits and loiterers of the frontier communities.

Major William Ferguson said that the Kentucky militia were almost destitute of camp kettles and axes and there was no supply available to issue in time for the expedition's departure.[72] Since Ferguson was commanding officer of the artillery at Fort Washington, it was his duty to inspect and repair the arms of the militia. Their arms, he said, were unfit for service. He gave an example of the typical kind of weapons that the militia brought, stating that one rifle came to him for repairs without a lock and another without a stock.[73] When he asked the owners of the guns why they thought he would be able to repair them at this late time, they replied that they had been told in Kentucky that all guns would be repaired at Fort Washington.[74] The Pennsylvania militia, Ferguson said, were worse and were not "Smart, active woodsmen, well accustomed to arms, eager and alert to revenge the injuries done to them and their connexions."[75] Many of the Pennsylvania militia came without arms

[63] *Ibid.*
[64] *Harmar Papers,* Vol. 29, Letter Book H, Harmar to Hardin, August 18, 1790.
[65] *Ibid.,* Harmar to Wyllys, August 15, 1790.
[66] *Ibid.*
[67] *Ibid.,* Harmar to Wyllys, August 15, 1790.
[68] *Ibid.*
[69] *Military Journal of Major Ebenezer Denny,* p. 344.
[70] *Ibid.*
[71] *Ibid.*
[72] *American State Papers,* Vol. 1, Military Affairs, p. 20.
[73] *Ibid.*
[74] *Ibid.*
[75] *Ibid.*

of their own and had to be issued government weapons from the stores at Fort Washington. Those who did bring their own guns arrived with weapons similar to those of the Kentucky militia, many of which were too far gone to repair. They, too, had to be issued government muskets.[76]

Captain Thomas Doyle of the Federal infantry described his reaction to the arrival of the militia as one of disappointment. Instead of the "complete riflemen," that he had expected from the frontiers of Kentucky and Pennsylvania, there were men armed with old muskets that needed a great deal of repair.[77] Ensign Daniel Britt, the paymaster, said that the militia "scarcely" deserved the name of anything like soldiers; that they were mostly substitutes for others, who had nothing to stimulate them to do their duty—.[78] Harmar, he said, found it difficult to establish harmony within the militia, since harmony did not exist between the commanding officers of the militia.[79]

Captain Armstrong said that Colonel Trotter aspired to the command of the militia, even though Colonel Hardin had seniority. Trotter, evidently, was the more popular among the Kentucky troops who threatened to go back home unless Trotter were given command.[80] Denny said, "The colonels were disputing the command and the one most popular was least entitled to it."[81]

Harmar, according to Denny, had to effect a reconciliation. He decided the Kentuckians would be formed into three batallions under Majors Hall, McMillen, and Ray, and these under the direct command of Lieutenant-Colonel–Commandant Trotter. The Pennsylvania militia were formed into one battalion under Lieutenant-Colonel Truby and Major Paul. The entire militia was commanded by Colonel John Hardin of Kentucky,[82] and all, of course, were subject to the orders of Harmar of the Federal corps. This seemed to satisfy the militia.

Secretary of War Knox had warned Harmar about the possibilities of jealousies arising, but not between the members of the militia. Rather, he foresaw a problem evolving between the militia officers and the Federal officers and had instructed Harmar to prevent jealousies from arising among the militia while they were serving under him.[83] He had written to the governor of Virginia, expressing the hope that jealousies would not arise between the militia and regular troops and thereby jeapordizing the expedition; and he requested additional Virginia militia to supplement the original number, if request by Governor St. Clair.[84]

During the early summer planning, Knox told Harmar that Major Doughty and Captain Ferguson estimated that the Wabash River had a more easterly course than "laid down on Hutchin's[85] map," thereby indicating the distance of the Miami towns was not greater than 140 miles from Fort Washington, or four days' march on horseback.[86] Knox then suggested that 100 Continental (Federal) and 300 militia mounted troops, all picked men with thirty days supply of bread and pork, and one bushel of corn for fodder for the horses, could carry out the campaign quickly and successfully.[87] The plans, of course, were enlarged, and the armed force rendered slower and more cumbersome. It was during this earlier planning stage of the expedition that Knox urged Harmar to assure friendly tribes of America's pacific disposition toward them.[88]

---

[76] *Ibid.*, p. 21.
[77] *Ibid.*, p. 26.
[78] *Ibid.*, p. 23.
[79] *Ibid.*
[80] *Ibid.*, p. 20.
[81] *Ibid.*, p. 24.
[82] *Military Journal of Major Ebenezer Denny,* p. 344.
[83] *American State Papers,* Vol. 1, Indian Affairs, p. 100.
[84] *Ibid.*, p. 99.
[85] John Hutchins, surveyor general.
[86] *Ibid.*, p. 98.
[87] *Ibid.*, p. 97.
[88] *Ibid.*, p. 98.

A letter had been sent to the Secretary of the Treasury by Henry Knox late in August estimating the expenses of the proposed expedition which, by the middle of July, had been planned for the latter part of September and was to consist of 1,700 militia and 400 Continental troops for a period of three months. The contractors, Knox said, were to execute the quartermaster's duties and that extra service would amount to $65,682.00, half of which would be required in advance of the expedition in order to expedite the purchase of provisions and supplies.[89] The cost of pay, subsistence, and rations for the militia would amount to $55,548 and additional costs of rations for the Federal troops, plus the rental of horses and boats and other transportations, plus contingencies, would amount to $100,000.[90]

The estimated cost of the expedition was based upon the plan submitted by Harmar to Knox and in turn forwarded to and approved by the President.[91] After receiving Washington's endorsement, Knox told Harmar that "a knowledge of your enemy's strength, situation, and designs, must be essential to your success; you will therefore make the best arrangements for obtaining intelligence."[92] He should watch out for a surprise attack, warned Knox in his letter to Harmar, and be certain to move rapidly and decisively, in order to "astonish the enemy."[93] Two tons of the "best *rifle*[94] and *musket* powder" had been forwarded, he continued, and lead, flints, and cartridge paper in proportion, plus medicine. One thousand dollars of contingent money had been sent to Harmar, for which Secretary Knox requested triplicate receipts.

The contractors, Knox said, were to supply packhorses for provisions at their own expense; however, they were receiving an additional fee for supplying the provisions in the field instead of at posts closer to their source of supply.[95] The army, he continued, was not carrying tents, so the packhorses would not be needed for that purpose and the cost would be eliminated. Since only the provisions needed to be transported on horses, Knox said that Harmar's force would travel "light and unincumbered."[96]

St. Clair arrived at Marietta on September 15 with the remainder of the Pennsylvania militia. A detachment of Pennsylvania militia was already marching to Fort Washington, and on the nineteenth Major Doughty left Marietta with the troops St. Clair brought four days previously,[97] and with the Federal troops from Fort Harmar, marched toward the rendezvous point at Fort Washington. St. Clair estimated that they would reach the Fort by the twenty-fourth and that all of the troops would be assembled by that time.[98]

The Pennsylvania quota was short more than 200 men, and St. Clair hoped to fill their ranks with Kentucky militia in time for the departure of the expedition. He sharply criticized Governor Mifflin of Pennsylvania.[99] Even though President Washington had advised the executives of Pennsylvania in advance that they were to supply militia for the proposed expedition, he said, they chose to ignore the request—and because of this the entire expedition could end in failure.[100]

[89] *Ibid.*
[90] *Ibid.*
[91] *Ibid.*
[92] *Ibid.*, p. 99.
[93] *Ibid.*
[94] *Ibid.*, p. 99. The Secretary of War also said that, "since the militia will probably be armed with rifles, which are certainly not good arms in a close fight," the general ought to try to persuade them to use instead some of the spare muskets in storage at Fort Washington.
[95] *Ibid.*, p. 100.
[96] *Ibid.*
[97] William Henry Smith, *op. cit.*, Vol. II, p. 183.
[98] *Ibid.*
[99] *Ibid.*, pp. 183, 184.
[100] *Ibid.*

Governor Mifflin was guilty of the grossest neglect.[101] Although he had been advised by not only Washington, but Knox, General Butler, St. Clair, and the lieutenants of the Pennsylvania frontier districts, he chose to ignore their letters. He was, said Smith, and had been since the close of the Revolution, a malcontent and was now a leader in a party opposed to Washington and St. Clair. By his inaction against a common enemy, Mifflin expressed an attitude of individual state superiority over the Union.[102]

The ammunition and quartermaster stores had not arrived by September 19, but a "favorable rise in the river" encouraged St. Clair to believe that the boats would appear any moment.[103] A single officer and a small detachment remained behind to escort the supplies to Fort Washington as soon as they arrived at Fort Harmar.

In the meantime, Knox had written to St. Clair with a résumé of the forthcoming expedition, which he said was intended to "exhibit to the Wabash Indians our power to punish them for their positive depredations, for their conniving at the depredations of others, and for their refusing to treat with the United States when invited Thereto."[104] That power, he said, would be demonstrated "by a sudden stroke," destroying their towns and crops.[105] The militia would be the principal force used in the execution of that plan.[106]

St. Clair had estimated 1,100 Indian warriors would possibly be brought into action against the expedition from the Wabash and its vicinity, and an even greater number if these were joined by Wyandot, Delaware, St. Joseph, and Illinois tribes.[107] This number of warriors, Knox told St. Clair, would not be greatly reduced in number by the plannned expedition during any of the skirmishes in which they would encounter the Indians. Knox reasoned that "the mode of Indian fighting" would not permit the loss of large numbers of Indians in battle.[108] By this statement, Knox admitted to clear knowledge of the Indian style of warfare. He knew that the tribes would wait until the most advantageous moment to make contact with their enemy and that, if they saw the battle was going against them, the Indians would quickly retreat to safe cover and await another time when the odds were more in their favor. Thus, battle losses would never reduce their overall strength by any important percentage.

It is apparent that the War Department did not figure on any major battle occurring. The Indians would wait at a place that afforded them perfect concealment and cover—and a place which would alow them to trap the enemy in the open. However, the War Department figured that the experienced woodsmen from Kentucky—and the swift-riding Kentucky militia mounted on the fine horses they raised in their own country—would discover any lurking Indians and would never allow such a surprise attack nor permit the expedition to move across open terrain that would allow such ambush. Knox said that the "principal means used will be the militia." The intended expedition was meant only to burn towns and crops, to show the Indians that a United States force could reach their far-flung villages.

What Knox completely overlooked was the Indian's genius for tactics and his ability to outfox his opponent in combat. The mere fact that a tremendous, well-equipped force was going to blunder through the woods, making the noise of a thousand elephants, was in Knox's mind all that was

[101] *Ibid.*
[102] *Ibid.,* footnote, p. 184.
[103] *Ibid.,* p. 185.
[104] *Ibid.,* pp. 181–182.
[105] *Ibid.,* p. 182.
[106] *Ibid.*
[107] *Ibid.,* pp. 181–182.
[108] *Ibid.*

necessary. This would frighten the savages; and when their homes and crops were burned their punishment would be complete. The Secretary of War did not figure that, while his expedition was noisily marching through the countryside, the Indian scouts would be carefully scrutinizing every movement—how the men marched; how they camped; how well trained and how used to the woods they were. All this information would be carried to Little Turtle and the other chiefs who would then skillfully select the proper place and time to strike most effectively.

Knox did not have an opportunity to observe the caliber of the militia. Whether the War Department can be blamed for planning a major campaign around men they had not seen, and whose capabilities they only assumed, is an interesting question. The fact is that the militia who arrived on the scene were not the type of men on which the War Department had planned or which Harmar had hoped he would command. Instead of skilled woodsmen, crack riflemen, and dashing mounted militia, they were inexperienced, undisciplined recruits who were strangers to that part of the country.

St. Clair, however, was optimistic. When he arrived at Fort Washington he wrote to General Knox and reported everything that had transpired. There, St. Clair found everything in a better state of preparation than he had expected, due to the attention of Harmar and Captain Ferguson.[109] The Kentucky militia, he said, had arrived at the Fort on schedule, except for 140 men, who had since arrived. Major Wyllys and his command arrived from the Falls on September 22, and Major Doughty's detachment from Fort Harmar arrived three days later.[110]

Since Pennsylvania had failed to supply its quota, St. Clair, acting under the powers vested in him by the president, called for 500 additiional Kentucky militia,[111] from the nearest and most populous counties, Fayette and Woodford. St. Clair requested that, if possible, the 500 be mounted cavalry.[112]

Rather than wait for additional militia to arrive, since those already collected at Fort Washington were becoming restless, St. Clair ordered Colonel Harding to march with the militia on September 27.[113] According to Denny, they were ordered out on the twenty-sixth: "The whole militia took the field under the direction of Colonel Hardin, an old continental officer, amounting to one thousand, one hundred and thirty-three. They marched on a direct route to the Indian towns."[114]

On the twenty-ninth, Harmar moved out with the Federal troops and joined the militia.[115] He took along three pieces of artillery and the provisions.[116] The cattle and horses for the transportation of the flour had arrived, St. Clair said, "in due season."[117] Lieutenant Frothingham arrived with the remainder of the Fort Harmar garrison on October 2 and marched to join the army the next day.[118]

Colonel Hardin had been ordered to advance twenty miles and make camp, there opening a road for the artillery that was to follow. Judging by the description he had received of the terrain, St. Clair said that after the first twenty miles the ground was level and thinly wooded, alleviating the necessity of opening roads for passage.[119]

[109] *Ibid.*
[110] *American State Papers,* Vol. 1, Indian Affairs, p. 96.
[111] *Ibid.*
[112] *Ibid.*
[113] *Ibid.*
[114] *Ibid.*
[115] *Ibid.*
[116] *Ibid.*
[117] *Ibid.*
[118] *Ibid.*
[119] *Ibid.*

The contractors reported to the Secretary of War October 14 and said that by September 18, twelve days ahead of schedule, they had furnished the army with 180,000 rations of flour, 200,000 rations of meat, 868 pack- and artillery horses equipped with pack saddles, bags, ropes, etc., one horsemaster general, eighteen horsemasters, and 130 packhorse drivers.[120] They said this could not have been possible if they had not used all of their own funds and "pledged their credit to the extent, to the people of the western country, where the supplies were principally furnished."[121] The expedition, they continued, could not fail from any default of theirs, "for we have forwarded supplies in greater quantities than were required of us—."[122]

While the army was on the march, St. Clair maintained correspondence with Knox. He said he had not heard from Harmar since his second day out, when he reported that the terrain was hilly and difficult for the artillery.[123] Some travelers, however, who had met the army on its second day's march said the terrain soon leveled out. They said that there had been only one occasion where they found a small causeway made of logs that the advance detachment had to build.[124] St. Clair estimated that the army should reach Chillicothe before the ninth of October and doubted that they would meet any opposition before arriving at the Miami towns. Hamtramck, at Vincennes, was ordered to march September 25, ahead of the main detachment from Fort Washington, and the specified militia were to have joined him to carry out their part of the plan.[125] "The little army," St. Clair said, "moved in high spirits, and have had excellent weather ever since, one day's rain excepted."[126]

HAMTRAMCK

Harmar, in his orders of July 15, said that 300 militia were to join Hamtramck and the French militia at Vincennes and their total force would be around 500 men. He said: "With this force you are to strike either at Vermillion,[127] L'Anguille,[128] or the Weatowns.[129] At any rate, I expect you will manouver in such a manner as to divert the attention of the Miamis to that quarter, whilst I shall use all possible means to destroy their villages—."

The militia, however, did not arrive until September twenty-ninth, and Hamtramck did not begin his march until the next day. His force consisted of 330 men as they marched off for the Vermillion,[130] the destination he had chose as the first point of attack. About ninety men (the sick and lame of both the Kentucky militia and the Federal corps) remained behind at Fort Knox. Arriving at Vermillion, October 10, Hamtramck found that the village had been deserted. The houses and crops were destroyed, but he advanced no further. Discovering that there was a shortage of flour and beef, he consulted with the militia officers who were afraid that their men would desert if they were required to proceed on half rations. Hamtramck said that "Had I to deal only with regular troops I should order them to live on the barks of trees if I thought it necessary," but with the militia unused to discipline he decided it was best to turn back, even though they had not made contact with the enemy.[131]

[120] *Ibid.*
[121] *Ibid.*
[122] *Ibid.*
[123] *Ibid.*
[124] *Ibid.*
[125] *Ibid.*
[126] *Ibid.*
[127] Kickapoo village on the Vermilion River, Indiana.
[128] On the Eel River near Logansport, Indiana.
[129] Miami villages on the Wabash river called Ouiatenon (the Weas were part of the Miami tribes).
[130] *Harmar Papers,* Hamtramck to Harmar, November 2, 1790.
[131] *Ibid.*

Whether Hamtramck turned back because he realized the force he commanded was not trained adequately to penetrate deep into Indian country and achieve a victory against a skillful foe or whether it was a lack of fortitude has been a question of debate. His letter to Harmar explaining his actions partially explains his reasoning and indicates a profound, practical knowledge of Indian warfare: "I had in a moment a number of very chagrinning reflections to surmount—the first to have gone so far without seeing an 'enimy,' the small state of my supplies, so small a body of troops and in whom (from a number of information) I had so little confidence of their keeping with me, the regulars excepted—."[132] He went on to say that by the time they had reached the Vermillion a number of the militia had already deserted. His confidence in achieving any kind of a victory was not only eroded by the behavior of the militia under his command, but by his able perception of the entire situation in the northwest.

In December Hamtramck wrote to St. Clair and at that time clearly stated his views about the Indian situation. His first observation, and clearly the most important in his own mind, was that no victory could be achieved until the British relinquished the forts on the Great Lakes.[133] It was, he said, the British who were daily sowing the seeds of discord between the Indians and the United States. If the Indians called for peace in the spring, he said, it would only be to deceive the United States. No peace should be granted, he continued, until a successful expedition took place and permanent posts established in the key locations. With proper garrisons, an army need not worry about supply or communication. It was no use, he pointed out, to go into the Indian town, burning their homes and crops, and then leave the next day. "They make themselves perfectly comfortable on meat alone," he said, and "can build houses with as much facility as a bird does his nest."[134]

It was of no use to attempt to destroy them in combat, he went on, because they would not fight unless they had a decided advantage over their enemy and, if they found themselves unable to whip their adversaries, they could always retreat into the vast wilderness where they would be secure from further enemy advances.[135] Hamtramck went on to suggest that, if the government wished to send out another expedition without first establishing garrisons in strategic locations, a surprise attack on horseback should be considered. If the men were mounted on good horses, and each man carried his own provisions, a large body of troops could move swiftly, undiscovered by the enemy, and return to their base with ample food.[136] This letter to St. Clair is a vivid refutation of the cumbersome expedition in which Harmar was engaged when Hamtramck turned back to Fort Knox. The planned expedition had failed before the objective was reached. Among other things it failed to draw the Miami Indians away from the marching columns that had left Fort Washington headed for the main Miami villages.

HARMAR

During the course of the march, of the main detachment, Ebenezer Denny, Harmar's adjutant, kept an accurate journal of the progress made by Harmar's small force, and Thomas Irvin, an enlisted man in the Kentucky militia, recorded fairly detailed observations about the march.[137]

---

[132] *Ibid.*
[133] William Henry Smith, *op. cit.,* Vol II, p. 197.
[134] *Ibid.*
[135] *Military Journal of Major Ebenezer Denny,* p. 345.
[136] *Ibid.*
[137] Ohio Archeological and Historical Society Publications, *ibid.,* Vol. 19, 1910, Columbus, Ohio, pp. 393–396, letter of Thomas Irvin.

The militia, numbering 1,133, left Fort Washington under Colonel Hardin on the twenty-sixth of September. They were followed three days later by Harmar and the Federal troops formed in two small battalions commanded by Majors Wyllys and Doughty and a company of artillery with three light brass pieces, under the command of Captain Ferguson.[138] The Federal troops numbered 353, making a total of 1,453 men under the command of Harmar in the expedition.[139]

On October third Harmar's troops caught up to the advanced units of the militia and the remainder of that day was spent organizing the line of march, the order of battle and encampment, and elaborately explaining the details to the militia officers. The army resumed the march on October fourth and on the fifth was joined by a reinforcement of mounted infantry from Kentucky.[140] The mounted troops were then formed into a company of mounted riflemen and a company of the light troops.

The army followed the old trace made by General George Rogers Clark from Kentucky in 1782 (when he successfully defeated the Indians and thereby prevented the British at Detroit from endangering the frontier settlements). Harmar's army marched in two columns, one on either side of the trace, about eighty yards apart,[141] with a strong front and rear guard and the baggage in the center.[142] Denny had diagramed the order of march, showing six spies and guides in advance, followed by an advance company of thirty men who were followed by twenty-four pioneers flanked on either side by cavalry.[143]

Militia under Major McMillen followed in three columns, numbering 200 men and immediately behind were the general, staff, music, colors, flanked by two columns of Federal troops who in turn were flanked by cavalry.[144] The main body followed in two large columns, on the left the Pennsylvania militia under Colonel Truby and Major Paul, and on the right a battalion of Kentucky militia under Major Ray. In the center of these two columns came the artillery, the ammunition, baggage, packhorses, and cattle. On the extreme flanks of these two columns was a small detachment of one noncommissioned officer and nine men.[145] Behind the packhorses and cattle marched Major Hall's battalion of 200 militia, which was, in turn, followed by a rear guard detachment of thirty men.[146]

There was a great deal of difficulty in keeping the various units in their proper position and in keeping the packhorses together.[147] As many as twelve miles were marched in a day, and as little as eight, depending upon the terrain.[148] At times traveling was easy, moving through open country which Denny described as beautiful, whereas other areas were described as a difficult march, "over beech roots and brush,"[149] and each evening's encampment was welcomed by the entire corps.

At the end of the day they fell out into a large hollow square, circled by the guard, which consisted of thirty men each at the front and rear, well beyond the square, and fifty men on each flank, each of the four groups commanded by a captain.[150] Encamped at the front of the square, in the

---

[138] *Military Journal of Major Ebenezer Denny*, p. 345.
[139] *Ibid.*
[140] *American State Papers*, Vol. 1, Military Affairs, p. 24.
[141] Ohio Archeological and Historical Society Publications, *ibid.*, p. 393.
[142] *Ibid.*
[143] *Military Journal of Major Ebenezer Denny*, p. 344 (diagram).
[144] *Ibid.*
[145] *Ibid.*
[146] *Ibid.*
[147] *Ibid.*, p. 346.
[148] *Ibid.*, pp. 344–48.
[149] *Ibid.*, p. 348.
[150] *Ibid.*

center, was McMillen's battalion of artillery, flanked by cavalry. Directly behind was the battalion of militia and military stores and the artillery were at the rear of the square.[151] Encamped on the upper left of the square was Colonel Truby's battalion of Federal troops.[152] Stationed at the upper right was Major Doughty's battalion of Federal troops and at the lower right the commandant had placed Major Ray's battalion of artillery.[153]

The same order of march and order of encampment was called for throughout the expedition to the Miami towns. The clearest path for Harmar's course of march led along the rivers toward the Miami towns.[154] Having traveled about 125 miles from Fort Washington,[155] the army encamped on Grave Creek, a branch of the Miami River on October 12, after a twelve-mile march that day.[156] Each rifleman of the militia was issued one-half pound of powder and one pound of lead, while the "musquetry" of the militia and Federal infantry received 24 cartridges per man.[157] The commanding officers of each battalion were ordered to make certain that their men's arms were in good order and were loaded.[158] At night the horses were hobbled and tied, and grass was cut and brought to them. Security for the cattle was just as rigid, the guard consisting of an officer and thirty men who were to "build a yard always within the chain of sentries, sometimes the square of the encampment, and place themselves round the inclosure which secures them."[159]

In spite of the security, horses broke loose "owing to the scarcity of food" and managed to pass through the chain of sentries and get lost.[160] On the morning of October 13, a patrol of about ten horsemen searching for the horses captured a young Shawnee brave.[161] Pushing on through "thick brush country" the troops, with their prisoner, encamped that evening near the ruins of a French trader's house on a branch of the Miami River, about 135 miles from Fort Washington.[162] Two of the troops could speak the Indian tongue very well and they spoke freely[163] with the Shawnee prisoner who said that the Indians originally had intended to make a stand at their towns but had given up that idea.[164] The slow-moving army had been under constant surveillance by the Indians, who had ample time to prepare for their defense.

Little Turtle, the Miami chief, awaited the undisciplined army marching slowly and noisily toward his towns. His spies had told him that the troops were not trained for the country and that the militia officers found it difficult to control their short-term volunteers. Not only had the British supplied the Indians with arms, ammunition, and provisions, but the strategy of the mission revealed in St. Clair's message to the commandant at Detroit had, in turn, been forwarded to the Indian encampment.

[151] *Ibid.,* p. 344 (second diagram).
[152] *Ibid.*
[153] *Ibid.*
[154] He followed the west bank of the Little Miami River, paralleling today's Highway 42 to Xenia, then northward to Piqua, and northwest to present St. Mary's, where the army followed the St. Mary's River, proceeding on the north bank, paralleling Highway 33. Howard H. Peckham, "Josiah Harmar and His Indian Expedition," *Ohio Archeological and Historical Quarterly,* June–September, 1946, p. 236.
[155] *Ibid.*
[156] *Military Journal of Major Ebenezer Denny,* p. 347
[157] *Ibid.*
[158] *Ibid.*
[159] *Ibid.,* p. 348.
[160] *Ibid.*
[161] American State Papers, Military Affairs, Vol. 1, *op. cit.,* p. 24.
[162] *Ibid.,* p. 21.
[163] Ohio Archeological and Historical Society Publications, *ibid.,* p. 393.
[164] *Ibid.,* p. 394.

One of the wisest and most cunning of the Indian leaders, Little Turtle, planned a counterstroke. Reasoning that the towns would make a poor place to stand against such a large army, Little Turtle ordered the houses burned and everyone evacuated. The Shawnee prisoner's story was related to Harmar and he immediately ordered Colonel Hardin of the militia to proceed with "600 light troops" early on the morning of the fourteenth,[165] hoping to catch the Indians before they were able to clear their towns.

When Hardin arrrived he found the town deserted except for two Indians hiding at the river bank; they were immediately killed.[166] Meanwhile, marching through beech and swamp oak, Harmar's main army encamped that night seven miles from the Miami town, about 163 miles from Fort Washington. They did not reach the Miami village until noon the next day, the seventeenth, and after eighteen days of travel Denny described what is today the site of Fort Wayne: "Two very considerable branches meet here, the St. Joseph from the north-west, and the St. Mary from the southwest, which form the Miami or Omee, emptying into Lake Erie."[167] "Several little towns on both branches, but the principal one is below the confluence on the north side. Several tolerable good log houses, said to have been occupied by British traders; a few pretty good gardens with some fruit trees and vast fields of corn in almost every direction."[168] Denny pointed out that the Indians had not burned the entire town.

Displaying absolutely no military discipline, the militia roamed the villages in bands of thirty and forty, searching for plunder, which they found hidden or buried everywhere about the towns. Denny commented that it appeared "as if the enemy went off in a hurry."[169] His observations were only partially correct, because the warriors were close by, concealed behind good cover, and waiting for the right moment to strike at the disorganized force looting their homes. Jonathan Heart said that "the Indians had moved off their effects and burned the French village and also the principal houses in the several villages. The 18th, 19th, and 20th were spent in destroying the remainder of the buildings and corn, etc.—"[170]

Major McMillen of the militia reported he had seen the tracks of women and children on a trail leading northwest of the village toward the Kickapoo towns. Harmar surmised that the warriors would not move far from their families, thus leaving them unprotected, and probably were encamped in the direction of the trail. On the morning of the eighteenth he detached Colonel Trotter, Colonel Hall, Major Ray, and Major McMillen and a detachment of 300, including thirty Federal troops, part of the cavalry, mounted infantry, and militia infantry, with three days' provision, to scour the country along the trail and make contact with the retreating Indians. Two warriors were apprehended and the four field officers gave chase, leaving their commands unattended and without direction for over half an hour.[171] The militia wandered around in confusion until the officers returned. In the meantime, the two Indians had been killed by the cavalry, and, when Colonel Trotter returned, he disobeyed Harmar's orders to follow the trail but instead marched in several different directions looking for more signs of Indians until nightfall.

Thomas Irvin, who marched with the militia under Trotter, said "we marched in excellent order, being a volenteer in said detachment,"[172] which was more than exaggerating the truth about the utter

[165] *Military Journal of Major Ebenezer Denny*, p. 347.
[166] Ohio Archeological and Historical Society Publications, *ibid.*, p. 394.
[167] *Military Journal of Major Ebenezer Denny*, p. 349.
[168] *Ibid.*
[169] *Ibid.*, p. 349.
[170] Jonathan Heart to William Judd, December 3, 1790, Guthman Collection.
[171] *American State Papers*, Vol. 1, Military Affairs, p. 26.
[172] Ohio Archeological and Historical Society Publications, *ibid.*

confusion that really existed on the march. Irvin said that when Trotter heard the six-pounder discharged at headquarters at sundown, he thought it was a signal for a detachment to return to camp and "we marched into camp a while after night."[173] Trotter, evidently satisfied with the results of having killed two Indians, had returned two days earlier than his orders from Harmar specified.

Both Harmar and Colonel Hardin were annoyed with the early return and unsatisfactory results of Trotter's detachment. Hardin requested to take the same command the next day, in order to save face for the Kentucky militia, and Harmar agreed that he could go out for the two remaining days. The Kentucky officer departed the next morning with the detachment and two days' provisions, following the same trail that Trotter was supposed to have followed the day before. Denny reported that the militia moved off reluctantly, and that "I am satisfied that when three miles from camp had not more than two-thirds of his command; they dropped out of ranks and returned to camp."[174]

Following the trail, Hardin came upon an encampment the Indians had abandoned the day before,[175] and ordered a halt. He designated different lookout positions for the various companies. When the troops were called back into formation, Hardin in his haste to catch up with the Indians forgot all about one company which had been sent out of sight beyond a distant hill.[176] Irwin belonged to the company, which was commanded by Captain Faulkner. After advancing several miles Hardin realized his mistake and dispatched Major Fontaine with part of the cavalry to locate the missing company.[177]

Shortly after Major Fontaine departed, Captain Armstrong reported that he heard what he thought might be an alarm gun fired some distance ahead and that he had also discovered the tracks of a horse that had come down the trail and then turned back up the trail.[178] Hardin took no precautions, Armstrong said, but continued straight ahead. Armstrong warned Hardin, telling him that there were Indians, probably in ambush, close by, but Hardin replied that the savages would not fight[179] and rode on, in front of the entire detachment. Possibly attempting to make up for a lack of courage displayed by Trotter the previous day, Hardin's bravado proved fatal. Although, as Armstrong implied, an Indian scout had probably turned around on the trail and ridden back to warn his comrades ahead, Hardin was not at all cautious and did not use basic tactics of advance scouts or of flank guards to protect the main body from a surprise attack.

Jonathan Heart briefly describes the events that followed:"—on the 19th a Party of ours fell in with a Body of Indians some distance from our main body. The Regulars being left unsupported fell nearly the whole."[180] Denny said: "Hardin proceeded, and about ten miles from camp, not expecting to be near the enemy, he suddenly came upon a party supposed to be about one hundred only, and owing to the bad order of his men, and their dastardly conduct, was entirely defeated."[181] The Indians commenced firing about 150 yards away from the soldiers, and continued to advance toward them.[182] Most of the militia fled without firing a shot, throwing down fully loaded muskets and fleeing as fast as they could, pushing Colonel Hardin back with them.[183] The thirty regulars and only nine militia stood their ground and were cut to pieces, with a mere half-dozen surviving the attack.

[173] *Ibid.*
[174] *Military Journal of Major Ebenezer Denny,* pp. 349–350.
[175] *American State Papers,* Vol. I, Military History, p. 27.
[176] Barce, *op. cit.,* p. 165.
[177] *American State Papers, ibid.*
[178] *Ibid.,* p. 26.
[179] *Ibid,* p. 27.
[180] Jonathan Heart to Wm. Judd, December 3, 1790, Guthman Collection.
[181] *Military Journal of Major Ebenezer Denny,* p. 350.
[182] *American State Papers, ibid.*
[183] *Ibid.,* p. 27; *Military Journal of Major Ebenezer Denny, ibid.*

One of the survivors, Captain Armstrong, said that, after seeing all but nine of the militia run, and twenty-four of the Federal troops and the nine militia fall, he, being surrounded by the enemy, and alone, threw himself into a thicket, where he hid for the remaining three hours of daylight.[184] During that time, he said, he was able to watch the enemy pass and re-pass and he did not believe there were more than 100 Indians involved in the entire operation. Some were mounted, he said, others carried rifles, and the advance groups were armed only with tomahawks. He judged that, if Colonel Trotter had advanced beyond the two Indian sentinels they killed the day before, they would have surprised the Indian encampment and could easily have taken the 100 warriors.[185] At any rate, Armstrong ascribed the defeat of the nineteenth to the cowardice of the militia and the poor judgment of Hardin, who, he felt was however a brave man.[186] He said he would not willingly fight alongside militia again, nor would he wish to be commanded again by a man so lacking in military talents as Hardin.[187]

Whether all the blame for the Indians' victory could be placed on the shoulders of the militia and their leader or whether some credit ought to be given to the military genius of Little Turtle is interesting speculation. The fact that untrained, undisciplined militia were recruited to march against highly disciplined Indian warriors was the responsibility of the Federal executive officers, who did not perceive the capabilities of their Indian enemies. Even Armstrong, a trained officer with fourteen years of military experience, could not detect (or would not allow himself to acknowledge) the masterful tactics of the Indians against the overconfident American force marching against them. His reports do not even hint that the enemy had anything to do with the victory; he merely criticized the cowardice and inability of the militia as compared to the regular army.

Thomas Irvin stated that, when Major Fontaine finally found the company that Colonel Hardin had left behind, he told them that "the Indians was retreating as fast as possible,"[188] indicating the complete lack of suspicion on the part of the militia officers that the Indians would even dare a surprise attack. Shortly afterward they came across some retreating militia, Irvin reports, who yelled to the advancing company: "For God's Sake retreat—you will Be all Killed—there is Indians enough to Eat you all up—."[189] According to Irvin's report, the Indians had obviously planned and executed the perfect ambush. One of the militia officers who had escaped told Irvin on the evening of the defeat that the trail Hardin's detachment was following led through a narrow prairie bordered on both sides with heavy timber, within twenty steps of the trail on the right side.[190] The Indians had kindled a fire at the far end of the prairie (which Armstrong had warned Hardin about and which was probably meant to attract the advancing militia). Irvin said that the Indians had also scattered some trinkets along the trail which caused the single column to halt. As soon as the advance men stopped, delaying the entire force, the Indians began firing from behind the cover on the right. The men retreated to the left and were then fired upon the Indians who were behind trees on that side of the trail.[191] Because the men were in single file, and because there were no flankers, Irvin said, the Indians had a tremendous advantage.[192] Even Irvin, acknowledging that the Indians had set the

---

[184] *American State Papers, ibid.*
[185] *Ibid.*
[186] *Ibid.*
[187] *Ibid.*
[188] Ohio Archeological and Historical Society Publications, *ibid.,* p. 395.
[189] *Ibid.*
[190] *Ibid.,* p. 396.
[191] *Ibid.*
[192] *Ibid.*

perfect trap, could not give credit to them in his account, and confined himself to criticism of Hardin's tactics.

On the nineteenth, also, while Hardin's detachment was running from the Indians, the man body of troops moved from the Miami village, which they had completely destroyed, two miles east to a Shawnee town (Chillocothe) which they proceeded to burn and loot. They also destroyed the adjacent cornfields. That night two militia captains decided to trap some Indians they suspected were lurking in the darkness near the village. They "close hoppled a horse with a bell on, and took their station in a hazel thicket but a few yards off. It was not long until an Indian appeared and seized the horse. The captains rushed upon him, cut off his head and brought it into camp, and claimed at the least the price of a wolf's scalp."[193]

The next day, the twentieth, was spent burning and destroying everything that could have been of use to the Indians. During this process a dozen or more Indians appeared near one of the burning parties. Major Fontaine and some of his cavalry were able to outflank them undiscovered and after some shots had been fired two of the warriors fell dead and the rest retreated.[194] By the twenty-first the army had completely burned the village and in five days had managed to burn five Indian villages, the main Miami town, and destroy 20,000 bushels of corn.[195] Harmar decided to move out that day and head back to Fort Washington, satisfied that he had accomplished his goal. Encamped for the night, eight miles from the ruined village, Harmar suddenly decided to send a detachment of 400 "choice men" back to the Miami village in hopes of surprising the Indians who he assumed would have returned to evaluate the damage.[196] About midnight 340 militia and sixty regulars marched out of camp in three echelons a few hundred yards apart, with the intention of crossing the Miami River at daybreak, and all three striking the village at the same instant, but at different locations.[197] Harmar thought to thus check the Indians with this sudden blow and prevent their harassing the army on its return march.[198]

The detachment was under the command of Major John Palsgrave Wyllys of the Federal corps. He took the center position with the Federal troops, a company of riflemen, and a company of cavalry under Major Fontaine.[199] Colonel Hardin, who had pleaded with Harmar to allow him to go on the expedition to atone for his fiasco on the nineteenth, accompanied Wyllys in the center column. On the right wing was a company of militia under the command of Major McMillen, and Major Hall with a battalion of militia marched on the left.[200]

Wylly's plan was to send Major Hall's battalion on an encircling movement around the bend of the river before crossing, thereby coming up behind the Miami town. He was to wait there while Major McMillen's battalion came up from the other side, and then the three divisions would attack simultaneously as Wyllys crossed the river at the regular fording place at the front of the village.[201] Captain Joseph Ashton of the Federal corps said that Wyllys had instructed the two militia majors not to separate but that as soon as the action began the three separate divisions were to converge on the enemy, or support each other, whichever circumstances required.[202] Wyllys's plan to encircle the enemy camp might have worked[203] but the militia officers did not follow orders. After crossing the river,

[193] *Military Journal of Major Ebenezer Denny*, p. 350.
[194] *Ibid.*, p. 351.
[195] *Ibid.*
[196] *Ibid.*
[197] *Ibid.*
[198] *American State Papers*, Military Affairs, Vol. 1, pp. 28–29.
[199] Jonathan Heart to Wm. Judd, December 3, 1790, Guthman Collection.
[200] *Ibid.*
[201] *American State Papers*, Military Affairs, Vol. 1, p. 28.
[202] *Ibid.*
[203] *Ibid.*

undiscovered, they came upon several Indians and gave chase, firing their weapons and thus alerting the main body of Indians. They pursued the few Indians up the St. Joseph river a short distance, leaving Major Wyllys and his middle division without support. Denny, in his first reference to the clever tactics of the Indians, said: "It would seem as if the enemy designed to draw the principal part of the force after a few of their people, while their main body attacked Major Wyllys."[204]

Major Fontaine, commanding the mounted troops, then charged the Indians who were now attacking the unsupported center in force. Jonathan Heart describes the attack:

> —the commanding officer of the Horse with the Fury of a mad man Charged the Indians without a single Man following him he fell and the horse were scattered in confusion—Major Wyllys moving still on, the Indians in a larger Body came around upon his Rear from the right, attacked his Party with irresistible impetuosity, numbers fell the first discharge, the remainder overpowered by [superior] numbers and no assistance were compelled to retreat across the main branch of the Miami about one quarter of a mile from the Place where the action commenced. During this, the slaughter was great on both Sides. By this time a Party of Major Hall's command and some horses had collected on the opposite Shore and gave the Indians a very warm reception but, being very numberous, our men scattered. They crossed in different Places, and Parties retreated, except Major McMillen who, having moved on for some distance and not hearing of the other Columns, returned to the French village and waiting there for some time after the retreat of the others, returned to Camp with very little loss.
>
> Our loss was a Major [Wyllys], Lieutenant [Frothingham] and about 70 men in both actions, the Militia lost something more—2 Federal officers and 48 Federal soldiers were killed, the balance militia.[205] The loss of the Indians cannot be exactly ascertained—from the most accurate calculations it is estimated about 120 of their Warriors—The general opinion of those late in the Field of Action is that the number was much greater—a testimony of more than one Militia Man declares that a Regular Soldier in the Retreat near the River being surrounded and in the midst of the Indians put his Bayonet through Six Indians, knocked down the Seventh and the Soldier himself made the Eighth dead Man in the same heap—there were many instances in which, while the Indians was giving the fatal Blow with his tomahawk, he fell by the Bayonet, and, he who pushed the bayonet, fell by the tomahawk in his turn—we returned to Head Quarters without a single Shott being fired afterwards—.[206]

Heart's description, although vivid, was not evidently detailed as he would have liked. He told Judd that "I think the transactions of that day would afford ample Field for the Pencil of a Trumbull in representing the horrors of War—".[207] The scene, however, in the eyes of Heart, Harmar, and the

---

[204] Denny, *op. cit.*, p. 351.
[205] Heart to Judd, *op. cit.*, December 3, 1790, Guthman Collection.
[206] *Ibid.*
[207] *Ibid.*

entire force was one of victory for the United States. Heart said, "—and though we have every reason to lament the death of Major Wyllys, Lieutenant Frothingham, and many brave men, we may say the Expedition under every circumstance has been as successful as we could expect, and we have reason to believe had we not sent back the detachment [referring to Wyllys on the 21st] more of our Men would have been killed by their harrassing us on the return than fell in the Action—."[208]

Governor St. Clair, reporting to Secretary of War Knox November 6, told him; "One thing, however, is certain, that the Savages have got a most terrible stroke, of which nothing can be greater proof than that they have not attempted to harass the army on its return. They arrived at this place on the 3rd instant in good health and spirits."[209] Harmar's report to Knox, written on November 4, said that "our loss was heavy, but the Head Quarters of iniquity were broken up."[210] He went on to say not less than 100 or 120 warriors were slain and 300 log houses and wigwams were burned. He also mentions that the villages were abandoned and that he was sorry because "the villainous traders would have been a principal object of attention."[211] The general went on to say 20,000 bushels of corn, in the ears, were burned by the army. However, his return for the entire expedition, by its content, contradicts any claim to an American army victory over the Indians. The cost of the expedition was the lives of twelve officers (two Federal and ten militia) and 171 noncommissioned officers and privates (seventy-three Federal and ninety-eight militia). There were also thirty-one men wounded (three Federal and twenty-eight militia).[212] Weapons, ammunition, accounterments, horses, and other supplies, valued at thousands of dollars, were lost; and the cost of feeding and equipping the entire force was a tremendous strain on the weak economy.

In comparison, the cost to the Indians was negligible. At the outside, they lost 120 warriors, and this figure was probably exaggerated since there was no accurate method of substantiating the figures the survivors estimated. The huts and wigwams that had been burned could easily be rebuilt and the loss of their corn crop meant only that the tribes had to depend more upon game for meat, which had been, whenever necessary, their entire diet. The British undoubtedly substituted other food stuffs for the lost crops.

Denny said that the return march was difficult. The frost had destroyed the forage for the horses early on the march out, thereby reducing their numbers considerably by the time the army was ready to return.[213] The militia, he continued, became altogether ungovernable and Harmar had to inflict punishment upon some of them in order to maintain any sort of military appearance. One offender was tied to a six-pounder and given a half-dozen lashes.[214]

The militia officers claimed that Harmar had no authority to punish a militia soldier, and they, too, began to grumble and complain about Harmar's handling of the entire expedition. Soon after the army returned to Fort Washington, criticism from Kentucky combined with the poor showing of the expedition in the eyes of the War Department, President Washington and some members of Congress, caused Harmar to request a military hearing of his conduct on the expedition. Rumors had originated among the Kentucky militia inferring that the commander was intoxicated often and had not conducted the campaign in a soldierly manner.

Harmar, who blamed the failure of the campaign on the poor behavior of the militia under battle conditions, requested the hearing to investigate whether or not his conduct was proper. A court was

[208] Ibid.
[209] American State Papers, Vol. 1, Indian Affairs, p. 104.
[210] Ibid.
[211] Ibid.
[212] Ibid., p. 106
[213] Military Journal of Ebenezer Denny, p. 351.
[214] His father was a Baptist preacher in Kentucky and Denny feared that, through his influence, ugly rumors and criticism would he leveled against Harmar from Kentucky as soon as the militia returned.

convened at Fort Washington on September 15, 1791, and consisted of Major-General Richard Butler, president of the court, and Lieutenant-Colonels George Gibson and William Darke. Although they had not served in the Federal corps previously, they all had fine Revolutionary War records, and each man had earned a good reputation on the frontier.

The court lasted nine days, and witnesses from all of the officer ranks who had been on the expedition were called upon to testify. However, none of the Kentucky militia officers appeared and the testimony was confined to Federal officers. Harmar's conduct during the campaign was found to be "irreproachable," and his plans of march, encampment, and battle "judicious and well calculated."[215] The major question concerned Harmar's choice of tactics (detaching smaller units of men to engage the enemy rather than striking with the full force of the entire expedition). Harmar's reasoning was explained satisfactorily to the court, which ruled that

> There were good reasons for the detachments of the 14th and 19th of October; that the detachment of the 21st was made on good principles, and had the designed effect of securing the return of the army, and from preventing the enemy from harassing their rear. That the General had ordered support for the said detachment in time, but that his orders were not properly executed; and that the conduct of the said Brigadier General Josiah Harmar merits high approbation.[216]

Harmar's expedition cannot be considered a total loss, although from a military point of view it only served to antagonize the Miami Indians and arouse their hostility rather than force them into submission. The campaign did prove to the War Department that a large force could penetrate the uncharted forests of the Northwest Territory, cut their own roads as they marched, and, without the benefit of accurate maps or supply posts along the way, reach a destination as far away as the Miami villages. Harmar's army returned well fed and, except for the losses suffered in battle, did not endure severe hardships on the march. The country was no longer uncharted, and accurate maps could be available for future expeditions.

On the other hand, the Indians, who fared much better in the fighting that occurred than the United States army, suffered a psychological setback as a result of the expedition. They had forced their opponents to engage in the kind of warfare in which they excelled, had inveigled the militia officers to move into the position chosen by Little Turtle, the Miami Chief, for a perfect ambush, and had further enticed the brash militia officers into splitting their forces thus favoring the well-concealed Indian warriors. But all of those brilliant tactics were executed on their home grounds and for the first time they had been reached, in their own villages, by a large force.

Previously, the Miamis could stalk the United States frontier along the Ohio River, and choose victims to rob and murder, knowing that they could escape back to the Miami towns. There, safe from any retaliation under the protective eye of the British at Fort Detroit, and too far for any meaningful discipline from the United States army headquarters on the Ohio River, they felt the security of almost 200 miles of wilderness. Now, however, Little Turtle, his chiefs and warriors, the fur traders, and the British, who protected the fur trade and directed the profits derived from it back to England, all knew

---

[215] *American State Papers*, Military Affairs, Vol. 1, pp. 20–30.
[216] *Ibid.*

that an era had come to an end: Harmar's army had marched into the previously unchallenged territory.

The mistakes of the campaign might have served as lessons for future expeditions. A late start in the year meant that frost would eliminate grazing for the horses. Untrained militia could only hurt, not help, the regular army. As St. Clair had suggested to Knox earlier that year, forts were needed along the way to supply the army, contain the hostile Indians, and establish the United States position in the territory. They would be built during the next campaign but had they been built during Harmar's expedition, as St. Clair recommended, the next campaign might have been successful. As it was, the forts built during St. Clair's disastrous expedition a year later helped General Wayne toward his victory; and thus Harmar's expedition blazed the trail for Wayne's ultimate success.

Harmar's expedition also established another United States military tradition—on the battlefield, under Armstrong on the eighteenth, when the militia fled under fire and the regulars stood their ground and were cut to pieces. Again, under Wyllys on the twenty-second, the regulars stood alone in the face of the enemy to suffer the withering assault that resulted in the deaths of forty-eight enlisted men and two officers.

Ironically, both officers came from Connecticut and both had a premonition of death before the battle. Lieutenant Ebenezer Frothingham received news of the death of his wife Polly in Connecticut just three months prior to the expedition. He was so saddened that he had no desire to live without his "partner Polly." He told his brother "I am about to leave you being ordered upon a long command and a great distance—the most heavy loss I am now labouring under is the late sudden death of my Wife; has sett the things of another world nearer in view; some sudden stroke may deprive you of your brother—."[217] A few days later he wrote to his sister: "Tomorrow I take off the remainder of this garrison (Fort Washington) and from there we expect to march against the indians—."[218] He ended the letter saying, "O Almighty God, of thy free mercy, through the all attoning blood of the Lamb, bring us all to meet in Heaven at Length."[219]

Frothingham told his brother "my will I leave in your possession to be opened after my Death." He went on, "Your poor brother must leave you in the hands of a Holy and Just God—with this last farewell request—."[220] Following Frothingham's last letter is the notation:

> After the above dated letter—Lieutenant Frothingham sett out with ye remainder of ye garrison to follow the troops into the wilderness—Takeing his farewell of his friends—Saying he neither expected or desired to return again—the 22nd of October following he was killed by the Indians—he was last seen by one of ye under officers on the Bank of The River St. Joseph, holding his wounded side—he was asked if he should help him—and answered, "escape for yourself"—[221]

Major Wyllys, on the other hand, wrote to a friend telling him that he expected trouble because of the inadequate militia: "We are about 'going forth to war' in this part of the world. I expect to have not a very agreeable campaign this fall. Tis probably the Indians will fight us in earnest, the greater part of our force will consist of Militia; therefore there is some reason to apprehend trouble."[222] Major Wyllys said that there was no time to make a proper will, but if, "the last sad accident befall me," he went on to distribute his personal property.

---

[217] Letters of Ebenezer Frothingham to his sisters and brother in the archives of the Connecticut Historical Society.
[218] *Ibid.*
[219] *Ibid.*
[220] *Ibid.*
[221] *Ibid.*
[222] Letter of Major John Palsgrave Wyllys to his friend in the archives of the Connecticut Historical Society.

On November 4, 1790, having returned from the campaign to headquarters, fellow Connecticut officer, Lieutenant John Pratt, wrote to Samuel Wyllys, the brother of John Palsgrave Wyllys. He told of the last few minutes of the major's life, as described by Captain Joseph Ashton, who was with Wyllys during the fighting. He recounted how the Federal troops were left unsupported and that the Indians "were about him within three minutes."[223] He went on to say that the last Ashton saw of his major was when he "was sitting on the ground with his hand to his breast, as he supposed holding a wound, and the Indians close upon him in a situation beyond relief—."[224]

Wyllys's last living moments, "beyond relief," can be likened to the events of the next year for the United States Army. Harmar's campaign had left the Indians enraged, more defiant and ready to cooperate with each other. Alexander McKee, Simon Girty, and Joseph Brant fired the aroused warriors' imaginations with speeches of hatred against the United States. The British at Detroit encouraged the Western Confederation of tribes, whose leaders had gone to Detroit with trophies of their last encounter against the United States. Such Indian leaders as Little Turtle, Blue Jacket, and LeGris conferred with the British and made plans against the next attack, which they knew was inevitable.

The lessons that the United States Army had learned in its campaign of 1790 were soon forgotten as preparations for another campaign got under way. Once again the only thought was the quantity of troops, not the quality. The clever tactics of the Indians were soon forgotten in the haste to build another army so that it could quickly enter into another expedition and achieve what Harmar's force could not.

[223] Letter of John Pratt to Samuel Wyllys, in the Archives of the Connecticut Historical Society.
[224] *Ibid.*

74.

74. Captain Ebenezer Denny from a print in *Military Journal of Major Ebenezer Denny,* published for the Historical Society of Pennsylvania in 1860. *Guthman Collection*

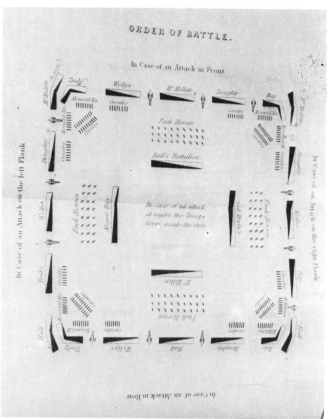

75.

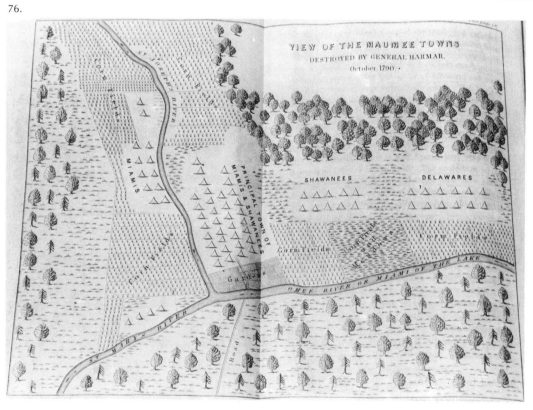

76.

77.

75. Order of battle, from a drawing by Captain Ebenezer Denny, United States Army, during the Harmar campaign. Taken from an engraving in *Military Journal of Major Ebenezer Denny*, published for the Historical Society of Pennsylvania in 1860.
Guthman Collection

76. A view of the Maumee (Indian) towns destroyed by General Harmar, drawn by Captain Ebenezer Denny after the campaign in October, 1790.

Engraved from Denny's drawing for *Military Journal of Major Ebenezer Denny*, published for the Historical Society of Pennsylvania in 1860.
Guthman Collection

77. Iroquois pouch (strap missing), circa 1775, made of red homespun and lined with red-and-white print cloth. It is decorated with white beads and tinkling tin cones.

All of the material for the pouch was obtained from the white man except for the red dyed horsehair at the end of the cones.
Guthman Collection

Arthur St. Clair, a major-general during the Revolution and governor of the Northwest territory, assumed command of the army in 1791 and subsequently led it to the worst defeat in history, at the hands of the Miami Indians under Chief Little Turtle. November 4, 1791, spelled tragedy for the task force which set out to achieve the victory that had escaped Harmar the year before. The proportion of killed and wounded to those taking part in an engagement has never again been equaled by any other United States force.

Chapter 10

Part I: The Peace Mission and Militia Campaigns of 1791

Henry Knox summarized the critical Indian situation of the Northwestern frontier for Congress in January 1791. He said that Harmar's expedition did not restrain the Miami Indians nor did it force them to sue for peace. On the contrary, "their opinion of their own success, and the number of trophies they possess, will, probably, not only encourage them to a continuance of hostilities, but may be the means of their obtaining considerable assistance from neighboring tribes."[1] The Secretary of War added that they probably would receive a great deal of help from those "malignant" whites who resided among them, referring to McKee, Elliot, Girty, and the French-Canadian traders.

Knox suggested that immediate preparations should be inaugurated for another expedition against the Wabash Indians. This time he favored establishing a strong military post at the Miami villages. He reminded Congress that, although it had been hoped the British would evacuate the fort at Detroit, this now did not seem possible and therefore a strong garrison stationed in the Miami Indian stronghold was imperative to the United States. The establishment of such a post, he said, could only occur after a successful military operation against the Indians, and, in order to accomplish this, the present military force had to be enlarged.[2]

The frontier along the Ohio River, Knox said, could more effectively be covered by a post at the Miami villages than at any other place—and in addition might curb the hostility of the Ottawas, Chippewas, and other tribes. It would also, he added, assist in reducing the national debt by offering security to those people who purchased and settled public lands in the territory.[3] Again he emphasized that the army was now too small to oversee the frontier and carry forth a successful expedition.

---

[1] *American State Papers,* Vol. 1, Indian Affairs, p. 112.
[2] *Ibid.*
[3] *Ibid.*

Pointing out to Congress how inadequate the present force was for the protection of the border settlers, Knox said that the frontiers were practically enclosed from the northeast to the southwest by "possessions, claims and garrisons of two formidable nations, whose interest cannot entirely coincide with those of the United States."[4] Compounding this, the Secretary at War said that the numerous tribes which resided in the vicinity were easily aroused to hostility by encroaching settlements and expanding populations. Schemers and adventurers, he predicted, would attempt to take over lands belonging to the government and promote schemes to their own advantage which would act against "public peace and prosperity."[5]

The seat of government was too far removed from the endangered territroy to protect it properly without a "wise and vigorous system" being adopted and executed to protect the inhabitants and prevent the usurpation of public lands. Besides all of these considerations, the state of Georgia needed more troops for the protection of its frontiers, he added. There were at present three companies of troops stationed in Georgia, and another being raised, totaling one-quarter of the entire Federal military establishment.[6]

The question of raising additional troops for another expedition against the Indians caused great controversy in Congress, as well as among the citizens along the Eastern seaboard who had become disenchanted with the results of Harmar's campaign. Strengthening the military force of the central government, and incurring additional expenses to secure a remote frontier that meant very little to the average citizen, presented a difficult obstacle to the administration. Pennsylvania Senator William Maclay, still a staunch opponent of the administration and any move toward a stronger military organization, said in February 1791: "I returned to the Senate and found the drafts of General Harmar's expedition before the committee. They look finely on paper, but, were we to view the green bones and scattered fragments of our defeat on the actual field, it would leave very different ideas in our minds."[7] The next day Maclay said, in reference to the administration bill to increase the military establishment, "I shall most undoubtedly vote against the augmentation of troops...the war is the pretext to raising an army meant to awe our citizens into submission."[8]

Many forces were working against the military bill that had been submitted for Congressional approval by the adminstration. Reviewing Knox's explicit summary of past events, and his analysis of the current situation, President Washington made certain that Congress became well aware of the plea for help sent by Rufus Putnam, leader of the Ohio Company settlement at Marietta and a judge of the Northwest Territory. Putnam had sent a frantic letter to Washington after one of the Ohio Company settlements had been wiped out. On the evening of January 2, Putnam said, eleven men, one woman, and two children were killed at a new settlement called Big Bottom, forty miles from Marietta on the Muskingum River. Three other men were missing and four had escaped.

Blaming the renewed wrath of the Indians on the unsuccessful expedition of Harmar, Putnam said the situation was critical. The garrison at Fort Harmar (across the river from Marietta) consisted of only twenty men and the Ohio Company settlements could muster only 287 men capable of bearing arms—and they were poorly armed.[9] Unless the Federal government could speedily send troops for the protection of the settlements, Putnam said, "we are a ruined people." There were about eighty houses at Marietta, scattered mills and houses several miles up the Muskingum, another settlement of twenty houses twenty-two miles up the river, and two miles further, five more families and a set of mills. Another settlement of between thirty and forty houses was located down the Ohio River, opposite the Little Kenhawa River, called Belle Prairie.[10] All of these people, Putnam said, were in

[4] Ibid.
[5] Ibid., p. 113.
[6] Ibid.
[7] Maclay, op. cit., p. 397.
[8] Ibid., p. 398.
[9] American State Papers, ibid., p. 121.

desperate need of immediate protection. President Washington made certain that Congress heard his plea for help.

Finally, with plans for a new campaign against the Indians, on March 3, 1791, Congress passed a bill authorizing the raising of an additional regiment of infantry to be added to the military establishment. This was the last act of the third session of the first Congress.[11] It called for an additional 912 men, exclusive of officers, each man enlisting to receive a $6 bounty. The basic pay and organization would be the same as that of the 1st Regiment. The recruiting officers were to receive a bonus of two dollars for every recruit they enlisted. If the regiment was not completely manned in time for the forthcoming campaign, the President could make up the deficiency with levies or militia. The President was empowered by the new act to call into service up to 2,000 levies for a period of six months as well as a body of militia to serve as cavalry (furnishing their own horses, arms and provisions). A major-general was to be appointed as commander of the force. Congress authorized an appropriation of $312,686.20 to be raised from taxes, and, if this amount could not be raised in time, the President could arrange a loan at an interest rate not to exceed six percent.[12]

The major-general appointed by Congress to command the army was Arthur St. Clair, governor of the Northwest Territory, former Indian commissioner, and Revolutionary War general. His appointment was confirmed on March 4, 1791, the day after Congress passed the military act raising the second regiment. St. Clair still retained his position as governor of the Northwest Territory.

Before St. Clair's army could be organized and ready for battle, several intermediate projects were undertaken. Cornplanter, a Seneca "war-captain,"[13] and other Indians of the same tribe visited Philadelphia in December 1790. They were told of the measures being taken by the United States to secure peace with the Western Indians and that the coercive action taken against the hostile Indians had been the result of continued Indian depredations, along with their refusal to respond to the peace offers of the United States.

When warned not to allow his young warriors to participate in the hostile activities of the Western tribes, Cornplanter assured the United States that all of the Indians under his influence would not only be on friendly terms, but would attempt to prevent further violence on the part of the Western tribes. Arrangements were then made for Cornplanter to visit the Western tribes and try to foster peaceful overtures toward the United States. Colonel Thomas Procter, an artillery officer during the Revolution and a close friend of Knox's, was selected to go along as the American emissary of peace. He left Philadelphia on March 12, 1791 with an aide, Captain Michael Gabriel Houdin, a French officer who served with the Massachusetts line during the Revolution, proceeding, as ordered, to Cornplanter's settlement on the headwaters of the Allegheny River on the western side of New York state.[14]

Before leaving Philadelphia Procter and Houdin purchased a small pocket compass, "McFadden's draught of North America," and a tin box and oil case, probably for maintenance of their firearms. On the fourteenth, at Reading, Pennsylvania, they purchased a tomahawk; and on the nineteenth at "Wilksburgh," Pennsylvania, they purchased a tinderbox, flints, steel, had a tomahawk "helved" and purchased a leather sling for the same tomahawk, and also a powder horn. Knox had told Procter to try and induce Cornplanter and other Seneca chiefs to come with him to the Miami towns in order to hold a peace conference. If Procter succeeded in bringing the Miami and Wabash chiefs to Fort Washington to a treaty, he was to be given $500 plus his daily expenses and $5 a day salary. If he was killed while on the mission, his orphan children were to receive seven years half-pay

[10] *Ibid.,* p. 122.
[11] *Acts Passed at a Congress of the United States of America,* p. 309, *op. cit.*
[12] *Ibid.,* pp. 309–12.
[13] *American State Papers, ibid.,* p. 139.
[14] *Ibid.,* p. 149.

of a lieutenant-colonel–commandant.[15] Procter was required to return to Fort Washington by May 5, whether or not his mission was successful, because "this is of the highest importance, as it is connected with collateral arrangements."[16]

The collateral arrangements were revealed in Knox's instructions to St. Clair, dated March 21, 1791. If Procter's mission failed, then St. Clair was to go ahead with the planned expedition against the Miami and Wabash tribes. Recruiting was to take place immediately. The second regiment of regulars was to be recruited from the four New England states except for one company recruited in Maryland and another in Delaware.[17] The recruits required to complete the ranks of the old first regiment were to be raised in the states from Maryland to New York.[18] The recruits for both the regular army and the levies were to be mustered into companies and marched to Fort Pitt as soon as possible[19] and there await further orders.

Knox believed the recruits of both the regulars and the levies could rendezvous at Fort Washington by July 10, and that St. Clair's force for the expedition would consist of 3,000 effectives, besides small garrisions along the Ohio. Meanwhile, if the Indians refused to listen to the peace offering of Colonel Procter, Knox said they would probably spread themselves along the Ohio in order to commit further depredations against the settlements. In order to prevent this, he explained that Brigadier-General Charles Scott of Kentucky had been authorized by the President to make an expedition against the Indian towns of Ouiatanon (Wea villages) on the Wabash River. Scott, who was brevetted major-general in 1783 on the basis of his illustrious Revolutionary War career was authorized to enlist 750 mounted Kentucky militia for his expedition.[20] Scott's force was not scheduled to set out until May 10, in order to give Colonel Procter's peace mission an opportunity to succeed.

If Procter were unsuccessful, and Scott's militia force carried off a successful attack on the Wea towns, then a second expedition—and possible a third—could be considered. Knox said that St. Clair was in the best position to evaluate the results of the Kentucky assault and, if he felt that the first raid had favorable results, he could consider a second if he thought it might induce the Indians to seek a peaceful settlement.

The second, and possibly third, raids were to consist of not more than 500 mounted Kentucky militia each.[21] Knox insisted that all captives, including women and children, be treated with humanity as kindness might attract the Indians after a demonstration of the power to punish. Knox hoped that this might peacefully end the hostilities and preclude the major expedition that St. Clair was preparing to undertake.. Knox said that the American people felt an Indian war should be avoided. Procter's mission was a dismal failure. His carefully recorded diary confirmed emphatically the need for another expedition, and clearly showed the extent of the British influence in preventing peace with the Western tribes. When Procter and Houdin arrived at Buffalo, New York, in late April, they visited the Seneca village where Farmer's Brother and Red Jacket lived. Procter found that the British influence was great because of the proximity of Fort Niagara, thirty-five miles away and Fort Erie, six miles away, "from which places they were supplied yearly with almost every necessary they require, so much as to make them indifferent in their huntings."[22] The Indians, he said, were far better clothed in this village than those villages further from the British posts. The chiefs, he said, looked to

[15] *Ibid.*, p. 146.
[16] *Ibid.*
[17] *Ibid.*, p. 171.
[18] *Ibid.*
[19] *Ibid.*
[20] *Ibid.*
[21] *Ibid.*, p. 172.
[22] *Ibid.*, pp. 149–162.

the British for subsistence almost daily and for their apparel. Farmer's Brother, the young king, was fully outfitted as a colonel, red-faced uniform with blue, as belonging to some royal regiment, and a pair of the best epaulettes."[23]

Procter's mission came to an abrupt end when the Seneca chiefs, whom he had brought with him, refused to cross Lake Erie in small boats or canoes. Procter sought permission to charter a larger schooner to transport his party across the lake to Sandusky to attend a council. The commandant of Fort Niagara, Colonel Gordon, flatly refused, stating that as far as he was concerned Procter was not acting in an official capacity. As the Senecas could therefore not be transported to Sandusky to influence the hostile chiefs to attend a treaty of peace at Fort Washington, Procter abandoned his mission and left Buffalo on May 21—two weeks past the deadline for his return set by Knox.

In the meantime, St. Clair held up Scott's expedition, awaiting word from Procter. This interval, St. Clair later claimed, delayed preparation for his own campaign. Scott was instructed by Knox on March 9 that he, Harry Innes, John Brown, Benjamin Logan, and Isaac Shelby (all members of the Board of War of the District of Kentucky, authorized by Congress) were to choose 750 mounted volunteers. If volunteers were insufficient, drafts should be made from the militia.[24]

The expedition was to depart from the Ohio River on the tenth of May (delayed by Procter) for the Wea towns on the Wabash and march from there to other Indian towns along that river. By "surprise, rapid marches and attacks"[25] they were to inflict as much injury upon the enemy as possible. If the commanding officer of the troops on the Ohio judged a second and third operation "in the public interests," Knox ordered that a second operation take place no later than June 10, with a force not to exceed 500 mounted militia.[26] Because of Procter's delay, it was not until the twenty-third of May that Scott's force crossed the Ohio River: 750 hand-picked Kentucky horsemen, with Lieutenant-Colonel—Commandant James Wilkinson the second in command. Colonel John Hardin, who had accompanied Harmar, was also one of the officers in the detachment.

On June 1 the force approached two Wea towns on the Wabash. Colonel Hardin with sixty mounted infantry and a troop of light horses was detached to attack the village on the left while the main force under Scott moved ahead toward the main town. Scott ordered forty men ahead to attack the first house that came into view, and two warriors were killed. Gaining high ground, Scott discovered the enemy in a state of confusion, trying to escape by canoe across the river. He immediately ordered Lieutenant-Colonel–Commandant Wilkinson down to the river bank with the first battalion of mounted infantry who, upon arriving at the bank, emptied five canoes crowded with escaping warriors with the deadly fire from their rifles.[27] As fire was being directed at the militia from the Kickapoo town across the river, Scott ordered two companies to ford the river below the town and attack. The men were able to approach the Kickapoo town unobserved, some swimming across the river, while others crossed in a canoe. When they attacked the town, the Indians immediately evacuated.

In the meantime, Colonel Hardin had attacked the village to which he had been dispatched, and then went on to another. He returned with fifty-two prisioners, after having killed six warriors.[28] The next evening at 5:30 P.M., Lieutenant Colonel Wilkinson was detached with 360 men and marched on foot (because of tired horses) eighteen miles to the mouth of the Eel River to attack the "important"

[23] Ibid., pp. 149–162.
[24] Ibid., pp. 129–130.
[25] Ibid., p. 130.
[26] Ibid.
[27] Ibid., p. 131.
[28] Ibid.

town of Kethtipecanunk. The detachment returned to camp at one o'clock in the afternoon of the next day, after destroying the town. Many of the inhabitants were French traders, Scott said, and had close connections with the British at Detroit.[29]

The following day Scott misinterpreted a white flag that the Indians placed to mark the spot where a prominent member of the tribe, who had died some time before, had been interred. The general thought it was a flag of truce and sent an aged squaw prisoner back to the village with a message to the Indians to surrender and their village would be spared. When he learned the flag was a marker, he burned the village. On the fourth of June he released sixteen of the weakest and most infirm prisoners in order to "rid the army of heavy incumbrance, to gratify the impulsions of humanity, to increase the panic my operations had produced—."[30] That same day, Scott began his return march. Recounting his accomplishments, he said that he had burned the towns and adjacent villages, destroyed the crops, and returned to the Rapids of the Ohio without the loss of a single man. Only five men had been wounded while they had killed thirty-two, "chiefly warriors of size and figure," and had taken fifty-eight[31] prisoners.[32] He added that "It is with much pride and pleasure that I mention that no act of inhumanity has marked the conduct of the volunteers of Kentucky on this occasion; even the inveterate habit of scalping the dead ceased to influence."[33]

The march from the Ohio to the first Wea towns on the Wabash, Scott estimated, was a distance of about 150 miles. Not until they approached the village did Scott order his force to form in the order of battle to attack.[34] It is interesting to compare the results of these swift, surprise tactics of a small force comprised of men who were used to the type of country (although none knew the immediate terrain)[35] and who were expert marksmen and horsemen with the results achieved by the raw recruits employed in the Harmar campaign, marching slowly and noisily to their objective.

Although the results were negligible, and the damage that was inflicted would not discourage further Indian incursions against the frontier settlements, the tactics employed by Scott did prove effective against the enemy. The skilled Kentucky horsemen were veteran Indian fighters. They knew that striking quickly, with surprise, and using deadly aimed rifle fire, was the best way to defeat the Indian, whose tactics they had borrowed. However, instead of utilizing these proven tactics in his forthcoming expedition, St. Clair ordered another small militia foray while preparations continued for his cumbersome major expedition later that year.

Lieutenant-Colonel–Commandant Wilkinson was selected by the Kentucky Board of War to lead a second raid with 500 mounted militia. Wilkinson's force numbered slightly more than that when it left Fort Washington, on August 1, 1791, heading for the Eel villages situated near the junction of the L'Anguile (or Eel) River with the Wabsh, about three miles up the L'Anguile.[36] This site was about six miles from present-day Logansport, Indiana.[37] Avoiding the "hunting grounds of the enemy," Wilkinson's force traveled across difficult, uncharted terrain, filled with deep bogs and covered with thickets of brambles, weeds, and shrubs. On the sixth of June, an ambush party detailed to fall behind the main force, killed one Indian warrior and drove off three others. Wilkinson, in unknown territory and alarmed that his position was known, pushed his men at a rapid pace, across

[29] *Ibid.*
[30] *Ibid.,* pp. 131–132.
[31] Scott reported that he delivered only forty-one prisoners to the garrison at Fort Steuben. He had released the others, as previously noted.
[32] *American State Papers, ibid.,* p. 132.
[33] *Ibid.*
[34] *Ibid.,* p. 131.
[35] *Ibid.*
[36] *Ibid.,* pp. 133–135.
[37] Barce, *op. cit.,* p. 188.

the Wabash River about "one and a half leagues above the mouth of the Eel River"—exactly the spot, he claimed, that he had aimed for all along.[38]

Soon, approaching cautiously, they came upon their objective, the Eel River town, situated on the opposite bank of the river. Wilkinson had made his plans for attack. When their presence was suddenly discovered and the Indians began hurriedly to evacuate the town, Wilkinson gave the command to charge, and the men forced their way through bramble thickets along the shore, swam the river, and sacked the town, killing six warriors and by mistake two squaws and one child. Thirty-four prisoners were taken, at a cost of two militia killed and one wounded. About an hour prior to the attack, Wilkinson said, all the warriors except eight had ridden up the river to a French store to obtain ammunition which had just arrived from the Miami village that same day. A detachment was sent in search of this group of Indians but could find no trace of them.[39]

The next day, after burning the town and the crops, Wilkinson headed for the Kickapoo towns in the prairie. Not finding a path, he headed for Tippecanoe, across the boundless prairie. Lost in unfamiliar terrain, he encountered bog after bog, sometimes leading his horse afoot, sinking to his armpits in mud and water. After changing course several times, he finally found the Tippecanoe road and encamped, after a tedious march of thirty miles. The day, he commented, "produced the most unfavorable effects."[40]

On the move at four the next morning, he soon came upon Tippecanoe, which had been evacuated before he arrived. After destroying the town, the detachment halted the remainder of the day to rest the men and horses. Wilkinson heard rumblings among the men and, upon investigating, found 270 horses had turned lame and tired and there were only five days' provisions left. This forced him to alter his plans, and, instead of pushing ahead toward the Kickapoo prairie towns, he turned toward Scott's old trace, destroyed several towns and returned to the Rapids of the Ohio by the twenty-first of August, after a march "by accurate compilation, of 451 miles from Fort Washington."[41] Wilkinson claimed that his expedition had accounted for the burning of 430 acres of corn, destroyed a major Indian town of the "Ouiattanon nation," and made prisoners of the sons and sisters of the king.

Although the small force did not move as efficiently as Scott's expedition, and the results were not as detrimental to the Indians, Wilkinson's troops did not suffer from an Indian ambush. Lost, struggling through swamps, thickets, and endless prairies, they kept moving quickly enough, changing direction when they thought they had been discovered, so that the tribes could not anticipate them soon enough to do more than evacuate their towns. Even though at times he was virtually thrashing around in the wilderness, Wilkinson did not leave his troops vulnerable to the enemy. Wilkinson never exposed his main body to surprise, but used an advance guard, flankers, and a rear guard at all times. His men, as did Scott's, knew rugged terrain, and how to take care of themselves in that kind of country.

The raids proved that special forces could penetrate Indian-controlled territory, inflict damage, and return with few, if any, casualties.

---

[38] *American State Papers, ibid.*
[39] *Ibid.*
[40] *Ibid.*
[41] *Ibid.*

Part II: The Plans Prepared in Philadelphia for St. Clair's Ill-Fated Expedition

While the Kentucky militia were engaged in their two harassing expeditions, preparations had been in progress at Fort Washington for the forthcoming major expedition. Colonel Timothy Pickering had been asked by the government to meet with the Six Nations and to try to persuade them not to join the Western tribes against whom the United States was at war, but rather for the Iroquois tribes to send their young warriors to join St. Clair's army, for which they would be well paid. Knox said that it would be impracticable for the chiefs to restrain the young warriors "from indulging in their passion for war. They will probably join the Western Indians unless they join us."[42] Knox added that not more than fifty or sixty warriors should join the troops at Fort Washington. However, Pickering did not attempt to persuade any of the Six Nations to join the United States Forces, feeling such a proposal would be distasteful to them.[43]

Meanwhile, St. Clair had received his instructions for the campaign from Knox. Dated March 21, 1791, Knox's letter carefully detailed the objectives, and how they were to be achieved by St. Clair. It was the policy of the United States, Knox said, to establish a just and liberal peace with the Indians. The great mass of American people felt, he said, an Indian war ought to be avoided, and only if all the overtures of peace failed was the campaign to be undertaken. Recruiting was to begin as soon as possible. As mentioned before, the 2nd Regiment was to be recruited from New England (except for a Delaware company and one company from South Carolina), while the balance of the recruits to complete the roster of the 1st Regiment were to be raised in Maryland, Delaware, Pennsylvania, New Jersey and New York.

In December 1791 Knox summarized the number of troops that had been authorized for the campaign.[44] His tabulation indicates the strength of the force with which St. Clair was to march into the field.

Regulars

(a) Act of April 30, 1790	One battalion of artillery		304
	First regiment of infantry		912
(b) Act of March 3, 1791	Second regiment of infantry		912
			2,128
Corps of 6 month levies			2,000
			4,128

The newly recruited regulars and the six-month levies were all scheduled to rendezvous at Fort Washington by the tenth of July 1791, marching, as individual companies were completed, to Fort Pitt and from there by boat to Fort Washington. There should be, Knox said, at least 3,000 effectives for the campaign, besides the garrisons along the Ohio.

---

[42] *Ibid.,* p. 165.
[43] *Ibid.,* p. 181.
[44] *Ibid.,* pp. 171–174.

Emphasizing that the main objective of the campaign was the establishment of a strong, permanent garrison at the Miami village, St. Clair was instructed to establish as many posts of communication with Fort Washington along the way as he thought necessary. The main fort, at the Miami village, was to be constructed by Major Ferguson of the artillery, under the direction of General St. Clair. For the campaign, Ferguson was to be furnished with: three 5½-inch brass howitzers, three brass three-pounders, three brass six-pounders, along with appropriate shot and shell. Between 1,000 and 1,200 men, Knox estimated, would be needed to garrison the main fort and the communication posts, with at least six months' rations of flour and salted meat.

In his instructions, the Secretary of War predicted that "disciplined valor would triumph over the undisciplined Indians."[45] Optimistically, Knox suggested boundary modifications, after the defeat of the Indians, in favor of the United States, those advantageous changes to occur along the Wabash, Miami, and extend to Lake Erie. However, he cautioned, the policy and interest of the United States dictated peace with the Indians. "This is of more value," he prophesized, "than millions of uncultivated acres, the right to which may be conceded by some, and disputed by others."[46]

"A delicate situation will probably develop unless the British are advised of our intentions at the Miami village," Knox warned. However, they should not be told until *after* the post is established, he said, having learned a bitter lesson warning the British beforehand when Harmar was preparing for his expedition. Because of the "jealousies" of the British over any American conquest of their Indian allies, Knox suggested it would be unwise, at that time, to make any "naval arrangement upon Lake Erie."[47]

Then Knox turned to the logistics of the campaign. All recruits for the 1st Regiment and the artillery were to be clothed from the surplus at the frontier posts. Roughly 550 complete suits of clothing were in the stores. One-quarter of the recruits of the 1st Regiment and artillery would be clothed, and all would have blankets, he added.[48] The 2nd Regiment, he said, would be clothed. Medicines, instruments, tents, and ordnance stores, would be forwarded to Fort Washington.

Samuel Hodgdon, who had been appointed quartermaster,[49] was ordered to report to Fort Washington as soon as he had arranged for the supplies at Philadelphia. He was under St. Clair's direct command; St. Clair would approve orders before Hodgdon could make any expenditures for boats, horses, and other means of transportation. The contractors, Knox said, would transport the provisions at their own expense. It was also the quartermaster's responsibility to transport the troops from Fort Pitt to the rendezvous, furnish return transportation for the levies, and to transport by land the ordnance and hospital stores and whatever baggage St. Clair deemed essential. Besides transportation of baggage and supplies, horses and equipment were to be supplied to mount one hundred cavalry for the expedition.

Lieutenant-Colonel Francis Mentges, inspector of the army, was to be ordered by St. Clair to inspect the troops as regularly as the service would permit. (Mentges acquired his rank in the Pennsylvania line during the Revolution, had the title "Mr.," and actually was a civilian during his service with the Federal corps. Hodgdon, on the other hand, had acquired the position of

---

[45] *Ibid.* An interesting comparison is Ebenezer Denny's entry in his journal quoting Josiah Harmar prior to St. Clair's departure from Fort Washington: "The enemy was brought up from infancy to war, and was perhaps superior to an equal number of the best men that could be taken against them."

[46] *Ibid.*

[47] *Ibid.*

[48] *Ibid.*

[49] *Military Journal of Major Ebenezer Denny,* p. 374. The office of quartermaster-general was abolished in 1785. It was reinstated in 1791, when the President felt that a quartermaster was necessary. The title was quartermaster and he was entitled to the same pay, rations, and forage as a lieutenant-colonel–commandant.

commissary-general during the Revolution, and was quartermaster of the United States Army, a military rank, on an appointment of March 4, 1791.)

St. Clair was also ordered to appoint a skilled person to make actual surveys of the march and if need be to make corrections by astronomical observations as they moved. Surveys were also required for the posts that might be occupied by the troops. Three thousand dollars for contingencies was to be delivered to St. Clair, to be used when the occasions arose either for intelligence or the Indian Department (treaties).

Knox estimated that all the troops would be assembled at Fort Washington by July 10, with 3,000 effectives, consisting of regulars and levies. However, if St. Clair was not able to raise this number of men (plus the additional troops to garrison the posts along the Ohio and Wabash rivers) he was to call for additional troops from the militia of Pennsylvania and Virginia and the district of Kentucky. The Congressional act of March 3, 1791, had decreed that these militia troops could be called upon in the name of the President of the United States. (However, complete confusion existed in regard to the militia officer's status under the new Constitutional government. With a lack of direction from state executives, the county militia of each state could not possibly have been organized soon enough to have coordinated with the Federal corps.)

Knox ordered that continuous communication be maintained between St. Clair and the War Department. In addition to the post rider from Philadelphia to Fort Pitt every second Friday, Knox directed that an additional trip be made between those two points on the middle Friday, so there would be weekly communication. Knox also requested that an efficient system of communication be established from garrison to garrison on the frontier, so that the War Department could receive up-to-date information on all of the military affairs along the Ohio River.

It was estimated that 4,000 rations per day would be required by St. Clair's army after it left Fort Washington. "The contractor," Knox said, "promises the highest exertions in order to furnish the rations which may be required in due season."[50]

The original contract was made with Theodosius Fowler on October 28, 1790, but on January 3, 1791, this contract was transferred to William Duer.[51] Another contract was made with Duer March 6, 1791. Duer, a close friend of Secretary of the Treasury Alexander Hamilton, Knox, and Washington, had been a member of the Continental Congress and Committee of Safety during the Revolution and had become immensely wealthy furnishing supplies to the Continental army. He would later be imprisoned (in 1792) for mishandling funds as assistant secretary of the Treasury Board in 1789 and would die in prison in 1799. This man was deeply involved in immense land speculation and financial difficulties when Knox told St. Clair on March 21, 1791, that he had been selected to make arrangements to provide for his army. Knox inadvertently anticipated one of the major weaknesses in St. Clair's campaign, when he said, "As your arrangements and success will greatly depend upon his [Duer's] punctuality . . ."[52] This misjudgment of the contractor's ability on the part of the War Department, along with its ignorance of the enemy's capabilities, were probably the greatest contributions to the defeat of the army seven months later.

Richard Butler of Pennsylvania, whose illustrious Revolutionary War career had earned him the rank of brevet brigadier-general in 1783 and whose experience as Indian agent and commissioner gained him the reputation of a man well versed in Indian affairs, was appointed major-general of the

[50] *American State Papers, ibid.,* p. 174.
[51] St. Clair, *op. cit.,* pp. 59–60.
[52] Duer, one of the originators of today's Wall Street, was heavily involved in speculation in government bonds and bank stocks. This involvement led to his downfall and was so time consuming he was unable to fulfill his obligation as contractor for the expedition.

six-month levies. He was placed second in command, under St. Clair, of the entire expeditionary force, and received his instructions from Knox, who on April 5, 1791, ordered him to embark immediately for Virginia and Maryland to raise the two battalions of levies from those states for the expedition.

Suggestions for the appointment of commanders for each battalion came from Washington and Knox, and the governors of the states raising the troops had also sent recommendations to the War Department for the field officers to command the various companies. Butler was ordered, by Knox, to "respect" the lists and then confirm the appointments as the officers appointed were responsible for raising their respective companies. Company officers were to be commissioned only if they could recruit twenty-eight noncommissioned officers and privates before the first of June.[53]

Hagerstown was selected as the principal rendezvous in Maryland and Winchester in Virginia. As soon as companies were formed, they were to be marched under command of the major to Redstone,[54] where they would embark by boat on the Monongahela River for Fort Pitt.[55] Troops from the Northern states marched to Fort Pitt.

This was to be accomplished each time a new company was completed, and, even though the Virginia and Maryland troops might be intermixed, they would be reassigned when all of the levies had been assembled at Fort Pitt. Duer had arranged to provide provisions for the recruits, Knox said, at both Hagerstown and Winchester and at any other places where they would be needed along the route to Fort Pitt. Clothing for the Maryland and Virginia levies was in the process of preparation and half the necessary supply would be forwarded from Philadelphia about the twentieth of April. The arms, ammunition, and accouterments for the levies would be issued from storage at Fort Pitt. Twelve copies of Steuben's regulations, thirty copies of the Articles of War, and thirty recruiting instructions were to be given to the levie officers before they began their recruiting chores. Weekly reports were to be submitted to the War Office on the progress of the recruiting, and "nothing was to be omitted which would give a spring and vigor to the recruiting service."[56] Most of the supplies would be waiting at Fort Pitt.

Quartermaster Hodgdon had forwarded most of the material in the quartermaster and ordnance department by the end of May when, on direct order from Secretary of War Knox, he was posted immediately to Fort Pitt.[57] There he was to complete the business of supplying the army. Hodgdon had to purchase 100 horses for the cavalry, plus ten extra; boats for the transportation of the troops and supplies down the Ohio River; and packhorses for the campaign. Knox suggested that Kentucky would be the best place to buy the packhorses. He estimated roughly 300 would be needed to transport the baggage of the army, the artillery, and the hospital stores.[58] This did not include the horses to be supplied by the contractor to transport the provisions. However, if St. Clair felt more would be needed, he could raise that figure. All other duties of the quartermaster's department would be determined by St. Clair at Fort Washington. Hodgdon was given $20,000, which Knox said would be sufficient for the campaign. However, it it was not, St. Clair could authorize additional funds to be drawn. By the end of May, all the principal personnel had been given their orders by the War Department and details had been firmed up so that the operation could proceed punctually. The troops were to be completely assembled, clothed, and accoutered at Fort Washington by the tenth of

---

[53] American State Papers, ibid., pp. 184–185.
[54] Redstone was another name for Brownville, Fayette County, Pennsylvania, known as Redstone, Old Fort, on the southeast bank of the Monongahela River, between Redstone Creek and Dunlap. (From Scott's 1795 United States Gazetteer. Joseph Scott, Philadelphia, 1795.)
[55] American State Papers, ibid.
[56] Ibid., p. 185.
[57] Ibid., p. 193.
[58] Ibid.

July. Timing was extremely important since the levies had been enlisted for a period of only six months, and since forage for the horses would disappear with the advance of the cold weather late in the fall, as it had in the Harmar campaign. All of the provisions and supplies were to be on hand and ready to be moved out at that date, and a compatible group of officers had been suggested by both the executive and military branch of the Federal government and the executive branch of those states contributing the militia and levies.

However, the original officers were not available for one reason or another. Whether this factor led to the jealousies that later developed in the upper echelon of command or not is pure speculation, but the expedition was destined for doom the moment it passed from the planning stage to reality. Preparations degenerated into frantic corrections and substitutions. Recruiting, as in the Harmar campaign, was not a careful selection of picked men but rather a hurried and futile attempt to gather together whatever willing specimens the recruiting officers could find. Schedules soon became outdated, and a race against time developed with an almost fanatic attempt on the part of St. Clair, under pressure from his superiors in Philadelphia, to begin the campaign.

The President and the secretary of war, harried by complaints from victims of Indian raids along the frontier, insisted that St. Clair's army set out before winter was upon them. Almost lost from sight were the capabilities of the enemy and the preparation necessary to subdue the combined tribes of the Western Confederacy. Josiah Harmar, whose experience a year earlier had taught him to respect the Indian warrior, predicted a defeat for his successor. Ebenezer Denny reported Harmar's and his own analysis of the army in his journal:

> The prediction of General Harmar, before the army set out on the campaign, was founded upon his experience and particular knowledge of things. He saw with what material the bulk of the army was composed; men collected from the streets and prisons of the cities, hurried out into the enemy's country, and with officers commanding them, totally unacquainted with the business in which they were engaged, it was utterly impossible they could be otherwise. Besides, not any one department was sufficiently prepared; both quartermaster and contractors extremely deficient. It was a matter of astonishment to him [Harmar] that the commanding general, who was acknowledged to be perfectly competent, should think of hazarding, with such people, and under such circumstances, his reputation and life, and the lives of so many others, knowing too, as both did, the enemy with whom he was going to contend.[59]

After his own defeat, Harmar had urged Knox to establish a regular cavalry unit in order to achieve a victory. "Without a regular cavalry," he said, "I know not how the Indians can ever be effectually checked."[60] His reference to "regular" implies his complete lack of faith in mounted militia utilized for a short time, or the hasty makeshift utilization of regular troops as cavalry for the purpose of a single campaign. His suggestion for a regular cavalry was made in May 1791, after he had been relieved of command. Almost immediately after the defeat, however, he had suggested "a body of regular horses on the frontiers—Cavalry have emphatically been Styled the eyes and the feet of an army."[61]

[59]*Military Journal of Ebenezer Denny, ibid.,* p. 374.
[60] Harmar to Knox, *Harmar Papers,* Vol. 30, Large Letter Book A, May 1, 1791.
[61] *Ibid.,* Harmar to Knox, November 23, 1790.

In the same letter to Knox, Harmar suggested changes for the next expedition, substituting oxen for pack horses. He said that, if the land were open, level or free of timber, as it was in the expedition he led, oxcarts could be built to hold the baggage and, as needed, the oxen could supply the army with beef. Horses, he said, were not only a great temptation for the Indians to steal, but they tired easily and could not be eaten. Objections that oxen were too slow, he added, were not well founded, since an army could not exceed ten or twelve miles a day in "this country," and oxen were fully competent to move that distance.[62]

As Harmar had lost favor with the President and with the War Department, his suggestions were not considered, and as a result the mistakes made before and during his campaign were compounded in the expedition of his successor. St. Clair supplied vivid details of the preparations for his campaign some twenty-one years after his defeat. His testimony, along with that of others who served under him, portrays a series of actions which can only be termed a tragedy of errors.

Part III: Preparations and Delays

"The President of the United States still continues anxious that you should at the earliest moment, commence your operations . . ." Thus wrote Secretary of War Knox to St. Clair, August 4, 1791, when preparations for the campaign were already a month behind. Knox wrote of the President's anxiety over the start of the campaign on the eleventh, and then on the twenty-fifth of August said: "The President of the United States laments exceedingly, the unfortunate detention of your troops on the upper parts of the Ohio, for which no reasons sufficiently strong have been assigned." Again, on the first of September, Knox relayed the President's concern over the start of the campaign, which was supposed to have been well on its way by that late date. On September 1 Knox wrote to Samuel Hodgdon about the preparations and closed his letter with, "I hope, In God, that the troops may not have been detained at Fort Pitt for want of boats, or any other thing in your department."[63] It was not until past mid-September that Knox assured St. Clair troops for the expedition were on their way to the rendezvous at Fort Washington.

It was under the extreme pressure of this persistent demand for action, complicated by the late arrival of troops, that St. Clair made preparations at Fort Washington, using everything within his means to create an expeditionary force—everything but his better judgment. Nothing seemed to matter except that an expedition take place. "The troops," St. Clair said, "were not arrived at Fort Washington by the time the second militia expedition under Wilkinson had ended and, said St. Clair, he was thereby denied the "use that might have been made of this expedition, as a collateral movement."[64]

It was then known, he said, that the force being recruited for the campaign would fall far short of the numbers originally estimated. The shortage could be made up in two different ways, both calling for the raising of troops in Kentucky, volunteer horsemen, and "militia draughts." The first method was to call for mounted volunteers but, said St. Clair, they would not submit to military discipline or

---

[62] *Ibid.*
[63] *St. Clair Papers,* Knox to Hodgdon, September 1, 1791, manuscript letter, Guthman Collection.
[64] St. Clair, *op. cit.,* pp. 7–8.

the slow movement of an army which had to cut through forests to make roads and build forts along the way. Since mounted men received two-thirds of a dollar a day, while militia footmen received but $3 a month, and mounted men were under the command of their own officers while the militia draftees were under martial law, it would be incompatible to utilize both in the same army. He felt the volunteers would demoralize the militia draftees. St. Clair said that he chose to relinquish the volunteer mounted corps because they were less efficient and more expensive.[65] He told Knox that volunteers would leave whenever they pleased—something which had occurred, he maintained, in the Wilkinson expedition earlier, even though Wilkinson did not mention it in his report.[66] Apparently, St. Clair felt he had more control over the draftees of militia than he would have over a volunteer force.

The regulars and levies arrived at Fort Pitt sporadically. One hundred and one levies left Trenton, New Jersey, on April 27, and arrived at Fort Pitt on the twenty-eighth of May.[67] Another group of seventy-six regulars under Captain Armstrong left Philadelphia on the same day, arriving at Fort Pitt on the twenty-fifth of May.[68] The last of the troops did not arrive at Fort Pitt until the twenty-sixth of August.[69] It was on that same date that the quartermaster, Hodgdon, arrived with General Butler,[70] both of whom had been expected much earlier and whose duties St. Clair had to assume.

Appraising his new recruits, St. Clair told Knox that the 1st Regiment was inexperienced and that "no pains have been spared to instruct them so far as it is possible, but I beg leave to observe the same steady service is not to be expected from any part of the army as from men who have been long accustomed to the restraints of discipline."[71] Many of those new men had to assume other duties, such as artificers and workers in the laboratory manufacturing cartridges and preparing the artillery ammunition. Neither the quartermaster nor the second in command were on hand to help in the preparation of the supplies which were found, on receipt, to be of inferior quality, broken, too large, or too small, and generally arriving later than anticipated. St. Clair had to assume personally all of the duties that were required to ready an army for battle. Finally, along with the tremendous task that he faced without the help of General Butler or Quartermaster Hodgdon, St. Clair still had to officiate as governor of the Northwest Territory, the position he had held before (and during) his command of the Federal troops.

Not only were his duties as governor particularly burdensome at this time, but he was confronted with many new crises that arose and overlapped his function as both commander of the Federal troops and governor of the territory. Friendly Seneca Indians of Cornplanter's tribe had been killed early in March while trading at a frontier store. Both Virginians and Pennsylvanians were among the whites who caused the trouble and the crime occurred during Procter's peace mission, when it was hoped he would obtain the help of Cornplanter and other Seneca chiefs.

Another problem that faced St. Clair was the disposition of land that had been illegally sold to unsuspecting settlers. Unfortunately, they had already begun to cultivate the government property. After inspecting surveys of lands purchased by the Symmes syndicate, St. Clair found the judge had sold acreage well beyond the limits of his property. To remove the people who had settled there, St. Clair said, would ruin them, since they were not willful trespassers but victims of the land company. It

[65] *Ibid.,* pp. 8–9.
[66] *Knox Papers,* St. Clair to Knox, September 4, 1791, XXXIX-91.
[67] *American State Papers,* Vol. 1, Indian Affairs, p. 175, and Vol. 1, Military Affairs, p. 37.
[68] *Ibid.*
[69] *Ibid.*
[70] *Ibid.*
[71] *Knox Papers,* St. Clair to Knox, August 3, 1791, XXIX-17.

would only create further antigovernment feelings among the settlers, who had felt neglected by the Federal government for a long time. As Indian depredations increased, their demands for stronger protection became more vocal, and one of St. Clair's major chores as governor was trying to reconcile them.

Now that the government was sending help against the Indians, St. Clair as commander needed the cooperation—not the antagonism—of the people he was trying to protect. He needed the collaboration of the settlers as much as he needed the help of the contractors supplying the army for the expedition, the quartermaster, and his second in command, General Butler, who was in charge of recruiting the levies. Unfortunately, according to St. Clair, he was not getting any help at all from Butler.

Because of the short training period available to the new troops before setting out on the expedition, St. Clair told Butler to send the recruits by boat to Fort Washington as soon as they arrived at Fort Pitt, detaining them just long enough to assemble entire companies. St. Clair commented that "a single company could descend the Ohio in as great safety as ten thousand—"[72] and that Butler should not hold any of the men in Pittsburgh in order to form larger units. Since they were arriving from so many different directions, and only as quickly as the recruiting officers were able to enlist them and then march them to Fort Pitt, the commanding officer instructed to Butler "to send them forward without loss of time as they arrived."[73]

These orders were repeatedly sent to Butler, St. Clair said later, "but without effect."[74] Actually, Butler had received conflicting orders from Knox on May 5, 1791, telling him to deploy part of the levies for temporary protection along the frontiers, which had become exposed to increased depredations from Indians as a result of the Harmar campaign. In the meantime, St. Clair had to leave for Kentucky to arrange for that territory's militia to supplement the levies, which were not enlisting in the numbers originally hoped for the campaign. On May 15, when he returned to Fort Washington "the present fit for duty amounted to eighty-five privates."[75]

Another reason for Butler's delay in sending on the troops was the fact that the contractor, Duer, had mismanaged an $85,000 advance of funds for provisions that had been supplied to him by the government but which he, in turn, had not sent on to his agents at the recruiting rendezvous points and at Fort Pitt. General Butler could not, therefore, furnish the new men with their traveling rations, nor did he have any boats available for their transportation, nor other supplies.[76]

General Butler was not without his own problems with recruiting. The incompetence of quartermaster Hodgdon led to a criminal lack of military supplies, and amid all of this confusion the new recruits were held up at all the various rendezvous points, some getting drunk and many deserting. Butler complained of the mismangement of the quartermaster department and said that there was a lack of tents, knapsacks, camp kettles, cartridge boxes, and pack saddles. Those that had been forwarded from Philadelphia by Hodgdon were of poor quality,[77] particularly the pack saddles, which were unfit for use (they were much too large) and cost double the amount that they could have been procured for at Pittsburgh, considering the cost of transportation.[78]

Another problem that faced Butler was the condition of the arms that had been forwarded to Fort Pitt. Evidently, they had not been properly inspected before they were shipped, and many of them

[72] St. Clair, *op. cit.*, p. 9.
[73] *Ibid.*
[74] *Ibid.*
[75] *Ibid.*
[76] *American State Papers*, Vol. 1, Military Affairs, pp. 36–37.
[77] *Ibid.*, p. 42.
[78] *Ibid.*

were unfit for use, requiring repair before being issued to the recruits.[79] Butler's complaints, however, were disputed by others who said that the arms were in good condition when issued to the recruits but, because of abuse and lack of training, had become damaged and had to be repaired.[80] However, a letter from Henry Knox to William Knox in the Guthman Collection, dated July 20, 1791, reads:

> You will immediately ship 2,000 thorough gun stocks to Mr. Hill of New York, in order to be sent from thence to West Point, each of those stocks must be packed so that none be transported but what are perfect. You will also send all the spare steel ramrods which are in store and 1,000 spare bayonets if there are any. This business must be executed as soon as possible."

This letter indicates that, even at this late date, muskets were yet to be assembled at West Point for the campaign.

No matter who was to blame, the recruits did not arrive ar Fort Washington when St. Clair expected them. Facing an expedition without troops, the general called in the regular troops from the other forts in the Northwest Territory. They arrived, he said, punctually; and, except for a handful of men left behind at other garrisons, St. Clair finally brought the strength of the 1st Regiment up to "four hundred and twenty seven rank and file."[81]

But, he complained, he had none of the newly raised troops as yet. Compounding his problems, the troops from Fort Steuben brought along the Indian prisoners taken by the Kentucky militia raids. There were not accommodations for all of the prisoners, and new buildings had to be hurriedly erected.[82] The gun carriages which had been used in the Harmar expedition were unfit for service, according to St. Clair, and new ones had to be built. This required "fatigue men and artificers," but since there

> was no corps of artificers in existence: draughts therefore had to be made from the corps of all that were to be found of that description, and they were required in a variety of branches, such as smiths, carpenters, harness makers, colliers, wheelrights, etc., and as the troops from the distant parts, as well as the garrison of Fort Washington, were ill provided with camp equipage, everything of that kind that could be made at the place was set about:—[83]

When Major Ferguson of the artillery arrived at Fort Washington on June 20, St. Clair found that the military stores he had brought with him consisted of the materials with which to make the ammunition, but none of it had been prepared ahead of time. Therefore, a laboratory had to be prepared for making musket cartridges. It was difficult to locate a shop in which the artillery shells could be prepared since, as St. Clair said, "Any person acquainted with fixing of ammunition, knows that it is a very tedious as well as laborious business; and that in places where there is no want of room, or other conveniences, accidents very frequent happen, and the laboratory blows up."[84] St.

[79] Ibid.
[80] Ibid.
[81] St. Clair, op. cit., p. 10. Note that American State Papers (Vol. 1, Military Affairs, p. 36) states that the regiment consisted of only 299 rank-and-file.
[82] St. Clair, op. cit., p. 10.
[83] Ibid.
[84] Ibid., p. 11.

Clair complained that the cartridges for the artillery and the shells for the howitzers could not be filled in barracks which were heated by open fire place, so that the artificers had to utilize an inadequate blockhouse that was also being used as a store house.[85] Not only were the gun carriages that had been used in the Harmar campaign in poor condition, but, he said, "It was discovered also that the carriages of the guns that came from Philadelphia were unfit for service, and those pieces must be new mounted."[86]

All of this additional work required a great deal of labor, since shops had to be built and tools had to be made. It required the constuction of an armory. Fortunately, Major Henry Gauther arrived on July 28 with a detachment of Maryland levies, among whom were a number of artificers.[87] A good portion of those men who had been enlisted to fight Indians had to be taken away from combat training in order to build and repair the equipment for the campaign. St. Clair observed that the dislike for labor was often the inducement for men to enlist in the army, and when they were employed as artificers instead of fighting men a great deal of discontent was created.[88]

The arms were in bad repair, St. Clair said, and great numbers of "axes, campkettles, canteens, knapsacks, kegs for the musket cartridges, and spare cannon balls, and boxes for the fixed ammunition had to be made; and cordage of various kinds, and the cartridge boxes had to be repaired."[89] He added that the splints for the wounded that had been sent from Philadelphia were useless and new ones had to be made of "half-jacked leather," prepared on the spot. "In short," he said, "almost every art was going forward, and Fort Washington had as much appearance of a large manufactory on the inside, as it had of a military post on the outside."[90]

Later, a congressional committee reporting on the causes of the failure of the campaign, said (in May 1792) that:

> Mr. Hodgdon was appointed Quartermaster General in the month of March, and continued at Philadelphia until the 4th of June, he then proceeded to Fort Pitt, where he arrived the 10th of the same month. No sufficient causes have appeared to the committee to justify this delay, and his presence with the army appears to have been essentially necessary previously to that time; the duties of the commander in chief were much increased in consequence of the absence of the Quartermaster General, and after a continued expectation of his arrival at Fort Washington, for more than six weeks, the commander in chief gave him express orders to repair to camp without delay.[91]

The report went on to say:

> The receipt of the letter is acknowledged but the orders contained therein were neither answered nor obeyed, and his arrival at camp was not until the 10th of September. The commander in chief, until that time, in addition to the duties of his office discharged those of the Quartermaster General and the military stores furnished

[85] *Ibid.*
[86] *Ibid.*
[87] *Ibid.,* p. 12.
[88] *Ibid.*
[89] *Ibid.*
[90] *Ibid.,* pp. 12–13.
[91] *American State Papers, ibid.,* p. 37.

by that department were so deficient, from mismanagement and neglect, that many things essential to the movements of the army were either wholly made or repaired at Fort Washington, and even the tools for the artificers to work with: the Quartermaster particularly informed the commander in chief that two complete traveling forges were sent forward, and upon examination both of them were found to be without anvils, many other things equally necessary were wholly omitted or unfit for intended use.[92]

Further complicating St. Clair's plans was a letter written to him by Secretary of War Knox on August 4, advising him that the 5½-inch shells and shot that had been requested would not arrive in time for the expedition[93] and that Hodgdon failed to obtain 200 additional shot and shells for each piece of artillery at the posts which Knox had ordered five months earlier.[94]

Another Congressional inquiry would be held in 1793 to examine the results of the first inquiry. Duer's financial manipulations and Hodgdon's mismanagement were soft-pedaled, undoubtedly to protect those government officials, particularly Knox and Hamilton, who were closely associated with the two men. Their errors were minimized.

St. Clair had blamed one of the failures of the expedition, as had other officers, on the poor quality of the gun powder supplied to the army. Even though Major Ferguson had tested the powder with a howitzer at Fort Pitt, reporting it to be satisfactory, the men in the field complained that it was, in fact, of inferior quality and one of the major causes of the failure of the army.[95]

The committee, in 1793, reported that evidence indicated that the powder was of good quality when it left Fort Pitt, but that some had been ruined by exposure to air and moisture after it had been issued to the troops. The rest, the committee reported, had been ruined (along with great quantities of fixed ammunition) because of the defective tents in which the supplies were stored.[96]

No matter what the actual causes were, St. Clair's problems in 1791 increased daily. In fact, his military situation before the campaign started was one of utter hopelessness. In his narrative, he spoke about having to manufacture bells for the horses because "the cavalry had been sent on without them."[97] To further complicate matters, he added, "The cattle for the campaign, which was expected to have begun about this time [end of July], were also poured upon us; and of course required considerable guards."[98]

Because the countryside around Fort Washington was "entirely eaten out," and because the recruits were constantly drunk, St. Clair decided to move the army six miles from Fort Washington to Ludlow's Stations where there was a fresh pasture for the horses and cattle and the supply of liquor, being scarce, could be kept under control—which was not possible at the town of Cincinnati, which surrounded Fort Washington. The army moved on August 7, leaving behind only the artificers and a

[92] Ibid.

[93] Ibid., Vol. 1, Indian Affairs, p. 195; and, in the Guthman Collection, a letter from Henry Knox to Samuel Hodgdon, dated War Department, August 18, 1791, which states: "It is extremely doubtful whether any 5½ inch shells can be obtained on this side of West Point, from which place I expect some hourly, and they shall be forwarded instantly—but they cannot be in readiness for the Campaign."

[94] American State Papers, ibid., p. 180.

[95] On August 18, 1791, Knox wrote to St. Clair and told him that, because of complaints about the poor quality of powder being furnished to the quartermaster by the manufacturer, Mr. Joseph Miller, he had some of it proved—"by taking one ounce of each sort, to wit, cannon, musket and rifle, and projecting a 24-pound ball out of a 5½'' mortar, elevated at 45° placing the powder in the chamber of the mortar loose, and putting a piece of paper over the mouth of the chamber; the powder to be well dried in the sun. This is the surest possible mode of proving powder, and the powder so proved have been manufactured from damaged public powder, and was found upon trial to be equal to the best proof powder. It is considered, that, if one ounce will, under the above circumstance, project a 24-pound ball thirty yards, it is sufficiently strong. Most of the powder which was tried, as above, projected the ball, on an average, forty yards." (Ibid., p. 181.)

[96] Ibid., Vol. 1, Military Affairs, pp. 42–43.

[97] St. Clair, op. cit., p. 13.

[98] Ibid.

small garrison for the fort. At that date the army consisted of about 2,000 rank-and-file, a figure far below the 3,000 Knox promised by the tenth of July. The price of the rations had more than doubled at Ludlow's Station, even though the distance from Fort Washington (for which the original contract had been issued to Duer) was only six miles.[99] Defending his move, which caused an increase in the cost of provisions, St. Clair added that the troops were "totally ignorant of field duty" and that it was more suitable to instruct the men in field exercises moving away from the environment of the village to Ludlow's Station at Mill Creek.

On August 29, Lieutenant-Colonel William Darke arrived with the detachment of Virginia levies, but there were still many more to come. St. Clair's adjutant, Ebenezer Denny, on September 1 commented that "General St. Clair appears exceedingly impatient at the delay or detention of some of the corps. The quartermaster general, Hodgdon, not yet come on, and General Butler, the second in command is also back. Preparations for the campaign very backward—"[100]

Because of the poor results of the recruiting officers for the levies, St. Clair had to return to Kentucky to obtain additional troops. Before leaving Fort Washington, he gave the following orders to Major Hamtramck: "As soon as the surveyor returns from the Miami River, and has reported to you that the route from the camp to the banks of that river is laid out, you will move with the troops under your command to a situation on or near its banks by either of the two lines Mr. Gano shall have marked, which upon a conference with him you shall judge the best."[101]

A surveyor had been dispatched to lay out the route which the army would travel from Ludlow's station to the Miami River where the first fort would be built. St. Clair continued: "A road must be opened as you advance, for the passage of the artillery, and as soon as the artillery horses arrive, two pieces will be sent forward to you. You will please to choose a defensible position, and such as may admit the troops, which are now here under command of Colonel Darke, consisting of about three hundred."[102]

Instructions for building the fort had been issued to Major Ferguson of the artillery, and St. Clair repeated them to Hamtramck:

> Major Ferguson has orders to mark out the ground for a small fort, to be inclosed with pickets, in doing which you will afford him such assistance as he shall require; and as soon as may be, you will employ all the men that can possibly be spared for that purpose, in cutting down pickets, pointing them, and carrying to the place where they are to be put up, agreeably to such directions as Major Ferguson may give.[103]

In his later testimony at the Congressional inquiry over the failure of St. Clair's campaign, Major David Zeigler of the 1st Regiment said:

> Even the officers showed a pride in working with the men, in order to expedite the work; the Major, Ferguson, frequently complained of the want of almost every kind of

[99] American State Papers, ibid., p. 37.
[100] Military Journal of Major Ebenezer Denny, p. 356.
[101] William Henry Smith, op. cit., Vol. II, p. 239.
[102] Ibid.
[103] Ibid.

> entrenching tools, particularly axes, and recently there was only one axe to three men, so that, consequently, two must look on and only work by turns.[104]

St. Clair, in his observations, made the pointed remark that there was only one froe and one cross-cut saw with the army on the fourteenth of October, as a result of the inefficiency of Quartermaster Hodgdon.[105] He said that tools were not sent on to the army until after that date. St. Clair also revealed that the quartermaster ordered only 100 axes, when at least 1000 were needed for the construction of just one fort.[106]

Adding to Hodgdon's errors, the general told of the inexcusable mistake Hodgdon made in ordering four-pound shot when three-pound cannon had been ordered for the expedition.[107] It was in this atmosphere of complete disorder that St. Clair left for Kentucky to try to make up the deficiency of troops by getting a draft of Kentucky militia. Placing Lieutenant-Colonel Darke of the Maryland levies in charge of the army, he ordered that, during his absence, Darke should lead the army to the Miami River where a post site had already been selected for construction.

From Lexington, Kentucky, St. Clair wrote to Knox telling him that he had arranged for 1,150 Kentucky militia to be drafted but that he did not expect more than 750 to show up at the rendezvous, Fort Washington, on the twenty-fifth of October.[108] Time was running out on the campaign that was to have begun on July 10, long before winter would arrive. The militia were drafted into the infantry, rather than form a detachment of mounted volunteers. St. Clair figured they could easily catch up with the slow-moving army that had to clear roads and construct forts along the way.

Major Zeigler described the march to the Miami River from Fort Washington when he

> conceived that the delay in marching from Ludlow's Station was occasioned by the difficulty in clearing the road, in making bridges, etc., one day the army marched but a mile and a half; added to this, there was so small a stock of provisions on hand, that, had the army moved on, they must have eaten their fingers; that the men were frequently at half allowance, and the quartermaster was sent back to hurry it; that the army was obliged to wait frequently for provisions, etc.[109]

The army that marched was woefully under strength. Secretary of War Knox (in his summary of the defeat to Congress later that same year) said that Congress had authorized a corps of 2,000 levies. These were to be organized into two regiments, each of three battalions. The battalions were to be raised from the following areas: one from New Jersey, two in Pennsylvania, one in Maryland, and another from Virginia, while the sixth battalion, consisting of riflemen, was to be raised in the territory south of the Ohio River.[110]

Each battalion was to consist of four companies and each company was to have been composed of eighty-three noncommissioned officers and privates. The total number of levies was to amount to 1,992 men, but during the months of April, May, June, and July, only 1,574 were recruited for the levies, for a period of six months.[111] Of the regular troops, there were supposed to have been recruited

[104] St. Clair, *op. cit.,* p. 210.
[105] *Ibid.,* p. 141.
[106] *Ibid.,* p. 114.
[107] *Ibid.,* pp. 114–15.
[108] William Henry Smith, *op. cit.,* Vol. II, p. 243.
[109] St. Clair, *op. cit.,* pp. 209–10.
[110] *American State Papers,* Indian Affairs, Vol. 1, *op. cit.,* p. 139.
[111] *Ibid.,* pp. 139–140.

enough new men for the 1st and 2nd regiments to supplement the 262 old members of the 1st Regiment that had already rendezvoused at Fort Washington to make a total regular army of 2,128 troops. Actually, just 718 infantry and forty-five artillery were recruited and marched to Fort Washington during April, May, June, and July.[112]

In summary, Knox said that 2,437 regulars and levies had been recruited, and, with the 262 old members of the 1st Regiment, they amounted to 2,699 men on the Ohio in readiness for the campaign. Of these, 699 had to be deducted for sick, garrison duty at the post, artificers, and noneffectives, which left only 2,000 fighting men available for the campaign.[113] To this number must be added the Kentucky militia which St. Clair had ordered drafted to make up for the deficiency of the 820 regulars and levies that recruiting failed to acquire. Unfortunately, of the 820 men needed, only 418 Kentucky militia showed up for the campaign, making a total force of 2,418 men.[114] Of the 4,128 troops authorized by Congress, only 3,308 had been raised, and of that total just 2,418 were available as fighting men for the expedition.[115] Knox suggested the deficiency that existed in the recruiting service might have been caused by low pay, and perhaps the nature of the service."

It might be noted at this point that of the 2,418 men for the expedition only 262 (the old enlistees of the 1st Regiment) had military experience. The rest were mostly raw recruits, of much the same caliber as the recruits on the Harmar campaign. St. Clair might be blamed for part of this, since he chose to ignore the more elite mounted Volunteers of Kentucky (who had proven successful under Scott and Wilkinson) in favor of the lower-paid, and easier to manage, drafts of Kentucky militia. Of the 1,050 militia St. Clair had Congressional authority to raise, only 418 joined him, with an additional sixty later on the march.[116] Knox later said that at least that number (sixty) deserted.[117]

While St. Clair was in Lexington arranging for the drafting of the Kentucky militia, Quartermaster Hodgdon and General Butler arrived at Fort Washington from Pittsburgh with a company of Federal troops on the seventh of September.[118] Butler's services were almost immediately required in presiding over a court of inquiry requested by Harmar over the causes of the failure of his campaign the previous fall. The court convened September 15 and lasted nine days. Two other officers, Lieutenant-Colonels Darke and Gibson, both of the levies, served on the board. During the course of the court those three officers were not able to participate in any of the crucial preparations for the campaign, and, since they comprised three of a total of six of the ranking officers of the expedition, their loss was critical.

An interesting sidelight concerning the field staff is contained in a letter written to St. Clair by the Secretary of War on December 2, 1791, after the defeat but before word of the disaster had reached Philadelphia. Knox said that James Wilkinson had been appointed lieutenant-colonel–commandant of the 2nd Regiment. He added that the President expected that the need for an adjutant-general would expire at the end of the campaign (St. Clair chose Winthrop Sargent as his adjutant-general) and those duties would be assumed by the inspector, Lieutenant-Colonel Francis Mentges. Then followed an amazing statement, carefully worded by Knox so that St. Clair would not misunderstand and would be able to relay to General Butler (whose resignation at the close of the campaign was expected) as to why he could not continue in the service. Knox said that, even though the President

[112] *Ibid.*, p. 140.
[113] *Ibid.*, p. 196.
[114] *Ibid.*
[115] *Ibid.*, p. 140.
[116] *Ibid.*
[117] *Ibid.*
[118] *Military Journal of Major Ebenezer Denny*, p. 357.

was desirous of retaining Butler, Butler had been appointed under a specific law for the formation of the levies and, since his duty was to command the levies, he would have to retire when their six-month term expired. The President would not have the power, said Knox, without a new law, to retain Butler in the service, and he told St. Clair: "You will, therefore, intimate to him in handsome terms, this order."[119]

Knox closed that letter with "I sincerely hope, by the time this letter arrives, you will have returned to Fort Washington, crowned with success, having made an equitable and lasting peace with the poor Indians, and entirely fulfilled all the objects of the campaign."[120]

Part IV: March to Massacre

> A Horrid Fight there hap'd of late,
> The Fourth day of November,
> When a vast number met their fate,
> We all shall well remember,
> 'Twas on renown'd Ohio land,
> And fatal prov'd of old,
> Sad to relate! our Federal Band,
> Were slain by Indians bold!

So went the *Columbian Tragedy,* a broadside published in Boston in 1791. All forty-one of the poem's four-line verses pay tribute to the fallen heroes who succumbed to the superior guerrilla fighting tactics of their savage foes, whose destruction the stanzas of verse boldly demanded.

In his journal, Ebenezer Denny stated that he did not wish to accompany General St. Clair upon his expedition, but would rather have returned with his former commander, Harmar, who was about to retire from the army and had refused to accept a command in the expedition with a rank equal to that of General Butler. When Denny suggested to Harmar that he, too, would like to return, Harmar said: "You must go on the campaign; some will escape, and you may be among the number."[121]

Equally pessimistic was Jonathan Heart who, writing from Fort Harmar September 2, 1791, told his friend William Judd, in what was to be the final letter in a series that began in 1785: ". . . with respect to military arrangements, Indian wars, etc., I am unable to give you any account, but I must confess the appearances at present are not promising, our numbers perhaps may be sufficient *were they disciplined,* but it *grows late* in the Year . . ."[122]

---

[119] *American State Papers, ibid.,* p. 184. The question arises from the order that had been issued to St Clair: if the President and Secretary of War did not think highly enough of Butler to want to retain his services after the campaign, why did they tolerate his command over the levies and retain the position of second in command for the entire expedition?
[120] *Ibid.*
[121] *Military Journal of Major Ebenezer Denny, ibid.*
[122] Heart to Judd, September 2, 1791, Guthman Collection.

Even though he had suffered every frustration that a general could when all his plans for a major campaign had gone wrong, St. Clair maintained a degree of optimism throughout. On September 4, he wrote Knox that he doubted whether there would be more than 1,000 or 1,500 Indians to oppose his force, since it was difficult for the Indians to find game "in that country."[123] Again, on the twenty-first of October, he wrote to Knox and said that even though desertion and sickness had reduced the ranks of his force, he felt that he had sufficient numbers to combat the Indians. He added, however, that he had no manner of information "as to the force collected to oppose us."[124] In the same letter he said that it was extraordinary that the Indians had allowed the army to penetrate into their country for sixty-nine miles without "looking at us, nor stealing a horse."[125]

Recording his thoughts after the campaign (having lost most of his papers during the battle), Adjutant-General Winthrop Sargent said that the army "was too generally wanting the stamina of soldiers."[126] He explained the reasons: "Picked up and recruited from the offscourings of large towns and cities; enervated by idleness, debaucheries and every species of vice, it was impossible they could have been made competent to the arduous duties of Indian warfare."[127]

Here was an admission that fighting Indians involved a special kind of warfare. Whether Sargent felt this way before the campaign is an interesting speculation. It is quite possible that he did, because he had been criticized by some for being too severe in the punishments he dealt out, and the rigid discipline he tried to maintain. Sargent, however, contradicted the statements of others as he continued: "An extraordinary aversion to service was conspicuous amongst them [the troops] and demonstrated by the most repeated desertions, in many instances to the very foe we were to combat. The late period at which they had been brought into the field left no leisure or opportunity to attempt to discipline them. They were, moreover, badly clothed, badly paid and badly fed."[128]

Sargent went on to say that much of the powder was of poor quality, and the contractor, so delinquent in the performance of his duty, was "one amongst the many primary causes" of the defeat. He said that "to correct, remedy or avert was the province of the General [St. Clair]."[129] St. Clair, Sargent said, was so consumed with making arrangements for all of the departments of the army for the campaign that he was exhausted before it began. Between May and early October, he continued, St. Clair had to make three trips to Kentucky.

St. Clair was wrong at a time when the accurate military assessment of his situation was, or could have been, a deciding factor. Good judgment would have dictated postponing the campaign until the following spring, thus allowing the construction of a fort for communications before winter and thereby speeding the campaign the following year. However, he had been under constant pressure to move out from both the Secretary of War and the President.

While he did realize the inferiority of his own force and equipment, without reconnaissance St. Clair had no idea at all of the enemy he was facing. On the other hand, the Indians under Little Turtle knew exactly where St. Clair's army was every moment of its march; how many men were in the ranks; in what type of formation they marched; and how many were deserting. One of the first moves made by the Indian council when it originally heard of St. Clair's army was to send a party of spies, headed by Tecumseh (the Shawnee chief of later fame).[130] It was the expert surveillance of the spies,

[123] *Knox Papers,* Roll XXIX-91, St. Clair to Knox, September 4, 1791.
[124] *Ibid.,* St. Clair to Knox, Roll XXIX-91, October 21, 1791.
[125] *Ibid.*
[126] Sargent, *op. cit.,* p. 242.
[127] *Ibid.*
[128] Sargent, *op. cit.,* p. 242.
[129] Butterfield, *op. cit.,* p. 261; Ohio Archeological Historical Society Publications, Vol. XV, 1906, p. 422.
[130] Butterfield, *ibid.;* Ohio Archeological Historical Society Publications, *ibid.*

and the swift communication they maintained with their main force, that enabled Little Turtle to execute his deadly ambush with masterful perfection. Not once during his march did St. Clair send out a scouting party adequate enough to ascertain the size and location of the enemy.

THE EXPEDITION BEGINS

When a portion of the army left Ludlow's station on September 6, its movement was slow.[131] Major Zeigler said that the delay in marching was caused by the difficult task of clearing a road and building bridges. One day, he said, the army marched "but a mile."[132]

By September 15, nine days after it had left Ludlow's station, the army had marched twenty-three miles to the Miami river where the men began to construct Fort Hamilton.[133] Lieutenant James Stephenson of the Kentucky levies said that the baggage was so difficult to move that it took no less than twelve oxen to each wagon to ascend a hill.[134] The fort was laid out, said St. Clair, "to cover the passage of the river and to serve as a place of deposit for provisions, and form the first link in the chain of communication between Fort Washington and the object of the campaign."[135]

The post was nearly completed by the thirtieth of September, and, after placing two small pieces of artillery on the platforms in two bastions, St. Clair named it Fort Hamilton.[136] At that point, St Clair was required to return to Fort Washington to bring up part of the Kentucky militia which had just arrived at that post and left General Butler in charge at Hamilton, with orders to move forward and build the next post. Butler was given explicit directions on the order of encampment, order of march, and order of battle, depending upon the circumstances in which he might find himself. St. Clair said that an order or march was only as good as the ease and celerity with which it could be converted into an order of battle. The commander said the tactical instructions he left Butler covered the possibility of a surprise attack by the enemy, and that his own actions, evoked the soundest military tactics of his time.[137] Although carefully explaining the maneuvers by which troops engaged the enemy under various circumstances, St. Clair did not understand that the Indian had devised his own brand of warfare which, for this particular type of terrain, was far superior to the conservative European military tactics.

According to Stephenson, the officers had their minds on problems other than ambush during the march—problems that, at the time, were more pressing. He said that "Dissension rather increases between the officers of the establishment and those of the Levies. The former claiming preference in Consequence of their Military knowledge; the latter in Consequence of their not being compelled to serve from necessity."[138] Stephenson even tells of a duel which almost took place between two officers. At the last minute their seconds intervened and reconciled the two combatants.[139]

Stephenson reported that on "The last evening [September 27] fifty eight horses is stolen by the Indians; a detachment ordered after them without effect."[140] Then, on the next day, Stephenson said they observed "Indian signs, on information of which, Two small Detachments [twenty-five each] Ordered to Reconnoitre the adjacent woods and if they made any discoveries, to impart the same to

[131] James Stephenson, *Orderly Book of Lieutenant James Stephenson,* Library of Congress, September 6, 1791.
[132] St. Clair, *op. cit.,* p. 209.
[133] *Military Journal of Major Ebenezer Denny,* p. 358.
[134] Stephenson, *ibid.*
[135] St. Clair, *op. cit.,* p. 14.
[136] *Ibid.,* p. 15.
[137] *Ibid.,* pp. 15–18.
[138] Stephenson, *op. cit.,* September 17, 1791.
[139] *Ibid.,* September 27, 1791.
[140] *Ibid.*

the General with expedition: Small parties thought very imprudent, tho' this observation aside—"[141] St. Clair later insisted no horses had been stolen nor any signs of Indians observed.

St. Clair did comment that he had made an arrangement with Colonel Oldham, commander of the militia, to send out daily scouting parties from ranks of the militia. St. Clair said that the militia were better suited for that type of service since "a great part of the other troops had never been in the woods in their lives, and many never fired a gun."[142] As a consequence, the militia were excused from all fatigue duty. This, of course, created more discord between the levies, regular troops and militia, and it was among the militia that the greatest percentage of desertions occurred.

The army had left Fort Hamilton on October 4, leaving behind a small detachment to man the garrison. Their destination was forty-four miles away at present-day Fort Jefferson, Ohio, where another fort was to be constructed. Sargent described in detail the activities of the army as it left Fort Hamilton:

> Upon the morning of the 4th of October we beat the General [drum roll]. Some deficiencies of pack horses postponed the march till twelve o'clock, when the army was put in motion by two columns from their encampment at the prairie near Fort Hamilton, crossed the Miami (the fording of which at this time was not deep) and advanced three miles, opening two roads, about two hundred and fifty yards apart, as they marched; the pack horses and bullocks moving in the center interval of wood, and the artillery in the front, centre and rear of the columns.[143]

The next day, Sargent went on,

> General Butler changed the disposition prescribed by the commanding general (who had returned to Fort Washington on October 1st) as to advance the artillery by a single broadcut road of twelve feet. Five pieces in front, and dressing with the heads of columns marching by single files about one hundred yards on right and left; the ammunition and baggage horses following immediately this artillery, and the five additional pieces bring up the rear, covered by the rear guard, et cetera; the bullocks between the road and the columns. The woods everywhere so compact as made the opening of a road extremely tedious. Bridges were frequently to be thrown over streams and ravines, and the infantry, though marching by single files, were *necessitated to cut their way at every step.*[144]

Needless to say, progress was slow.

Adjutant Ebenezer Denny and Adjutant-General Winthrop Sargent, who had gone back to Fort Washington for the militia with General St. Clair, record in their journals the march to the next post. Catching up to the troops on October 18, after having a difficult time equipping the militia, Denny wrote:

---

[141] *Ibid.,* September 28, 1791.
[142] St. Clair, *op. cit.,* pp. 26–27.
[143] Sargent, *op. cit.,* p. 241.
[144] *Ibid.,* pp. 241–242.

Joined the troops with St. Clair on the evening of the 8th, 44½ miles from Fort Washington. The army is five days from Fort Hamilton, not four miles a day.

9th—The army marched at ten and encamped at three-gained only five miles.

10th—Army in motion at eight o'clock. Crossed a number of small rivulets. Timber chiefly beech. Gained about eight miles and encamped at four o'clock. [Sargent notes that Colonel Oldham joined the army with 300 Kentucky militia on this day.]

11th—Ten o'clock this morning before the troops took up the line of march. Horses missing, which occasioned the delay. About twelve arrived at a pretty little creek. Fresh trails of Indians discovered. Two o'clock came directly upon an extensive wet prairie. Army obliged to halt and encamp. Marched this day not more than six miles.

12th—This morning spent in searching the prairie and examining for a passage across.[145]

Several parties went out; General Butler's group was successful, finding a way about three miles around the swamp, and the troops found an Indian path that wound through several other small, wet prairies. Sargent noted that they had discovered many Indian tracks, and both old and new campsites of warriors and hunters. Several times they almost surprised the occupants, who fled just ahead of the approaching parties of soldiers. They did wound one Indian, but he was able to either escape with the aid of others in his party or conceal himself from the searching troops, who recovered his gun and a quantity of peltry.

Ice had formed on a thin surface that night and on October 13, not moving out until one o'clock, the army marched only one mile, where they encamped. The order of encampment, according to Sargent, was

two lines facing to the front and rear, the militia in the rear of the whole and the horse upon the flanks, covered by Faulkner's company of riflemen. The artillery disposed in the first and second line, in the intervals between the battalion, the whole occupying (from the unevenness of the ground) a length of more than one thousand yards. In the distance from our last encampment, we have passed a ridge of indifferent soil. On this ground we are to halt for some days, to erect a small fort of deposit.[146]

Construction began on October 14 under Major Ferguson, who supervised 200 men who cut the timber and trimmed and laid the logs horizontally,[147] and Fort Jefferson began to rise.

Winthrop Sargent described the fort as a square work with 114-foot sides and four small bastions. It was built of rough logs, laid horizontally, and the barracks and storerooms comprised the curtains. It took one day for the 200 men employed in the construction to clear the face of the ground and lay the foundation.[148]

[145] *Military Journal of Major Ebenezer Denny,* pp. 359–360.
[146] Sargent, *op. cit.,* p. 244.
[147] *Military Journal of Major Ebenezer Denny,* p. 360.
[148] Sargent, *op. cit.,* p. 245.

The new fort, according to Sargent's calculations, was located 68½ miles from Fort Washington, on the Miami River (near present-day Greenville, Ohio). During most of the period of construction the troops were exposed to heavy rains, that, along with the scarcity of tools, made their tasks more difficult. Sargent said that there were only eighty axes furnished by the quartermaster, and of those thirteen had to be borrowed from the troops.[149] Besides the axes there were only one saw and one frow.[150]

While the troops were on the march, General St. Clair had given strict orders not to discharge firearms without permission. The penalty for disobeying that order was 100 lashes, but Sargent said several militia and levies were guilty every day.[151] "Game," he said, "is very plenty and presents a strong temptation, but the consequences are extremely injurious to the service and tend, amongst other improprieties, to destroy all order in the army."[152]

Denny continued:

> 16th—Rain all last night. Express from Fort Washington with information of the mountain leader (Piamingo, a Chickasaw chief) and twenty Indians of the Chickasaw nation on their way from Fort Washington, and also of sixty horse loads of flour.
>
> 17th—The new fort goes slowly. Weather very bad; constant rain night and day. A rifleman of the militia, a few miles from camp with leave to hunt, fired upon by a single Indian and wounded through the hip, but made his escape into camp. Men desert; four of the first regiment went off since our arrival here.
>
> 18th—A continuation of wet, disagreeable weather. The army would have been without bread after to-day, had not a small supply of forty-eight horse loads arrived.
>
> 19th—All the horses of the army, quartermaster's as well as contractors, sent back for a supply flour. Unpardonable mismanagement in the provision department. Troops put on half allowance of flour. Colonel Oldham, commanding officer of the militia, directed to furnish an escort to go back with the horses. His men declare if they are sent on that duty they will not return. Falconer's company of levies escort the horses back.
>
> 20th—The time for which the levies were enlisted begins to expire. Ten were discharged this morning; several a few days ago. The levies from Virginia claim their discharge. All of Captain Hannah's company from Alexandria discharged. An express this day from Fort Washington, Captain Buel's company of the second regiment arrived there from the eastward.
>
> 21st—Very severe frost last night! ice upon the waters near a half inch thick. *The food of our horses and cattle had been injured by slight frosts as early as the 4th.* A strong guard escort the cattle and horses to the best pasture, and every afternoon one-half the army off duty turn out and bring grass from the prairie to serve them over night.

---

[149] *Ibid.*
[150] *Ibid.*
[151] *Ibid.*
[152] *Ibid.*

22nd—For want of sufficiency of flour, the General has been under the necessity of keeping the troops upon half a pound of that article daily, but the ration is made up of beef. This, however, would not satisfy the militia; twenty of them deserted last night, and some more this morning. An officer near Lexington, who joined us this day with about sixty men, happened to meet those who went off this morning, and brought them back. He informed us that a number of militia who had deserted from Fort Washington, and on the march, had been apprehended in Kentucky and were confined in the jails. Two brigades of horses loaded with flour arrived this day, estimated at one-thousand-eight-hundred pounds; also, a small drove of cattle. The Quartermaster general is ordered to Fort Washington to make some more certain arrangement with regard to supplies of provisions—*the contractor or not to be depended on.*

23rd—Two artillery men attempted to desert to the enemy, were taken, tried and sentenced to death; were hanged along with one of the levies for shooting his comrade.[153] The country for ten miles around has been well explored—.

24th—The army took up their line of march about nine o'clock. Pursued the old Indian path leading north through a fine open woods. Gained six miles and encamped along the bank of a handsome creek—. A captain's command left at the new fort, called Fort Jefferson, with all the men unable to march. The commander-in-chief has been unwell for some time past,[154] but to-day scarcely able to accompany the army.[155]

The Congressional investigation in 1792 summarized the progress to this point:

> . . . they employed about fifteen days building Fort Hamilton and then proceeded in their march to the place where Fort Jefferson is now erected, about 44 miles distant from Fort Hamilton, where they arrived on the 12th of October, and commenced their march from that place on the 24th of the same month; that the army at this time consisted of about 1,770 non-commissioned officers and privates fit for duty; at this time the army had not more than three days supply of flour, and were sometimes at one-fourth, and sometimes at one-half allowance of that article.[156]

The report went on:

> The deficiencies of the flour allowance were made up by increasing the quantity of beef, with which they were plentifully supplied. The army was delayed five or six days, on the march from Fort Jefferson, for the want of provisions, and the season was so far advanced that sufficient green forage for the horses could not be procured, from which circumstance many of the horses were totally lost, and others rendered unfit for service.[157]

[153] St. Clair complained to Knox that there was no middle choice of punishment between 100 lashes and death. He hoped it would be corrected (*American State Papers,* Indian Affairs, Vol. 1, p. 180).
[154] St. Clair was suffering from a severe attack of gout.
[155] *Military Journal of Major Ebenezer Denny,* pp. 362–63.
[156] *American State Papers,* Vol. 1, Military Affairs, p. 37.

Then, as if in extenuation: "The orders to the Commander-in-Chief to proceed with the expedition were express and unequivocal, so much so as, in the opinion of the committee, to preclude the Commander-in-Chief from exercising any discretion relatively to that object."[158] An evaluation of the situation shows that:

(a) St. Clair's army was to have begun its expedition by July 10 with a force of 4,128 men.

(b) Three months behind schedule, his force consisted of only 1,700 men.

(c) Winter was fast approaching, a disaster period for any military operation on the frontier, miles from bases of supply. Winthrop Sargent said, "With the best disciplined troops, the general would at this season have much to apprehend. The roads are becoming very bad and forage almost exhausted." Sargent went on: "The militia discontented, and under no subordination and the time of service for the levies very near expiring. Melancholy considerations, these to the whole army; but distressing beyond measure must they be to the commanding general, whose reputation is to be hazarded upon events extremely precarious.[159] The discipline of the levies and mlitia had so deteriorated that Sargent commented: "The General's humanity is well know, but desertions have become so prevalent as to become alarming, and examples (in terrorem) are necessary."[160]

Even with a force of only 1,700 effectives, St. Clair's army presented an enormous caravan moving slowly through the otherwise quiet wilderness. Originally, 800 packhorses to transport provisions, and 300 packhorses to transport supplies had been ordered for the campaign.[161] Camp followers, consisting of washerwomen, mistresses, wives, children with pets, and partially tamed captured animals, followed the regular soldiers behind the columns of carts and the assortment of irregularly dressed militia and levies. The levies had been issued two pairs of overalls and two pairs of shoes, but, as Denny said, it was difficult to find supplies for the militia. The knapsacks that had been delivered to Fort Washington for the campaign were not painted or strapped, as ordered.[162] Knox had some painted in Philadelphia, while Hodgdon was to paint the rest at Fort Washington. In contrast to the Spanish-red appearance of the painted knapsacks, the 1st Regiment had been issued knapsacks covered with bearskin.[163] Josiah Harmar said that "the knapsacks of the levies were small; the covering of the knapsacks [bearskin] increased the martial appearance of the troops as he conceived, as also the difference of clothing of the regulars, between the regulars and the levies."[164] Major Zeigler had said that, even so, "the clothing for the levies was infamous, as many who arrived at Fort Washington were almost naked."[165]

St. Clair reported that, as the army marched through the wilderness,

> it was preceded by a small party of riflemen, with the surveyor, to mark the course of the road; for we had no guides, not a single person being found in the country, who

[157] *Ibid.*
[158] *Ibid.*
[159] Sargent, *ibid.*
[160] *Ibid.*, p. 248.
[161] *American State Papers*, Indian Affairs, Vol. 1, p. 183.
[162] *Ibid.*, p. 188.
[163] St. Clair, *op. cit.*, p. 205.
[164] *Ibid.*
[165] St. Clair, *op. cit.*, p. 204.

had ever been through it, and both the geography and topography were utterly unknown; the march was, therefore, made upon a compass course, conjectural indeed, but which proved to be sufficiently correct, as it brought us into a large path leading to the Miami towns about twenty miles from them; from that party scouts were sent out to scour the country every way; then followed the road cutters with a party to cover them [Major Zeigler said the axes, of poor quality, bent like dumplings because the metal was so soft],[166] then the advanced guard and after them the army in two columns, with one piece of artillery in front, one in the center, and one in the rear of each. In the space between the two columns marched the remaining artillery destined for the fort at the Miami town; then the horses with the tents and provisions, and then the cattle with their proper guards,[167] who were to remove them in case of the enemy appearing. Without the columns, at a distance of about one hundred yards, marched the cavalry in file, and without them, at the same distance, a party of rifleman, and scouts without them, then followed the rear guard at a proper distance.[168]

As this noisy, cumbersome army plodded along, trees being cut ahead, drums rolling behind, hungry horses neighing, cattle bellowing, and undisciplined soldiers swearing at officers who were swearing back at them, the spies under Tecumseh were quietly observing from behind cover. Worrying more about *where* he was going and *how* he was going to get there, with only a compass and no maps, St. Clair apparently did not give his enemy's plans a second thought. As long as he could not see them, he apparently did not worry about them.

The chain of command at that point was as follows: St. Clair, in command, Butler, second, and Winthrop Sargent, adjutant-general; Lieutenant-Colonel George Gibson commanding the 2nd Regiment of levies and Lieutenant-Colonel William Darke commanding the Virginia, Maryland, and North Carolina troops of the 1st Regiment of levies; Lieutenant-Colonel William Oldham commanded the Kentucky militia and Major William Ferguson commanded the regular artillery battalion.

St. Clair had been seized with gout when he had first set out to take command of the army and remained stricken with that ailment throughout most of the year. As commander, his crippled appearance could hardly have been inspiring to the frightened and inexperienced men who followed.

The failure of the expedition became inevitable as the season progressed. Both Denny and Sargent became more pessimistic, but St. Clair's army did not turn back. On the twenty-fifth:

A detachment of fifty men from the militia with the deputy surveyor have marched this morning to explore the country for twenty miles to the northwest, and a party of twenty as an escort for two days to return some horses, on their way to Fort Hamilton. The army halts from the impossibility of being supplied with beef and flour for any forward movement at present. By dispatches received this day, it appears that no magazines are established at Fort Hamilton and that our horses sent back must proceed of course to Cincinnati, and even there supplies are precarious. *So that any further operations* have become doubtful. Small delays alone will render it impracticable for the General to advance, as the time of service of some of the levies is

[166] *Ibid.,* p. 205.
[167] Along with the cattle and the packhorses came scores of civilian drovers and drivers.
[168] *Ibid.,* pp. 270–71.

nearly up, and their example of going off, if followed by the militia, will render our force contemptible indeed.[169]

Rain almost all last night. Troops continue encamped.[170]

[The twenty-sixth:] Remain encamped. A party of fifty militia sent to reconnoitre the country, fell in with five of the enemy about 15 miles from camp, but, owing to mismanagement, the Indians made their escape, leaving behind in their camp, blankets, tomahawks, paint, etc., to the value of 20 dollars. The commander-in-chief is very ill.[171]

The militia were moved across the creek this day up a pretty defensible piece of ground half a mile in advance. The country to the northwest for nineteen miles has been found by the deputy surveyor to be principally upland, timbered with the young white oak and hickory.[172]

It is apparent at this point that there would be no chance of a surprise attack against the Miami towns. Even without the spies under Tecumseh, the Indians would have had full knowledge of the advancing army and their delays due to the lack of supplies, through the reports of those hunters and warriors whose campsites had been overrun by detachments of St. Clair's soldiers.

[The twenty-seventh:] The army wait for a supply of flour to enable them to proceed. The last pound served out this day, and should none arrive, on to-morrow the men will be without bread. Much dissatisfaction among the militia and levies. The latter claim their discharge; say they have served longer than the term for which they have enlisted. The enlistments are indeed somewhat extraordinary; they specify six months after assembling at the rendezvous on the frontier, but there has been no uniformity observed; some corps have inserted Winchester, some Fort Pitt, and others Fort Washington, but the bulk of the men say and declare that they engaged to serve but for six months from the date of their enlistment. The season is so far advanced it will be impracticable to continue the campaign.

Forage entirely destroyed; horses failing and cannot be kept up. Provision from hand to mouth.[173]

We expect a supply flour on the morrow which will enable us to move forward for a few marches. Beyond that, our prospects are gloomy, no magazines established, and even an uncertainty of a supply at Fort Washington with the difficulties of transportation every day increasing by the season and to become still greater, as we add to our distance, *may make events* fatal to the whole army. But the General is compelled to move on, as the only chance of continuing our little army. Thirteen men of the Virginia troops have insisted upon their discharge this day; almost the whole

---

[169] Sargent, *op. cit.,* pp. 248–49.
[170] *Military Journal of Major Ebenezer Denny,* p. 263.
[171] *Ibid.*
[172] Sargent, *op. cit.,* p. 249.
[173] *Military Journal of Major Ebenezer Denny,* pp. 363–64.

battalion will speedily follow their example, and in a short time the period of enlistments with the other battalions will expire. So that the only prospect of effecting the purpose of the campaign is by immediately marching the army so far into the enemy's country that they may be afraid to return in such detachments as shall from time to time be entitled to claim their discharges.[174]

Although Sargent and Denny cite multiple reasons for the failure of the campaign, none of those imply that the Indians might have superior force. Occasionally the style of "Indian warfare" is mentioned but the capabilities of the Indian warrior as opposed to the American soldier are never discussed. Even the tactical advantage of having Chickasaws in the army is not mentioned, as Sargent continues:

> The 20 Chickasaw Indians mentioned to have been at Fort Washington arrived in camp this day. Piaming, who is now their king, with Colbert and some other character of distinction, are among the number. These people have the most inveterate animosity to all the Indian tribes northwest of the Ohio, but most particularly to the Kickapoos, and have been at war with the whole of them from time immemorial.[175]

> [The twenty-eighth:] Some hail and snow today. Seventy-four horses loaded with flour arrive; about 12,000 pounds. This supply will afford 4 days allowance. A few horses came loaded with clothing for the first Regiment, the officers of which were directed to fill up their companies, if possible, from the levies. The new clothing has a good effect; near forty have already enlisted.[176]

> [Denny continued:] Two privates of Major Butler's Battalion [of levies] were fired upon about three miles from camp, one of them shot and scalped, the other wounded, but made his escape to camp. Most probably will die of his wound.
> Two of the militia some miles out, were pursued by four Indians; only one got in, it is supposed the other is a prisoner, as the savages endeavored to catch him when they might have shot him with certainty.
> In the general orders of this day the troops directed to be under arms at the first tap of the drum, which is to be given at daylight, and to continue paraded until dismissed.[177]

> [The twenty-ninth:] One of the sentries which form the chain round the encampment, alarmed the troops last night about nine o'clock, and put them all under arms. He imagined that he saw an Indian and fired three times at some object.
> The first and second Regiment of regulars composed about one-third the army, and although chiefly recruits are tolerably well disciplined, but the remainder (excepting the militia) being levies and raised but for six months, and their times expiring daily, they take great liberties.

[174] Sargent, *op. cit.*, p. 250.
[175] *Ibid.*, p. 249.
[176] *Ibid.*, p. 250.
[177] *Military Journal of Major Ebenezer Denny*, p. 264.

This morning there was a constant firing kept up round the camp, notwithstanding it is known there is a general order against it; in fact, at present they are more troublesome and far inferior to the militia.

A bridge thrown across the creek. One hundred and twenty men, properly officered, were ordered forward to open the road for the army. Two hundred militia go as a covering party. Piamingo and his nineteen warriors accompanied Captain Sparks of the levies, with four riflemen, set out on a scout, their object to take a prisoner.

The battalion of levies from the territory southeast of the Ohio being so small, it was blended with one from Virginia. Supernumerary officers went home. Three days' flour issued to the troops in order that horses may be had to carry baggage; most of the baggage horses having been sent with the quartermaster general for provisions.[178]

[The thirtieth:] A fatigue party with one hundred and thirty non-commissioned officers and privates were detached yesterday morning to open a road forward, under cover of two hundred militia. They were to work until three o'clock this day, and then return to the army. *This has been the usual strength of our fatigues for this purpose,* but they have heretofore been covered by the piquets and never preceded the army more than three or four hours.[179]

The army took up the line of march about nine o'clock, crossed the creek upon the bridge and left a very handsome encampment. Gained seven miles this day. The General has been so very ill since we left Fort Jefferson, that it was supposed he would not be able to proceed.[180]

[The thirty-first:] Army continued encamped, waiting for several brigades of pack horses loaded with flour, which had reached Fort Jefferson last night. The troops are supplied for today and to-morrow, and the contractor has enough for one other day; but should we move, the supply behind would be too late or lost; besides, it was found yesterday that the horses with the army were not sufficient to carry the baggage, part of which had to be left on the road.[181]

Militia show great impatience; their officers appear to have little influence. One-third turn with a determination to go back, a few are prevailed on to stay; between 60 and 70, however, march off in spite of everything, and swear they will stop the pack horses with the provisions.

The 1st Regiment (under Major Hamtramck) was dispatched after them,[182] not with an expectation of bringing them back, but with that idea and to prevent further desertions and principally to protect the convoys. This evening 212 horses, loaded

[178] *Ibid.,* p. 265.
[179] Sargent, *ibid.*
[180] *Military Journal of Major Ebenezer Denny,* pp. 365–66.
[181] *Ibid.*
[182] This was a decision of St. Clair's for which he was later to be severely criticized. He split and thereby weakened his force (as Harmar had before him—and for which the latter also had been criticized). St. Clair wrote to Knox that day telling him that the 1st Regiment had been dispatched under Major Hamtramck, who had specific orders to send a sufficient guard back with the first provision convoy and then to meet the second convoy and return with it and rejoin the army. (*Knox Papers,* Roll XXIX-91, October 31, 1791.)

with flour, arrived; 155 pounds, the average weight.[183] [Sargent calculated a total of 32,000 pounds.]

The dispatch of the 1st Regiment after the deserting militia resulted in an expression of mixed emotion by Sargent: "This movement," he said,

> may have further good effect upon the militia that are in camp, and be the means of keeping them to their duty; but, however necessary it may be, I have to regret that we are hereby deprived for a time of the experience of a corps of three hundred effective men (effective from the experience of the officers, and the opportunities they have had for discipline) which must be estimated as the best in the service.[184]

St. Clair later claimed that Hamtramck had orders to proceed only twenty miles (or until he met the convoy, if it was less than twenty miles distant). But, since the contractor failed to send the supply convoy on time, Hamtramck, not meeting it as planned, continued further than twenty miles. "Thus," said St. Clair, "the regiment was separated from the army for a time, and to a distance far beyond what was intended."[185]

The next day, November 1, St. Clair halted the army "in order to give the road cutters an opportunity of getting some distance ahead."[186] Denny said, "The party remained encamped. A party advanced to open the road. Prepare for marching tomorrow. A deposit made here of heavy articles and such as could be dispensed with, to lighten our horses."[187] Sargent, however, surmised: "The army is ordered to halt this day to give the General time, I imagine, to make up despatches for the war office, as no other cause is obvious. It is very true that we have not the means of transporting all the tents, and entrenching tools without dismounting some of the cavalry, but the same objections will remain tomorrow."[188]

On the second, Denny commented that the army marched eight miles through country that was flat and marshy. A small command sent ahead fell upon an Indian encampment and "got some plunder," said Denny, "and seven horses branded United States supposed to have been stolen from Fort Washington."[189] Sargent sarcastically commented that, according to "general practice," all the Indians were allowed to escape.

During the next day, November 3, there was a light snow, but not enough to cover the ground. The army had marched eight miles, starting out at nine o'clock in the morning and, according to the line that the surveyor had run, said Sargent, had traveled ninety-seven miles from Fort Washington.[190] The road, which had been cut wide enough to permit the passage of two carriages, did not deviate materially, he continued, from the surveyor's line.[191]

Denny described the countryside:

[183] *Military Journal of Major Ebenezer Denny, ibid.*
[184] Sargent, *op. cit.,* p. 251.
[185] St. Clair, *op. cit.,* pp. 265–66 and p. 28.
[186] *Knox Papers, ibid.,* November 1, 1791.
[187] *Military Journal of Major Ebenezer Denny,* p. 356.
[188] Sargent, *ibid.*
[189] *Ibid.,* p. 252.
[190] *Ibid.*
[191] *Ibid.*

The first four miles [of the day's march] very wet and flat. About twelve, passed over dry ground and descended gradually for three miles to a small creek, supposed to be a branch of the waters emptying into Lake Erie; proceeded two miles further, and encamped on pleasant dry ground, on the bank of a creek about twenty yards wide, said to be Pickaway fork of the Omee [Wabash].[192]

Winthrop Sargent further described the site:

Here are an immense number of old and new Indian camps, and it appears to have been a place of their general resort. About fifteen of them, horse and foot, quitted this ground near the time we arrived upon it, as was discovered by their tracks in the banks of the stream. Colonel Oldham, who had long been conversant with Indian affairs, supposes it a party of observation, and the first that has been about us since He joined the army; imagining all the others have been noticed mere hunters.[193]

Colonel Oldham of Kentucky and several other officers were experienced Indian fighters. Oldham joined the regiment during its march on October 10, and the fact that he observed no signs of Indian scouting parties during that time, proves the excellence of Little Turtle's scouts under Tecumseh. Denny tells that "parties of riflemen were detached" after the Indians but "without success."[194] He comments that "it was later than usual when the army reached the ground this evening, and the men much fatigued prevented the General from having some works of defense immediately erected. Major Ferguson, commanding officer of artillery, sent for and a plan agreed on intended to be commenced early on tomorrow."[195]

It is amazing that St. Clair would have allowed the men to retire before adequate defenses had been established, no matter how tired they might have been, since, for the first time, the army was aware that they were under surveillance and, according to Sargent's estimations, were only about twenty miles[196] from the Miami towns. The events of the evening of the third are pertinent enough to the massacre to record them in detail.

Denny described the location:[197] "High dry ground barely sufficient to encamp the army: lines

---

[192] *Military Journal of Major Ebenezer Denny, ibid.*
[193] Sargent, *op. cit.,* pp. 252–53.
[194] *Military Journal of Major Ebenezer Denny,* pp. 367–68.
[195] *Ibid.,* p. 368.
[196] Sargent, *op. cit.,* p. 256.
[197] The original camp site had been selected by the quartermaster, but, finding it unsuitable, St. Clair sent out additonal parties of officers to scout for a better camping ground. Although the site the army finally reached was better than the original area selected by the quartermaster, it required an additional march of a mile and a half (St. Clair, *op. cit.,* p. 214), and, after a long day's march, the additional move late in the day completely exhausted the cold and hungry men.
    Denny told how cramped the men were on this campsite. Sargent relates that

the militia position appeared to me to have been a very defensible one. For four hundred yards in front the wood was open and afforded no cover to the enemy; it could hardly be supposed an attempt would be made upon their rear, for in that case the Indians must have been exposed to two fires—a situation they extremely dread—and besides, the bottom land in that direction, and which was just at the back of their tents, fell suddenly to nearly thirty feet, and men stepping off only a little distance from it must have put themselves under good cover. *I regretted to the General upon the preceding evening that we could not occupy this ground,* but the troops much fatigued, had at that time got their camp, and it was too late to alter their dispostion.

[Sargent, p. 258.]

rather contracted. Parallel with the front lines runs the creek, about 20 yards wide. On both flanks, low wet ground and along most part of the rear. Militia advanced across the creek about 300 yards." Winthrop Sargent further described the site: ". . . The army in two lines, and four pieces of artillery in the center of each: Faulkner's company of riflemen upon the right flank with one troop of horse also upon the left . . ." Denny continued,

> Had accompanied the quartermaster in the afternoon, on to this ground; it was farther than could have been wished, but no place short of it appeared so suitable. I was much pleased with it; returned and made report, found the army halted and about to encamp on flat land, and with no good water; although it was late, the march was continued till just dark, when we reached the creek.[198]

Both Denny and Sargent reveal glaring errors that made Little Turtle's decision to attack on the following morning an obvious one. The army, reduced in size, riddled with hunger, and chilled to the bone, had moved, after their long day's march, to what appeared to be a better location, thereby fatiguing the men to the point that no defensive measures were taken that evening. The cramped location (except for the militia bivouacked across the creek) was one which the Indians could attack under cover, and the main force was separated by the creek from the militia. (The creek was the Upper Wabash River.)

Sargent was explicit in his description of the order of encampment:

> Patterson's, Clarke's and Butler's battalions composed the first line, Patterson on the right and four pieces of artillery upon the right of Butler. The Second U. S. Regiment with Gaither's and Beddinger's battalions formed the rear line; Beddinger on the right [in a rear face] and four pieces of artillery upon the left of his battalion. One troop of horse, commanded by Captain Truman, and a company of riflemen, under Captain Faulkner, were encamped upon the right flank, and occupied a front of about seventy yards, which was the whole distance between the lines, the length of them being nearly four hundred, the rear somewhat more and the front line somewhat less. Snowden's troop of horse was on the left.[199]

In retrospect, Sargent said: "*The encampment, very defensible against regular troops, was found on experience to be feeble to an Indian attack.* Descending, as has been observed, to the front, although in some places the stream was more than a hundred yards distant, yet in others it approached within twenty five."[200]

Sargent recalled that detachments were supposed to have gone the night of the third to learn the enemy's strength and position. However, the militia who, because of their knowledge of the woods, were chosen for this task did not go out and the job was never accomplished. Sargent said that the militia would not listen to orders and would do only what they wanted to—not what their officers commanded. He added that they were not enlisted for any of the common duties of the army and, complaining that they were too fatigued, did no reconnoitering whatever.[201]

[198] *Military Journal of Major Ebenezer Denny, ibid.*
[199] Sargent, *op. cit.,* p. 256.
[200] *Ibid.*
[201] *Ibid.,* p. 257.

This negligence on the part of the militia, and St. Clair's neglect to follow through with his orders, created another vulnerable situation for the army. The unaccountable lack of scouting prior to this night certainly resulted in the indifferent attitude of most of the men.

Another eyewitness account of the evening of the third reveals the complete vulnerability of St. Clair's force that night and the next morning:

> The gen'l observed that he did not think the Indians was watching the movements of the army with a view to attack them. The officers present concurred with him in that opinion. We marched from there about 2 miles, halted to encamp. An express came up from the front guard, stated that they had got to a fine, running stream, and good place to encamp at. We started and got there about sunset. I expect it was near eight o'clock before the troops got fixed for lodging and cooking their scanty mess of provisions.[202]

It must be noted that on this date, November 3, 1791, the official strength of the encamped force had been reduced, by sickness and desertion (and the detachment of the 1st Regiment of regulars), to only 1,400 effectives. The main body was encamped in such cramped quarters the militia had to bivouac across the stream 300 yards forward of the main group. Snow had covered the ground that day and the damp, and the cold night air caused extreme discomfort to the hungry soldiers, whose alertness to danger must have been numbed by their situation.

The dispostion of his huddled force on the evening of the third was described by St. Clair:

> On the 3rd instant the army had reached a creek about twelve yards wide, running southward, which I believe to have been the river St. Mary, that empties into the Miami of the lake; [it was actually on the eastern fork of the Wabash near the eastern boundary of Ohio, in present-day Mercer County, Ohio] arrived at the village about four o'clock in the afternoon having marched near nine miles, and were immediately encamped upon a commanding piece of ground in two lines, having the above-mentioned creek in front. The right wing composed of Butler's [Major Thomas of the levies, not his brother, General Richard], Clarke's and Patterson's battalions, commanded by Major-General Butler, formed the first line; and the left wing, consisting of Bedinger's and Gaither's battalions, and the second regiment, commanded by Colonel Darke, formed the second line, with an interval between them of about seventy yards, which was all the ground would allow.

St. Clair continued:

> The right flank was pretty well secured by the creek, a steep bank, and Faulkner's corps; some of the cavalry and their pickets covered the left flank; the militia were thrown over the creek, and advanced in the same order; there were a few Indians who appeared on the opposite side of the creek, but fled with the utmost precipitation on the advance of the militia; at this place, which I judged to be about fifteen miles from

---

[202] Ohio Archeological and Historical Society Publications, Vol. 10, p. 389, 1902, "St. Clair's Defeat," by Frazer E. Wilson.

the Miami village, I had determined to throw up a slight work, the plan of which was concerted that evening with Major Ferguson, wherein to have deposited the men's knapsacks, and everything else that was not absolutely necessary, and to have moved on to attack the enemy as soon as the First regiment was come up—.[203]

An alarm was given that evening, but the message never reached St. Clair, who used the testimony of Captain Slough,[204] of the levies, in his own defense. Slough, who was serving under Major Thomas Butler, gave the following account of events that occurred on the evening of the third:

> While I was busily pitching my tent, Colonel Gibson came up with a raccoon in his hand, and told me if I would come to his tent he would show me how to dress a raccoon Indian fashion; I went into his tent and sat down, and we were shortly after joined by Captain [Edward] Butler; he observed that he thought if a party was sent out they might have an opportunity of catching some of the rascals who might attempt to steal horses; I told him that I should like to command such a party.[205]

Later that evening Slough was asked to take command of 23 "good men," mostly all sergeants. Before departing on the mission Genral Butler invited Slough into his tent for a glass of wine and told him to be very cautious.

The general instructed Slough to report to Colonel Oldham before leaving. The latter, after Slough reported, requested that Slough give up the mission for fear of being cut off because he expected the army to be attacked in the morning. Colonel Oldham, Slough said later, was then lying down in his tent with his clothes on, in readiness. As Slough, however, had been ordered to go, he was given the password by the picquet guard, and departed. About a mile from camp Slough divided his men into two parties and ordered them to lie close to the ground about forty yards apart on each side of the path they had been following and remain quiet. Soon six or seven Indians approached, upon whom the men fired, possibly killing one, while the rest escaped. Slough ordered the men to remain in ambush, after reloading their pieces (guns) and in about a quarter of an hour a large party of Indians came along, looking, Slough thought, for his detachment. He kept his men quiet and remained undiscovered. Another party, about the same time, passed on the right, about the same size. At this point the men became uneasy, and Slough felt it would be wise to return to camp since there were so many Indians in the woods.[206]

He ordered his men to proceed back along the path in single file and, if attacked, to defend themselves with bayonets so as not to alert other Indians to their position. They heard movement in the woods about every fifteen or twenty yards but could see nothing. As soon as he returned to camp, Slough reported to Colonel Oldham, who agreed with him that the Indians would certainly attack in the morning. It was then about midnight, and Oldham told Slough to report his findings immediately to St. Clair. Slough, however, went to General Butler's tent to report to him first. Butler's tent was dark and Slough was afraid to awaken the general, so he went to Colonel Gibson's tent and awakened him, asking him if the colonel would not go with him to General Butler.[207]

Gibson said he was "stripped" and would not, but that Slough should himself report to Butler,

[203] St. Clair, *op. cit.,* p. 214–18.
[204] Jacob Slough, Pennsylvania, captain in the levies, 1791.
[205] *Ibid.*
[206] *Ibid.*
[207] *Ibid.*

who had issued the orders for the mission. Slough went back to General Butler's tent, awakened the general, and reported, asking him if he should relay his findings to St. Clair. Butler told him he should go to bed since he must be fatigued, which Slough did, and did not awaken until the next morning when he heard the attack. St. Clair was never given the report by General Butler,[208] who was killed the following day. If he had alerted St. Clair, would his life, along with the lives of 636 others, have been saved? St. Clair posed this question, as did the Congressional committee. The next morning it was too late. Denny continues his journal:

> 4th—Camp on a creek twenty yards wide, supposed to be the Pickaway fork of the Omee, 98 miles from Fort Washington [east branch of the Wabash]. The frequent firing of the sentinels through the night disturbed the camp, and excited some concern among the officers. The guards had reported the Indians to lie skulking about in considerable number.[209]

Sargent recalled that he had heard about fifty shots during the night, fired "principally by our own sentinels, sometimes, no doubt, at the enemy, but oftener, probably, without any object whatever."[210] The commotion that night, which

> exceeded much our usual practice, induced the General, in addition to his orders for the men to be prepared at all times for immediate service, to direct that the troops should lay upon their arms with all their accoutrements on. And upon the morning of the 4th, they were turned out somewhat earlier than common, and continued on parade until objects could be distinctly seen at the distance of at least 300 yards.[211]

Parade was usually formed every morning ten minutes before sunrise, Sargent said, and continued under arms until sunrise. This morning, however, for the purpose of collecting horses to be sent back to Fort Jefferson for ammunition, and in order to erect some places of deposit at this new site the troops were dismissed earlier than was ordinarily the custom. Sargent, a half-hour before sunrise, proceeded to inspect the militia quarters and, upon his return to headquarters, the attack by the Indians commenced upon the militia.

"The firing of the enemy was preceded for about five minutes by the Indian yell, the first I had ever heard," he recounted. "Not terrible, as has been represented, but more resembling an infinitude of horse-bells suddenly opening to you than any other sound I could compare it to."[212] Denny observed that the Indians, who had surrounded the entire army under good cover, had attacked the militia first, causing them to panic and to break ranks and run across the creek through the main body of troops, and throwing the corps into a state of confusion.[213] "The resistance of the militia deserves not the name of defense," said Sargent, "but should be branded as the most ignominious flight."[214]

"Close upon the heels of the flying militia followed the Indians, who for a moment," said Sargent, "seemed as if determined to enter out camp with them."[215] Our troops were under arms in an instant," recalled Denny, "and a smart fire from the front line met the enemy. It was but a few minutes, however," he said, "until the men were engaged in every quarter. The enemy from the front

---

[208] St. Clair states this fact per his report to General Knox, November 9, 1791.
[209] *Military Journal of Major Ebenezer Denny*, p. 368.
[210] Sargent, *ibid.*
[211] *Ibid.*, p. 258.
[212] *Ibid.*
[213] *Military Journal of Major Ebenezer Denny*, p. 369.
[214] Sargent, *ibid.*
[215] *Ibid.*, p. 259.

filed off to the right and left, and completely surrounded the camp, killed and cut off nearly all the guards, and approached close to the lines." Describing their tactics, Denny said,

> They advanced from one tree, log or stump to another under cover of the smoke of our fire. The artillery and musketry made a tremendous noise, but did little executions. The Indians seemed to brave everything, and when fairly fixed around us, they made no noise other than their fire, which they kept up very consistent and which seldom failed to tell, although scarcely heard.[216]

It was impossible to determine the exact number of the enemy, but Sargent estimated there were over 1,000 warriors involved in the attack.

> Taking this for granted, and when it is known that our whole force (the militia excepted) amounted only to 1,380 men, 80 of whom were officers' servants who are very seldom,, if ever, brought into action—and that the various guards equal to 220 by being made up in the general detail from the corps, and dispersed in the suddenness of the attack (never after to be effectually collected), reducing our efficient numbers to 1,080 of raw and undisciplined troops, ignorant totally of the Indian and indeed all other mode of fighting—for the whole army was constituted by new raised troops, engaged only for six months, the Second Regiment excepted, and this also was but for a moment, just brought into the field without time for instruction and never having fired even a blank cartridge—whoever, I say, shall be acquainted with all these circumstances must acknowledge that we entertained an unequal war, and long maintained the contest, too soon rendered doubtful *by the superiority of the Indian mode of fighting.*[217]

The corps fought for over two hours before retreat was thought of, said Sargent. He went on, "The Second U. S. Regiment, Butler's and Beddinger's battalions, the artillery and the cavalry were the principal sufferers; and Gaither's battalion also experienced great loss. Clarke's battalion, being advantageously posted and acquainted with this kind of fighting, lost but few men, and a company of riflemen posted on the right flank scarcely any. . . . Whether, he continued, "*it was that the Indians respected and stood aloof from men fighting in some measure after the manner of themselves, or from some other cause, I know not; but it is certain that those corps suffered less than any others,* excepting Patterson's which was always drawn up between them and which shared little in the misfortunes of this day."[218]

Those Indians engaged in the attack were principally the Miamis, Delawares, Wyandots, Shawnees, Ottawas, Kickapoos, Chippewas, Pottawatomies, some Mohawks from Canada, and a few Creeks from the South.[219] Their leaders were Little Turtle of the Miamis, Blue Jacket of the Shawnees, and Buckongahelas of the Delawares.[220]

The enemy's fire, said Sargent, seemed to commence with the artillery of the first line, "and to continue along Butler's battalion to the left and through the whole of the second. This battalion charged the enemy with great spirit; and the artillery, if not well served, was bravely fought and every officer and more than two-thirds of the men killed or wounded. Concealed as the Indians were," he continued, "it was almost impossible to discover them and aim the pieces to advantage, but a large

---

[216] *Military Journal of Major Ebenezer Denny,* p. 369.
[217] Sargent, *op. cit,* p. 259.
[218] *Ibid.,* 259–60.
[219] Butterfield, *op. cit.,* p. 261.
[220] *Ibid.*

quantity of cannister and some round shot were, however, thrown in amongst them. . . .[221] The Second U.S. Regiment," he went on, "made three successive and successful charges, the enemy giving ground to the powerful effect of their bayonet—but not till they had felt its force."[222]

Denny describes the action as he saw it:

> Our left flank, probably from the nature of the ground, gave way first; the enemy got possession of that part of the encampment, but it being pretty clear ground, they were too much exposed and were soon repulsed. Was at this time with the General engaged toward the right; he was on foot and led the party himself that drove the enemy and regained our ground on the left. The battalions in the rear charged several times and forced the savages from their shelter, but they always turned with the battalions and fired upon them back; indeed, they seemed not to fear anything we could do. They could skip out of reach of the bayonet, and return as they pleased, They were visible only when raised by a charge. The ground was literally covered with the dead. The wounded were taken to the centre, where it was thought the most safe, and where a great many who had quit their posts unhurt had crowded together.
>
> The General, with other officers, endeavored to rally these men, and twice they were taken to the lines. It appeared as if the officers had been singled out; a very great proportion fell, or were wounded and obliged to retire from the lines early in the action. General Butler was among the latter as well as several other of the most experienced officers. The men, being thus left with few officers, became fearful, despaired of success, gave up the fight, and to save themselves for the moment, abandoned entirely their duty and ground, and crowded in toward the centre of the field, and no exertions could put them in any order even for defense; perfectly ungovernable. The enemy at length got possession of the artillery, though not until the officers were all killed but one, and he badly wounded, and the men almost all cut off, and not until the pieces were spiked, As our lines were deserted the Indians contracted until their shot centered from all points, and now meeting with little opposition, took more deliberate aim and did great execution.
>
> Exposed to a cross fire, men and officers were seen falling in every direction; the distress, too, of the wounded made the scene such as can scarcely be conceived; a few minutes longer and a retreat would have been impractible. The only hope left was, that perhaps the savages would be so taken up with the camp as not to follow. Delay was death.
>
> No preparation could be made; numbers of brave men must be left a sacrifice, there was no alternative. It was past nine o'clock [A.M.], when repeated orders were given to charge toward the road. The action had continued between two and three hours. Both officers and men seemed confounded, incapable of doing anything; they could not move until it was told that a retreat was intended.[223]

"In this desperate situation of affairs," Sargent said, "when even hope, the last consolation of the wretched, had failed the army . . . the General took the resolution of abandoning his camp and attempting a retreat." Sargent observed that there was no alternative. "The men must either retreat or

[221] Sargent, *op. cit.,* 260.
[222] *Ibid.*
[223] *Military Journal of Major Ebenezer Denny,* pp. 369–71.

be sacrificed without resistance, as the enemy were shooting them down at pleasure from behind trees and the most secure covers, whilst they could scarcely be let to discharge a single gun with effect."[224]

Even the retreat required the most strenuous effort on the part of the officers attempting to gather the cowering men together.

> Upon this occasion [Sargent went on] very extraordinary exertions were made to draw together men sufficient to give the appearance of efficiency. Feints were made in various directions and different parts of the encampment, and whilst they served in some measure to produce the first effect, they operated to deceive the enemy.
>
> Having thus collected in one body the greatest part of the troops and such of our wounded as could possibly hobble along with us, we pushed out from the left of the rear line, sacrificing our artillery and baggage; and with them, we were compelled to leave some of our wounded.[225]

Describing the bravery of those wounded that were left behind and acted as a rear guard, Sargent said:

> The determined resolution of our unfortunate friends (incapacitated from wounds to quit the field, yet who, as soon as the fate of the day became uncertain, charged their pieces with a coolness and deliberation that reflects the highest honor upon their memory), and the firing of musketry in camp after we quitted it, leaves us very little room for doubt that their latest efforts were professionally brave and that where they could pull a trigger they avenged themselves.[226]

During the retreat, Denny said, "a few officers put themselves in front, the men following, the enemy gave away and perhaps not being aware of the design, we were for a few minutes left undisturbed."[227]

Sargent estimated that the retreating army "gained the road" in about a mile and a half, "the enemy scarcely pursuing beyond that distance. There can be little doubt," he went on, "they had it in their power to have cut us off, almost to a man; it is probable, however, that they might have been suspicious of this movement, and there thought it most eligible to embrace the opportunity to plunder, before possibly it could be snatched from them." He added that the unfortunate few left behind must, for a time, have engaged their attention.[228]

Denny added: "the stoutest and most active now took the lead, and those who were foremost in breaking the enemy's lines, were soon left behind. At the moment of the retreat," he went on, "one of the few horses saved had been procured for the General; he was on foot till then; I kept him, and he delayed to see the rear. The enemy soon discovered the movement and pursued, but nor for more than a few miles."[229]

[224] Sargent, *op. cit.*, p. 261.
[225] *Ibid.*
[226] *Military Journal of Major Ebenezer Denny*, p. 262.
[227] *Ibid.*, p. 371.
[228] Sargent, *ibid.*
[229] *Military Journal of Major Ebenezer Denny, ibid.*

"The conduct of the army after quitting the ground was in a most supreme degree disgraceful," said Sargent. "Arms ammunition and accoutrements were almost thrown away, and even the officers in some instances diverted themselves of their fusees and cartridge boxes, exemplifying by this conduct a kind of authority for the most precipitate and ignominious flight."[230]

> Soon after the firing ceased, I was directed to endeavor to gain the front, and if possible. to cause a short halt that the rear might get up. I had been on horseback from the first alarm, and well mounted; pushed forward, but met with so many difficulties and interruptions from the people, that I was two hours at least laboring to reach the front. With the assistance of two or three other officers I caused a short halt, but the men grew impatient and would move on.
>
> I got Lieutenants Sedam and Morgan, with half a dozen stout men, to fill up the road and to move slowly, I halted myself until the General came up. By this time, the remains of the army had got somewhat compact, but in the most miserable and defenseless state. The wounded who came off left their arms in the field, and [as Sargent observed] one-half of the others threw theirs away on the retreat. The road for miles was covered with firelocks, cartridge boxes and regimentals.
>
> How fortunate that the pursuit was discontinued; a single Indian might have followed with safety upon either flank. Such a panic had seized the men, that I believe it would not have been possible to have brought any of them to engage again.
>
> In the afternoon, Lieutenant Kersey, with a detachment of the First regiment, met us. This regiment, *the only complete and best disciplined portion of the army,* had been ordered back upon the road on the 31st of October. They were 30 miles from the battle ground then they heard distinctly the firing of cannon, were hastening forward and had marched about nine miles when met by some of the militia, who informed Major Hamtramck, the commanding officer, that the army was totally destroyed. The Major judged it best to send on a subaltern to obtain some knowlege of things and to return himself with the regiment to Fort Jefferson,[231] eight miles back, and to secure at all events the post."[232]

Hamtramck was criticized by some for this action later. It was a moot point whether had Hamtramck marched back,[233] he would have been able to take the offensive and save the rear guard that was left behind—or whether his regiment would have been totally destroyed.

In his letter to Knox, St. Clair later said:

> I am not certain, sir, whether I ought to consider the absence of the first regiment from the field of action as fortunate, or otherwise, I incline to think it was fortunate; for I very much doubt whether, had it been in the action, the fortune of the day had been turned; and if it had not, the triumph of the enemy would have been more complete, and the country would have been destitute of every means of defense.[234]

---

[230] Sargent, *op. cit.,* p.262.
[231] *Military Journal of Major Ebenezer Denny,* pp. 371–352.
[232] The battle ground was twenty-nine miles from Fort Jefferson (St. Clair, *op. cit.,* p. 19).
[233] Knox criticized Hamtramck for not returning to the scene of the battle ground with his regiment (*Knox Papers,* Roll XXX-1, March 2, 1792).
[234] Smith, *op. cit.,* Vol. II, p. 265.

On the other hand, Colonel William Darke, whose son was mortally wounded during the action, severely criticized St. Clair after the battle and, in a letter to President Washington, called the action of Major Hamtramck "cowardly."[235] Darke had Hamtramck arrested for cowardice and, in another letter to Secretary of War Knox, St. Clair said that this action was terribly embarrassing. Hamtramck was honorably acquitted, but Darke, extremely bitter, continued openly to criticize St. Clair's actions. St. Clair had many other critics and spent a good deal of his later life defending his conduct during the entire campaign.

In retrospect, the commanding general referred to basic military principles to defend his actions during the campaign. Explaining his order of encampment, he said:

> When encamped, which was always in order of battle, guards from each battalion were posted from fifty to one hundred yards advanced in front and rear and on each flank, and a chain of sentries from them quite around the encampment. Without them one hundred yards more advanced, were outlying piquets, and another chain of sentries from them; and as soon as the tents were pitched, small parties were sent out in all directions to scour the country round.[236]

He explained the late arrival at camp the night of the third "when the army arrived in proper time, at a place where the quartermaster had marked out the encampment, it was such a situation as I could not approve; a single shower of rain would have put it in such a condition as no man could have kept his feet; a halt was therefore made, until more proper ground, where there was water could be found."[237]

A Congressional committee investigating the defeat said:

> The committee conceive it but justice to the commander-in-chief, to say, that, in their opinion, the failure of the late expedition can, in no respect be imputed to his conduct, either at any time before or during the action; but that as his conduct in all the preparatory arrangements was marked with peculiar ability and zeal, so his conduct during his action furnished strong testimonials of his coolness and intrepidity.[238]

A volunteer aide, Viscount Malartie, said of his general, "he was cool, deliberate and calm during the battle,"[239] and he went on to describe St. Clair's heroism in attempting to rally the men and in covering the retreat.

Secretary of War Knox blamed the defeat upon three causes: 1) deficient number of good troops, according to expectation, in the early part of the year; 2) their want of sufficient discipline, according to the nature of the service; 3) the lateness of the season.[240] He added a fourth reason, saying that an unusually large number of Indians took part in the campaign—as many as 3,000.

The exact number of Indians has never been determined, but knowledgeable estimates guessed that not more than 1,500 took part in the ambush.[241] They were, however, supplied by the British and bolstered in their ranks by renegade whites, such as Simon Girty, French traders, and possibly some

---

[235] *Knox Papers,* Roll XXX-12, November 9, 1791.
[236] St. Clair, *op. cit.,* p. 271.
[237] *Ibid.*
[238] *American State Papers,* Vol. I, Military Affairs, p. 39.
[239] St. Clair, *op. cit.,* pp. 221–22.
[240] *American State Papers,* Vol. I, Indian Affairs, p. 198.
[241] Butterfield, *op. cit.,* p. 263.

British officers and Canadians.[242] One story has it that it was Girty who had the wounded General Butler put to death by the tomahawk blow of an Indian warrior.[243]

Along with Butler, Denny counted thirty-six other officers and 593 enlisted men killed, while thirty-two officers and 252 enlisted men were wounded. Stephenson gives a slightly different accounting: 637 killed, 263 wounded, and only 500 of the 1,400 escaping. Casualties among the regular army officers were:

Killed		Wounded
Major Ferguson	Captain Phelon	Captain Ford
Captain Bradford	Captain Kirkwood	Captain Doyle
Lieutenant Spear	Lieutenant Warren	Lieutenant Graton
Major Heart	Ensign Balsh	
Captain Newman	Ensign Cobb	

Of the ranking officers, other than Butler of the levies, Lieutenant-Colonel Gibson died of wounds, and Lieutenant-Colonel Oldham was killed. Of the officers who played a major part in the campaign, Lieutenant-Colonel Darke, Major Butler, Captain Slough, Colonel Sargent, and Viscount Malartie were all wounded.

Bitterness and controversy followed the defeat. Conflicting reports and letters resulted, and to this day exact figures of the number of the enemy killed is not known. Sargent maintained that "It is not probable that many of the Indians fell this day, though there are persons who pretend to have seen great numbers dead. I had myself an opportunity of making observations, but they were not correspondent with this assertion."[244]

Lieutenant-Colonel William Darke, writing to President Washington on November 9, said:

> I am at a loss to know what General St. Clair intends to do, but I well know what I would do was I in his place and would venter [venture] to forfit [forfeit] my life if the Indians have not moved the cannon [they captured] farther than the Meammi [Miami] Towns. If I did not Retake them by going there in three days instead of three months. I well know they have lost many of their braves and Warriors, and make no doubt they have near 100 wounded. Their killed I cannot think bare any perportion [proportion] to ours as they lay so concealed, but many I know were killed and those the most daring fell over which has weakened them greatly and that a violent push with 100 brave men—[245]

The sad results of the battle so incensed the critics of St. Clair that they ignored the problems he faced in preparing for the campaign. His critics were many—including Washington and Knox. The results, when tabulated, were staggering. Besides the dead and wounded, there were lost in action, according to Sargent:

---

[242] *Ibid.*
[243] *Ibid.*
[244] Sargent, *op. cit.,* p. 262.
[245] *Knox Papers,* Darke to Washington, *op. cit.,* Roll XXX-12, November 9, 1791.

3 brass six-pounders, 3 brass three-pounders, 2 pieces of iron ordinance, 2 traveling forges and 4 ox teams, complete; 2 baggage wagons with horses; 316 pack horses fully harnessed, besides those of the contractor's department; 39 artillery, and a considerable number of dragoon and private riding horses; with the horseman's swords, pistols, etc.; 384 common and eleven horseman's tents and marquees; 1,200 muskets and bayonets, with cartridge boxes, belts, and all the other accoutrements, complete, and all the drums of the army; 163 felling axes; 89 spades; 88 mattocks; armourer's, carpenter's blacksmith's and tinman's tools in the whole sets; with a variety of valuable et cetera requisite for establishing works upon the great scale at the Miami towns, also 2 medicine chests, and a quantity of quartermaster's stores, which, together with the provision of bread and beef in camp, have been estimated by a tolerably accurate calculation, at the sum of $32,810.00.[246]

Although Arthur St. Clair spent his declining years in poverty, he maintained the posture and authority of his former command. Killed when thrown from his pony-drawn wagon near his home in the eighty-fourth year of his life, his tombstone bore the inscription:

The
Earthly Remains
of
Major-General Arthur St. Clair
are deposited
Beneath this humble monument
which is
Erected to Supply the Place
of a Nobler one
Due from his Country[247]

[246]Sargent, *op. cit.,* p. 265.
[247] William Henry Smith, *op. cit.,* Vol. 1, p. 254.

78.

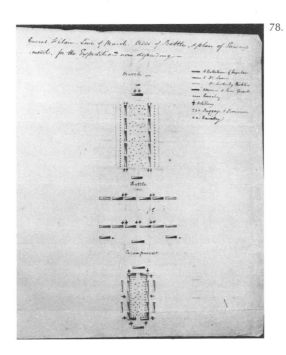

78. The original order of battle, march, and encampment for the St. Clair expedition drawn in watercolor by an unknown officer when the troops were departing Fort Washington. *Guthman Collection*

78A. Tecumtha scouting St. Clair's troops and followers moving toward the Indian towns. *Drawing by Don Troiani*

78A.

79.

79.A

Death of GENERAL BUTLER.

80.

79. Colonel William Darke shown in a pose of victory with retreating Indians in the background, by an unknown primitive artist, who tried to hide the truth about St. Clair's massacre in this portrait. *Museum of Early Southern Decorative Arts*

79A. Early morning attack on St. Clair's troops. *Drawing by Don Troiani*

80. Rare woodcut depicting the death of General Richard Butler in the action of November 4, 1791, taken from *History of the Discovery of America* by Henry Trumbull, Norwich, Connecticut, 1811. *Guthman Collection*

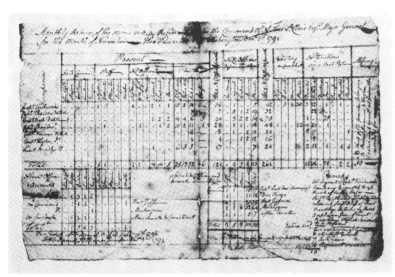

81.

82.

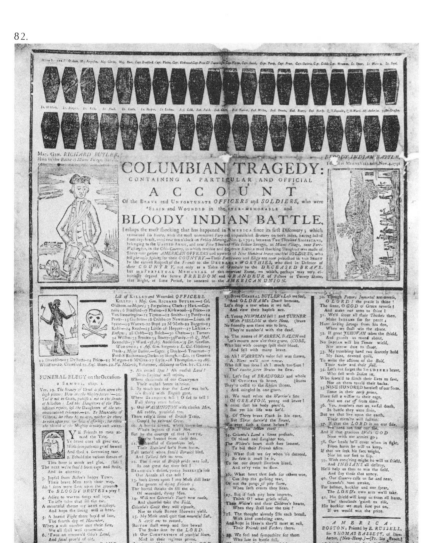

83.

81. Original manuscript return (report) from the surviving senior officer of the 2nd U.S. Regiment. Dated December 1, 1791, after St. Clair's defeat. This regiment suffered the greatest number of casualties during the battle. Out of a total of 261 enlisted men, 101 were killed, and fifty were missing, the return indicates. Seven officers were also killed.
Guthman Collection

82. *Columbian Tragedy* broadside, printed by Ezekiel Russell, Boston, immediately following the news of St. Clair's tragic encounter with the Ohio Indians. The broadside consists of a brief description of the battle, a list of officers killed and wounded, and forty-one stanzas of verse, in elegy form.
Guthman Collection

83. Broadside published in December 1818 in memory of Major General Arthur St. Clair, who was killed August 31 of that same year. The honors denied St. Clair by his country are proclaimed in the broadside.
Guthman Collection

Bibliography

HISTORICAL BACKGROUND

American State Papers, Class VIII, Public Lands, Vol. 1, Gales and Seaton, Washington, 1832.

American States, Documents Illustrative of the Formation of the Union of The, Government Printing Office, Document #398, Washington, 1927.

Barnhart, John D., and Dorothy L. Riker, *Indiana to 1816,* Indiana Historical Society, Indianapolis, 1971.

Bond, Beverley W., Jr., *The Civilization of the Old Northwest,* Macmillan Company, New York, 1934.

Brigham, Clarence S., *History and Bibliography of American Newspapers,* American Antiquarian Society, Worcester, Mass., 1947.

Cauthorn, Henry S., *History of the City of Vincennes, Indiana, from 1702–1901,* M. C. Cauthorn, Terre Haute, Ind., 1902.

Clinton, George, Public Papers of, War of the Revolution Series, Compiled and Arranged by Hugh Hastings, published by the State of New York, Albany, 1899.

The Columbian Magazine, July–December 1787, Seddon, Spotswood and Trenchard, Philadelphia, 1787.

Congress, The Journals of, Volumes 1–13, containing their proceedings from September 5, 1774, to November 3, 1788, published by authority, Folwell's Press, Philadelphia, 1801.

Cotton, Joseph P., Jr., *The Constitutional Decisions of John Marshall,* G. P. Putnam and Sons, New York, 1905.

Cutler, Manasseh, *Description of Ohio,* Old South Leaflets, General Series Number 40, the Directors of the Old South Work, Old South Meeting House, Boston, Mass. (no date).

de Chambrun, Clara Longworth, *Cincinnati,* Charles Scribner's Sons, New York, 1939.

Evans, Charles, *American Bibliography,* reprinted by Peter Smith, New York, 1941.

Fiske, John, *The Critical Period of American History, 1783–1789,* Houghton Mifflin Company, Boston, 1888.

Greene, George E., *History of Old Vincennes,* S. J. Clark, Chicago, 1911.

Hamilton, Alexander, John Jay, and James Madison, *The Federalist on the New Constitution,* Jacob Gideon, Jr., Washington, D.C., 1818.

Hatcher, Harlan, *The Western Reserve,* the Bobbs-Merrill Co., Inc, Indianapolis, 1949.

Helderman, Leonard C., "Danger on the Wabash," *Indiana Magazine of History,* Vol. 34, Number 4, December 1938.

Hulbert, Archer Butler, *The Ohio River,* G. P. Putnam's Sons, New York, 1906.

History of the Expedition of Captains Lewis and Clark, reprinted from the edition of 1814 (Paul Allen), introduction and index by James K. Hosmer, A. C. McClurg and Company, Chicago, 1902.

Johnson, Allen, editor, *Dictionary of American Biography,* Charles Scribner's Sons, New York, 1964.

"The Journals of Lewis and Clark," edited by Bernard de Voto, Houghton Mifflin Company, Boston, 1953.

King, John Alsop, "The Framing of the Federal Constitution and the Causes Leading Thereto," New York Historical Society, 1888.

King, Rufus, Ohio, *First Fruits of the Ordinance of 1787,* Houghton Mifflin Company, Boston, 1891.

Lossing, Benson J., *The Home of Washington,* A. S. Hale Co., Hartford, Conn., 1870.

———, *The Pictorial Field Book of the Revolution,* Harper Brothers, New York, 1860.

———, *The Pictorial Field Book of the War of 1812,* Harper Brothers, New York, 1868.

Maclay, William, *Journal of William Maclay,* edited by Edgar S. Maclay, D. Appleton and Company, New York, 1890.

McMaster, John Bach, *A History of the People of the United States,* D. Appleton and Company, New York, 1883.

Marshall, John, *The Life of George Washington,* the Citizen's Guild of Washington's Boyhood Home, Fredericksburg, Va., 1926.

Mathews, Mitford M., editor, *Dictionary of Americanisms,* the University of Chicago Press, Chicago, 1951.

May, Colonel John, *Journals and Letters of Colonel John May,* with notes by William M. Darlington, Robert Clarke and Company, Cincinnati, 1873.

The New York Magazine or Literary Repository, January–December 1791, Thomas and James Swords, New York, 1791.

Ohio Company Series, Volumes I and II, edited by Archer Butler Hulbert, Marietta College Historical Collections, Marietta, Ohio, 1917.

Ohio in the Time of the Confederation, edited by Archer Butler Hulbert, Volume III, Marietta College Historical Collections, Marietta Historical Commission, Marietta, Ohio, 1918.

Peat, Wilbur D., *Pioneer Painters of Indiana,* Art Association of Indianapolis, Indiana, 1954.

Putnam, Rufus, *The Memoirs of Rufus Putnam,* compiled and annotated by Rowena Buell, Houghton Mifflin Company, Boston, 1903.

Sabin, Joseph, *A Dictionary of Books Relating to America,* reprinted by N. Israel, Amsterdam, Holland, 1961.

Slocum, Charles Elihu, *The Ohio Country between the Years 1783 and 1815,* G. P. Putnam's Sons, New York, 1910.

Smith, Daniel, *Surveying Journal of Daniel Smith,* Draper Collection, the State Historical Society of Wisconsin, manuscript journal, Madison, Wisconsin, 1779.

United States, The Territorial Papers of, compiled and edited by Clarence Edwin Carter, Government Printing Office, Washington, D.C., 1934.

United States, Acts Passed At A Congress Of The United States Of American begun and held at the City Of New York on Wednesday, the Fourth Of March in the Year 1789, Hodge, Allen and Campbell, New York, 1789.

United States, Acts Passed at the first session of the Second Congress of The United States Of American Begun and held at the City Of Philadelphia in the State of Pennsylvania on Monday, the Twenty-Fourth of October, One Thousand Seven Hundred and Ninety One, Francis Childs and John Swaine, Philadelphia, 1792.

Walker, Francis A., *The Making of a Nation, 1783–1817,* Charles A. Scribner's Sons, New York, 1902.

"Washington, a Catalogue of the Washington Collection in the Boston Anthenaeum," compiled and annotated by Appleton P.C. Griffin, the Boston Anthenaeum, Boston, 1897.

Washington, *Moments of Washington's Patriotism,* fourth edition, Frank Knight, Washington, 1844.

Washington, George, *The Writings of George Washington,* by W. C. Ford, G. Putnam, New York, 1891.

———, *Diaries, 1784–1799,* edited by John C. Fitzpatrick, Houghton Mifflin Company, Boston, 1925.

———, *The Journal of George Washington: An account of his mission to the Commandant of the French Forces on the Ohio, 1753–1754,* facsimile edition, Colonial Williamsburg, Williamsburg, Virginia, 1959.

Welling, James C., "The Land Politics of the United States," a paper read before the New York Historical Society, New York, 1888.

Wilson, James Grant, and John Fiske, editors, *Appleton's Cyclopedia of American Biography,* D. Appleton and Company, New York, 1887.

Wyoming Valley, Documents Relating to the Connecticut Settlement in the, edited by William Henry Egle, Pennsylvania Archives, Second Series, Vol. 28, Harrisburg, Pa., 1890.

CRAFTSMEN

Baines, Anthony, *European and American Musical Instruments,* the Viking Press, New York, 1966.

Beauchamp, William M., *Metallic Ornaments of the New York Indians,* University of the State of New York, Albany, 1903.

Bedini, Silvio A., *Early American Scientific Instruments and Their Makers,* Smithsonian Institution, United States National Museum Bulletin 231, Government Printing Office, Washington, D.C., 1964.

Belden, Bauman L., *Indian Peace Medals Issued in the United States,* reprinted by N. Flayderman & Co., New Milford, Conn., 1966.

Bigelow, Francis Hill, *Historic Silver of the Colonies and Its Makers,* the Macmillan Company, New York, 1917.

Brewington, M. V., *Navigating Instruments,* Peabody Museum, Salem, Mass., 1963.

Brix, Maurice, *A List of Philadelphia Silversmiths and Allied Artificers,* Philadelphia, 1920.

Buchan, William, *Domestic Medicine, or, the Family Physician,* John Dunlap for Robert Aitken, Philadelphia, 1772.

Buhler, Kathryn C., and Graham Hood, *American Silver in the Yale University Art Gallery,* Yale University Press, New Haven, Conn., 1970.

Carter, W. A., *North American Indian Trade Silver,* Volumes I and II, Engel Printing, London, 1971.

Curtis, George Munson, *Early Silver of Connecticut and Its Makers,* International Silver Company, Meriden, Conn., 1913.

Darling, Herbert F., *New York State Silversmiths,* Darling Foundation, New York, 1964.

Dillon, John G. W., *The Kentucky Rifle,* Trimmer Printing, Inc., York, Pa., 1959.

Ensko, Stephen G. C., *American Silversmiths and Their Marks III,* Robert Ensko, Inc., New York, 1948.

Fales, Martha Gandy, *American Silver in the Henry Francis Du Pont Winterthur Museum,* Winterthur, Delaware, 1958.

————, *Early American Silver,* Funk & Wagnalls, New York, 1970.

Flynt, Henry N., and Martha Gandy, Fales, *The Heritage Foundation Collection of Silver,* the Heritage Foundation, Old Deerfield, Mass., 1968.

Gardner, Robert E., *Small Arms Makers,* Bonanza Books, New York, 1963.

Gibson, Robert, *A Treatise of Practical Surveying,* Wm. Davis, New York, 1798.

Gottesman, Rita Susswein, *Arts and Crafts in New York, 1777–1799,* the New York Historical Society, New York, 1954.

Guthman, William H., "Decorated Military Americana," *Antiques Magazine,* New York, July 1966.

Jamieson, Melville Allan, *Medals Awared to North American Indian Chiefs,* reprinted by Spink & Son, Ltd., London, 1961.

Kauffman, Henry J., *American Copper and Brass,* Thomas Nelson & Sons, Camden, New Jersey, 1968.

————, *The Pennsylvania Rifle,* the Stackpole Company, Harrisburg, Pa., 1960.

Klapthor, Margaret Brown, *Presentation Pieces in the Museum of History and Technology,* Paper 47, Smithsonian Institution, Washington, D.C., 1965.

Langdon, John Emerson, *Canadian Silversmiths,* the Stinehour Press, Lunenberg, Vermont, 1960.

Loubat, J. F., *The Medallic History of the United States of America,* reprinted by N. Flayderman & Co., New Milford, Conn., 1967.

Newman, Eric P., *The Early Paper Money of America,* Whitman Publishing Co., Racine, Wisc., 1967

Prime, Alfred Cox, *Arts and Crafts in Philadelphia, Maryland, and South Carolina, 1721–1785,* the Walpole Society, Philadelphia, 1929.

Smart, Charles E., *The Makers of Surveying Instruments in America since 1700,* Vol. I, Regal Art Press, Troy, N.Y., 1962, Vol. II, 1967.

Traquair, Ramsay, "Montreal and the Indian Trade Silver," *The Canadian Historical Review,* Vol. 19, No. 1, Toronto, March 1938.

GEOGRAPHY AND CARTOGRAPHY

The American Heritage Pictorial Atlas of United States History, American Heritage Publishing Co., New York, 1966.

Brown, Lloyd Arnold, *Early Maps of the Ohio River Valley,* University of Pittsburgh Press, Pittsburgh, 1959.

Brown, Samuel, *The Western Gazetteer or Emigrant's Directory,* H. C. Southwick, Auburn, N.Y., 1817.

Carter, C. E., editor, *The Territorial Papers of the United States,* Government Printing Office, Washington, D.C., 1934–1971.

Cramer, Zadok, *The Navigator,* Cramer, Spear, and Eichbaum, Pittsburgh, 1817.

Cumings, Samuel, *The Western Navigator,* E. Littel, Philadelphia, 1822.

Gipson, Henry Lawrence, *Lewis Evans,* the Historical Society of Pennsylvania, Philadelphia, 1939.

Hulbert, Archer Butler, "A Topographical Description of the Ohio River," *Ohio Archeological and Historical Society Publications,* Vol. 20, Columbus, 1911.

Imlay, G., *A Topographical Description of the Western Territory of North America,* Samuel Campbell, New York, 1793.

Indiana Junior Historical Society, "Directory of Historical Markers of Indiana," *Indiana History Bulletin,* Indiana Historical Society, Indianapolis, March 1966.

Kilbourn, John, *The Ohio Gazetteer or Topographical Dictionary,* J. Kilbourn, Columbus, 1821.

Moore, S. S., and T. W. Jones, *The Traveller's Directory or, a Pocket Companion,* Mathew Carey, Philadelphia, 1804.

Morse, Jedidiah, *The American Gazetteer,* Samuel Etheridge, Boston, 1804.

———, *The American Geography,* John Stockdale, London, 1794.

———, *The Traveller's Guide or Pocket Gazetteer of the United States,* Nathan Whiting, New Haven, 1823.

The North American and West-Indian Gazetteer, printed for G. Robinson, London, 1777.

Scott, Joseph, *A Geographical Dictionary of the United States of North America,* Archibald Bartram, Philadelphia, 1805.

———, *The United States Gazetteer,* F. and R. Bailey, Philadelphia, 1793.

World Atlas, Rand McNally and Co., New York, 1958.

INDIAN BACKGROUND AND CULTURE

Adair, James, *The History of the American Indians,* Edward and Charles Dilly, London, 1775.

Barce, Elmore, *The Land of the Miamis,* the Benton Review Shop, Fowler, Indiana, 1922.

Colden, Cadwallader, *The History of the Five Indian Nations,* reprinted by Cornell Paperbacks, Cornell University Press, Ithaca, New York, 1964.

Cox, Isaac Joslin, "The Indian as a Diplomatic Factor in the History of the Old Northwest," *Ohio Archeological and Historical Society Publications,* Volume 18, Columbus, Ohio, 1909.

Drake, Samuel G., *The Aboriginal Races of North America,* revised by Professor H. L. Williams, Hurst and Company, New York, 1880.

———, *Indian Biography, of Indian Chiefs,* Josiah Drake, Boston, 1832.

Franklin, Benjamin, *Indian Treaties Published by Benjamin Franklin, 1736–1762,* the Historical Society of Pennsylvania, 1938.

Gillette, Charles E., "Wampum Beads and Belts," New York State Museum, State Education Department, Albany, N.Y., (no date).

Guthman, William H., "Indian Trade Documents," *The Museum of the Fur Trade Quarterly,* Vol. 7, No. 2, Summer, 1971, Chardron, Nebraska.

Heckewelder, Reverend John, *History, Manners, and Customs of the Indian Nations,* new and revised edition by the Reverend William C. Reicher, the Historical Society of Pennsylvania, Philadelphia, 1876.

Holmes, William H., "Art in Shell of the Ancient Americans," Bureau of Ethnology, *Smithsonian Institution Annual Report,* Government Printing Office, Washington, D.C., 1881.

Johnson, Sir John, "Instructions for the good government of the Branch of the Indian Department Within the District of Detroit," addressed to Indian Agent Alexander McKee, written in Canada, Collection of William H. Guthman, Westport, Conn., 1786.

Kinietz, Vernon W., *The Indians of the Western Great Lakes, 1615–1760,* Ann Arbor Paperbacks, the University of Michigan Press, Ann Arbor, Mich., 1965.

Kinzie, Mrs. John H., *Wau-Bun,* the Lakeside Press, Chicago, 1932.

Lewis and Clark, *History of the Expedition of Captains Lewis and Clark, 1804–5–6,* reprinted from the edition of 1814, with an introduction by James K. Hosmer, A. C. McClurg and Co., Chicago, 1902.

Moorehead, Warren K., "The Indian Tribes of Ohio," Ohio Archeological and Historical Society Publications, Volume 7, Columbus, Ohio, 1899.

Parrish, John, "Missionary Journals of John Parrish," six manuscript journals describing treaties among the Shawnee, Delaware, and Wyandot tribes in 1773, at the Newtown Point Indian Treaty in 1791 and treaties at Sandusky and Detroit in 1793, Guthman Collection.

Quimby, George Irving, *Indian Culture and European Trade Goods,* the University of Wisconsin Press, Madison, Wisc., 1966.

———, *Indian Life in the Upper Great Lakes, 11,000 B.C. to A.D. 1800,* the University of Chicago Press, Chicago, 1960.

Schoolcraft, Henry R., *Historical and Statistical Information Respecting the Indian Tribes of the United States,* collected and prepared under the direction of the Bureau of Indian Affairs, Lippincott, Grambo and Co., Philadelphia, 1851–57.

———, *Notes on the Iroquois,* Bartlett and Welford, New York, 1846.

Shippen, Edward, collection of manuscript invoices, inventories, letters and broadsides from Indian trade merchant Edward Shippen, Philadelphia and Lancaster, Pa., from 1730 to 1780, Guthman Collection.

Stone, William L., *Life of Joseph Brant-Thayendanegea,* George Dearborn and Company, New York, 1888.

Ticonderoga, "The Gorget," *The Bulletin of the Fort Ticonderoga Museum,* Vol. 4, No. 5, Fort Ticonderoga, New York, September 1937.

Woodward, Arthur, *The Denominators of the Fur Trade,* Socio-Technical Publications, Pasadena, California, 1970.

Young, Calvin M., *Little Turtle,* Greenville, Ohio, 1917.

Zeisberger, David, *History of the Northern American Indians,* edited by Archer Butler Hulbert and William Nathaniel Schwarze, Ohio State Archeological and Historical Society, Columbus, 1910.

INDIAN CAMPAIGNS

Adams, Randolph G., and Howard H. Peckham, *Lexington to Fallen Timbers, 1775–1794,* University of Michigan Press, Ann Arbor, Mich., 1943.

American State Papers, Class II, Indian Affairs, Vol. I, Gales and Seaton, Washington, 1832.

Bouquet, Henry, *Historical Account of Bouquet's Expedition against the Ohio Indians in 1764,* preface by Francis Parkman, Robert Clarke & Co., Cincinnati, 1868.

———, *An Historical Account of the Expedition against the Ohio Indians in the Year 1764, under the Command of Henry Bouquet, Esq.,* published from Authentic Documents by a Lover of His Country (William Smith), William Bradford, Philadelphia, 1765.

Bunn, Matthew, *A Journal of the Adventures of Matthew Bunn Who Enlisted with Ensign John Tillinghast, of Providence, in the Year 1791, on an Expedition into the Western Country—Was Taken by the Savages,* reprinted by Thomas Collier, 1796.

Butterfield, Consul Willshire, *History of the Girty's,* Robert Clarke and Company, Cincinnati, 1890.

Clinton Campaign, Orderly Book, 5th New York Regiment, August 9, 1779–November 15, 1779, Guthman Collection.

Cone, Stephen Decatur, "Indian Attack on Fort Dunlap," Ohio Archeological and Historical Society Publications, Vol. 17, Columbus, Ohio, 1908.

Denny, Ebenezer, *Military Journal of Major Ebenezer Denny,* Historical Society of Pennsylvania, J. B. Lippincott & Company, Philadelphia, 1860.

English, William Hayden, *Conquest of the Country Northwest of the River Ohio 1778–1783 and Life of General George Rogers Clark,* the Bowen-Merrill Company, Indianapolis, Ind., 1896.

Gilman, Dr. Chandler R., "Defeat Of General St. Clair," a paper read before the New York Historical Society, William Van Norden, New York, 1847.

Gipson, Henry Lawrence, *The British Empire before the American Revolution,* Vol. VI, Alfred A. Knopf, New York, 1956.

Helderman, Leonard C., "Danger on the Wabash," *Indiana Magazine of History,* Vol. 24, No. 4, Bloomington, Ind., December 1938.

Johonnet, Jackson, *The Remarkable Adventures of Jackson Johonnet of Massachusettes, Who Served as a Soldier in the Western Army, in the Expedition under General Harmar, and the Unfortunate General St. Clair, Written by Himself,* reprinted by Alden Spooner, Windsor, Vt., 1793.

Katzenberger, George A., "Major David Zeigler," Ohio Archeological and Historical Society Publications, Vol. 21, Columbus, Ohio, 1912.

Kehoe, Vincent J-R., *Virginia, 1774,* privately printed, 1958.

Peckham, Howard H., *Josiah Harmar and His Indian Expedition, Ohio Archeological and Historical Quarterly,* Columbus, June–September 1946.

———,"Redcoats and Redmen: The Development of American Military Confidence," Indian Historical Society, Lectures, 1969–1970, Indianapolis, Ind., 1970.

Roosevelt, Theodore, *Winning of the West,* G. P. Putnam's Sons, New York, 1902.

Sargent, Winthrop, "Diary of Winthrop Sargent," Ohio Archeological and Historical Society Publications, Vol. 33, Columbus, Ohio, 1924.

———, *The History of an Expedition against Fort Duquesne in 1755 under Major General Edward Braddock,* edited from the original manuscripts, J. P. Lippincott and Company, Philadelphia, 1856.

St. Clair, Arthur, *A Narrative of the Manner in Which the Campaign against the Indians, in the Year One Thousand, Seven Hundred and Ninety-one, Was Conducted, under the Command of Major-General St. Clair,* Jane Aitken, Philadelphia, 1812.

———, manuscript letters about the preparations for his campaign in 1791, of Knox, Hodgdon, and St. Clair, Guthman Collection.

Smith, Dwight L., *With Captain Edward Miller in the Wayne Campaign of 1794,* edited by Dwight L. Smith, the William L. Clements Library, Ann Arbor, Mich., 1965.

Smith, Colonel James, *A Treatise on the Mode and Manner of Indian War,* Joel R. Lyle, Paris, Ky., 1812.

Smith, William Henry, *The St. Clair Papers,* arranged and annotated by William Henry Smith, Robert Clarke & Co., Cincinnati, 1882.

Stephenson, James, "Orderly Book of Lt. James Stephenson," manuscript collection of the Library of Congress, Washington, D.C.

Stillé, Charles, *Major General Anthony Wayne,* J. B. Lippincott Company, Philadelphia, 1893.

The Sullivan-Clinton Campaign in 1779, prepared by the Division of Archives and History, the University of the State of New York, Albany, 1929.

Sullivan, John, *Journals of the Military Expedition of Major General John Sullivan against the Six Nations of Indians in 1779,* reprinted by Benchmark Publishing Co., Inc., Glendale, N.Y., 1970.

Trumbull, Henry, *History of the Discovery of America,* Norwich, Conn., 1810.

Wayne, *A Precise Journal of General Wayne's Last Campaign,* American Antiquarian Society, Worcester, Mass., 1955.

Wilson, Frazer E., editor of manuscript letter of Thomas Irvin in "Harmar's Campaign," Ohio Archeological and Historical Society Publications, Vol. 19, Columbus, Ohio, 1910.

————, "St. Clair's Defeat," Ohio Archeological and Historical Society Publications, Vol. 11, Columbus, Ohio, 1903.

Wyllys, John Palsgrave, and Ebenezer Frothingham, manuscript letters of both prior to Harmar's expedition, archives of the Connecticut Historical Society, Hartford, Conn., 1791.

NEWSPAPERS

The Boston Gazette and Country Journal—1793 (Boston)

The Boston Gazette and Weekly Republican Journal—1794 (Boston)

The Connecticut Courant and Weekly Intelligence—1784–March 14, 1791 (Hartford)

The Connecticut Courant—March 21, 1791–1792 (Hartford)

The Connecticut Gazette—1791–92 (New London)

Gazette of the United States—1789–90 (New York)

Gazette of the United States—1790–92 (Philadelphia)

Massachusetts Centinel—1789 (Boston)

Massachusetts Gazette—1787 (Boston)

The New Haven Gazette and Connecticut Magazine—1786 (New Haven)

The New Hampshire Mercury and General Advertiser—1785 (Portsmouth)

The New Hampshire Mercury and the General Advertiser—1785 (Portsmouth)

The Pennsylvania Packet and Daily Advertiser—1784–90 (Philadelphia)

Dunlap's American Daily Advertiser—1791–92 (Philadelphia)

The Salem Gazette—1785 (Salem)

The Salem Gazette—1791 (Salem)

The United States Chronicle: Political, Commercial and Historical—1789–91 (Providence)

The Vermont Journal and Universal Advertiser—1787 (Windsor)

MILITARY BACKGROUND

American Military History 1607–1953, ROTCM145–20, Dept. Of The Army, U.S. Government Printing Office, Washington, D.C., July, 1956.

American State Papers, Class V, Military Affairs, Vol. I, Gales and Seaton, Washington, D.C., 1832.

Armstrong, John, manuscript papers 1784–1801 and notebooks 1792–99, William Henry Smith Memorial Library, Indiana Historical Society, Indianapolis, Ind.

Boatner, Mark Mayo, *Encyclopedia of the American Revolution,* David McKay Company, Inc., New York, 1966.

Boynton, Captain Edward C., *History of West Point,* D. Van Nostrand, New York, 1864.

Brown, Harvey E., *The Medical Department of the United States Army from 1775 to 1873,* Surgeon General's Office, Washington, D.C., 1873.

Butterfield, Consul Willshire, *Dickinson-Harmar Correspondence of 1784–85,* and *Journal of Captain Jonathan Heart, U.S.A.,* Joel Munsell's Sons, Albany, N.Y., 1885.

Callan, John F., *The Military Laws of the United States,* John Murphy and Company, Baltimore, Md., 1858.

Duane, William, *A Military Dictionary,* William Duane, Philadelphia, 1810.

1st American Regiment, enlistment records, 1785–89, manuscript collection, Pennsylvania Historical and Museum Commission, Harrisburg, Pa.

Force, Peter, *American Archives,* fourth and fifth series, M. St. Clair Clarke and Peter Force, Washington, D.C., fourth series, 1837–46, fifth series, 1848–53.

Ganoe, William Addleman, *The History of the United States Army,* reprinted by Eric Lundberg, Ashton, Md., 1964.

The Gentleman's Dictionary; In Three Parts; I, The Art of Riding the Great Horse; II, The Military Art; III, The Art of Navigation, H. Bonswicke, London, 1705.

Harmar, Josiah, manuscript collection of his papers, William L. Clements Library, University of Michigan, Ann Arbor, Michigan.

Heart, Jonathan, manuscript collection of his military letters, 1785–91, Guthman Collection.

———, manuscript letter book, April 17, 1787–January 26, 1788, United States National Archives, Washington, D.C.

Heitman, Francis B., *Historical Register of Officers in the Continental Army,* April 1775–December 1783, the Rare Book Shop Publishing Co., Inc., Washington, D.C., 1914.

———, *Historical Register and Dictionary of the United States Army,* 1789–1903, reprinted University of Illinois Press, Urbana, Ill., 1965.

Hetzel, Capt. A. R., *Military Laws of the United States,* George Templeman, Washington City, 1846.

Hoyt, E., *Practical Insructions for Military Officers: To Which is Annexed a New Military Dictionary,* John Denio, Greenfield, Mass., 1811.

Jacobs, James Ripley, *The Beginning of the U.S. Army,* 1783—1812, Princeton University Press, Princeton, N.J., 1947.

Jones, Robert Ralston, *Fort Washington at Cincinnati, Ohio,* Society of Colonial Wars in the State of Ohio, 1902.

Knox, Henry, "A Plan for the General Militia of the United States," Francis Childs and John Swaine, New York, 1790.

———, manuscript papers, owned by the New England Genealogical Society and deposited in the Massachusetts Historical Society, Vol. XVI–XXXVI, November 1783–January 1795, and Index, Vol. LVI, Boston, 1960.

Mahon, John K., *The American Militia–Decade of Decision, 1789–1800,* University of Florida Press, Gainesville, Florida, 1960.

Matloff, Maurice, editor, *American Military History,* Office of the Chief of Military History, United States Army, Washington, D.C., 1969.

Military Merit, The Order of, forward by Winslow Warren, Society of Cincinnati in the State of New Hampshire, Exeter, N.H., 1925.

Northwest Territory manuscript collection, *Arthur St. Clair Papers,* 1788–1815, William Henry Smith Memorial Library, Indiana Historical Society, Indianapolis, Ind.

Minot, George Richards, *The History of the Insurrections in Massachusetts in the Year MDCCLXXXVI, and the Rebellion Consequent Thereon,* Isaiah Thomas, Worcester, Mass., 1788.

Pennsylvania Troops in the Service of the United States, August 7, 1787, Return of, from the original manuscript with notes, John P. Nicholson, Philadelphia, 1887.

Scott, Colonel H. L., *Military Dictionary,* D. Van Nostrand & Co., New York, 1864.

Smith, Charles, *The Monthly Repository,* William Davis, New York, 1796.

Smith, Captain George, *An Universal Military Dictionary,* J. Millan, London, 1779.

Thian, Raphael P., *Legislative History of the General Staff of the Army of the United States, from 1775 to 1901,* Government Printing Office, Washington, 1901.

Thornbrough, Gayle, *Outpost on the Wabash,* Indiana Historical Society, Indianapolis, Ind., 1957.

United States Army manuscript *Waste Books* I, II, and III, 1786–1793, United States Military Academy Library, West Point, N.Y.

United States Artillery, 2nd Regiment, manuscript order book, 1787–1800, United States Military Academy Library, West Point, N.Y.

Walton, William, *The Army and Navy of the United States,* George Barrie, Publisher, New York, 1889.

Ward, Harry M., *The Department of War, 1781–1795,* University of Pittsburgh Press, Pittsburgh, 1962.

Washington, George, *General Washington's Military Equipment,* the Mount Vernon Ladies Association of the Union, Mount Vernon, Va., 1963.

Wright, Colonel John Womack, "Some Notes on the Continental Army," New Windsor Cantonment Publication #2, National Temple Hill Association, Vails Gate, N.Y., 1963.

MILITARY—FORTS AND FLAGS

Brown, Margaret Kimball, "Glass from Fort Michilimackinac," *The Michigan Archaeologist,* Vol. 17, Nos. 3–4, Ann Arbor, Michigan, September–December 1791.

Davis, Gherardi, *Regimental Colors in the War of the Revolution,* New York, privately printed, 1907, supplement 1910.

———, *The Colors of the United States Army 1789–1912,* privately printed, New York, 1912.

Emery, B. Frank, "Old Michigan Forts," a series of sketches, The Old Forts and Historic Memorial Association, Detroit, Michigan, 1931.

Graham, A. A., "Military Posts in the State of Ohio," Ohio Archeological and Historical Society Publications, Volume III, Columbus, 1890–91.

Grant, Bruce, *American Forts Yesterday and Today,* E. P. Dutton and Co., New York, 1965.

Grimm, Jacob L., "Archaeological Investigation of Fort Ligonier," *Annals of Carnegie Museum,* Vol., 42, Pittsburgh, 1970.

Hume, Ivor Noel, *A Guide to Artifacts of Colonial America,* Alfred A. Knopf, New York, 1970.

Kerrick, Harrison Summers, *The Flag of the United States,* Wisconsin edition, the White House Publishers, Chicago, 1931.

Mercer, Henry C., *Ancient Carpenter's Tools,* the Bucks County Historical Society, Doylestown, Pa. 1960.

Miller, J. Jefferson, II, and Lyle M. Stone, *Eighteenth-Century Ceramics from Fort Michilimackinac,* Smithsonian Institution Press, Washington, 1970.

New Windsor, *Cantonment Bulletin,* special number, "Preliminary study of Continental Army Flags and Colors," Temple Hiss Association, Inc., Vails Gate, N.Y. (no date).

Pennsylvania, "Report of the Commission to Locate the Site of Frontier Forts of Pennsylvania," Clarence M. Busch, State Printer of Pennsylvania, 1896.

Prucha, Francis Paul, *Guide to the Military Posts of the United States,* the State Historical Society of Wisconsin, Madison, Wisc., 1964.

Quaife, Milo M., editor, "Fort Knox Orderly Book, 1793–1797," *Indiana Magazine of History,* June 1936, Bloomington, Ind.

———, Melvin J. Weig, and Roy E. Appleman, *The History of the United States Flag,* Harper and Row, New York, 1961.

Riker, Dorothy, "Fort Finney," *Year Book of the Society of Indiana Pioneers,* Indianapolis, Ind., 1944.

Russel, Carl P., *Firearms, Traps and Tools of the Mountain Men,* Alfred A. Knopf, New York, 1967.

Schermerhorn, Frank Earle, *American and French Flags of the Revolution, 1775–1783,* Pennsylvania Society of Sons of the Revolution, Philadelphia, 1948.

Smith, H. R. Bradley, *Blacksmiths' and Farriers' Tools at Shelburne Museum,* Museum Pamphlet series, No. 7, the Shelburne Museum, Inc., Shelburne, Vt., 1966.

Ticonderoga Museum, "Development of the Flag of the United States," *The Bulletin of the Fort Ticonderoga Museum,* Vol. 7, No. 2, July 1945.

Watts, Florence G., "Fort Knox," *Indiana Magazine of History,* Vol. 62, No. 1, Indianapolis, Ind., March 1966.

Wildung, Frank H., *Woodworking Tools at Shelburne Museum,* Museum Pamphlet series No. 3, the Shelburne Museum, Shelburne, Vt., 1957.

Woehrmann, Paul, *At the Headwaters of the Maumee,* Indiana Historical Society, Indianapolis, Ind., 1971.

MILITARY—TRAINING

Bland, Humphrey, *A Treatise of Military Discipline,* Sam. Buckley, London, third edition, 1784.

Connecticut, *Plan of Exercise for the Militia of the Colony of Connecticut Extracted from the Plan of Discipline for the Norfolk Militia,* Timothy Green, New London, 1772.

Hoyt, E., *A Treatise of the Military Art: In Four Parts,* Benjamin Smead, Brattleborough, Vt., 1798.

Muller, John, *A Treatise Of Artillery,* John Millan, London, 1757.

———, *A Treatise Containing the Elementary Part of Fortification Regular and Irregular,* J. Nourse, London, 1746.

Nicola, Lewis, *L'Ingenieur de Campagne: Or Field Engineer,* written in French by the Chevalier de Clairac and translated by Lewis Nicola, R. Aitken, Philadelphia, 1776.

———, *A Treatise of Military Exercise Calculated for the Use of the Americans,* Styner and Cist, Philadelphia, 1776.

Porterie, M. De la, *Institutions Militaires pour la Cavalérie, et les Dragons,* Chez Guillyn, Libraire, Qua des Augustins au Lys d'Or, Paris, 1754.

Prussia, *Regulations for the Prussian Infantry,* translated from the German, J. Nourse, London, 1754.

Saint-Rémy, Sr. Surirey de, *Memoires d'Artillérie,* Imprimerie Royale, Paris, 1697.

Simes, Thomas, *The Military Guide for Young Officers,* plus extracts from *A Military Essay* by Campbell Dalrymple, reprinted by J. Humphreys, R. Bell, and R. Aitken, Philadelphia, 1776.

Simes, Thomas, *The Military Medley,* London, 1768.

Steuben, Baron von, *Regulations for the Order and Discipline of the Troops of the United States,* Philadelphia, Styner and Cist, 1779.

Stevenson, Roger, *Military Instructions for Officers Detached in the Field: Containing a Scheme for Forming a Corps of a Partisan,* R. Aitken, Philadelphia, 1775.

Tousard, Louis de, *American Atillerist's Companion,* C. and A. Conrad and Company, Philadelphia, 1809.

Windham, William, and the Honorable George Lord Viscount Townshend, *A Plan of Discipline for the Use of the Norfolk Militia, in Three Parts,* J. Millan, near Whitehall, 1768.

MILITARY—UNIFORMS AND ACCOUTERMENTS

Albert, Alphaeus H., *Record of American Uniform and Historical Buttons,* privately printed, Hightstown, N.J., 1969.

Calver, William Louis, and Reginald Pelham Bolton, *History Written with a Pick and Shovel,* New York Historical Society, New York, 1950.

Campbell, J. Duncan and Edgar M. Howell, *American Military Insignia, 1800–1851,* Smithsonian Institution, Bulletin 235, Government Printing Office, Washington, D.C., 1963.

Company of Military Historians, quarterly journal and uniform plates.

Curtis, John Obed, and William H. Guthman, *New England Militia Uniforms and Accoutrements,* Old Sturbridge Village, Sturbridge, Mass., 1971.

Earle, Alice Morse, *Two Centuries of Costume in America,* the Macmillan Company, New York, 1903.

Johnson, David F., *Uniform Buttons,* American Armed Forces 1784–1948, Century House, Watkins Glen, N.Y., 1948.

Klinger, Robert L., and Richard A. Wilder, *Sketch Book '76, the American Soldier 1775–1781,* privately printed and distributed.

Lefferts, Charles M., *Uniforms of the American, British, French, and German Armies in the War of the American Revolution, 1775–1783,* New York, 1926.

McClellan, Elizabeth, *History of American Costume 1607–1870,* Tudor Publishing Company, New York, 1937.

Peterson, Eugene T., *Gentlemen on the Frontier, a Pictorial Record of the Culture of Michilimackinac,* Mackinac Island State Park Commission, Mackinac Island, Mich., 1964.

Warwick, Edward, and Henry C. Pitz, *Early American Costume,* the Century Company, New York, 1929.

WEAPONS

Baird, Donald, "An 18th-Century Fusil by Richard Wilson-London," *The Canadian Journal of Arms Collecting,* Vol. 6, No. 1, Museum Restoration Service, Ottawa, Ontario, Canada, February 1968.

Belote, Theodore T., *American and European Swords,* Smithsonian Institution Bulletin 163, U.S. Government Printing Office, Washington, D.C., 1932.

Blackmore, Howard, L., *British Military Firearms,* Henry Jenkins, Ltd., London, 1961.

Brown, John Brewer, *Sword and Firearm Collection of the Society of the Cincinnati,* Society of Cincinnati, Washington, D.C., 1965.

Brown, Rodney Hilton, *American Polearms,* N. Flayderman & Co., New Milford, Conn., 1967.

Darling, A. D., "The Long Land Pattern Musket," *The Canadian Journal of Arms Collecting,* Vol. 6, No. 4, Museum Restoration Service, Ottawa, Ontario, Canada, November 1968; see also "The Short Land Pattern Musket" (Vol. 7, No. 2, May 1969) and "Staff Weapons of the British Army" (Vol. 9, No. 1, February 1971).

Dean, Bashford, *On American Polearms,* reprinted from Volume I, Part 1, Metropolitan Museum Studies, New York.

Gluckman, Major Arcadi, *United States Martial Pistols and Revolvers,* Otto Ulbrich Co., Buffalo, N.Y., 1944.

——, *United States Muskets, Rifles, and Carbines,* Otto Ulbrich Co., Buffalo, N.Y., 1948.

Gooding, S. James, *An Introduction to British Artillery in North America,* Historical Arms Series, No. 4, Museum Restoration Service, Ottawa, Ontario, Canada, 1965.

Grose, Francis, *Military Antiquities Respecting a History of the English Army,* T. Egerton, London, 1801.

Hamilton, T. M., *Early Indian Trade Guns, 1625–1775,* Museum of the Great Plains, Lawton, Okla., 1968.

Hanson, Charles E., Jr., "John Kinzie and His Gun," *The Museum of the Fur Trade Quarterly,* Vol. 6, No. 4, Chadron, Neb., Winter 1970.

——, *The Northwest Gun,* Nebraska State Historical Society, Lincoln, Neb., 1955.

Hicks, Major James E., *French Military Weapons.* reprinted by N. Flayderman & Co., New Milford, Conn., 1964.

——, *Notes on United States Ordnance,* James E. Hicks, Mount Vernon, N.Y., 1946.

Hughes, Major-General B. P., *British Smooth-Bore Artillery,* Stackpole Books, Harrisburg, Pa., 1969.

Moore, Warren, *Weapons of the American Revolution,* Funk and Wagnalls, New York, 1967.

Neumann, George C., *The History of Weapons of the American Revolution,* Harper and Row, New York, 1967.

Peterson, Harold L., *American Indian Tomahawks,* Museum of the American Indian, Heye Foundation, New York, 1965.

——, *Arms and Armor in Colonial America, 1526–1783,* The Stackpole Company, Harrisburg, Pa., 1956.

——, *Round Shot and Rammers,* Stackpole Books, Harrisburg, Pa., 1969.

——, *The American Sword,* Robert Halter, New Hope, Pa., 1954.

Sawyer, Charles Winthrop, *Firearms in American History, 1600 to 1800,* Norwood, Mass., 1910.

——, *Our Rifles,* Williams Books Store, Boston, 1944.

Van Rensselaer, Stephen, *American Firearms,* Century House, Watkins Glen, New York, 1947.

Woodward, Arthur, "Tomahawks," *The Bulletin of the Fort Ticonderoga Museum,* Vol. 7, No. 3, Fort Ticonderoga, N.Y., 1946.

Index

A

Accouterments, 54, 102–106
  camp and field, 170
  improvisations, 104
  small arms, 91–98
  soldier's issue, 102–106
Adjutants, records kept by, 10–11
Administration, 12
Alleghany River, 56, 65
  Fort Franklin, 42–43
Appearance, military, 26, 30, 90
Armories and armorers, 48–49, 80, 93
Arms and ammunition, 10, 55–56, 91–106
  bayonets, 99–100, 170
  brass six-pounders, 55
  bullet molds, 96, 170
  at Fort Washington, 108
  fusils, 97
  gunpowder, 105–106, 216
  Indian, 93, 98
  indiscriminate firing forbidden, 15, 60, 230, 237
  issued to soldiers, 102–106
  lost in campaigns, 93
  powder magazine within fort walls, 35
  records of, 105
  repair of, 108–109
  rifles, 94–97
  shops and equipment for, 48, 108–109
  small arms, 91–98
  stamped "U.S.," 108–109
  Steuben's manual of instruction, 11–12
  stolen by Indians, 93
  surplus Revolutionary war weapons, 91–94
  swords, 100–101
Armstrong, Capt. John, 46, 81–84, 96, 129, 151, 190–191, 196
Armstrong, John, Jr. (Judge), 74
Articles of Confederation, 2–3
Artificers, 47–48, 57, 67, 215
Artillery, 23, 92, 97, 107, 238–239

accouterments and ammunition, 102–103
clothing issued, 25
at Fort Hamilton, 50
set of silver instruments, 111
Ashton, Capt. Joseph, 60, 104, 192, 197
Atrocities and tortures, 128–129, 168–169, 171
Avery, George, 47
Axes, 41, 48–49, 101–103, 215, 228
  belt, 101–102, 170

B

Banbury, Capt. (British army), 98
Banquettes, 61, 69
Barracks, 47, 50
Bartering for supplies, 64, 68
Bastions, 50, 61, 69
Battery, fortification, 70
Battleaxes, 101
Bayonets, 11, 17, 49, 91, 99–100, 170
Bearskins, 104, 227
Beatty, Eskurius, 29
Beaver Creek fort, 36–37, 82
Bissel, Ensign, 64
"Black hole," 61
Blacksmiths, 41, 47–49
Blockhouses, 35
Blue Jacket, Shawnee chief, 238
Blunderbuss, 93
Boats, 64, 85–87
  barges, 42
  builders, 67
  canoes, 86–87
  keel, 85–87
  "Kentucky boats," (large flatboats), 39, 64–65, 80, 85–87
  perrogues, 46
  "polling," 56–57
  small craft, 87
  (See also River travel)
Braddock's defeat, 115, 124–126
  failure of army to learn from, 124–126

Bradford, Captain, 104–105, 243
Brant, Joseph (Mohawk chief), 47, 58–59, 98, 142, 153, 157, 162, 167, 175, 197
Brant, Molly, 58
Brickmakers, 49
British: ceded Northwest Territory to U.S., 116
  control of forts on Great Lakes, 4–5, 36, 83, 186
  Indians armed by, 98, 242
  influenced Indians against U.S., 5, 44–45, 47, 75, 88, 116, 122, 153, 166–169, 175, 202
  information about 1790 and 1791 campaigns, 178–179, 207
  refusal to relinquish western forts, 4–5, 142, 179
  treaty at Fort Erie, 58–60
  violations of Treaty of Paris, 1, 83, 88
Britt, Daniel, 42
Brown, John, 203
Brown, Patrick, 158–159
Buckongahelas, Delaware chief, 238
Buffalo Creek, Indian council meeting, 98
Bugle horns, 104
Bullet molds, 96, 170
Burgoyne's defeat, 95, 124
Burial mounds, Indian, 63, 137
Butler, Gen. Richard, Superintendent of Indian Affairs, 44, 58, 96–97, 104–105, 153, 195
  with St. Clair's expedition, 208–209, 212–213, 219–224, 228, 235–236, 243
Butler, Maj. Thomas, 235–236, 243
Butler, Col. William, 58
Butterfield, Consul Willshire, 100, 129

C

Cahokia, 46
Calumets (peace pipes), 46

Campaigns: Harmar's expedition,
  173–198
    Kentucky militia (1791), 202–205
    peace million, 199–202
    St. Clair's expedition (1791), 206–
      244
Campfollowers, 61–62, 227
Camps (see Encampments)
Cannons, 48, 60, 91, 106–107
  shot and carriages, 48
Canteens, 48, 105, 215
  tin, 105, 170
  wooden, 170
Carbines, 91, 93, 97, 100
Carleton, Joseph, 4
Carlisle, repository of military stores,
  102
Carpenters, 35, 48–49, 57
  tools, 41, 68
Cartridges and shells, 48, 105–106
  boxes, 94, 99, 105, 109, 170
  control over, 60
  kegs for, 215
  paper, 109
Cattle and horses, 64–67, 188
  cattle guard, 64–65, 67
    St. Clair's expedition, 209–210,
      216–217, 223, 227–229
Cavalry, 23, 50, 228
  need for regular unit, 210
Cayahoga River, 82
Cayuga Indians, 59, 153
Celebrations at the forts, 62–63
Cherokee Indians, 132–133, 153,
  161
Chests, liquor, 54
Chickasaw Indians, 97, 132–133
Chippewa Indians, 116, 144, 153,
  156, 161, 238
Choctaw Indians, 97, 132–133
Cincinnati, 217
  Fort Washington, 47–48
Cincinnati Historical Society, 53
Clark, Gen. George Rogers, 63, 151,
  153, 187
Clinton, Governor DeWitt, 134
Clothing and accouterments, 103–
  104
  allowance, 6, 24–25, 145
  contracts to supply, 26–28, 63, 65

cross belt plate, 32
  eagle buttons, 26
  Federal period military clothing, 33
  issued recruits, 22–34
  lack of military appearance, 26,
    30, 105
  late deliveries, 29–30
  officers clothing, 26, 33
    cockade, 27, 32
  orderliness of, 12–13, 105
  quality of, 29–30
  records of, 10
  regulations issued by Gen. Knox,
    25–26
  Revolutionary war surplus, 22, 24
  (See also Uniforms)
Colliers, 48
Columbian Centinel, 100
Columbian Magazine, 63
Columbian Tragedy (poem), 220, 247
Command structure, 3–4
  chain of command, 5, 228
  executive direction, 4
Commissions, 19
Communications with forts, 49, 208,
  222
  lack of, 143
Compasses, surveying instruments,
  73, 79–80, 201
Confederation, Articles of, 2–3
  establishing First American
    Regiment, 1–8
  lacked taxing authority, 1
  interstate disagreements, 3–4
Congress
  campaign against the Indians
    authorized, 201
  controversy over size of army,
    199–201
  financial problems, 28–29
  Indian policy, 45, 88–90, 201
  Land Ordinance of 1787, 74–78
  report of military situation in 1788,
    36–37
  report on forts (1788), 38–39,
    43–44
  resolution establishing regiment, 2,
    36
  resolution of June 22, 1786, 39
  resolution ordering general treaty,

153–154
  right to appoint officers, 4
Connecticut, 8
  land feuds, 78
  recruits and recruiting, 23–25
  Western Reserve lands, 77, 143–
    144, 146–147
Connecticut Courant, 25
Connecticut Society of Cincinnati, 75
Continental Army: disbanded in
    1784, 2
  pay, subsistence and rations, 5–6
  training and discipline, 9, 11–12
  veterans poorly treated, 21
Contracts and contractors, 3, 42,
    62–70, 182, 184–185
  competitive bids, 28
  Indian trade, 66, 68
  excess army supplies traded, 66, 68
  government slow in paying, 21–23,
    65–68
  St. Clair's expedition, 207–208
  vouchers, 68
Cooks and bakers, 49
Coopers, 49
Cornplanter, Seneca chief, 59, 138,
    153, 178, 201, 212
Countersigns, 61
Courts-martial, 10, 13–14
  conducting, 14, 47
  general, 13, 14
  punishments and, 13–14
  verdicts, 10, 13–14
Crafts, frontier, 48
Cramer, Zadock, 85
Cranch, Joseph, 93
Creek Nation, 93, 130–135, 238
  commissioners sent to, 134
  fighting strength, 130
  refusal to negotiate treaty, 131–132
  relations with Spain, 95, 135
  trade negotiations, 134–135
  treaties protested by Georgia and
    North Carolina, 130–135
  Upper and Lower Creeks, 130
Cummings, Samuel, 85
Cunneat (Cunniat), 82–83
Currency, 65–67
  Connecticut Treasury Office note, 8
  of state of Pennsylvania, 65

warrants of the states, 66–67
Curtain, part of fortification, 70
Cutler, Dr. Manasseh, 73–74, 76

D

Darke, Lt.-Col. William, 195, 217,
    219, 228, 235, 242–243
    portrait, 246
Delaware Indians, 114, 116, 124,
    144, 153, 157, 161, 238
    friendly to United States, 177
Deliette, Louis, 128
Denny, Maj. Ebenezer, 38, 42–43,
    66, 85, 96, 100, 129
    on Harmar's campaign of 1790,
    180–181, 186, 189–190,
    193–194, 197–198
    on St. Clair's expedition, 210–211,
    220–244
Desertions, 13–14, 16
    punishments for, 15
Detroit (see Fort Detroit)
Dickinson, John, 6, 36–37, 96
Discipline, 9–20, 242
    running the gauntlet, 13–14
    Steuben's manual, 9–20
    trials and whippings, 13
    (See also Training and discipline)
Diseases and sickness, types of, 55–
    56
Document boxes, 54
Dod, Lebbeus, 80
Doolittle, Enos, 80
Doughty, Capt. John, 37–39, 47, 65,
    92, 106, 145, 178, 184, 187–
    188
Doyle, Capt. Thomas, 96, 181, 243
Dragoons, 97, 171
Drew, Capt. Seth, 9
Drills and drilling, 11–12
Drummed out of the service, 13, 14–
    16
Drums and drumbeat, 12, 16
    instrument of command, 16, 60
Drunkenness, 13, 23, 62, 66, 68–69
Duane, James, 116–117

Duer, William, 73–74, 76, 208–209,
    213
    financial manipulations, 216
Dunlap's Station attack, 129
Duty, neglect of, 13

E

Eel villages, attack on, 204–205
Elliot, John, 56
Elliot, Matthew, 167
Elliot, Robert, 176
Elliot and Williams of Maryland, 67,
    69
Elliott, Captain (British agent), 90
Emigrants westward bound, 75–77,
    84–85
    (See also Settlers)
Encampments, 235
    equipment and supplies 48, 170
    inspection of, 10
    method of setting up, 12
Enlistments, 4–5, 23–24
    1784 expirations, 23
    1785 expirations, 23–24
    three years, 5n
    (See also Recruits and recruiting)
Equipment and supplies: camp and
    field, 48, 170
    improvisation, 104–105
    (See also Contracts and contractors)
Esprit de corps, creating, 3, 6
Explorations of territory, 81–84
    archeological, 63, 137
    European, 119–122
        claims to Indian lands, 115,
        120–122
        territorial claims, 115–116

F

Fallen Timbers (1794), 5, 92, 121
Farmer's Brother, king of the
    Senecas, 202–203

Fascine, 70
Fatigue men, 48
Faulkner, Captain, 234–235
Federal corps, 1–8
    1st American Regiment (see First
        American Regiment)
    governed Northwest Territory, 74
    headquarters, 39
    lack of communications, 143
    limiting size of the army, 2, 4–5,
        21, 174, 200–201
    military discipline, 11–12
    militia and, 156, 173–177, 180–
        187
    organization of, 23n
    pay, subsistence and rations, 5–6,
        134, 145–146
    recruits, 5, 9, 21–23, 150, 177
    regimental duties, 81–90, 143
        building and navigating boats,
            85–86
        exploring, mapping and spying,
            81–84
        maintaining civil law and order,
            88–89
        protecting settlers, 88–89, 199–
            201
        protecting surveyors, 74–75, 143
        river travel, 84–88
        treating with Indians, 89–90,
            143
    2nd American Regiment (see
        Second American Regiment)
    in Southwestern Territory, 130
Federal government
    claim to Indian lands, 120–122
    faith in future of, 76, 78
    need for money to pay debts, 1–2,
        116
    state lands ceded to, 77
    weak financial position, 1–2, 63–
        64, 67–68, 116
Ferguson, Maj. William, 41, 66, 97,
    180, 184, 187, 207, 217, 233
Financing army, 28–29
Finney, Capt. Walter, 37–40, 51, 66
Firelocks, 99
Firewood, 61, 103
First American Regiment, 1–8, 53
    common structure, 3–4, 230–231

duties and deployment, 71–90,
143
exploring, mapping and spying,
81–84
land companies, 73–74
maintaining civil law and
order, 89–90
Ordinance of 1787 and, 74–78
protection of settlers, 84–89,
199–201
protection of surveyors, 71–75,
143
river travel, 84–88
establishment of, 1–8
limiting size of army, 4–5, 21,
174
to police frontier, 1–2
Resolution of June 3, 1784, 2
maintaining peace between Indians
and Whites, 89–90, 156–157
Major Hamtramck in command,
230–231
recruitment, 206–207, 209
St. Clair's expedition, 212, 219,
241–242
small arms, 91–98
state quotas, 2
1st Battalion, 5th Field Artillery,
oldest unit of U.S. Army, 2
First campaign, 173–198
(See also Harmar's campaign of
1790)
1st Pennsylvania Battalion, 101
Five Nations, 153
Flags, flown over forts, 51–52
Florida, 81
Spanish territory, 45
Flour ration, 65–66
Fontaine, Major, 190–193
Food: buffalo and deer meat, 46, 69
supplied by hunters, 62, 64–66
(See also Provisions and supplies)
Forage and subsistence, 6, 145
Forks, folding, 54
Fort Detroit, 5, 36, 59, 157, 175
British possession of, 5, 36, 59
influence on Indians, 166–169
view of (1794), 7
Fort Erie, 202
British treaty with Indians, 58–60

Fort Finney, 37–38, 40, 51
celebrations at, 62
council house, 38
evacuation of old Fort Finney, 39
New Fort Finney, 39–40
plans drawn by Jonathan Heart, 51
Fort Franklin, 40–43, 55–58
construction of, 57–58
description of, 42, 55–58
Harmar's visit to, 42–43
relations with Indians, 58–60
security at, 60–61
views of, 53
Fort Hamilton, 49–50, 222–223
construction, 222, 226
description of, 49–50
Fort Harmar, 15–16, 38–40, 55, 155
erection of, 38–39, 52
gathering of Indians for a treaty,
155–158
protection of surveyors, 72
regimental headquarters, 39, 52
security precautions, 61
supplies stored, 63, 65–67
Fort Jefferson, 49–50, 223–226
final fort built (1791), 35, 223–226
Fort Knox, 43–44, 46–47
Congressional report on, 43–44
establishment of, 46–47
French settlers, 44–45
Indian troubles, 44–46
lawless banditti, 45–46
problems with Spain, 45
Fort McIntosh, 14–15, 36–37
celebrations, 62
clothing shortage, 29
headquarters for Federal corps, 39
Indian treaties at, 36, 89–90
provisions, 63, 65–67
rebuilding of, 36–37
vandalism and deterioration, 36–
37
Fort Mackinac, 36
Fort Mackmilimack, 5
Fort Niagara, 5, 36, 59, 202–203
Fort Oswego, 5
Fort Pitt, 2, 36, 42
clothing issued recruits, 22–23
deserters, 14
protection of surveyors, 72

2nd regiment at, 202
supply depot, 36, 41, 55, 63–67,
102, 106
Fort Stanwix, 153
Fort Steuben, 40, 73
Fort Washington, 47–48, 194
Col. Proctor, 201–202
frontier crafts, 47–48
headquarters at, 52
plan of, 53
preparations for Harmar's campaign
of 1790, 180–184
preparations for St. Clair's
expedition of 1791, 206
Forts and fortifications, 35–54
bastions, 36
blacksmith shops, 47
blockhouses, 35
clear ground surrounding, 60–61
Congressional resolutions, 36
Congressional reports on (1788),
38–39, 43–44
construction of, 35–36, 49, 71
defense of, 35, 60–61
European, 35
frontier crafts at, 48
frontier living, 55–63
gardens and gardening, 47
garrisons, 35
glossary of terms, 69–70
guardhouses, 61
Harmar's good-will march to, 46
Indian troubles, 35–36, 44
lawless banditti, 45
need for additional, 196
officers' barracks, 47
palisades, 47, 57
problems with Spain, 45
relaxation at, 61–62
storage space, 35
tools, 41, 48–49
trading posts within walls, 35
water supply, 61
Fourth of July celebrations, 39, 62
Fowler, Theodosius, 208
Fowling pieces, 91, 98
Fraise, 70
Franklin, Pennsylvania, site of
Venango, 60
French Creek, 18, 75

Fort Franklin, 41–43, 56
French-Indian relations, 44, 116
French-Indian wars, 81, 116
    Braddock's defeat, 115, 124–126
Frontiersmen: life at the forts, 55–63
    weapons and tactics, 54, 125–128
Frothingham, Lt. Ebenezer, 8, 43, 48,
        82, 148, 184, 193–194
    death of, 193, 196
Fur trade and traders, 4–5, 75
    relationship with Indians, 98,
        115–116, 121–122
Fusils, 91, 97

G

Gaither, Maj. Henry, 215, 234–235,
        238
Gamelin, Antonine, 175–176
Gardening at the forts, 47, 62, 68–69
Garrisons at forts, 35, 50
George III, King of England, 59
Georgia: Indian problems, 130–135
    protested legality of Indian treaties,
        130–135
    troops stationed in, 200
Gerry, Elbridge, 2
Gibson, Lt.-Col. George, 195, 219
        228, 236, 243
Girty, Simon, 98, 129, 167, 197,
        242–243
Glossary of fortification terms, 69–70
Guards and patrols, 15, 60–61
    sleeping on duty, 13, 15
Guerilla tactics, 11, 94–97, 115,
        125–127, 152, 204
    army lacked training in, 11
    use of rifles, 94–97
    use of small forces, 115, 124–126,
        204
Gun powder, 105–106
    poor quality, 216
Gunlocks, 97
Gunsmiths, 49

H

Half Town, Oneida chief, 157
Hamilton, Alexander, 118, 208, 216
Hammers, 41, 49
Hamtramck, Maj. John Francis, 40,
        64, 87, 89, 106, 151, 158–161,
        241–242
    criticism of, 241–242
    1st Regiment commanded by,
        231–232
    at Fort Knox, 47
    Harmar's campaign of 1790, 176,
        185–186
    protection of surveyors, 72–73
    St. Clair's expedition, 241–242
Hardin, Col. John, 180–181, 184,
        187–192, 203
Harmar, Gen. Josiah, 5–6, 9–20,
        61–62
    appointed commander, 5–6, 9–20
    attempts to standardize uniform,
        26–27
    campaign against Miami villages,
        48, 81, 173–198
    (See also Harmar's campaign of
        1790)
    on contracts for provisions, 63–69
    council with Indians at Post
        Vincennes, 46
    on desertions, 15
    on erecting forts, 36–37, 41–42,
        61–62
    on Fourth of July celebrations, 62
    good-will march to forts, 46
    on immigration on the Ohio,
        84–85
    investigation of, 195
    on militia, 150–152
    military training and background,
        6, 9, 101
    portrait of, 18
    preparations for treaty, 155–157
    on protecting surveyors, 72
    on recruiting, 23–24, 95–96
    retirement, 220
    with St. Clair's expedition, 210–

211
    training and discipline, 9–20
    treating with Indians, 46, 155–162
Harmar's campaign of 1790, 8, 48,
        173–198
    arms and ammunition, 182–183,
        188
    authorized by Congress, 173–175
    British knowledge of, 178–179
    cost of, 182, 194
    failure of campaign, 194–197
    forces, 176, 181, 186–197
        undisciplined, 184, 189, 191,
        196
        Hamtramck's forces, 176, 185–186
        Indian scouting parties, 184,
            188–189
        Indians' surprise attack, 183–185,
            190–197
    investigation of, 219
    march and encampment, 186–194,
        198
    militia used to supplement Federal
        corps, 173–177, 180–187,
        189–191
    objectives, 173, 179, 181
    order of battle, 198
    overtures of peace, 175–176, 178
    preparations for, 176–185
    riflemen, 95–96
Harness makers, 48–49
Harrison, Gen. William Henry, 122–
        123, 127
Hatchets, 99
Haversacks, 103–104
Hawkins, Benjamin, 119
Health care, 12, 55–56
Heart, Maj. Jonathan, 38, 64, 85,
        189–190, 193–194, 243
    accouterments and ammunition,
        103
    death of, 100, 243
    on deteriorating situation on the
        frontier, 141–148
    drawings of, 53, 137
    expeditions against Miami villages,
        48
    explorations and mapmaking, 63,
        82–83
    forts planned and erected by, 40–

43, 51, 55–56
    Fort Finney, 51
    Fort Franklin, 40–43, 55–56
    interest in land companies, 40,
        75–78
    military experience, 55
    relations with Indians, 58–61
    on St. Clair's expedition, 220, 243
Heckewelder, David, 136
Heisely, Frederick A., 79
Herring, James, 31
Hodgdon, Samuel, 207–216
    mismanagement by, 215–218
Hopewell treaty (1785), 132
Horses (see Cattle and horses)
Houdin, Capt. Michael Gabriel,
    201–203
Hunt, Abner, 129
Hunters, food supplied by, 62, 64–66
Huron Indians, 153
Hutchins, Capt. Thomas (geographer
    of the United States), 40, 71–73,
    81, 151

I

Illinois, settlement of, 74
Imlay, Gilbert, 63
Indian agents, 117–118, 135
Indian attacks, 44, 222, 229–230
    fear of, 40, 60–61
    on Kentucky settlers, 85–88, 151–
        152
    retaliation of settlers, 151–152
    suggestions for fighting Indians,
        125–126
Indian burial mounds, 63, 101
Indian Commissioners, protection of,
    36, 89–90
Indian Department, 89–90
    northern and southern districts,
        89–90
Indian treaties, 117–118, 153–165
    Greenville (1795), 139
    counteracting British propaganda,
        141–142

deterioration and disappearance of
    Indians, 119–122, 141–148
obligations of United States, 132–
    134
(See also Treaties and treaty-
    making)
Indiana, settlement of, 74
Indians: appearance and dress, 136,
    237
    assaults upon, 13, 15
    British aroused hatred of
        Americans, 5, 44–45, 88
    characteristics, 136
    Congressional policy, 45, 72, 88–
        89
    culture, 121–122, 136
    cunning and military acuity, 3,
        94–97, 115–129
    customs and ceremonies, 136,
        166–167
    dress, 136
    effect of colonization on, 115–116
    firearms, 97–98
    fondness for whiskey, 46, 121–122
    at Fort Franklin, 58–60
    friendly, 93, 177–178
    fur trappers and, 115–116, 121–
        122
    gifts to, 97, 118, 135, 139
    guerilla tactics, 11, 94–97, 115,
        125–127, 152, 204
    guides, 46, 72
    John Marshall on deterioration of
        Indian nation, 119–122
    Kentucky country, 44–46
    land ceded by treaty, 38
    military ability, 115–129
    peace overtures to, 36, 72, 201–
        203
    population, 149, 164
    settlers and, 39, 44–45, 116
    southern Indian tribes, 130–135
    title to lands, 120–122
    trade with, 118, 130, 134–135,
        165–166
    war yell, 237
    warfare, 73, 122–128, 222, 229–
        230
        disciplined warriors, 123–124
        Harmar's campaign of 1790,

183–185
    interrogation of prisoners, 124
    St. Clair's expedition, 237–244
    scouting parties, 83, 123, 184,
        188–189, 221–223, 229–
        230, 233
    Washington's views on, 116–119
    weapons, 35, 93, 97
Infantry, 23, 95–97
    clothing allowance, 25, 34
    equipment, 99
    riflemen, 96–97
Innes, Judge Harry, 175, 203
Insignia, army, 26, 32
    use of eagle, 26
Intelligence, 60
    Federal corps, 119, 182
    Indians, 83, 123, 184, 188–189,
        221–222, 229–230, 233
Irish soldiers, 62
Irvin, Thomas, 186, 189–191

J

Jackson, Col. Henry, 26, 97
Jeffers, Ensign, 83
Johnson, Sir John, 83, 157, 166–168
Johnson, Sir William, 58, 167
Johnston, Col. Francis, 37
Judd, William, correspondence with
    Maj. Heart, 40–41, 48, 75–78,
    82, 141–148, 193

K

Kanawha River, 124
Kaskaskias, 88–89, 176
    Harmar's good-will trip to, 46, 137
Kayashuto, Seneca chief, 58–59
Kentucky, 43–44, 75
    Indian attacks, 151–152
    settlers, 75, 116, 148, 151–152

Kentucky boats (flatboats), 80, 85–87
Kentucky militia, 131, 175
    Harmar's campaign, 175–177, 180,
        189–191
    Indian raids (1791), 158–159,
        162–163, 202–205, 228
Kersey, Lt., 241
Kettles, camp, 48, 102–103, 215
Kickapoo Indians, 44, 205, 238
Kingsbury, Lt., 97, 129
Knapsacks, 48–49, 99, 103–104,
    170, 215, 227
Knox, Gen. Henry, 4, 13
    on army weapons, 91–98
    on immigration on the Ohio, 84–
        85
    on lack of adequate maps, 81
    letter to President Washington on
        Indian problem, 160–165
    on militia 150–151
    on negotiations with southern
        tribes, 130–135, 148
    portrait, 31
    on protecting surveyors, 72
    recommendations for permanent
        army, 132, 134
    recommendations for reduction in
        pay, 134
    on recruiting, 24
    report on northwestern Indians,
        148
    reports to Congress on Harmar's
        campaign of 1790, 173–185
    reports on St. Clair's expedition
        (1791), 206–220, 242
    on treaties with Indians, 153–165
    on uniform regulations, 25–28
Knox, William, 158, 214

L

LaDemoisel's band, 159
Lake Erie, exploration of, 82–83
Land, 40, 71–78
    acquired from Great Britain, 71
    mineral rights, 72

pension grants, 1, 63, 72, 76–78
public sale of, 71
speculation, 1, 63, 77, 118
surveys, 71–72
Land companies, 71, 73–74, 76, 147
Land Ordinance of 1785, 71, 73–74
Land Ordinance of 1787, 74–78
Lane, Capt. Derck, 27
Law and order on the frontier, 45, 75
    lack of, 88–89
"Lawless banditti," 45, 75
    in Kentucky country, 43–44
    violated Indian treaties, 133
Leach, Lewis, 155
Lee, Arthur, 153
La Gras, Col. Jean, 45
Legionary corps, recruiting, 23, 25–
    26, 96–97
Letter-writing activities, 62
Levie groups, 96, 104
    clothing and appearance, 227
    1st Regiment of, 228
    small arms, 93
Lewis and Clark expedition, 81
Licking River, 47
Limestone, Kentucky, 84–85, 151
Lincoln, Benjamin, 4
Liquor chest, 54
Little Turtle, Miami chief, 121–122,
    137, 195, 221–222, 233, 238
    military genius, 184, 188–189, 191
    portrait, 137
Logan, Col. Benjamin, 151, 203
Losantiville, 47
Louisiana Territory, 81
Louisville, Kentucky, 36, 66, 85

M

McDowell, Ensign Nathan, 46, 83
McGillivray, Alexander, 130–135, 140
    pension given to, 147
McGillivray, Lachlan, 130
McIntosh, Gen. Lachlan, 36
McKee, Alexander (British agent), 98,
    160, 166–168, 175, 197

Maclay, William, 173
McMahon's Creek, 177
Malaria, 56
Malarties, Viscount, 242–243
Maps and mapping, 7, 73, 81–84
    need for accurate maps, 81–84
    (See also Surveys and surveyors)
Marching maneuvers, 11, 28
Marietta, Ohio, 39, 74, 147
Marshall, John, 119–122
Maryland recruits, 23
Massachusetts: land feuds, 78
    recruits, 23, 25, 97
Maumee (Indian) town, 198
Medicine and medical supplies, 54–
    56, 64
    care of wounds, 56
Melanthy, Shawnee chief, 151
Melcher, Jacob, 155
Mentges, Lt. Col. Francis, 207, 219
Miami Indians, 116, 162
    Harmar's campaign against, 48,
        147, 173–198
    intertribal warfare, 128
    massacre of St. Clair's forces,
        237–247
    military ability, 115–129
Miami River, 37, 39, 76
    Fort Finney, 37–38
    Fort Hamilton, 49
    treaty at, 7, 153
Miami villages, 189
    attack on, 179–198
    burning of, 179, 192
    fort at, 207
Michigan, settlement of, 74
Michikiniqua or Chief Little Turtle,
    137
Mifflin, Governor Thomas, 157, 182–
    183
Migrations westward, 77, 81, 146
    volume of emigrants, 84–85
Militia, 95n, 105, 148, 150–152,
    189
    antagonism between army and,
        148, 150–152, 181
    formation of companies, 99, 173
    Harmar's campaign of 1790, 175–
        177, 180, 189–191
    Indian raids in Kentucky, 44–45,

158–159, 162–163, 202–205, 228
pay and subsistence, 173
St. Clair in command, 201–205, 213–216
to supplement Federal corps, 173–177, 180–187
weapons, 93, 99, 102
Mingo Bottom (Fort Steuben), 40, 72
Mississippi River, 46, 76, 81
forts along, 36
Spanish control, 45
Missouri River, exploration of, 81–82
Mohawk Indians, 58–59, 238
treaties, 153
Muller, John, 107, 128
Munsee tribe, 60, 161
Musicians, 34
Musketoons, 100
Muskets, 11, 17, 49, 91, 93, 96, 99, 214
British Brown Bess, 91, 98
fusils and, 97
kegs for cartridges, 48
loading, 105
repair of, 108
tools, 170
versus rifles, 95–96
Muskingum River, 38–39, 56, 63, 65, 137

N

Napoleon, 81
Navigator, The (Cramer), 85
New England mode of settlement, 75–77, 143
New Hampshire recruits, 23
New Jersey recruits, 27
New Orleans, 45
New York: land feuds, 78
recruits, 27
Newspapers, 22, 30, 62
Nicola, Lewis, 94
North American Almanack, 55–56

North Carolina, protested Indian treaties, 130–135
Northwest Ordinance, 74–78, 154
provisions, 74
Northwest Territory: acquisition from Great Britain, 1, 116
exploring and mapping, 7, 81–84
forts and fortifications, 35–54
government of, 74, 88–89, 117
map of, 7
need to protect settlers, 1–8, 36
sale and settlement, 1–2, 36
state lands, 77–78, 143–144, 147–150
surveying, 71–73

O

Officers: clothing and accouterments, 26, 50
duties, 71–90, 143
erection of forts, 40–43
land fever, 75–78
recruiting duty, 24, 30
O'Hara, James, 63–64, 66
Ohio Company, 73–74, 142–143, 147
settlement at Marietta, 39
survey of lands, 73
Ohio Indians (see Miami Indians)
Ohio River, 64–65, 69, 76, 82
boats and navigation, 36–37, 84–88
Fort Harmar, 38–39
Indian attacks, 200–202
settlements, 74, 116
(See also Ohio Company)
Washington's survey, 78n
Oldham, Lt.-Col. William, 224–225, 228, 233, 236, 243
Oneidas, 153
Onondagas, 59, 153
Orders to men, 10
in regimental record books, 10–11
Ordinance of 1785, 76
Ordinance of August 7, 1786, 130

Ordnance, 48–49
(See also Arms and ammunition)
Ottawas, 116, 144, 153, 156, 161, 238
Ouiatanon (Wea villages), 202–204
Oxen, use of, 50, 211

P

Pacane (Pakan), Miami chief, 137, 159–160
Pallisades or stockades, 38, 47, 70
Parades and salutes, 10, 62
Parapets, 70
Parrish, Jasper, 114
Parsons, Samuel Holden, 74, 76, 141, 143, 153
Patronage system, 4
Pay and allowances, 5–6, 24, 134, 145–146
reduction of, 145–146
Paymasters, duties of, 29
Peace mission to the Indians, 201–203
Pennsylvania: forts along the Allegheny River, 41
land feuds, 78
militia, 6, 150–151, 176–177, 181–183
quota of men for regiment, 5–6, 30, 96
settlers, 116
Pension lands, 1, 63, 72
distribution of, 76–78
Perrogues (canoes from hollow trees), 46
Philadelphia: first troops stationed at, 36
plans for St. Clair's expedition prepared in, 206–211
recruiting for Federal corps, 22, 36
repository for clothing issued recruits, 22–23
Piamingo, Chickasaw chief, 127, 225, 230–231

Piankeshaws, 44
Pickering, Col. Timothy, 118, 206
Pillories and punishments, 47
Piquets, 47, 49–50, 61
Pistols, 91, 93, 100, 102
Point Pleasant, Battle of (1774),
    124–125
Portages, 82
Post Vincennes, 36, 40, 43–44, 67,
    84, 89
  council with the Indians, 46
  French inhabitants, 44–45
  gifts to Indians, 97
  lawless banditti at, 45–46
  river travel, 86–87
Potawatomis, 116, 144, 153, 161,
    238
Powder horns, 94, 96, 102, 105–
    106, 110
Prairie du Roche, 46
Pratt, Lt. John, 24, 197
Price, William, 24, 27
Priming horns, 170
Prisoners, 61, 204
  torture of, 128–129
Proctor, Col. Thomas, 98, 138
  peace mission, 199–205, 212
Provisions and supplies, 63–70
  bartering for, 64, 68
  contracts, 63–70
  flour ration, 69
  at Fort McIntosh, 37
  from garrison gardens, 68–69
  lack of, 67
  from local sources, 67–68
  meat ration, 55–56, 64–67
  medical supplies, 55–56
  monthly provision return, 64, 68
  payments for, 67
  quality and quantity of rations, 66
  records of, 10, 64, 68
  transportation difficulties, 46, 64
  (See also Contracts and contractors)
Prud, Homme, John Francis Eugene,
    31
Public opinion, influencing, 164
Punishments, 13–16
  being drummed out of service,
    13–16
  executions, 13

necessity to retain offender, 13
running the gauntlet, 16, 20
(See also Courts-martial)
Putnam, Rufus, 39, 76, 200–201

Q

Quartermaster department, 10, 68

R

Ramparts, 70, 93
Ranchers, 49
Randolph, Edmund, 118
Rapids of the Ohio (Louisville), 16,
    39–40, 66–67
  Fort Finney, 40, 66, 72
  protection of surveyors, 72
Rations and subsistence, 5–6, 145
Records and record-keeping, 12
  monthly returns, 55
  regimental record books, 10–11
Recruits and recruiting, 5, 9, 21–23,
    150
  advertisements in newspapers, 22,
    30
  clothing greatest inducement, 22–
    24
  desertions, 23
  difficulties involved, 21–23
    military career looked down
      upon, 21
  drinking problem, 23
  expiration of 1784 enlistments, 23
  expiration of 1785 enlistments,
    23–24
  four-state quota system, 21–22
  from unemployed, 22
  officers responsible for filling
    quotas, 22, 24, 30

one-year enlistments (1784), 23
pay and clothing allowance, 24
riflemen, 95–96
training, 9–20, 35, 148, 177
Red Jacket, chief of Turtle tribe, 98,
    202
Redoubts, 46
Renegade whites, 72, 242
  incited Indians to attack settlements,
    45
Repairing equipment, 48–49
Resolution of 1784; 2–6
  establishing First American
    Regiment, 2
  limiting size of the army, 4–5
  pay, subsistence and rations, 5–6
Retreat, 10
Review of the regiment, 11
Revolutionary War, 55
  British surrender at Yorktown, 1
  military discipline, 11
  pension lands, 63
  small arms, 91–94
  (See also Continental Army)
Rhea, Lt. James, 96
Rhea, Thomas, 98
Rhode Island recruits, 23
Rifles and riflemen, 11, 50, 73, 91,
    93–97, 106, 127–128, 181, 204
  brass-bore rifles, 165
  negative attitude of military, 94–95
  Pennsylvania, 110
  powder horns, 94, 96, 102, 105–
    106, 110
  St. Clair's expedition, 227–228
  smooth, 93
  value of, 94–95
River travel, 84–88
  charting rivers, 81–84
  from Fort Pitt to Fort McIntosh,
    36–37
  Indian attacks, 85–86
Roads and roadbuilding, 195
  charting new travel routes, 83–84
Roll calls, 9–10
  courts-martial announced at, 13–
    14
  punishments given at, 13, 16
Rope and ropemaking, 88
Running the gauntlet, 13–16, 20

S

Sabers, 111
Sailors, 49
St. Clair, Gen. Arthur, 48–50
  on desertions, 50
  on erecting forts, 48–50
  expedition of 1791, 206–244
    (*See also* St. Clair's expedition
      of 1791)
  governor of Northwest Territory, 62,
    79, 88–89, 154, 212–213
  honors denied, 244, 247
  illness and death, 226*n*, 228–229,
    231, 244
  on militia and regular army
    command, 151, 208–209
  *Narrative of the Campaign Against
    the Indians,* 49
  peace proposals to Wabash Indians,
    174–179
  portrait, 172
  riflemen under, 96
  on treaty negotiations, 152, 161
St. Clair's expedition of 1791, 3, 93,
    206–244
  arms and ammunition, 213–216,
    221
  casualties, 243
  chain of command, 228
  Chickasaw Indians allied with, 230
  communications, 222
  Congressional inquiry, 215–218,
    226, 242
  criticism of, 241–243
  defeat of, 50, 90, 100, 119, 127,
    208, 215–216, 220–244
    due to inadequate intelligence,
      119, 221–222, 234–235
    predicted by Gen. Harmar, 210–
      211
  desertions, 221, 226
  forces, 206, 214, 238
    1st Regiment, 202, 217–219,
      221, 227, 231–232, 238,
      241–242
    militia and levies, 209–212,
      217–219, 227–229

  vulnerability of, 234–235
  horses and cattle, 223, 227–229
  Indian attack, 222–223, 230, 234–
    244, 246
    number of Indian warriors, 238,
      242
    spies, 228–230, 233
  marches and encampments, 208–
    209, 222–244
    order of battle, 245
    preceded by riflemen and
      surveyors, 208, 217, 227–
      228
  massacre of troops, 237–241
  objectives, 206–207
  preparations for, 206–220
    at Fort Washington, 206–211,
      215–216
    in Philadelphia, 206–211
  provisions and supplies, 207–210,
    213, 216, 226–231
  recruits and recruiting, 201–202,
    218–219
  retreat, 239–241
    bravery of wounded, 240
    panic of troops, 241
  training of troops, 213–214, 218
  Washington's interest in, 211–220
St. Joseph River, 179
St. Louis, Spanish commandant, 46
St. Mary's River, 36, 179
St. Mary's River, Georgia, 130
St. Vincent (*see* Post Vincennes)
Sargent, Col. Winthrop, 47, 73–74,
    127, 176, 219
  on St. Clair's expedition, 221–244
Saws, 41, 49
Sax Indians, 161
Scalps and scalping, 40, 45, 168–
    169, 171
  knives, 73, 102, 114, 127
Scioto Land Company, 73–75, 147
Scott, Brig.-Gen. Charles, 202–204
  expedition against Wea villages,
    202–203
Scott, Joseph, 85
Scouting parties, 222–223
  Indian, 83, 123, 184, 188–189,
    221–223, 229–230, 233
Scurvy, 55

Second American Regiment, 225, 278
  authorization, 201
  at Fort Pitt, 202
  pay, 201
  recruitment, 202, 206
  St. Clair's defeat, 100, 238–239,
    247
Secretary at War, office of, 4
  records forwarded to, 10–11
  (*See also* Knox, Gen. Henry)
Sedam, Ensign Cornelius Ryer, 46,
    241
Seminole Indians, 130
Seneca Indians, 41, 43, 58–59, 82,
    153, 202–203
  Chief Kayashuto, 58–59
  peace overtures, 58–60
  Turtle tribe, 98
Sentries, 15, 60–61
Settlers, 38–39
  antigovernment feelings, 213
  army not adequate to protect, 84–
    89, 199–201
  illegal sale of land to, 212
  Indian troubles, 44–45, 116, 158
  migration westward, 75–76
  New England mode of settlement,
    75–77, 143
Shawnee Indians, 44, 116, 151, 153,
    238
Shay's Rebellion, 23
Shelby, Isaac, 203
Shoe buckles, 8
Shoemakers, 49
Shot pouches, 96, 104, 106
Sickness and disease, 55–56
  prevention of, 12
Silver Creek, 64
Silvie, Captain (British officer), 98
Six Nations of the North, 41, 47,
    132, 156, 206
  treaties with, 58, 153, 162
Slavery, abolition of, 74
Sleeping on guard duty, 13, 15
Slough, Captain, 236–237, 243
Smallpox, 60
Smith, Daniel, 112–113
Smith, Col. James, 122–127
Smiths, 57
  (*See also* Blacksmiths)

Index 273

Southwestern Territory, 93, 130–135
 Federal corps, 130
 military force recommendations, 132–135
Spanish-Indian relations, 81, 132
 feared American expansion, 45
 Southern Indian tribes armed by, 95, 98
Spear, Lt., 243
Spears, 100, 102
Spies and spying, 81–84
 (See also Scouting parties)
Splints for the wounded, 48, 215
Squatters, Kentucky country, 43–45
 removed by army, 38, 40, 89
States:
 attempt to use their own currency, 8, 29, 65–67
 boundary and territorial disputes, 142–143
 feuds over land, 78
 interference in Northwest Territory, 77, 118
 militia (see Militia)
 power to appoint officers in Federal corps, 3
 private treaties with Indians, 77–78, 143–144
 quotas for First American Regiment, 2
 responsibility for paying soldiers, 3, 28–29
Stearns, Samuel, 55–56
Stephenson, Lt. James, 222–223
Steuben, Major General Baron von, 6, 128
 manual of instructions, 9–20, 99–100
Steubenville, Ohio (Fort Steuben), 40
Stockades, 46, 50
Storehouses, 50
Superintendent of Indian Affairs, 89–90
Suppliers of food and clothing, 3
 (See also Contracts and contractors)
Supplies and equipment (see Equipment and supplies)
Surveys and surveyors, 72–73, 79–80

 important role in American history, 73–74
 Indian guides, 72
 instruments, 72–73, 79–80
  brass circumferentor, 80
  chain carriers, markers, 72
  compasses, 79–80
 laid out route for army, 73, 208, 217, 227–228
 Ohio Company's purchase, 73
 precision of survey, 71
 protection by army, 38–39, 65, 71–73
Swords, 99–102
 espontoons and, 99
 Federal-period decoration, 111
Symmes, John Cleves, 74, 76
Symmes syndicate, 212

T

Tailors, 49
Tammany Society, 134
Tecumseh (Tecumtha), 135, 138, 221, 233, 245
 portrait, 138
Tents, 103–104, 172
Thievery, petty, 13, 15
Thomson, Charles, 154–155
Tippecanoe, 122–123, 205
"Tomahawk rights," 45
Tomahawks, 99, 101–102, 113, 127, 201
 carried by surveyors, 73
 engraving on, 112–113
 leather sling for, 201
 pipe, 102, 112–114
Tools and tool-makers, 41, 48–49
 forging, 48
 needed for erecting forts, 41, 55
 scarcity of, 225
Tortures and atrocities, 128–129, 168–169, 171
Tousard, Louis de, 107
Towns and townships, 71–77

land reserved by government, 72
New England mode of settlement, 75–77, 143
settlement of, 75–78
surveys of, 38, 71–73
Trading posts, 75
 within forts, 35
Trail markers, 172
Training and discipline, 9–20
 cleanliness and prevention of sickness, 12–13
 courts-martial and punishments, 13–16
 drum signals and commands, 12, 16, 60
 regimental record books, 10–11
 review of regiment, 11
 routine orders, 10
 Steuben's manual of instruction, 9–20
 weapons, 15, 17
Treaties and treaty-making, 153–165
 alternative to Indian wars, 163–165
 appropriations by Congress, 154–155
 boundary disputes, 153–155
 British attempts to influence Indians, 153, 157–158, 160
 commissioners of the United States, 77, 141, 153
 with Creek Nation, 147
 expeditions to enforce, 152
 formation of Confederate Council, 153
 at Fort Harmar (1789), 157–165, 173
 at Fort McIntosh (1785), 153
 general treaty ordered by Congress, 153–154
 gifts to Indians, 147, 149, 165–166
 Grand Treaty (1789), 161
 Indian claims, 153–154, 164
 Indian rights, 163–165
 ineffective position of U.S., 156, 160–165
 lawless whites, 156, 158–160, 162–163
 negotiations, 161–162
 overtures of peace, 156, 158–160

participants, 153
preparations for, 155–156
regulating trade with the Indians, 154
    trade articles, 165–166
role of the regiment, 89–90
with Shawnee Nation, 153
with Six Nations, 153
states and, 143–144, 147–150
    private treaties, 77–78, 143–144
    rights of premption of territory, 149–150
trade articles, 165–166
vigilance against attack, 156, 158, 160
violations of, 148–149
with Wabash Indians, 148–149
white settlers and, 158–159, 162
Treaty of Greenville (1795), 139
Treaty of Paris, 1, 5, 71
    British violations, 83, 88
Troop and retreat, 9–10
    roll calls at, 9
Trotter, Col., 181, 189–191
Truby, Col., 181, 187–188
Trunks and baggage, 54
Turnbull, Marnie & Company, 65
Tuscaroras, 153
Twightwees, 153
Two Feet, Seneca Indian, 58

U

Uniform Militia Act, 94
Uniforms, 17, 103–104
    attempts to standardize, 26–28
    cockades, 27, 32
    eagle insignia on buttons, 26
    Federal period, 33
    horseman or dragoon helmet, 171
    improvisation, 104
    issued recruits, 24
    military appearance, 26, 30, 90
    regulations issued by Gen. Knox, 27–28
    shoe buckles, 8

(See also Clothing and accouterments)
United States (see Federal government)
United States Gazetteer, 85
United States Supreme Court, 119

V

Valley Forge, American troops at, 11
Varnum, James Mitchell, 74
Venango Post (Pennsylvania), 41–43, 55, 66, 82
    arrival of Capt. Heart, 58–60
    description of, 43
    Fort Franklin, 40–43
    provisions, 67
    settlement of lands, 75
    trip to, 56–57
    weapons, 107
Venereal diseases, 56, 61
Venison, availability of, 64–65, 69
Vermillion (Kickapoo village), 185–186
Vermont land feuds, 78
Vermont Journal, 44
Veterans of Continental army, recruitment of, 21
Vincennes (see Post Vincennes)
Vinegar, need for, 54, 64, 66
Virginia, 75–77, 142–143
    military tracts, 77
    militia, 150, 176–177
    recruits, 23
    (See also Kentucky)

W

Wabash Indians, 43, 46, 148, 157, 174
    attacks on river boats, 86
    peace proposals, 174–179
    population, 164
    treaties with, 90, 131, 149

Wabash River, 76
    exploration of, 81–84
    Fort Knox, 43–44, 47
    Post Vincennes, 36
    (See also Post Vincennes)
Waist belts, 104
Wall pieces, 93
Wallets, leather, 54
Wampum, 46, 59, 158, 166
    belts, 139
War clubs and tomahawks, 101
Washington, George, 6, 81, 100
    commander-in-chief, 4
    inauguration, 8
    on Indian problems, 116–119, 173
    land holdings, 78n
    militia call-up, 95n
    opposed standing army in peacetime, 2
    orders on discipline and training, 9
    reorganization of army, 96–97
    St. Clair's campaign and, 211–220, 242–243
    settlers ask for help, 200–201
    treaty with Creek Nation, 130–135
Water supply at forts, 61
Wayne, Gen. Anthony, 6, 90, 122, 126–127, 139
    advocated use of bayonet, 99–100
    trail marker from campaign of 1794, 172
    on use of rifles, 95
    victor at Fallen Timbers (1794), 5, 92, 121
Wea villages, attacks on, 202–204
Weapons, 17, 91–106
    accouterments and ammunition, 102–106
    bayonets, 99–100
    brass six-pounders, 55
    British Brown Bess, 91, 98
    destruction of vast quantities, 92–93
    difficulty in identifying, 92–93
    edged, 99–102
    European, 107
    fusils, 97
    Indian, 93, 98

indiscriminate firing prohibited, 15, 60, 230, 237
military strategy and, 125–128
records of, 10
rifles, 94–97
    brass-bore, 165
sabers and spears, 99
small arms, 91–98
stamped or branded "US," 92–93
standardization of, 94
Steuben's manual of instructions, 11
swords, 100–101
tomahawks, 73, 99, 101–102, 112–114, 127, 201
types of, 106
West Point, 2, 55, 214
    clothing and accouterments issued recruits, 22, 24, 93
    ordnance returns, 99
    repository of military stores, 91–93, 101

view of (1791), 7
Western Confederacy of Indian tribes, 116, 197, 210–211
    military ability, 122
Wheelrights, 48
Whipping posts, 47
Whiskey drinking, 13, 23, 62, 66, 68–69
    furs traded for whiskey, 121–122
    Indians destroyed by, 122
    liquor chests, 54
Wilkinson, Lt.-Col.—Commandant James, 203–205, 212, 219
Willett, Marinus, 134
Wisconsin, settlement of, 74
Wolcott, Oliver, 153
Women at the forts, 61–62, 227
    washerwomen, 61
Work parties, 60–61
Wounds, care of, 56
    splints, 48, 215
Wyandot Indians, 44–45, 58, 116,

238
    friendly, 177
    treaties with, 153, 157, 161–162
Wyllys, Maj. John Palsgrove, 48, 87, 151, 180, 184, 187, 192–194, 196
    death of, 193, 196

Y

Yazoo Company (land speculators), 135

Z

Zeigler, Maj. David, 39–40, 51, 156–157, 217–218, 227–228
Zeisberger, David, 136

About the Author

William H. Guthman was born in Chicago, served in China during World War II, and was graduated from Northwestern University. His business career began as a society photographer in Chicago; he remained in Chicago until 1951 when he accepted a position as purchasing agent for a major manufacturing concern. Moving to Connecticut, and commuting to New York City, his leisure interest soon turned to the field of Colonial and Federal Period American military history. His Colonial and Federal period American military collection is one of the foremost in the United States, and portions of it have been exhibited at major museums and exhibitions. His extensive research in the field has enabled him to become consultant to many museums, and he has helped form several notable museum collections. Mr. Guthman is a Fellow of the Company of Military Historians and a member of the American Society of Arms Collectors and the Kentucky Rifle Association.

The author left the manufacturing field in 1966 to devote his full time to the completion of this book, which he began to research in 1964. He is now wholly involved in the field of military Americana, placing rare artifacts, documents, and publications in museums, libraries, and advanced collections. He lives in Westport, Connecticut, with his wife, two children, and a large black Labrador retriever.

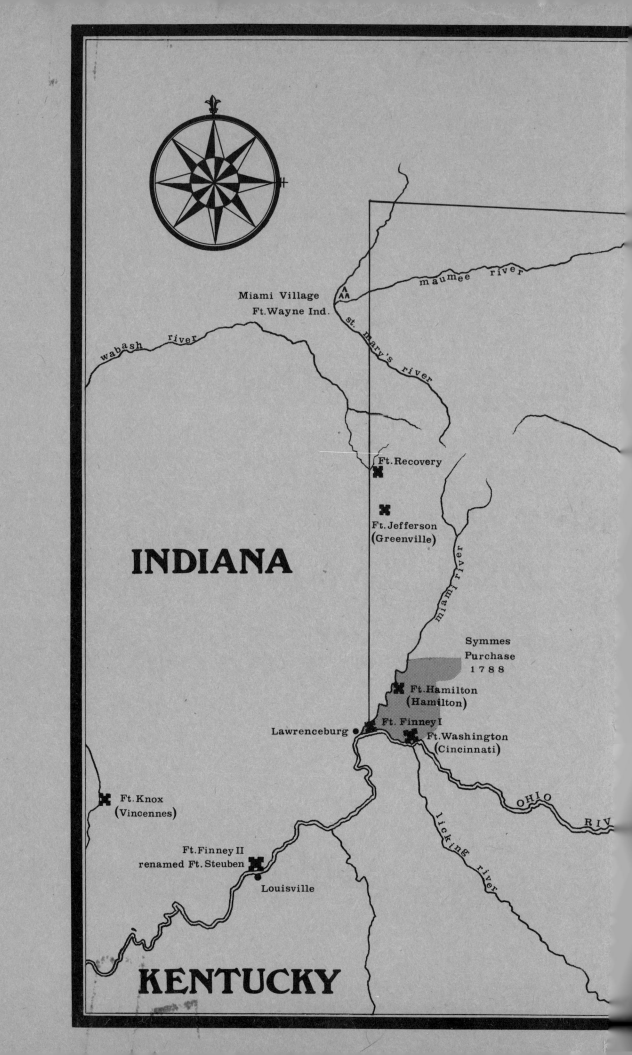